Kakuriyo
Bed & Breakfast
for Spirits

3

Art by
Waco Ioka

Original Story by **Midori Yuma**
Character Design by **Laruha**

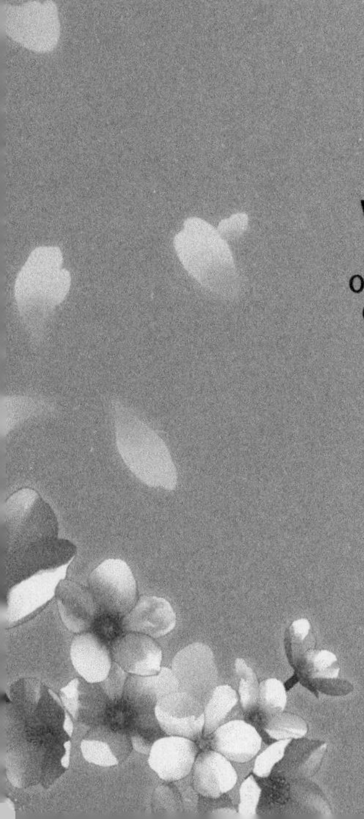

CONTENTS

CHAPTER 11
3

CHAPTER 12
27

CHAPTER 13
51

CHAPTER 14
115

CHAPTER 15
149

END NOTES
200

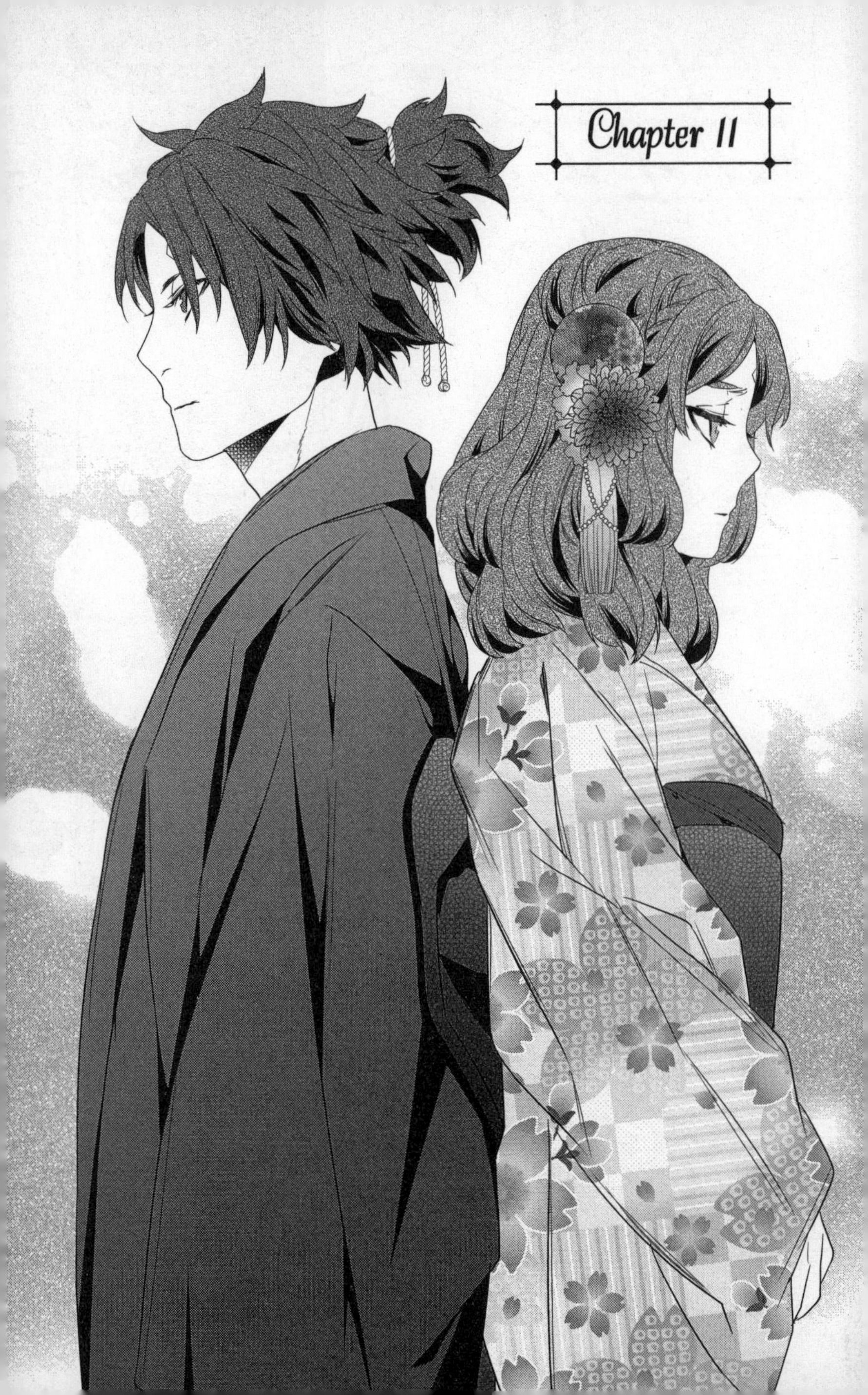
Chapter 11

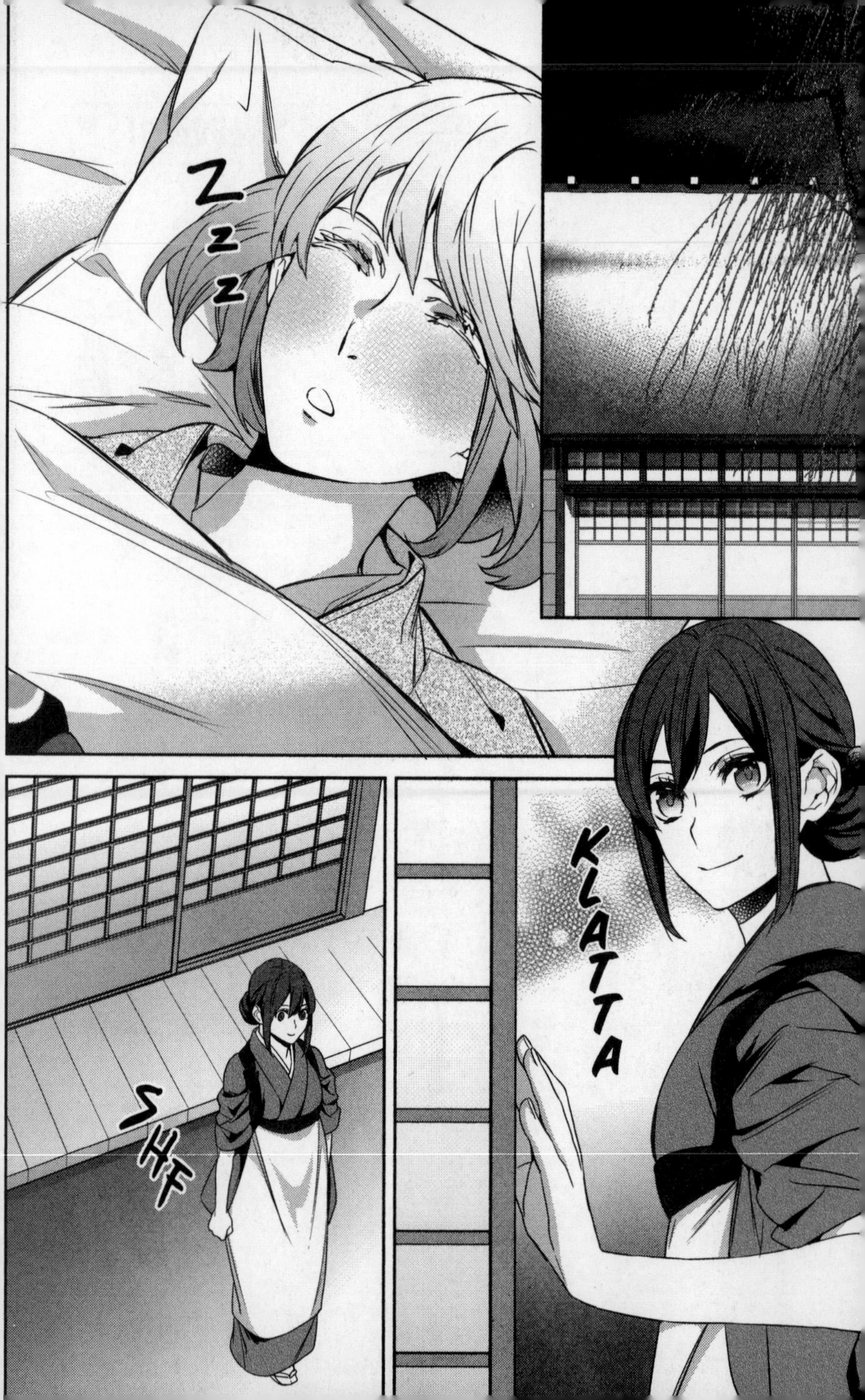
Zzz
KLATTA
SHF

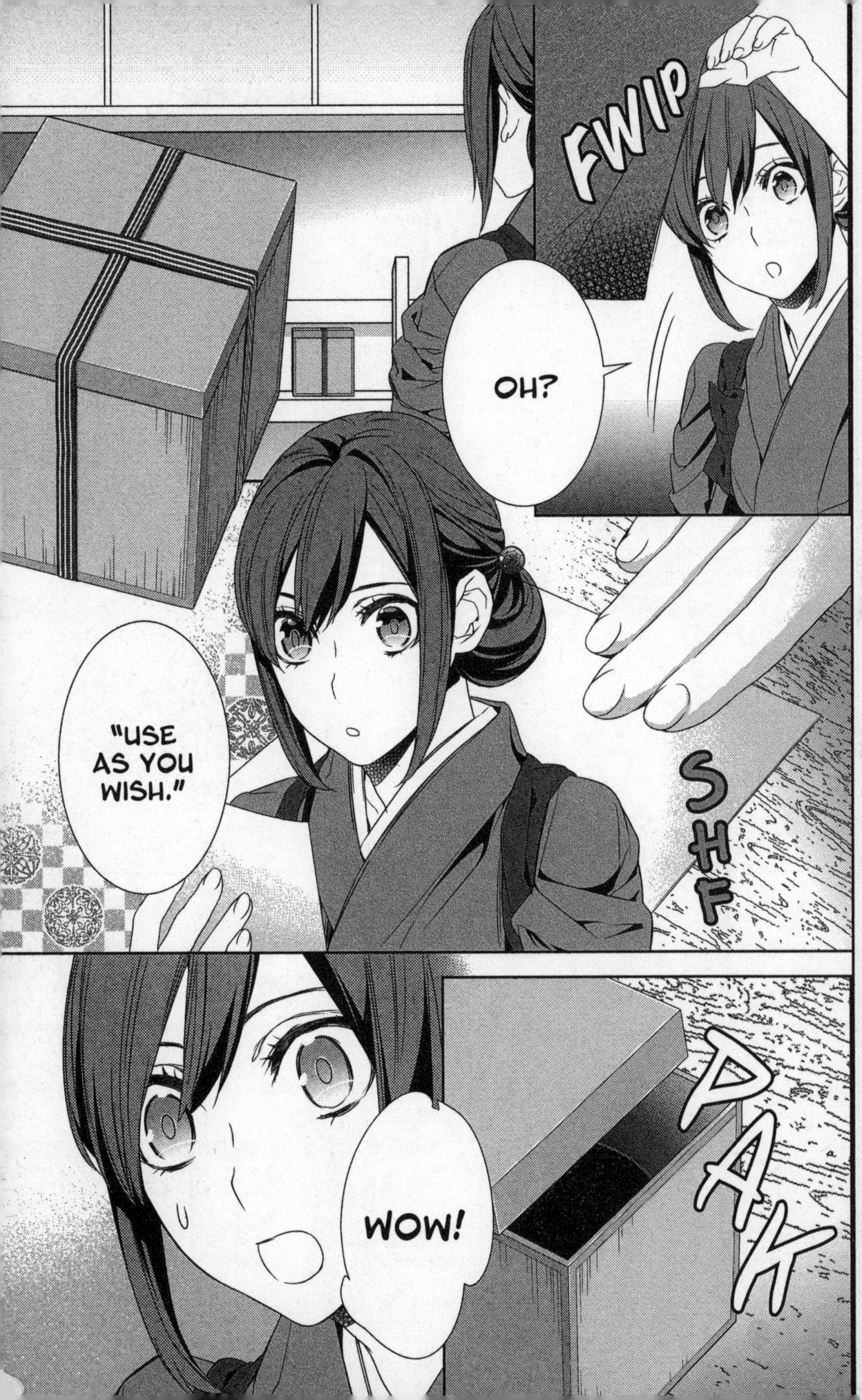
FWIP
OH?
SHF
"USE AS YOU WISH."
DAK
WOW!

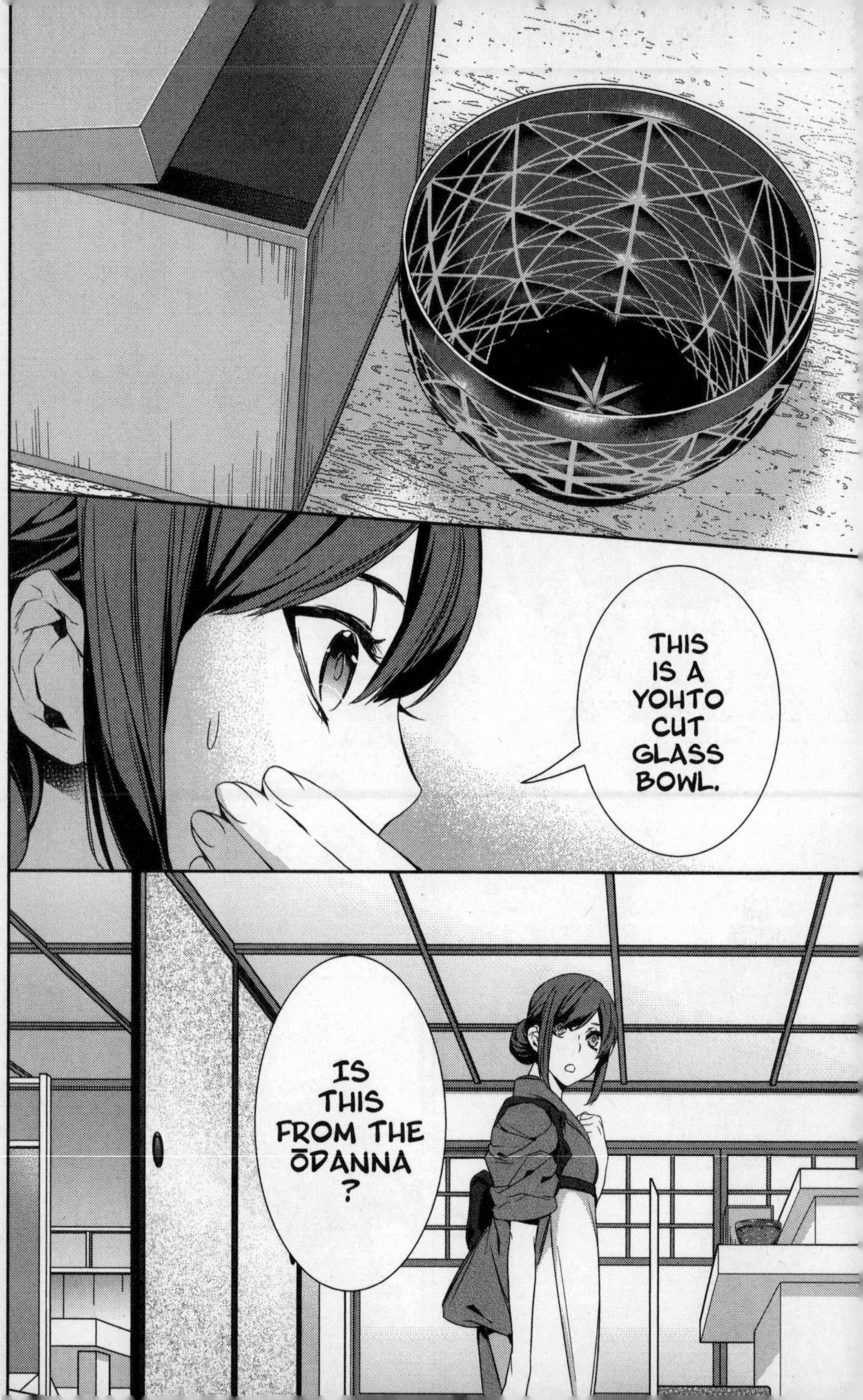
THIS IS A YOHTO CUT GLASS BOWL.
IS THIS FROM THE ŌDANNA?

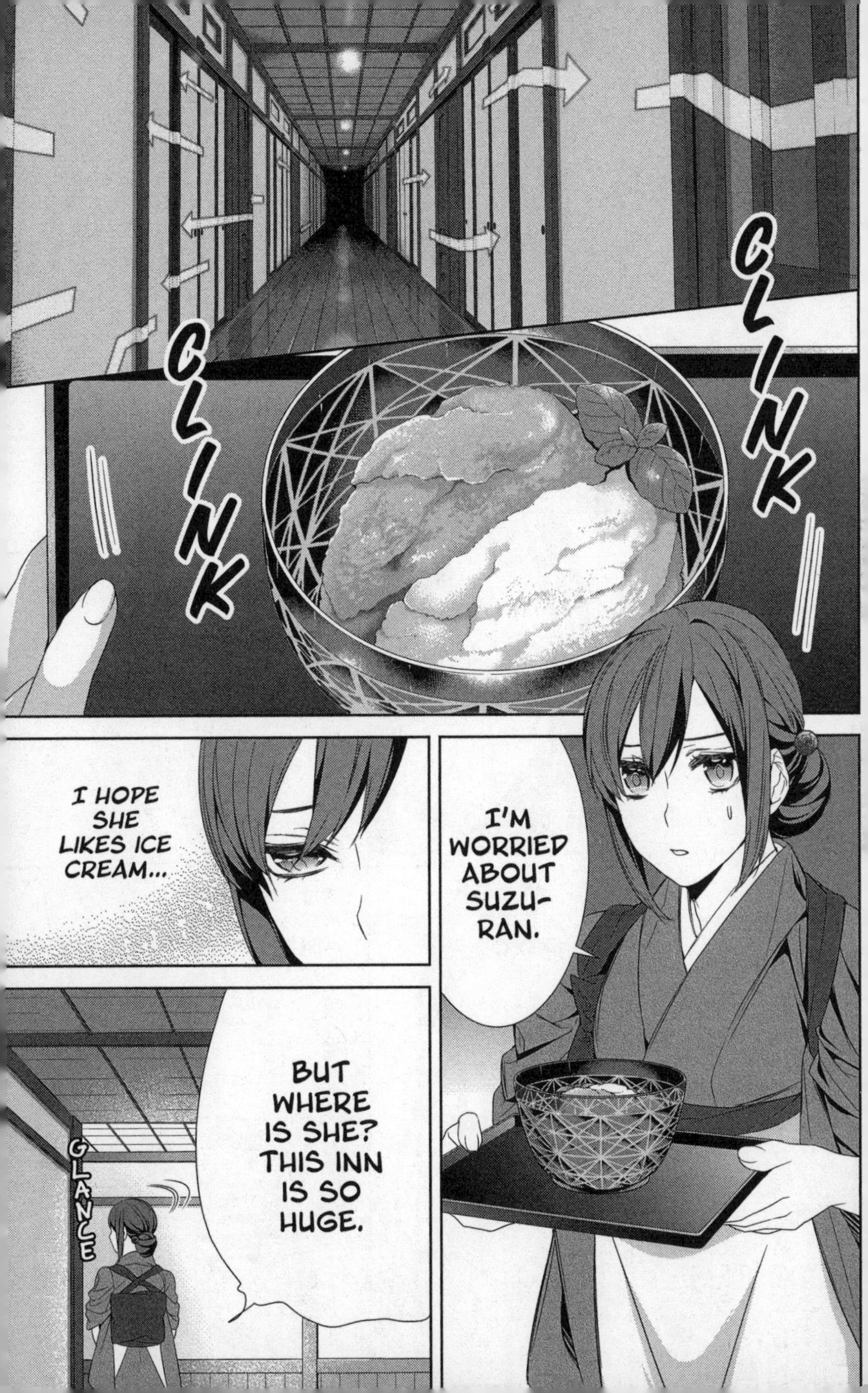
CLINK
CLINK
I'M WORRIED ABOUT SUZURAN.
I HOPE SHE LIKES ICE CREAM...
BUT WHERE IS SHE? THIS INN IS SO HUGE.
GLANCE

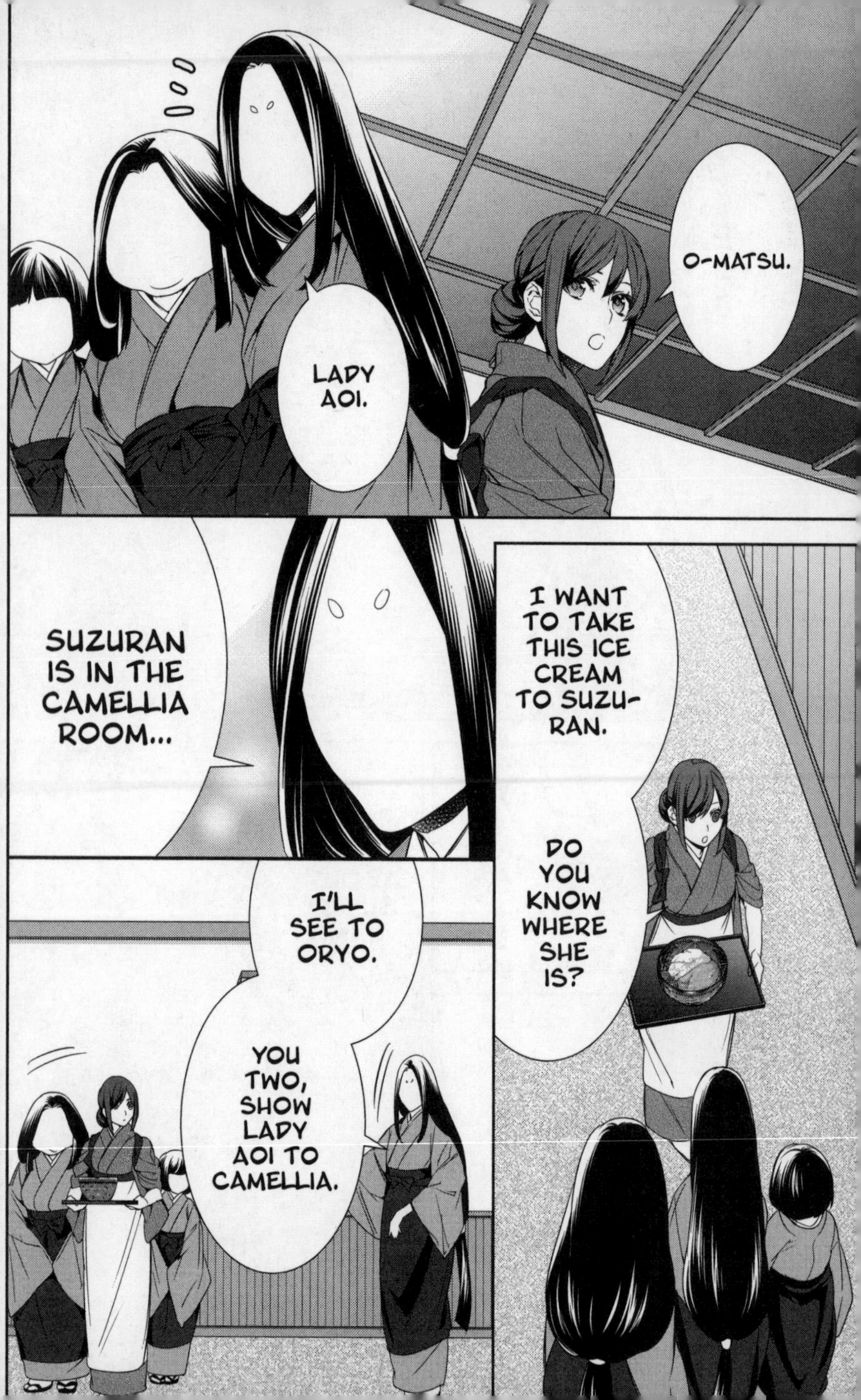
O-MATSU.
LADY AOI.
I WANT TO TAKE THIS ICE CREAM TO SUZU-RAN.
DO YOU KNOW WHERE SHE IS?
SUZURAN IS IN THE CAMELLIA ROOM...
I'LL SEE TO ORYO.
YOU TWO, SHOW LADY AOI TO CAMELLIA.

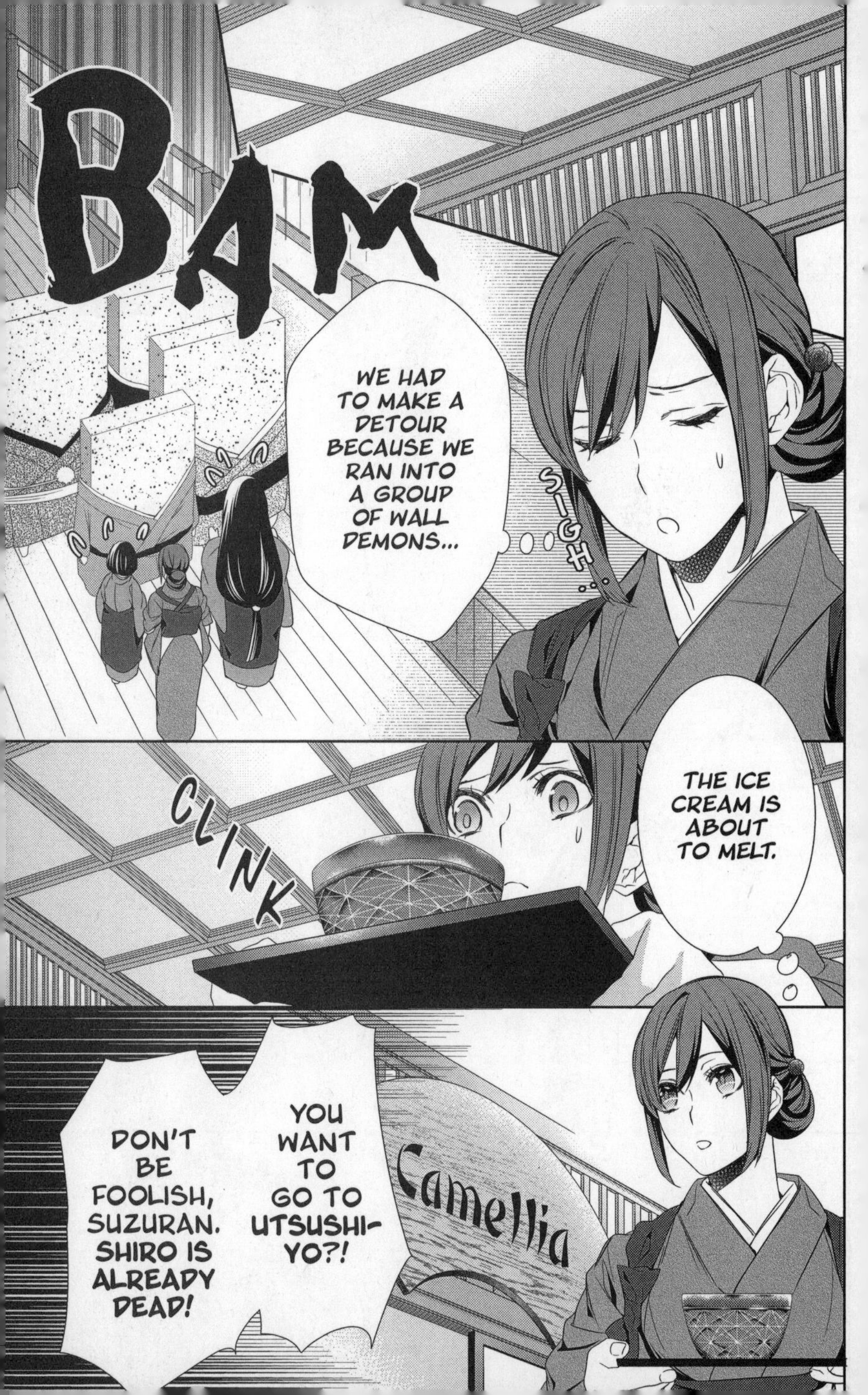
BAM
WE HAD TO MAKE A DETOUR BECAUSE WE RAN INTO A GROUP OF WALL DEMONS...
SIGH...
THE ICE CREAM IS ABOUT TO MELT.
CLINK
Camellia
YOU WANT TO GO TO UTSUSHI-YO?!
DON'T BE FOOLISH, SUZURAN. SHIRO IS ALREADY DEAD!

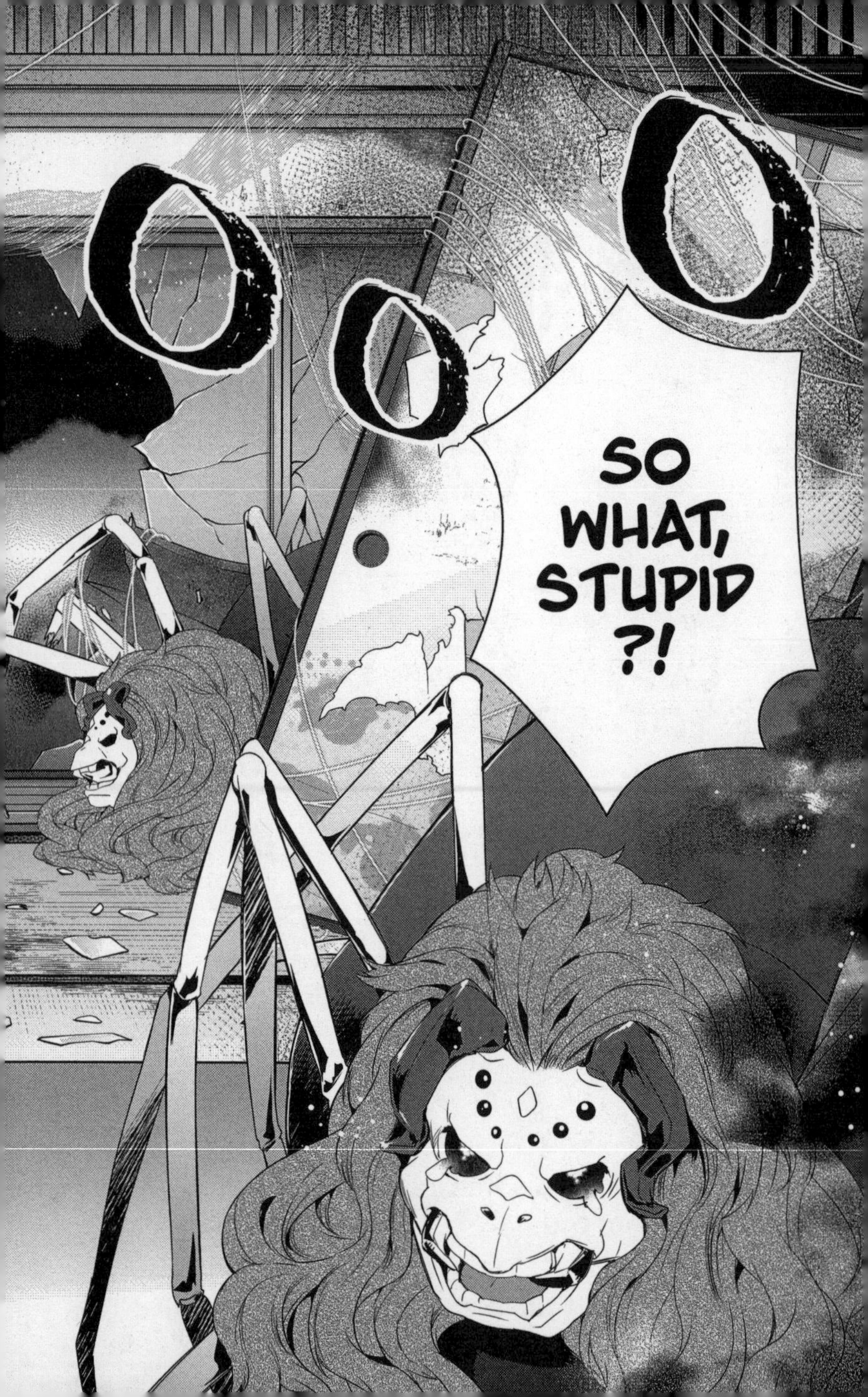
SO WHAT, STUPID ?!

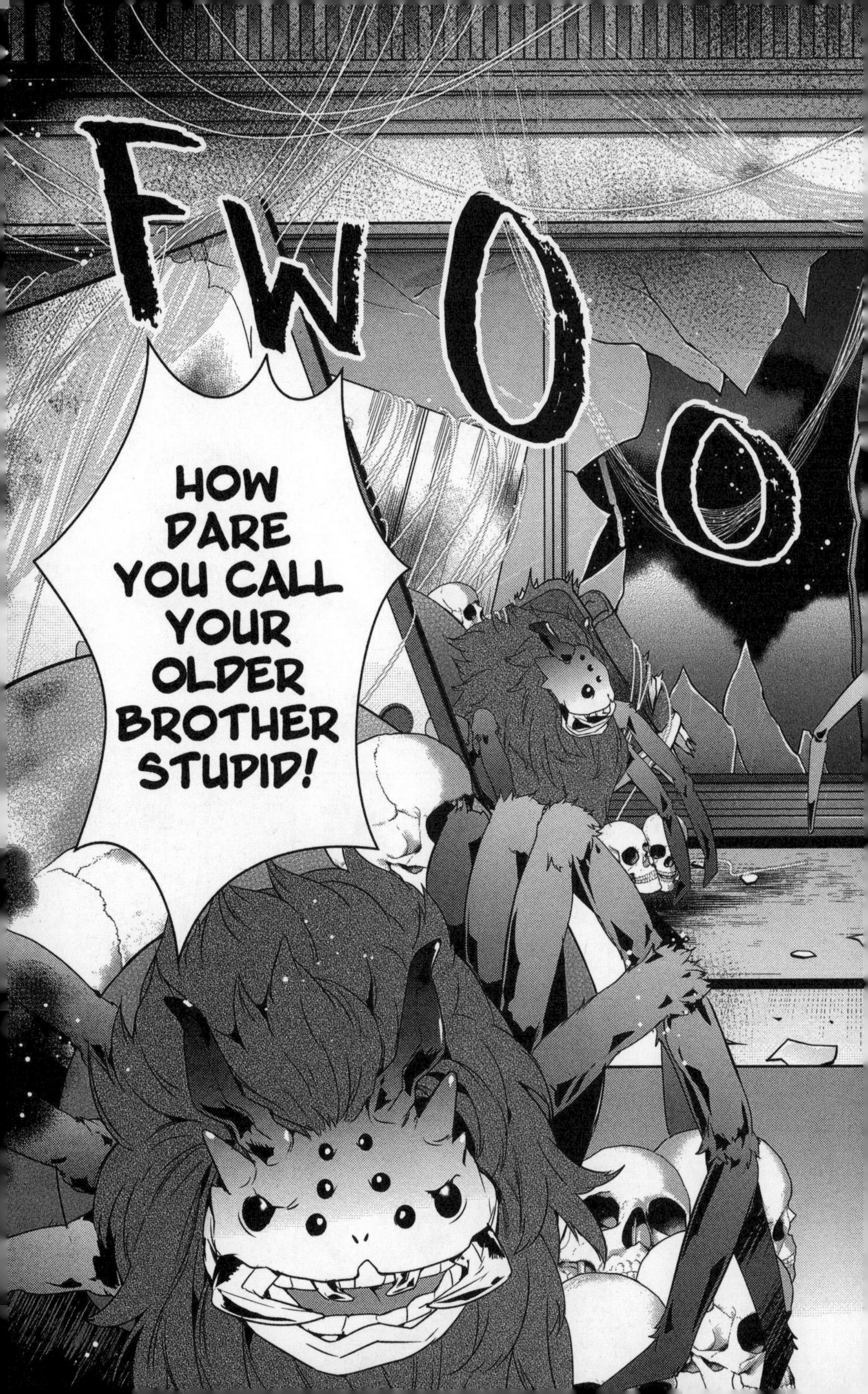
FWOOO
HOW DARE YOU CALL YOUR OLDER BROTHER STUPID!

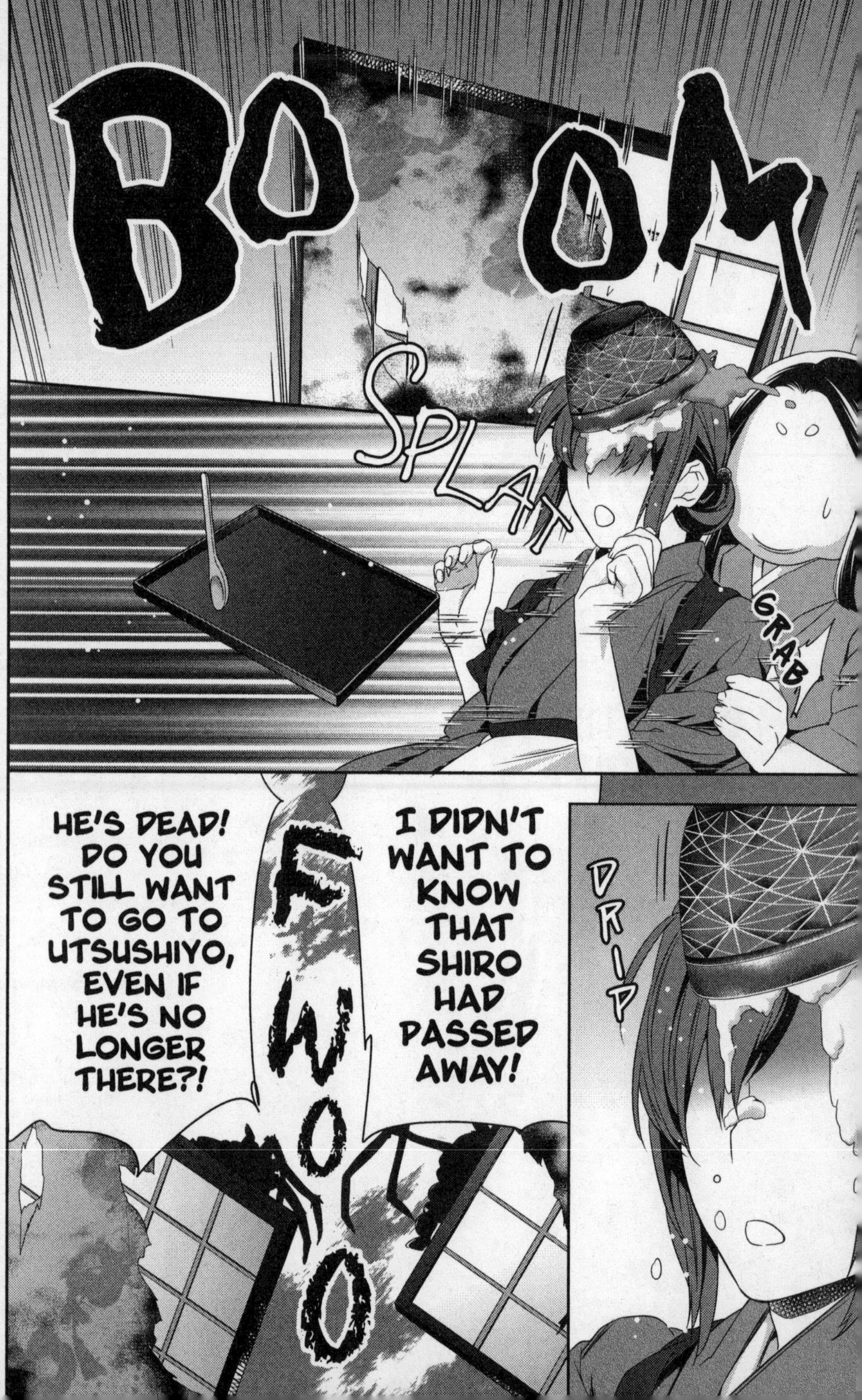
BOOM
SPLAT
GRAB
DRIP
I DIDN'T WANT TO KNOW THAT SHIRO HAD PASSED AWAY!
FWOOO
HE'S DEAD! DO YOU STILL WANT TO GO TO UTSUSHIYO, EVEN IF HE'S NO LONGER THERE?!

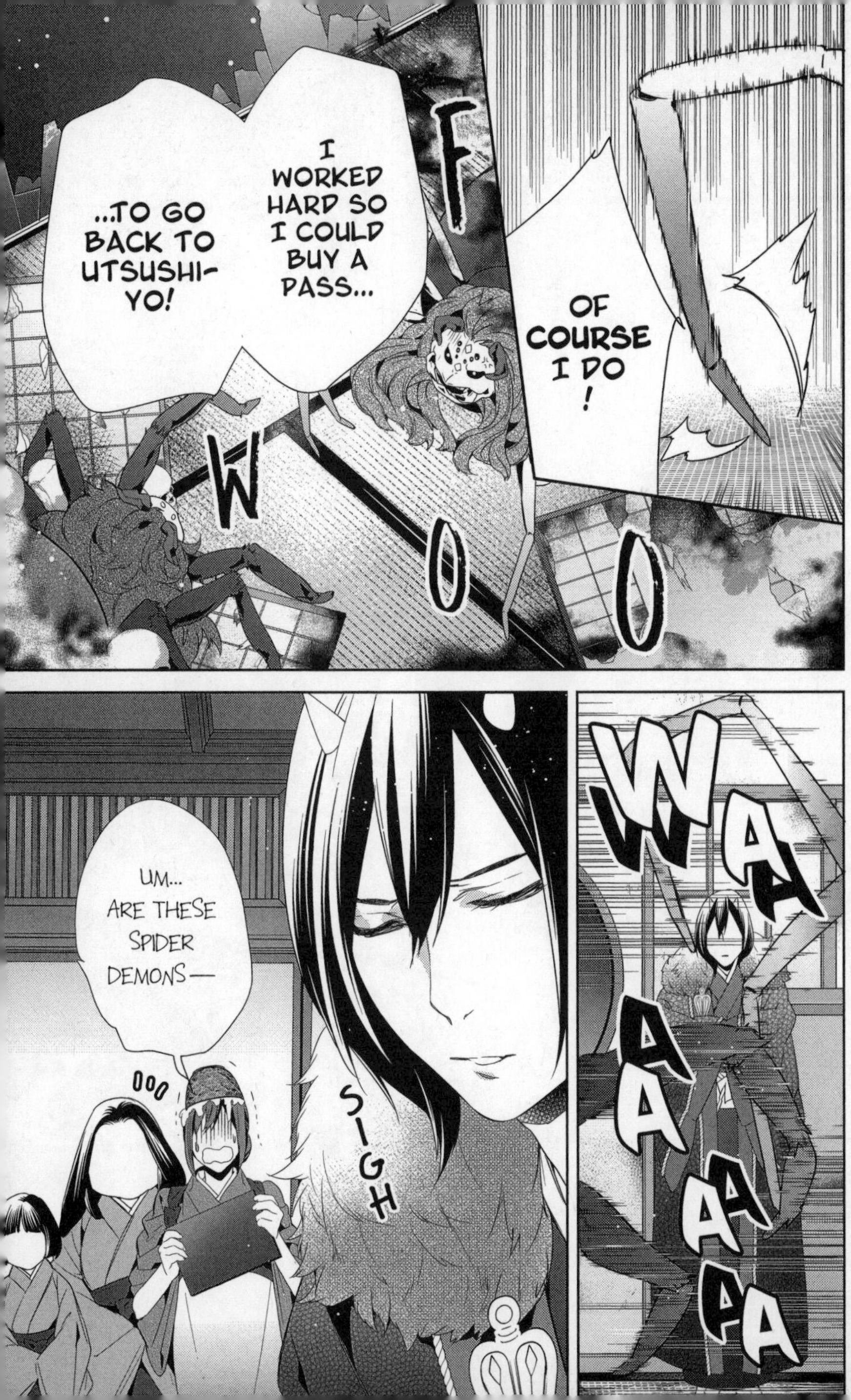
OF COURSE I DO!
I WORKED HARD SO I COULD BUY A PASS...
...TO GO BACK TO UTSUSHI-YO!
FWOO
WAAAAAAA
SIGH
UM... ARE THESE SPIDER DEMONS—

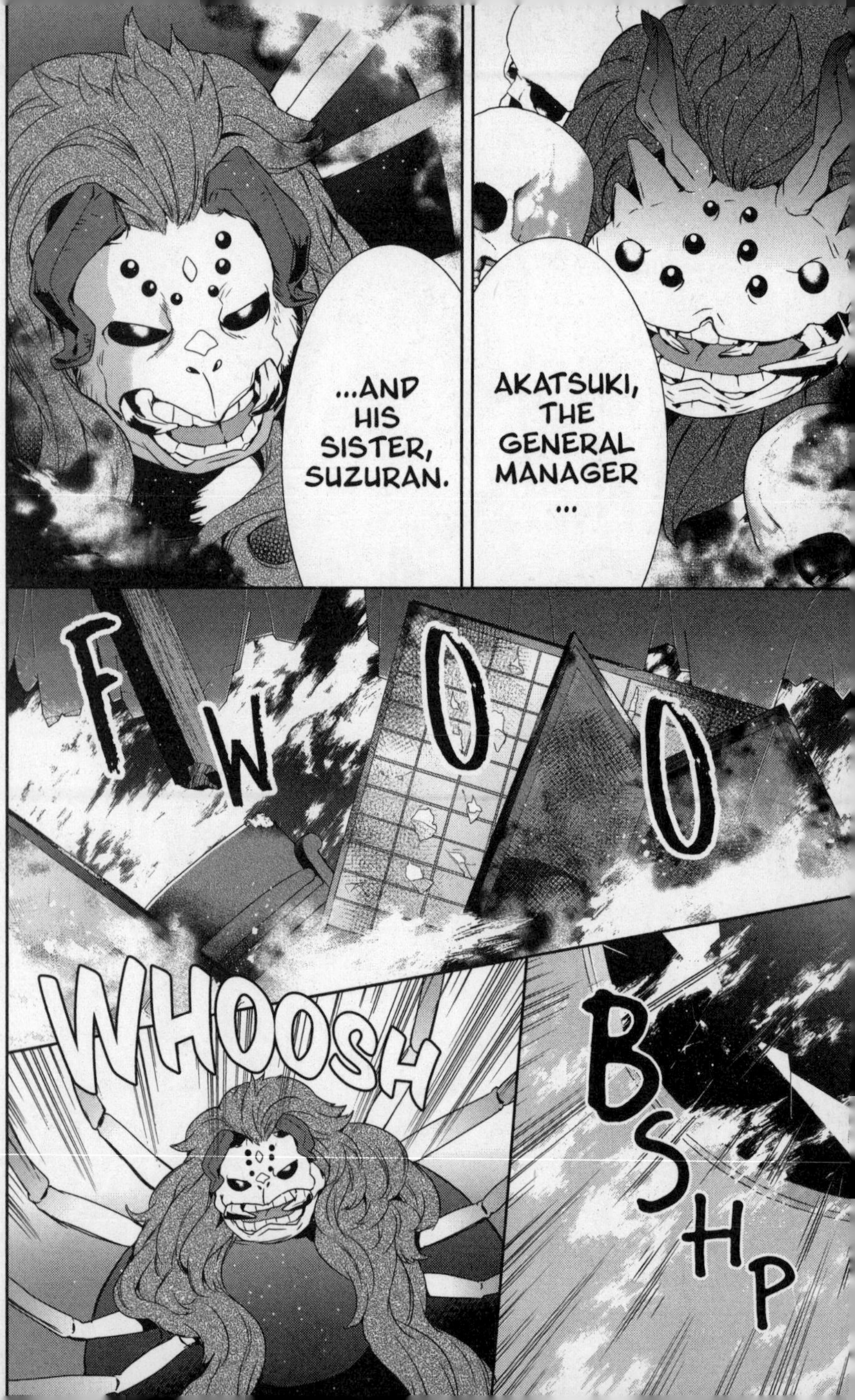
AKATSUKI, THE GENERAL MANAGER ...
...AND HIS SISTER, SUZURAN.
FWOO
WHOOSH
BSHP

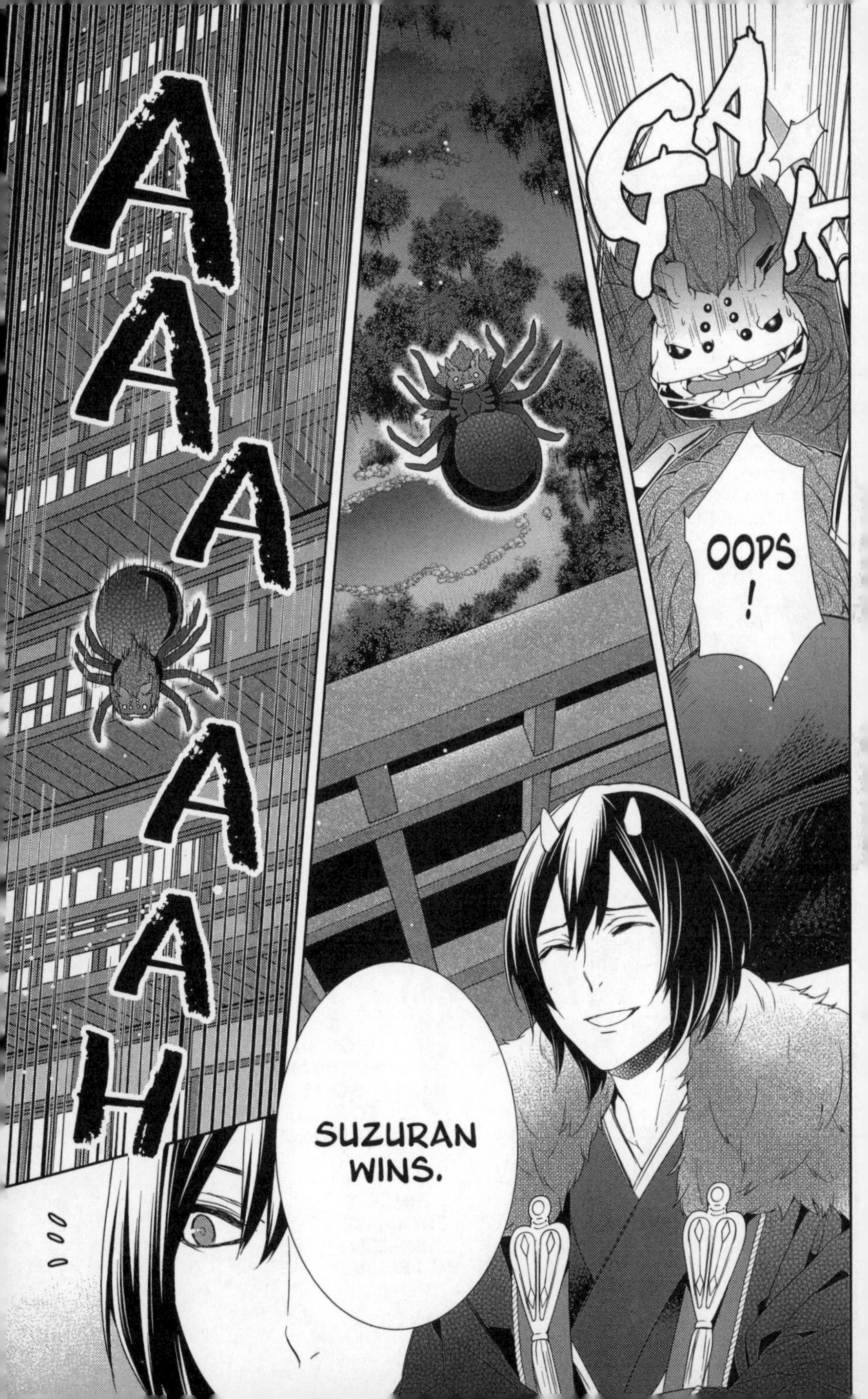
GAK
OOPS!
AAAAAH
SUZURAN WINS.
...

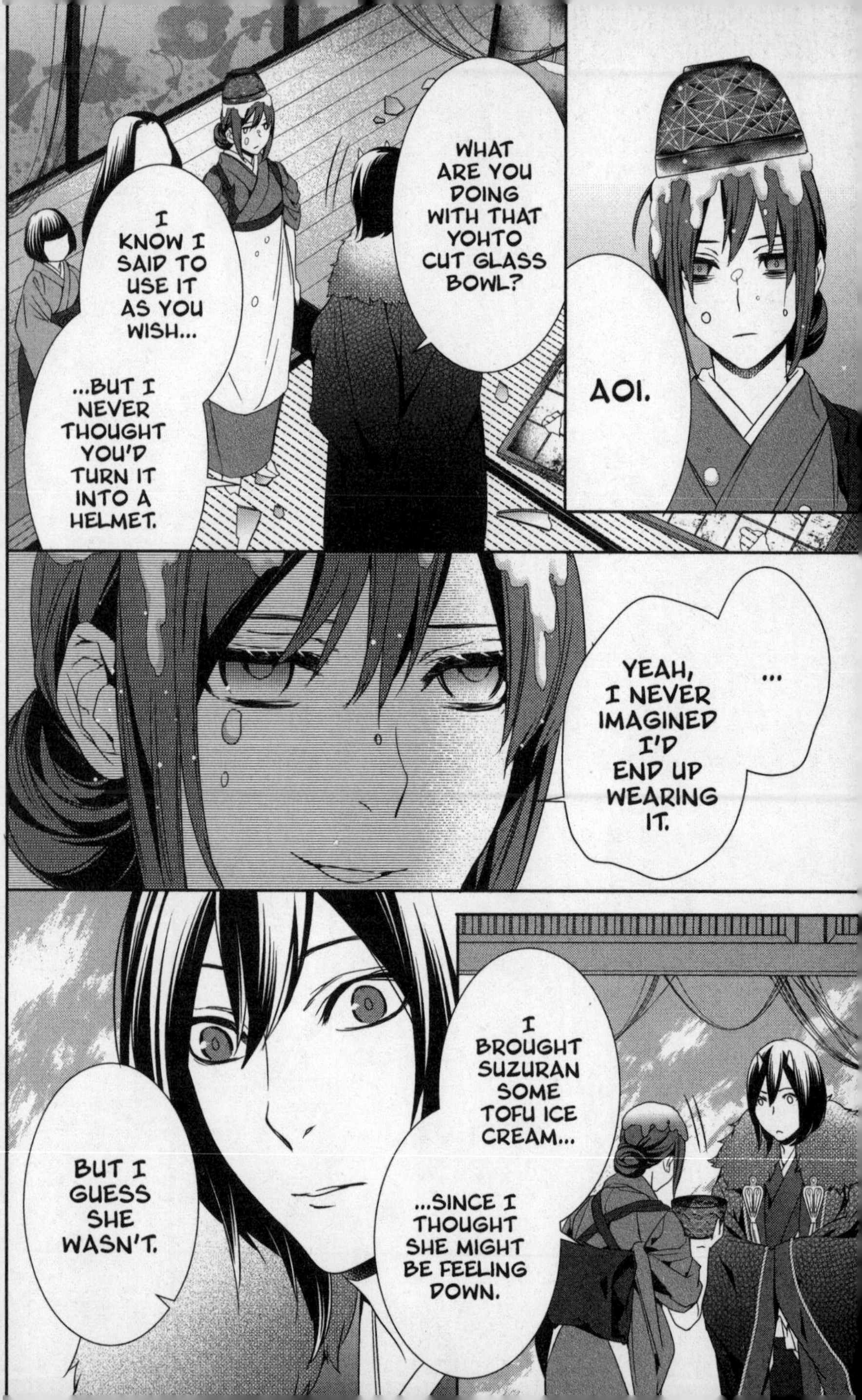
AOI.
WHAT ARE YOU DOING WITH THAT YOHTO CUT GLASS BOWL?
I KNOW I SAID TO USE IT AS YOU WISH...
...BUT I NEVER THOUGHT YOU'D TURN IT INTO A HELMET.
...
YEAH, I NEVER IMAGINED I'D END UP WEARING IT.
I BROUGHT SUZURAN SOME TOFU ICE CREAM...
...SINCE I THOUGHT SHE MIGHT BE FEELING DOWN.
BUT I GUESS SHE WASN'T.

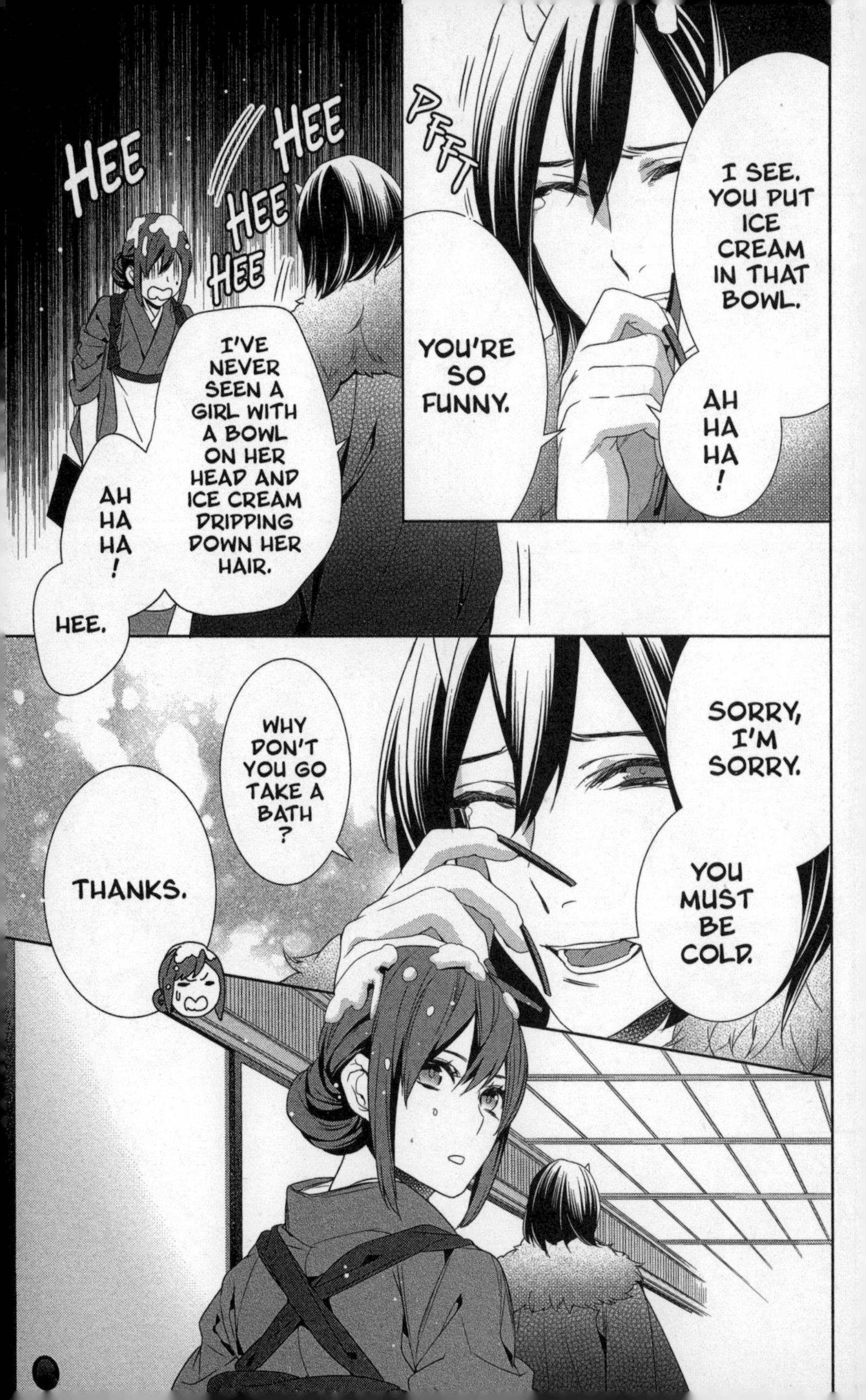
PFFT
I SEE. YOU PUT ICE CREAM IN THAT BOWL.
AH HA HA!
YOU'RE SO FUNNY.
HEE HEE HEE HEE
I'VE NEVER SEEN A GIRL WITH A BOWL ON HER HEAD AND ICE CREAM DRIPPING DOWN HER HAIR.
AH HA HA!
HEE.
SORRY, I'M SORRY.
YOU MUST BE COLD.
WHY DON'T YOU GO TAKE A BATH?
THANKS.

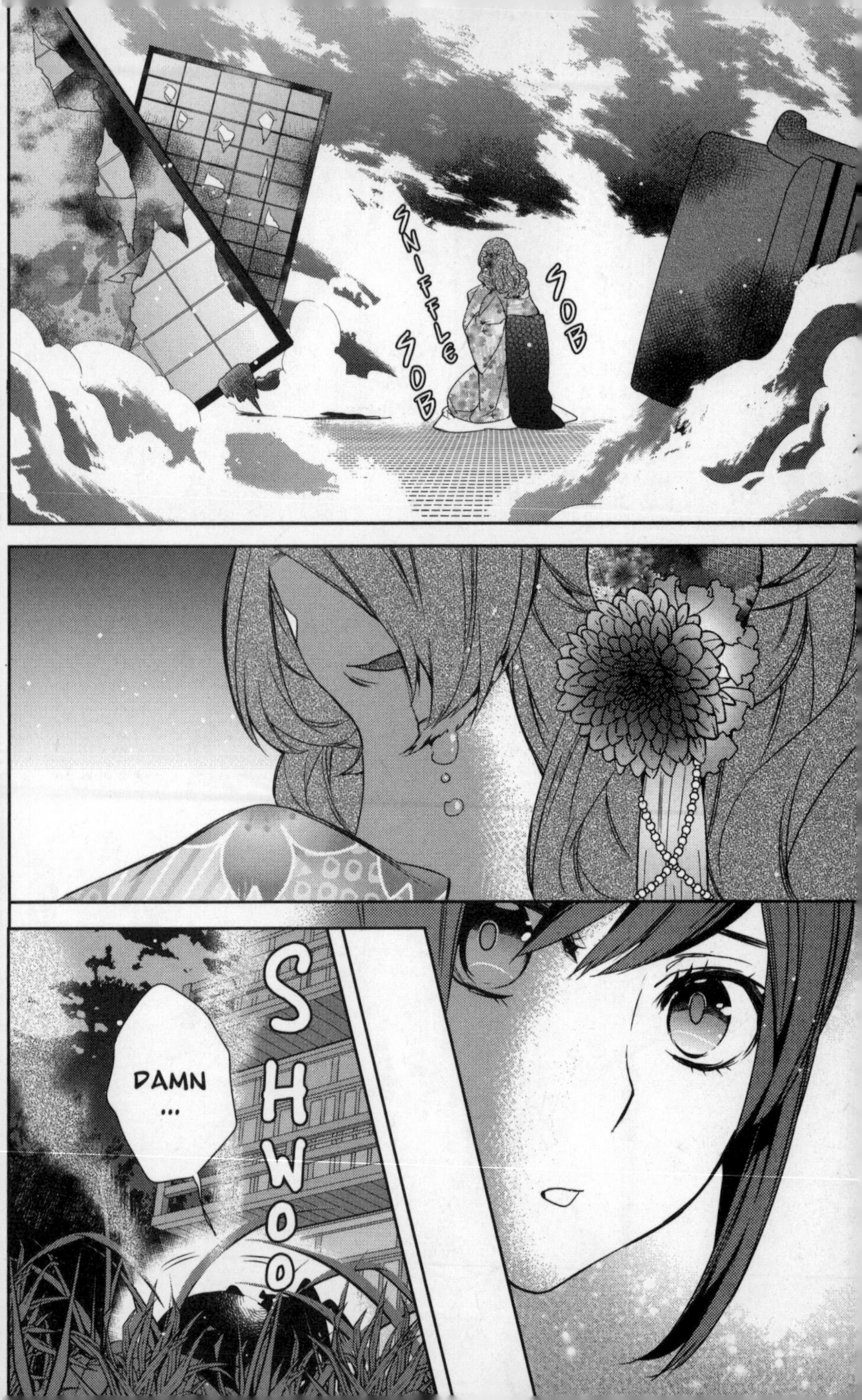
SOB
SNIFFLE SOB
SHWOO
DAMN ...

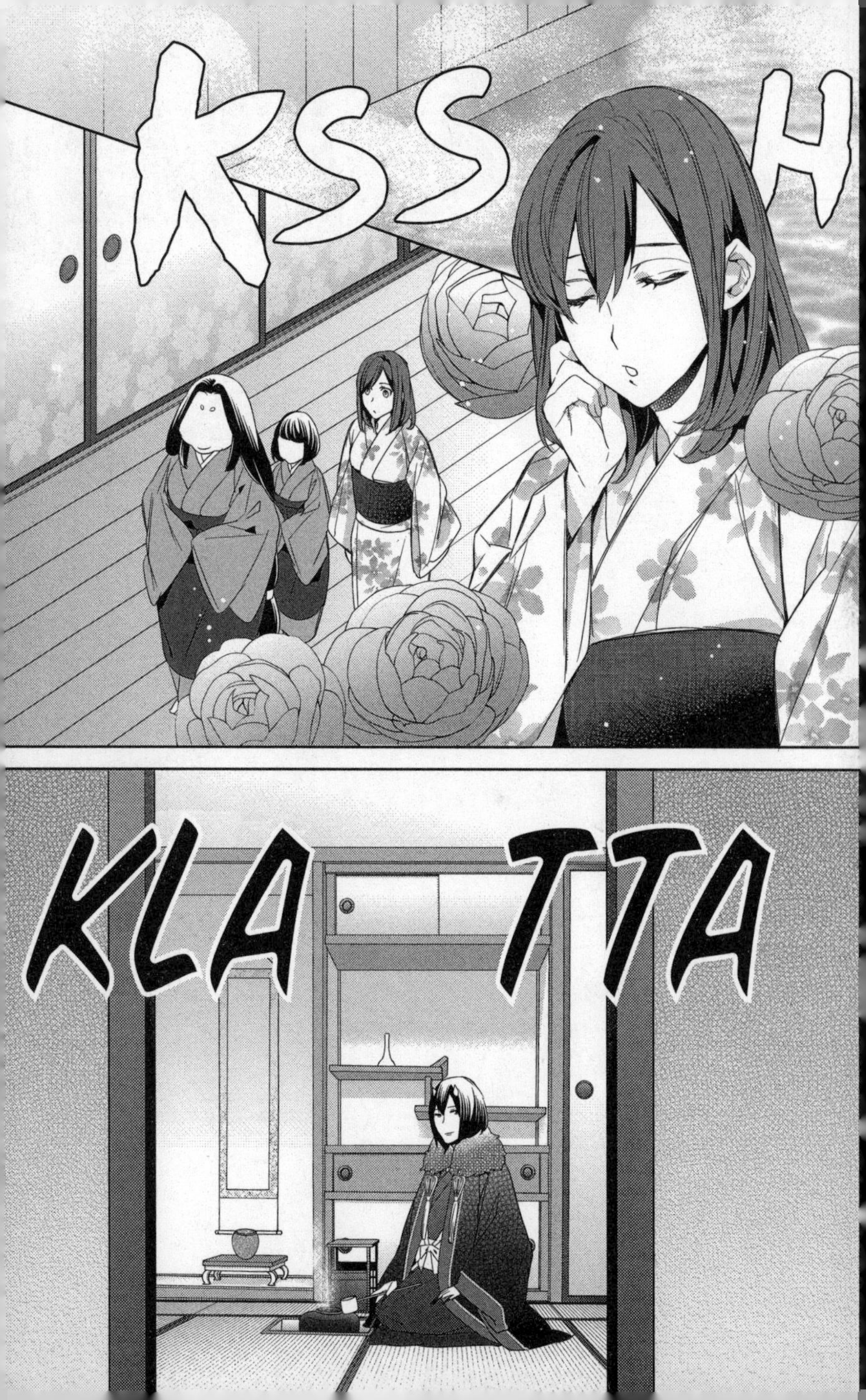
KSSH
KLATTA

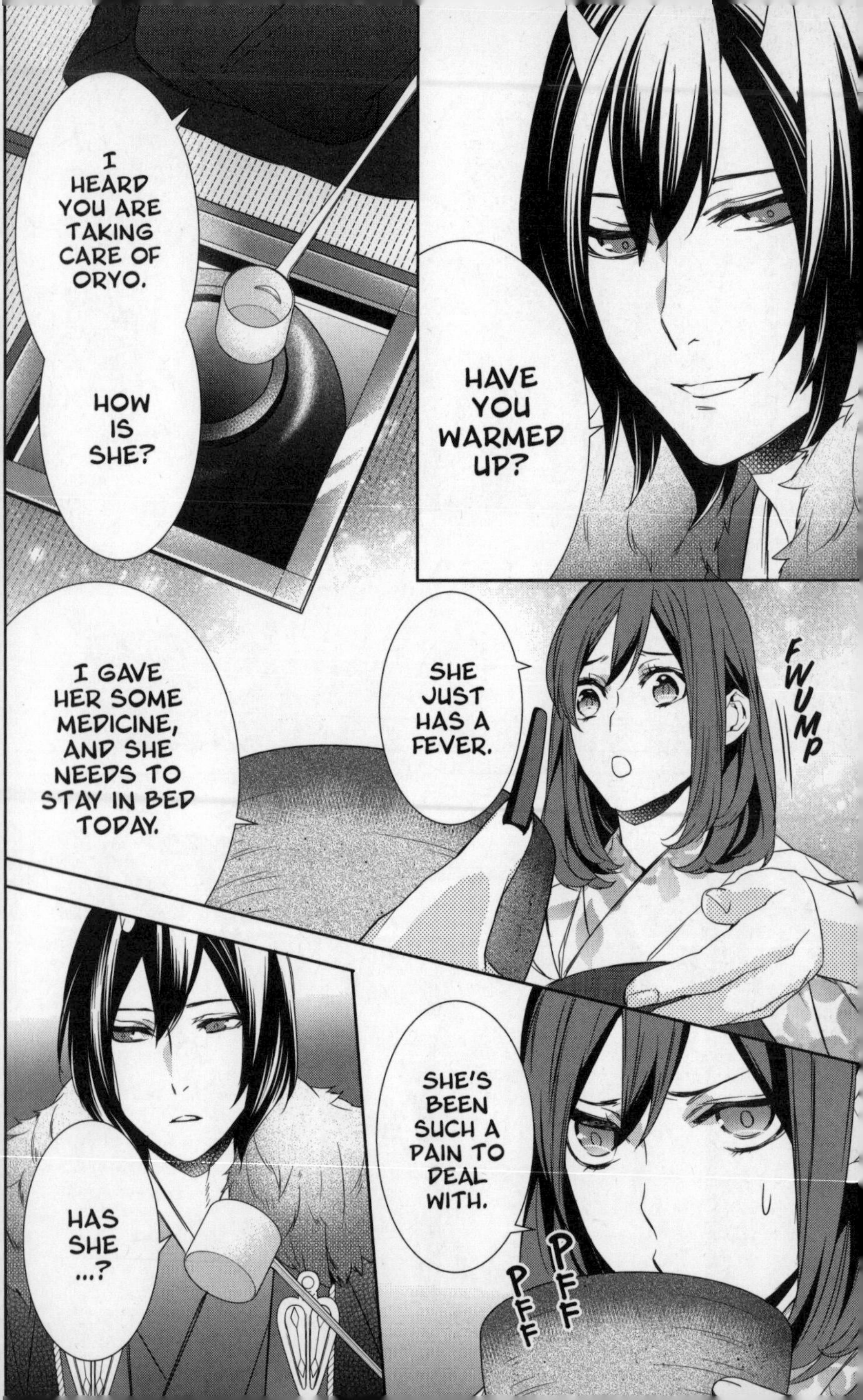
HAVE YOU WARMED UP?
I HEARD YOU ARE TAKING CARE OF ORYO.
HOW IS SHE?
FWUMP
SHE JUST HAS A FEVER.
I GAVE HER SOME MEDICINE, AND SHE NEEDS TO STAY IN BED TODAY.
SHE'S BEEN SUCH A PAIN TO DEAL WITH.
PFF
PFF
HAS SHE ...?

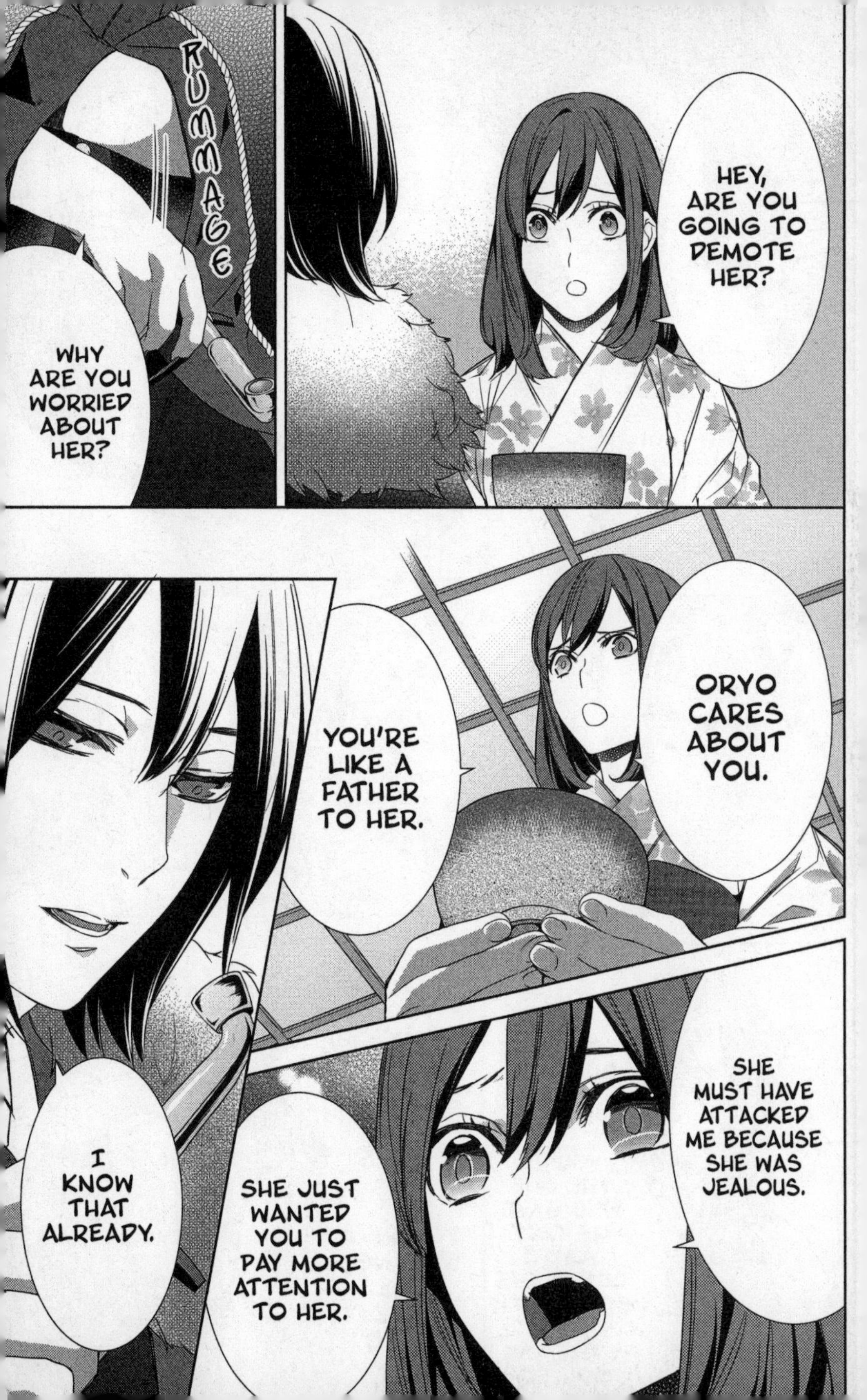
HEY, ARE YOU GOING TO DEMOTE HER?
RUMMAGE
WHY ARE YOU WORRIED ABOUT HER?
ORYO CARES ABOUT YOU.
YOU'RE LIKE A FATHER TO HER.
SHE MUST HAVE ATTACKED ME BECAUSE SHE WAS JEALOUS.
SHE JUST WANTED YOU TO PAY MORE ATTENTION TO HER.
I KNOW THAT ALREADY.

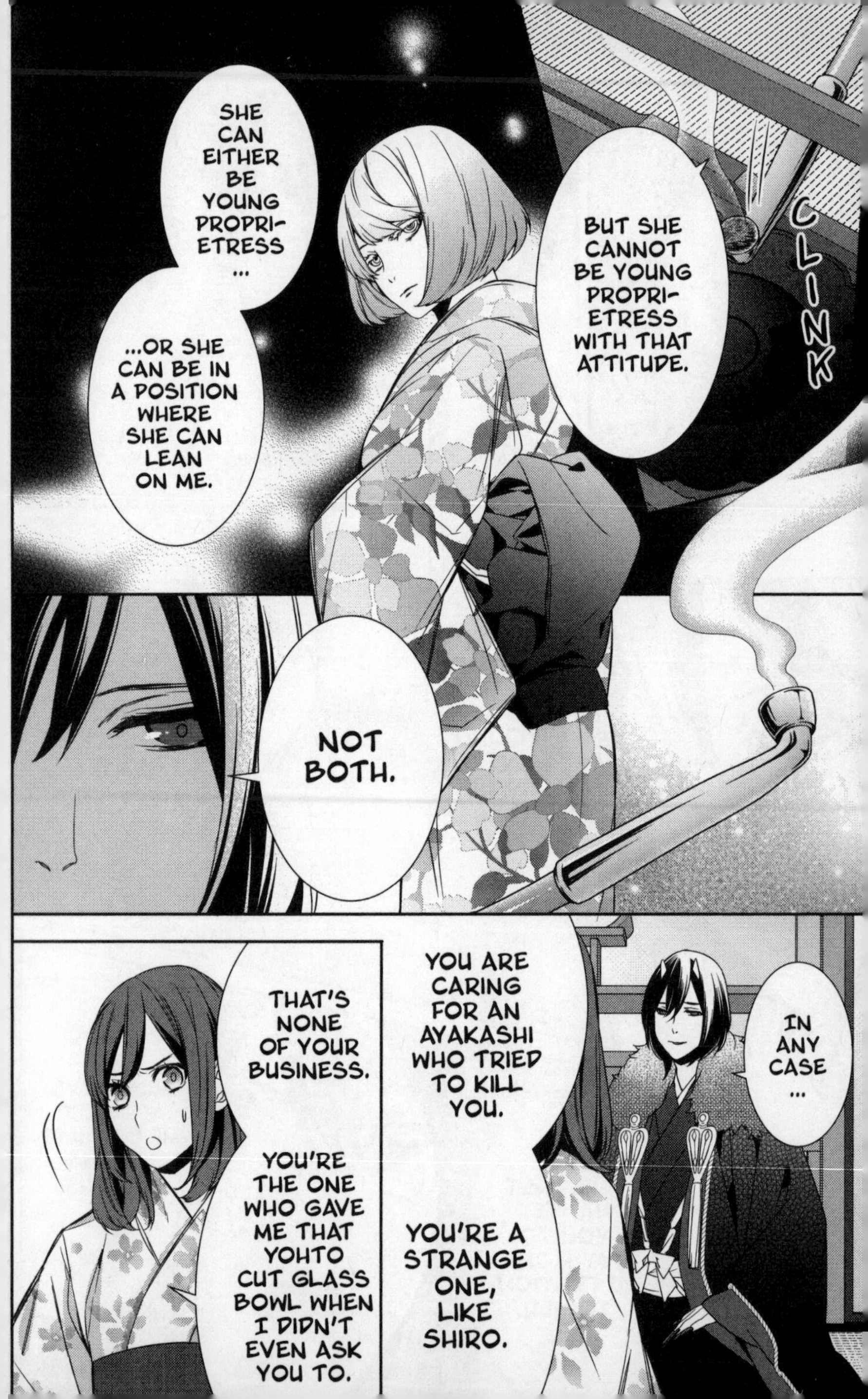
CLINK
BUT SHE CANNOT BE YOUNG PROPRI-ETRESS WITH THAT ATTITUDE.
SHE CAN EITHER BE YOUNG PROPRI-ETRESS...
...OR SHE CAN BE IN A POSITION WHERE SHE CAN LEAN ON ME.
NOT BOTH.
IN ANY CASE...
YOU ARE CARING FOR AN AYAKASHI WHO TRIED TO KILL YOU.
YOU'RE A STRANGE ONE, LIKE SHIRO.
THAT'S NONE OF YOUR BUSINESS.
YOU'RE THE ONE WHO GAVE ME THAT YOHTO CUT GLASS BOWL WHEN I DIDN'T EVEN ASK YOU TO.

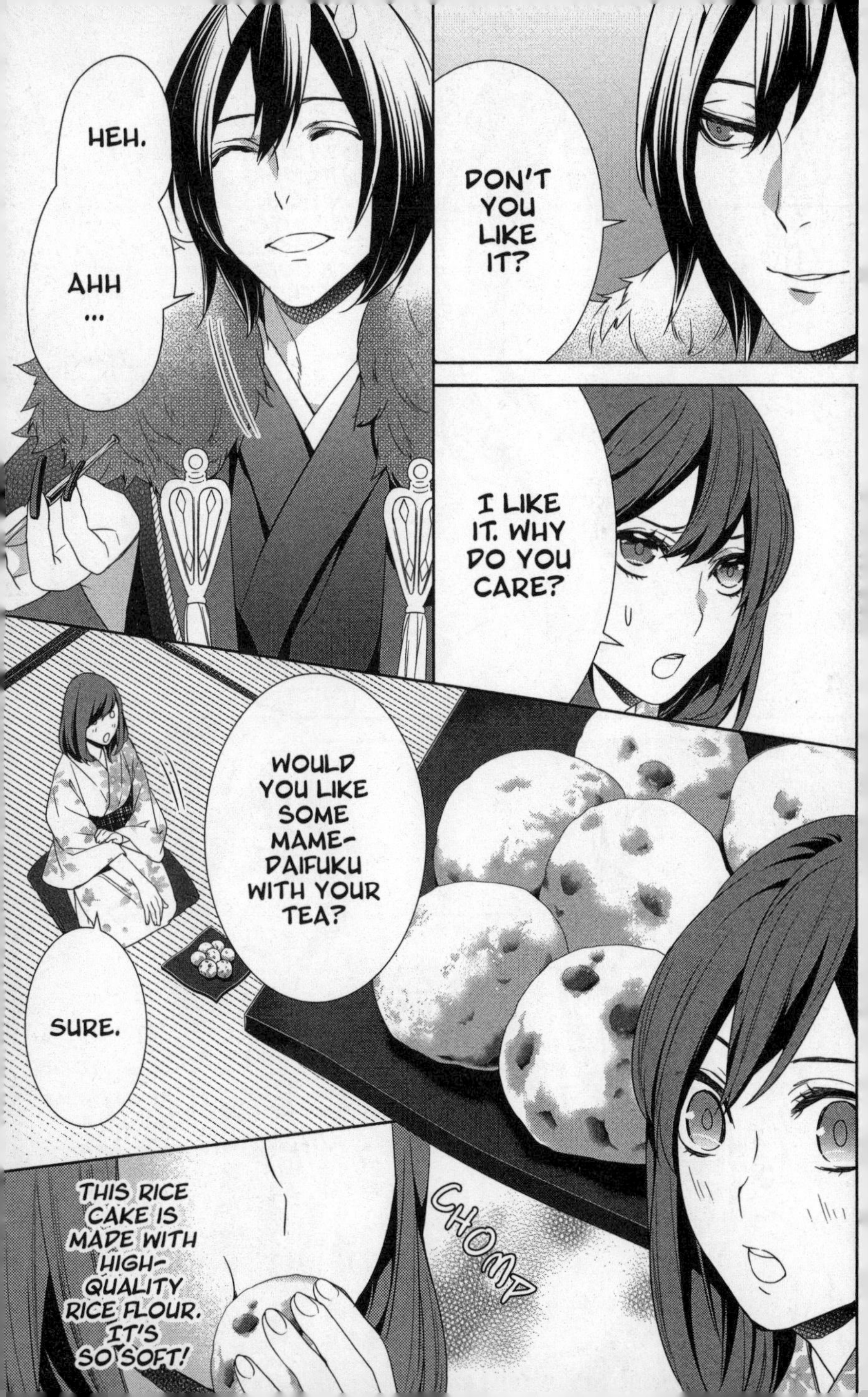
DON'T YOU LIKE IT?
I LIKE IT. WHY DO YOU CARE?
HEH.
AHH...
WOULD YOU LIKE SOME MAME-DAIFUKU WITH YOUR TEA?
SURE.
CHOMP
THIS RICE CAKE IS MADE WITH HIGH-QUALITY RICE FLOUR. IT'S SO SOFT!

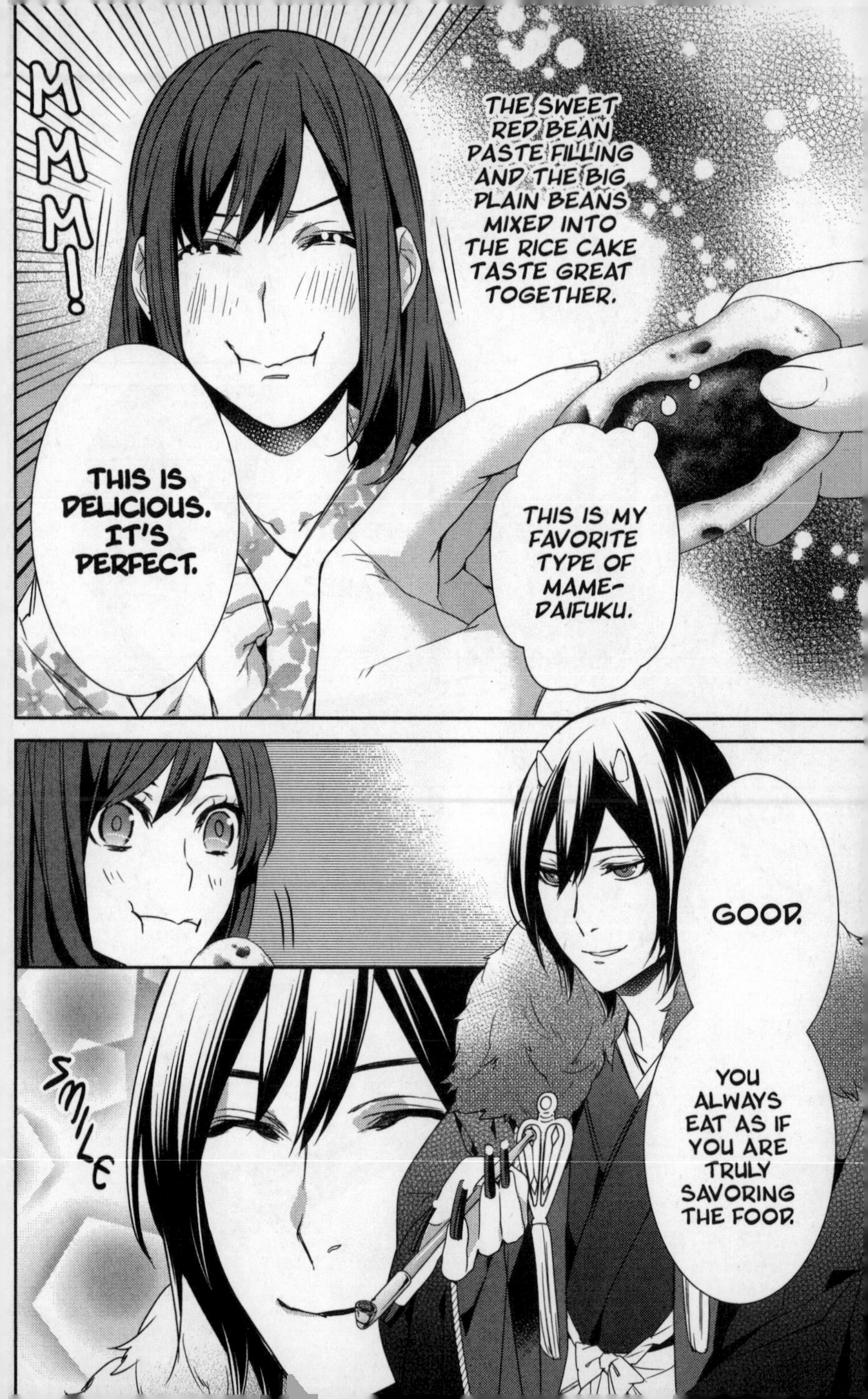
THE SWEET RED BEAN PASTE FILLING AND THE BIG PLAIN BEANS MIXED INTO THE RICE CAKE TASTE GREAT TOGETHER.
MMM!
THIS IS MY FAVORITE TYPE OF MAME-DAIFUKU.
THIS IS DELICIOUS. IT'S PERFECT.
GOOD.
YOU ALWAYS EAT AS IF YOU ARE TRULY SAVORING THE FOOD.
SMILE

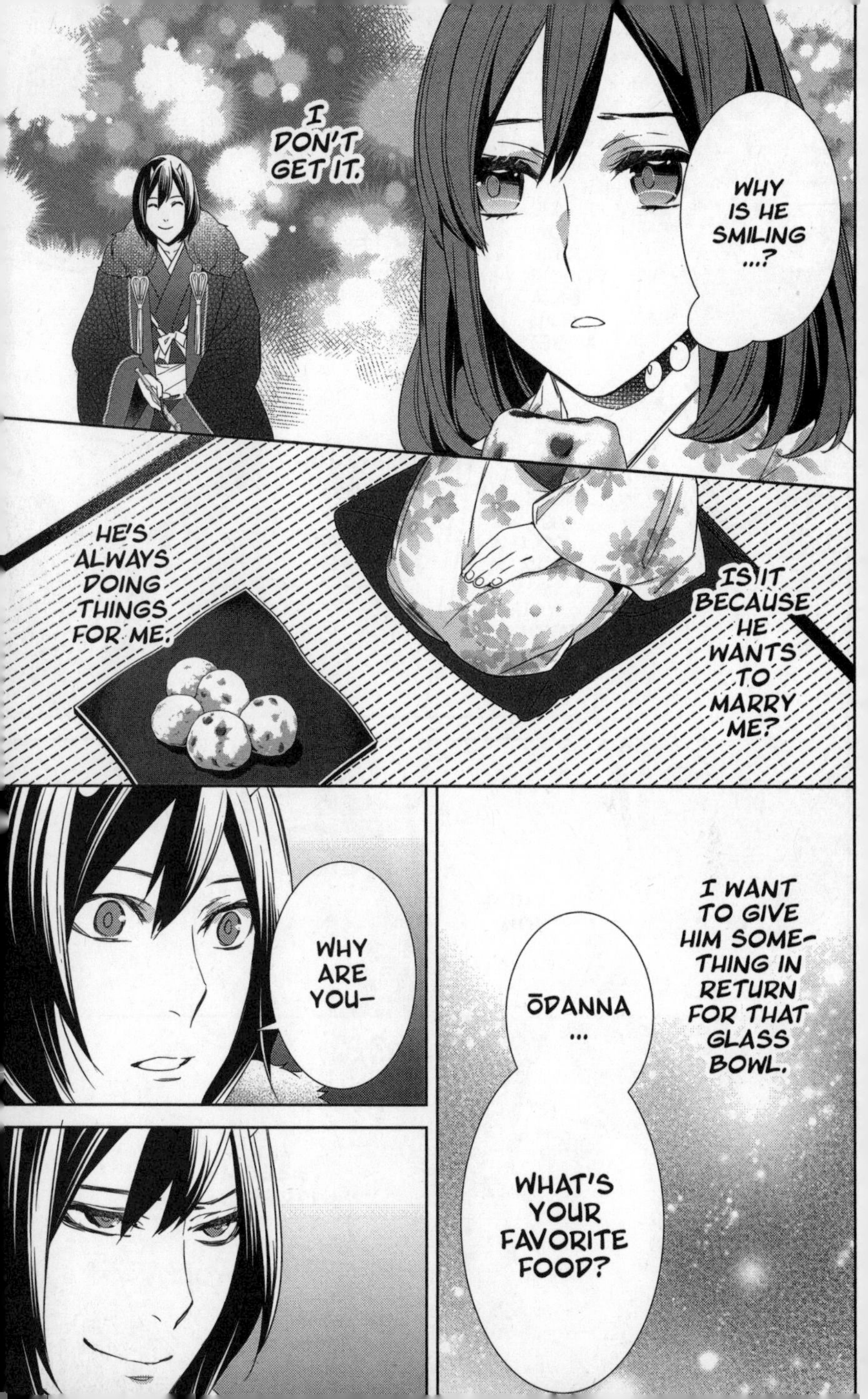
WHY IS HE SMILING ...?
I DON'T GET IT.
IS IT BECAUSE HE WANTS TO MARRY ME?
HE'S ALWAYS DOING THINGS FOR ME.
I WANT TO GIVE HIM SOMETHING IN RETURN FOR THAT GLASS BOWL.
ŌDANNA ... WHAT'S YOUR FAVORITE FOOD?
WHY ARE YOU-

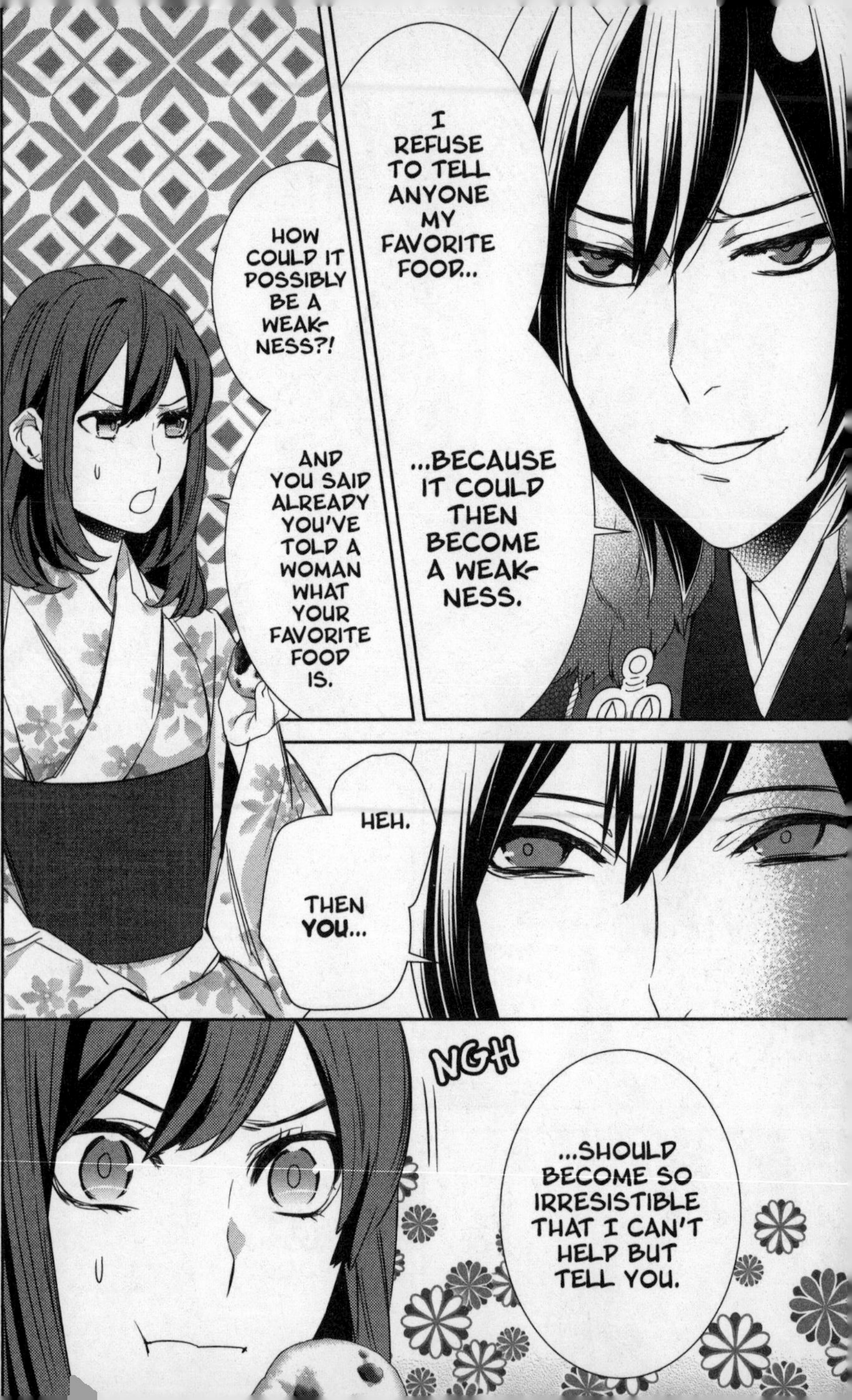
I REFUSE TO TELL ANYONE MY FAVORITE FOOD...
...BECAUSE IT COULD THEN BECOME A WEAK-NESS.
HOW COULD IT POSSIBLY BE A WEAK-NESS?!
AND YOU SAID ALREADY YOU'VE TOLD A WOMAN WHAT YOUR FAVORITE FOOD IS.
HEH.
THEN **YOU**...
NGH
...SHOULD BECOME SO IRRESISTIBLE THAT I CAN'T HELP BUT TELL YOU.

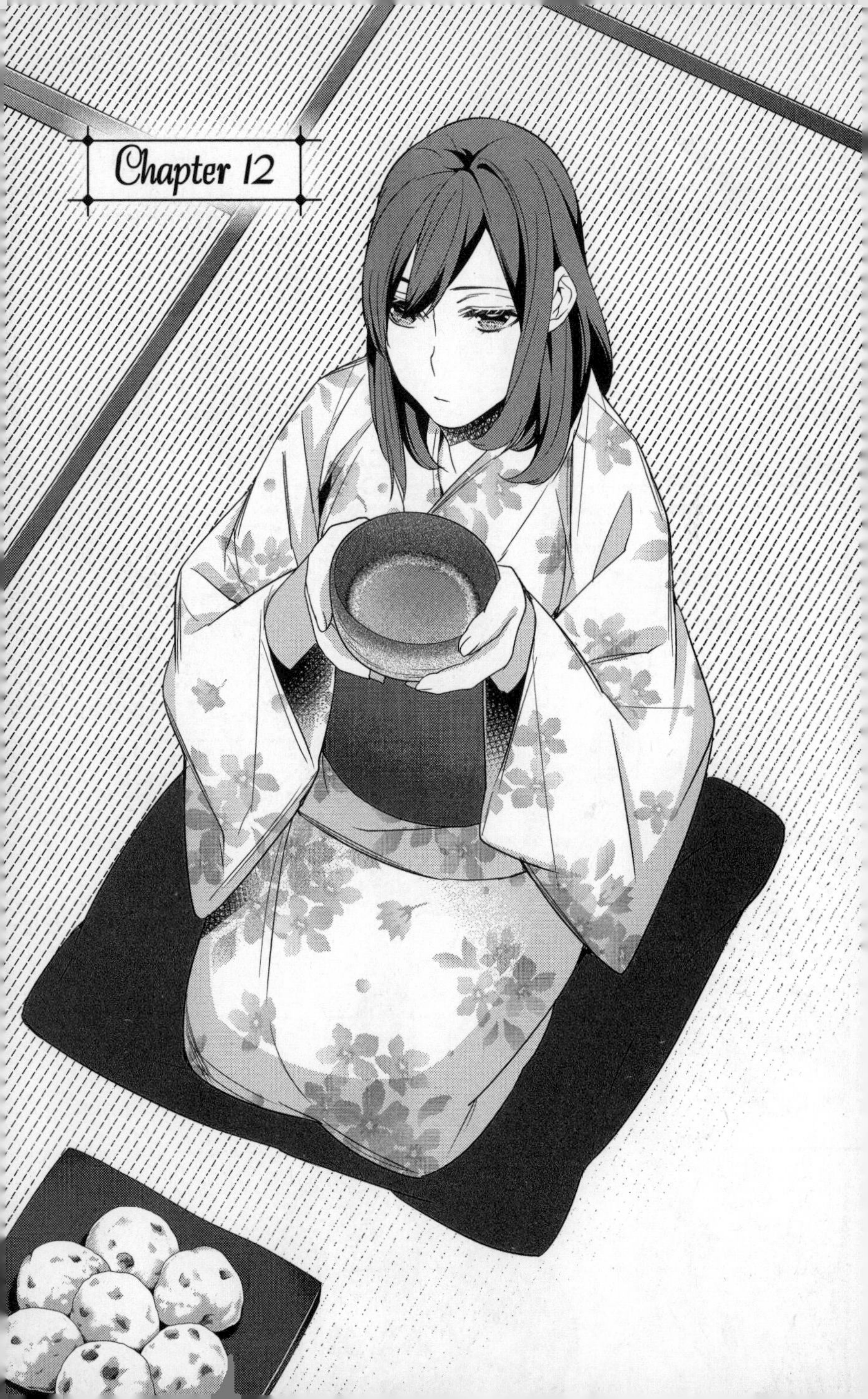
Chapter 12

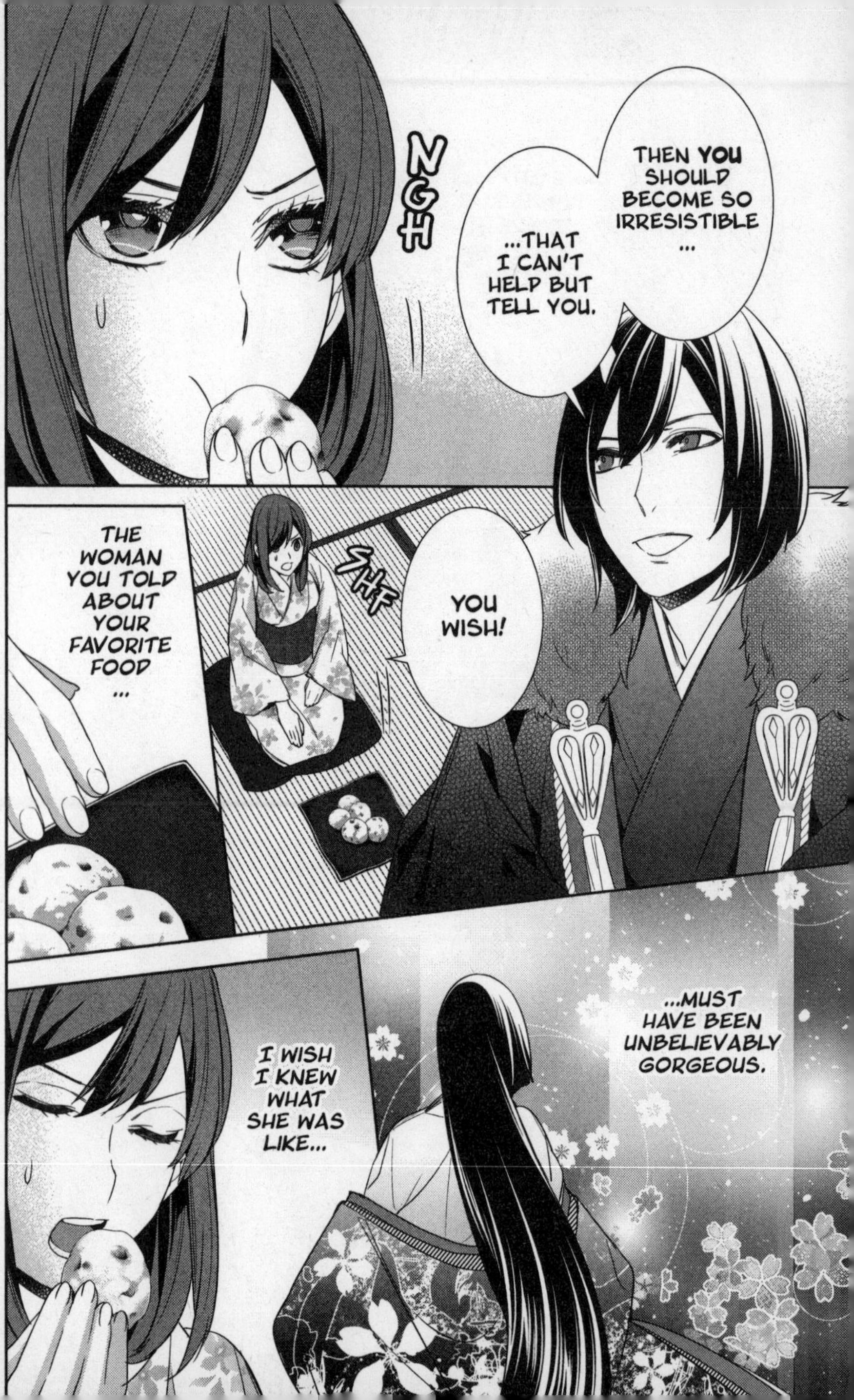
THEN YOU SHOULD BECOME SO IRRESISTIBLE...
...THAT I CAN'T HELP BUT TELL YOU.
NGH
YOU WISH!
SHF
THE WOMAN YOU TOLD ABOUT YOUR FAVORITE FOOD...
...MUST HAVE BEEN UNBELIEVABLY GORGEOUS.
I WISH I KNEW WHAT SHE WAS LIKE...

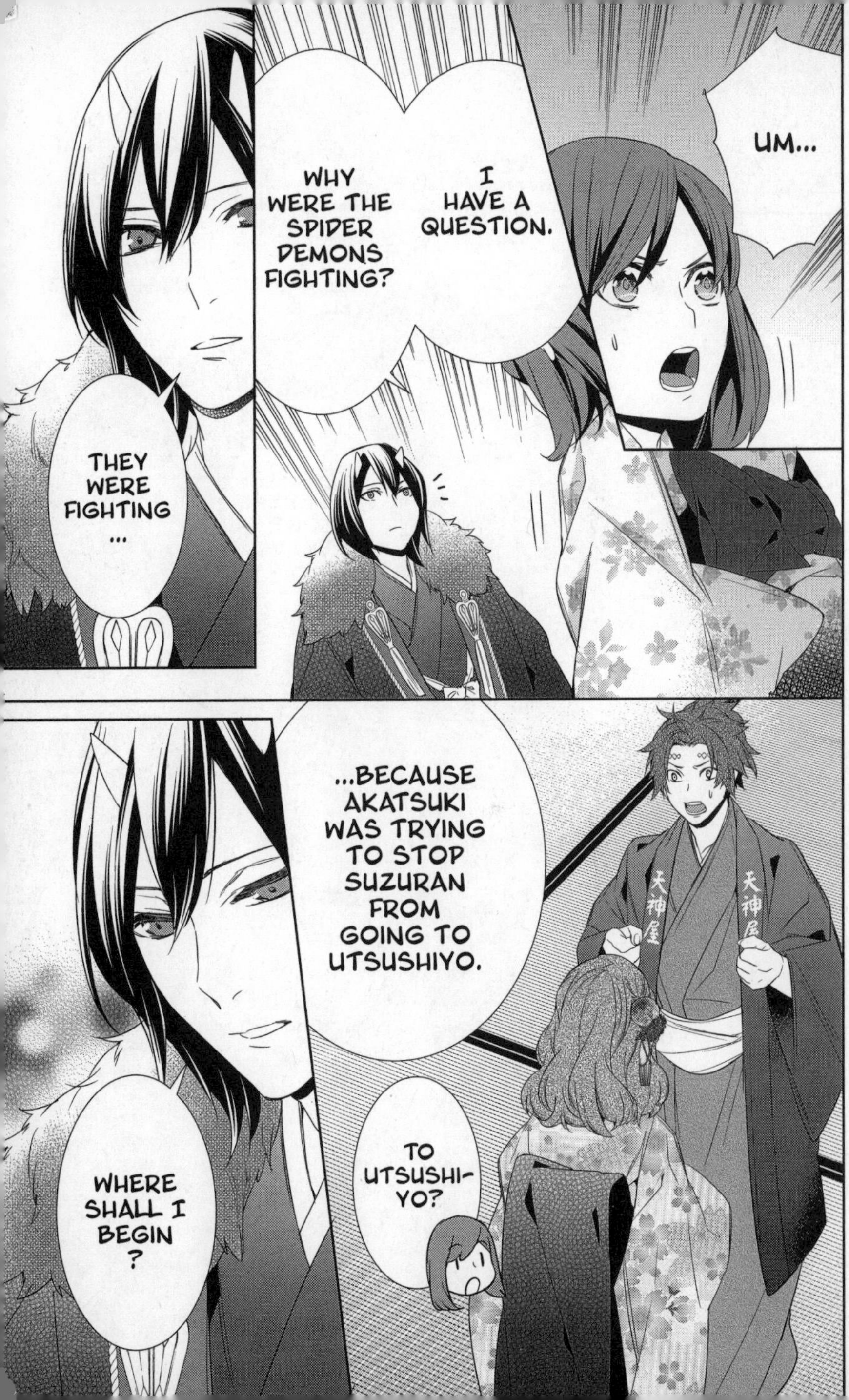
UM...
I HAVE A QUESTION.
WHY WERE THE SPIDER DEMONS FIGHTING?
THEY WERE FIGHTING ...
...BECAUSE AKATSUKI WAS TRYING TO STOP SUZURAN FROM GOING TO UTSUSHIYO.
TO UTSUSHI-YO?
WHERE SHALL I BEGIN ?

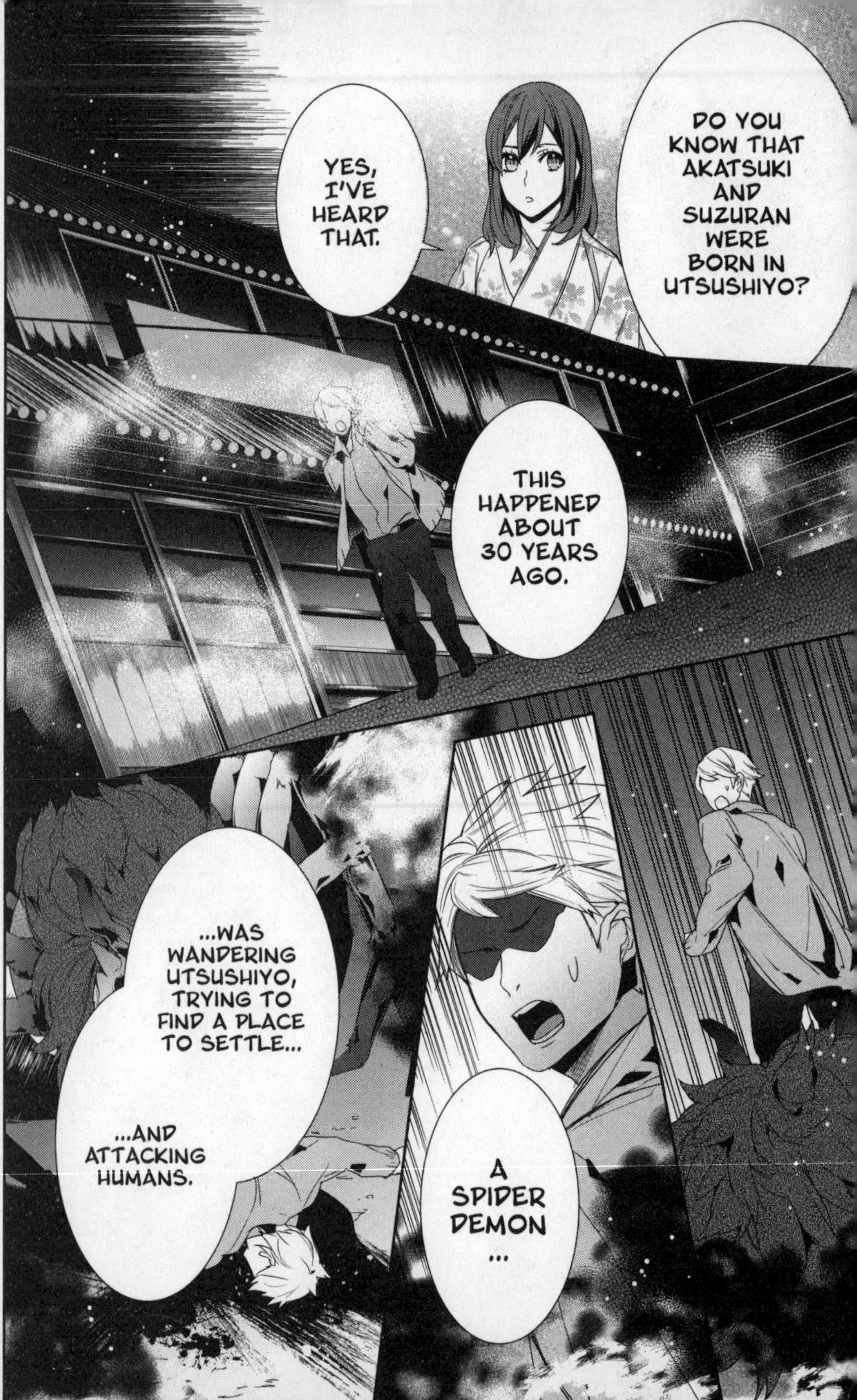
DO YOU KNOW THAT AKATSUKI AND SUZURAN WERE BORN IN UTSUSHIYO?
YES, I'VE HEARD THAT.
THIS HAPPENED ABOUT 30 YEARS AGO.
A SPIDER DEMON ...
...WAS WANDERING UTSUSHIYO, TRYING TO FIND A PLACE TO SETTLE...
...AND ATTACKING HUMANS.

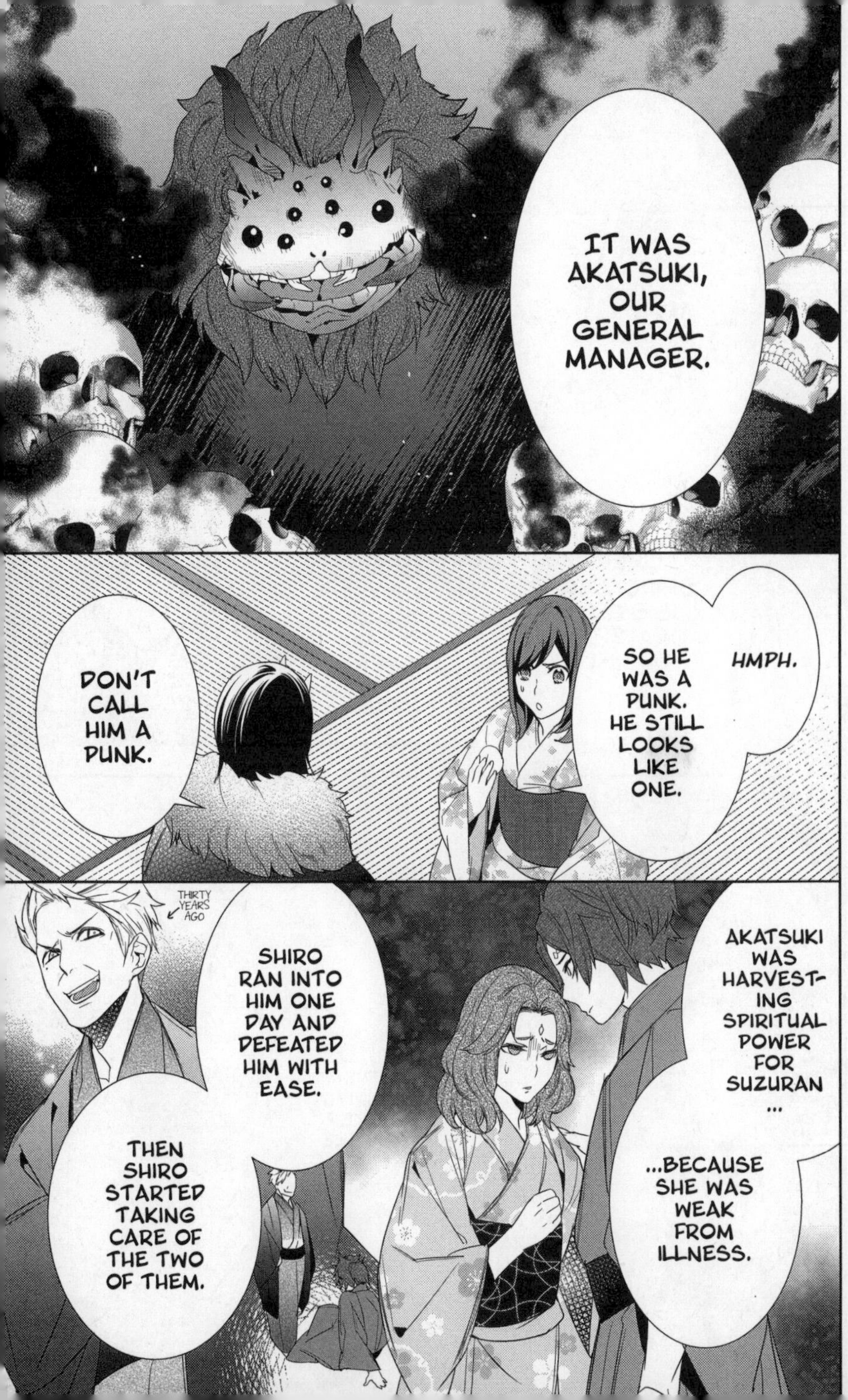
IT WAS AKATSUKI, OUR GENERAL MANAGER.
HMPH.
SO HE WAS A PUNK. HE STILL LOOKS LIKE ONE.
DON'T CALL HIM A PUNK.
AKATSUKI WAS HARVEST-ING SPIRITUAL POWER FOR SUZURAN...
...BECAUSE SHE WAS WEAK FROM ILLNESS.
THIRTY YEARS AGO
SHIRO RAN INTO HIM ONE DAY AND DEFEATED HIM WITH EASE.
THEN SHIRO STARTED TAKING CARE OF THE TWO OF THEM.

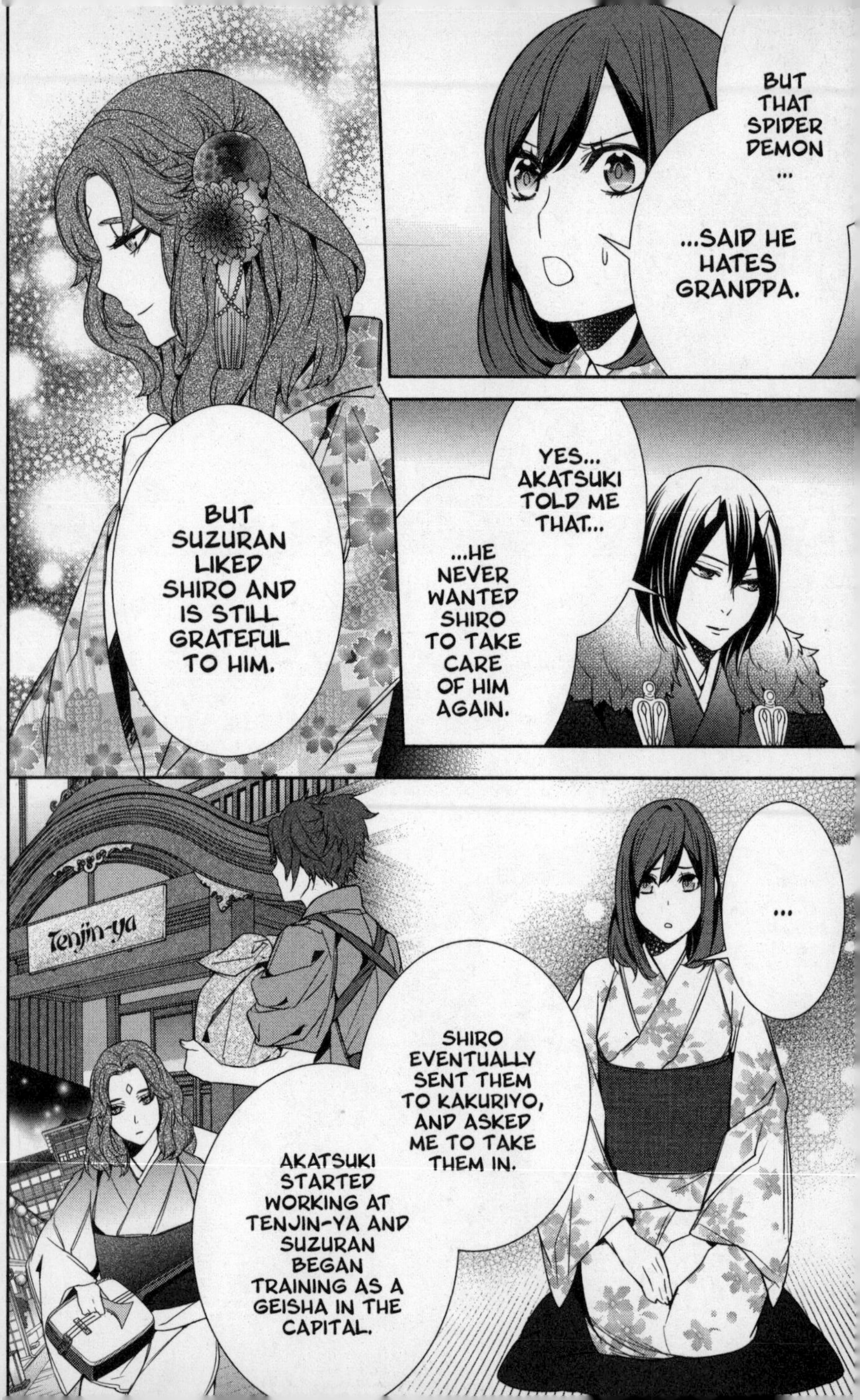
BUT THAT SPIDER DEMON...
...SAID HE HATES GRANDPA.
YES... AKATSUKI TOLD ME THAT...
...HE NEVER WANTED SHIRO TO TAKE CARE OF HIM AGAIN.
BUT SUZURAN LIKED SHIRO AND IS STILL GRATEFUL TO HIM.
...
SHIRO EVENTUALLY SENT THEM TO KAKURIYO, AND ASKED ME TO TAKE THEM IN.
AKATSUKI STARTED WORKING AT TENJIN-YA AND SUZURAN BEGAN TRAINING AS A GEISHA IN THE CAPITAL.
Tenjin-ya

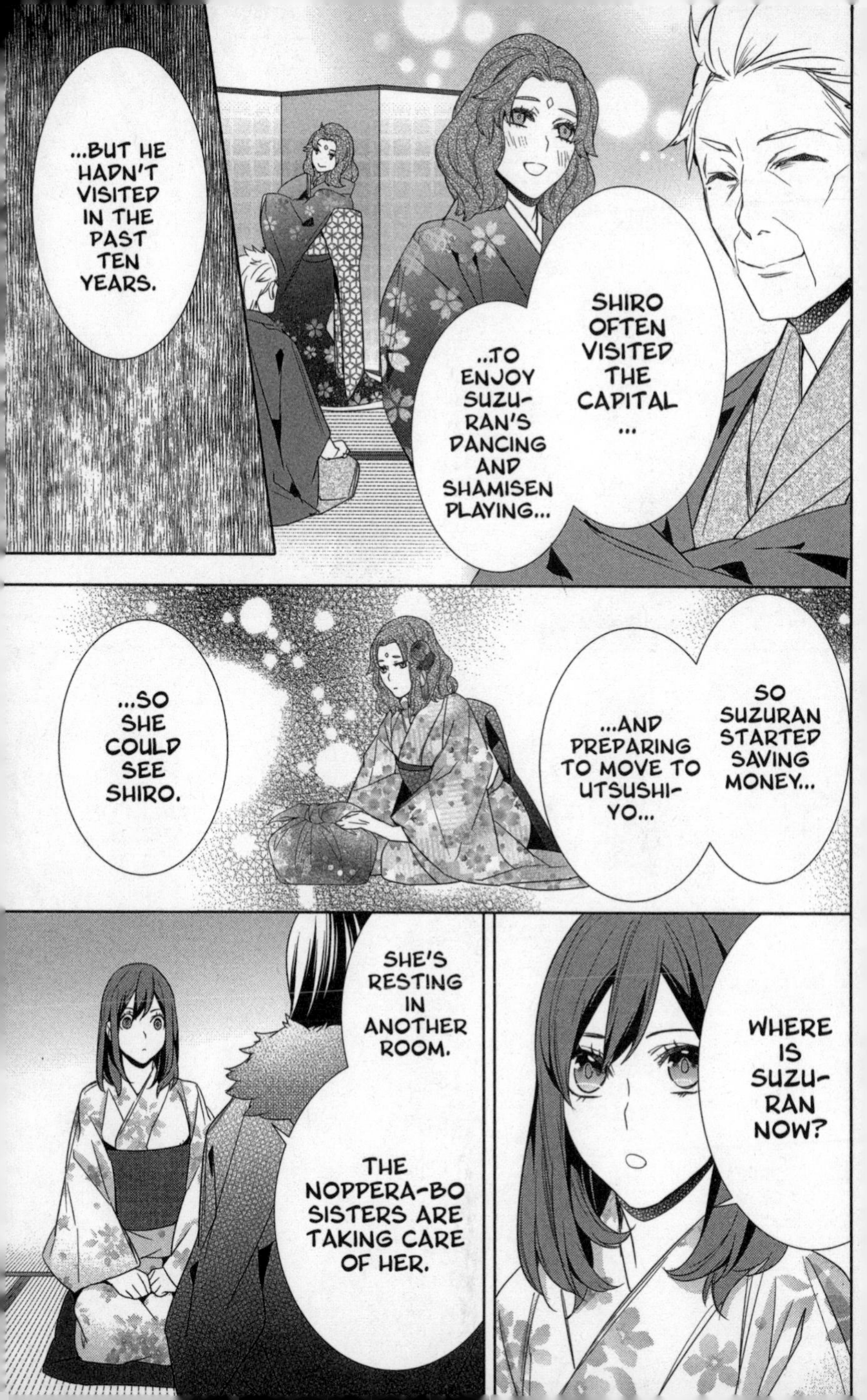
SHIRO OFTEN VISITED THE CAPITAL...
...TO ENJOY SUZURAN'S DANCING AND SHAMISEN PLAYING...
...BUT HE HADN'T VISITED IN THE PAST TEN YEARS.
SO SUZURAN STARTED SAVING MONEY...
...AND PREPARING TO MOVE TO UTSUSHIYO...
...SO SHE COULD SEE SHIRO.
WHERE IS SUZURAN NOW?
SHE'S RESTING IN ANOTHER ROOM.
THE NOPPERA-BO SISTERS ARE TAKING CARE OF HER.

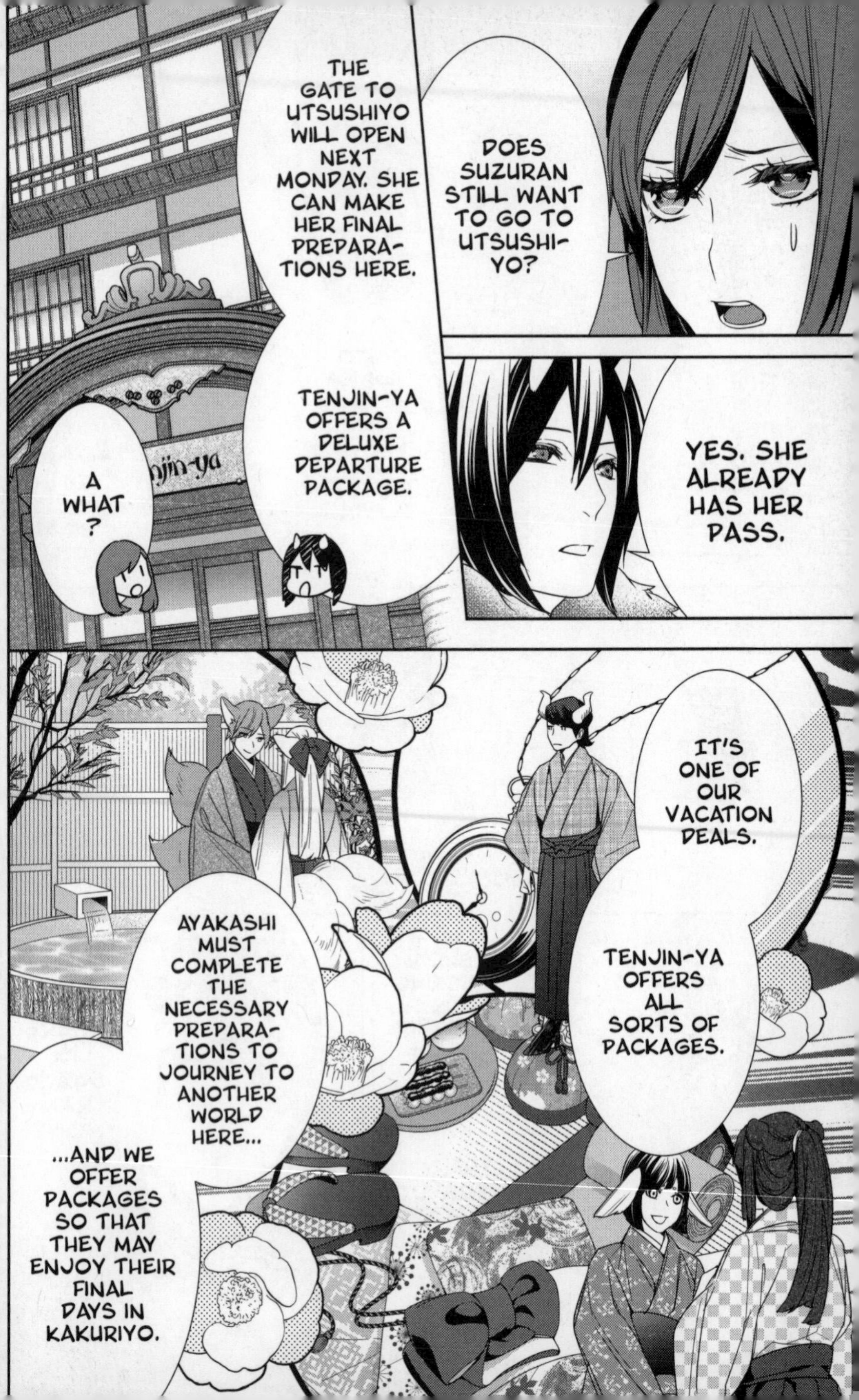
DOES SUZURAN STILL WANT TO GO TO UTSUSHI-YO?
YES. SHE ALREADY HAS HER PASS.
THE GATE TO UTSUSHIYO WILL OPEN NEXT MONDAY. SHE CAN MAKE HER FINAL PREPARA-TIONS HERE.
TENJIN-YA OFFERS A DELUXE DEPARTURE PACKAGE.
A WHAT?
IT'S ONE OF OUR VACATION DEALS.
TENJIN-YA OFFERS ALL SORTS OF PACKAGES.
AYAKASHI MUST COMPLETE THE NECESSARY PREPARA-TIONS TO JOURNEY TO ANOTHER WORLD HERE...
...AND WE OFFER PACKAGES SO THAT THEY MAY ENJOY THEIR FINAL DAYS IN KAKURIYO.

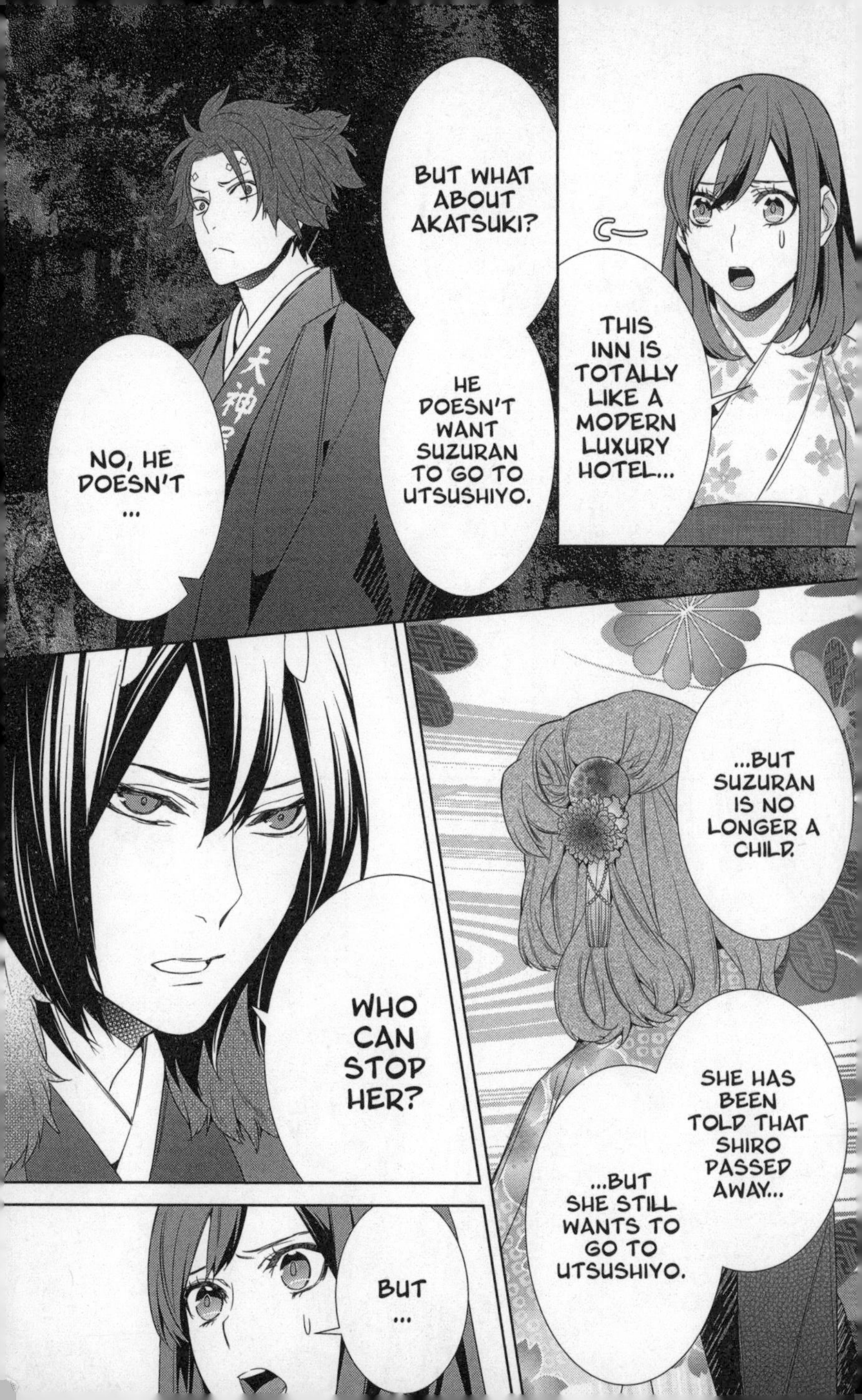
THIS INN IS TOTALLY LIKE A MODERN LUXURY HOTEL...
BUT WHAT ABOUT AKATSUKI?
HE DOESN'T WANT SUZURAN TO GO TO UTSUSHIYO.
NO, HE DOESN'T ...
...BUT SUZURAN IS NO LONGER A CHILD.
SHE HAS BEEN TOLD THAT SHIRO PASSED AWAY...
...BUT SHE STILL WANTS TO GO TO UTSUSHIYO.
WHO CAN STOP HER?
BUT ...

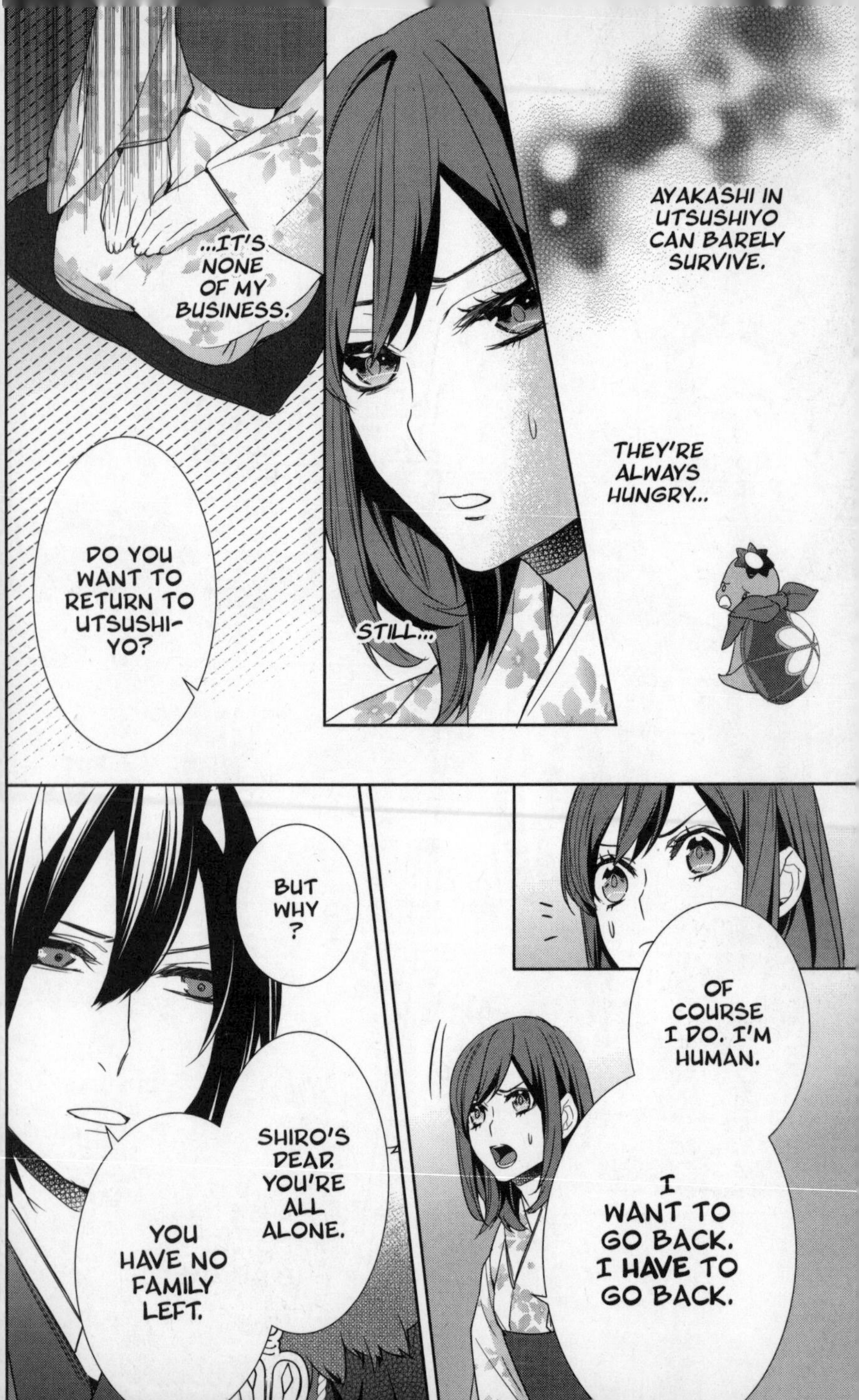
AYAKASHI IN UTSUSHIYO CAN BARELY SURVIVE.
THEY'RE ALWAYS HUNGRY...
STILL...
...IT'S NONE OF MY BUSINESS.
DO YOU WANT TO RETURN TO UTSUSHI-YO?
OF COURSE I DO. I'M HUMAN.
I WANT TO GO BACK. I HAVE TO GO BACK.
BUT WHY?
SHIRO'S DEAD. YOU'RE ALL ALONE.
YOU HAVE NO FAMILY LEFT.

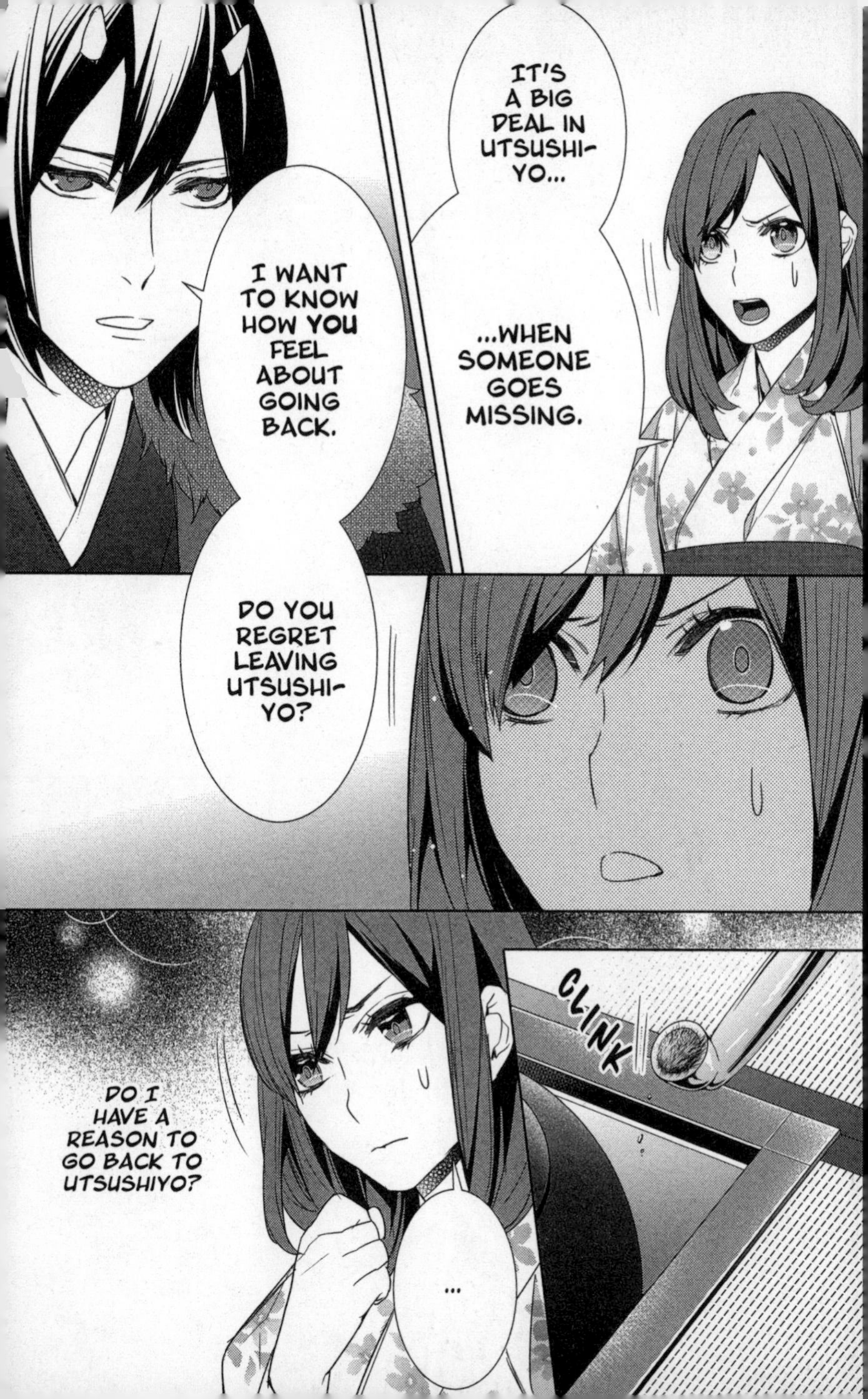
IT'S A BIG DEAL IN UTSUSHI-YO...
...WHEN SOMEONE GOES MISSING.
I WANT TO KNOW HOW YOU FEEL ABOUT GOING BACK.
DO YOU REGRET LEAVING UTSUSHI-YO?
CLINK
DO I HAVE A REASON TO GO BACK TO UTSUSHIYO?
...

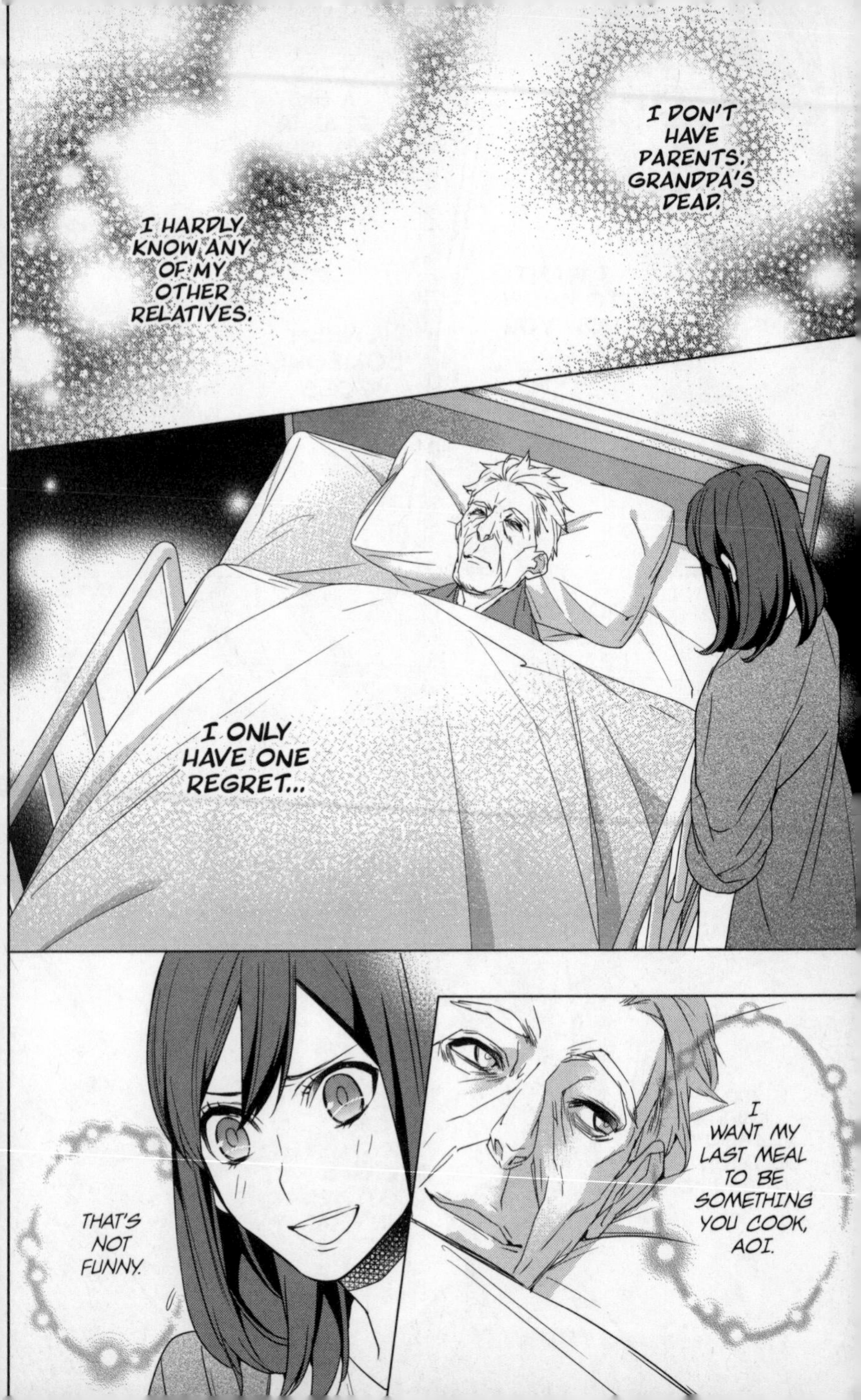
I DON'T HAVE PARENTS. GRANDPA'S DEAD.
I HARDLY KNOW ANY OF MY OTHER RELATIVES.
I ONLY HAVE ONE REGRET...
I WANT MY LAST MEAL TO BE SOMETHING YOU COOK, AOI.
THAT'S NOT FUNNY.

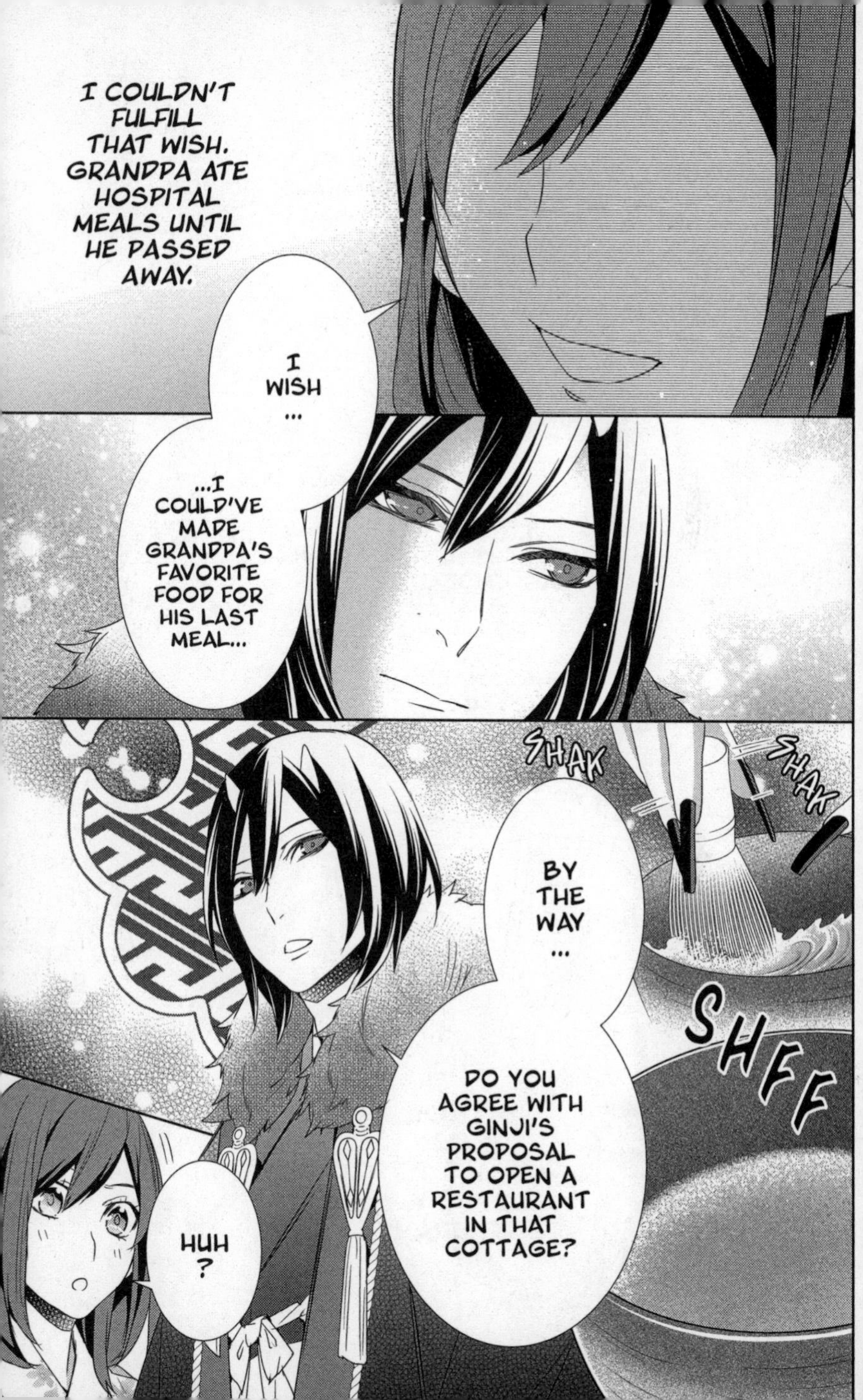
I COULDN'T FULFILL THAT WISH. GRANDPA ATE HOSPITAL MEALS UNTIL HE PASSED AWAY.
I WISH...
...I COULD'VE MADE GRANDPA'S FAVORITE FOOD FOR HIS LAST MEAL...
SHAK
SHAK
BY THE WAY...
SHFF
DO YOU AGREE WITH GINJI'S PROPOSAL TO OPEN A RESTAURANT IN THAT COTTAGE?
HUH?

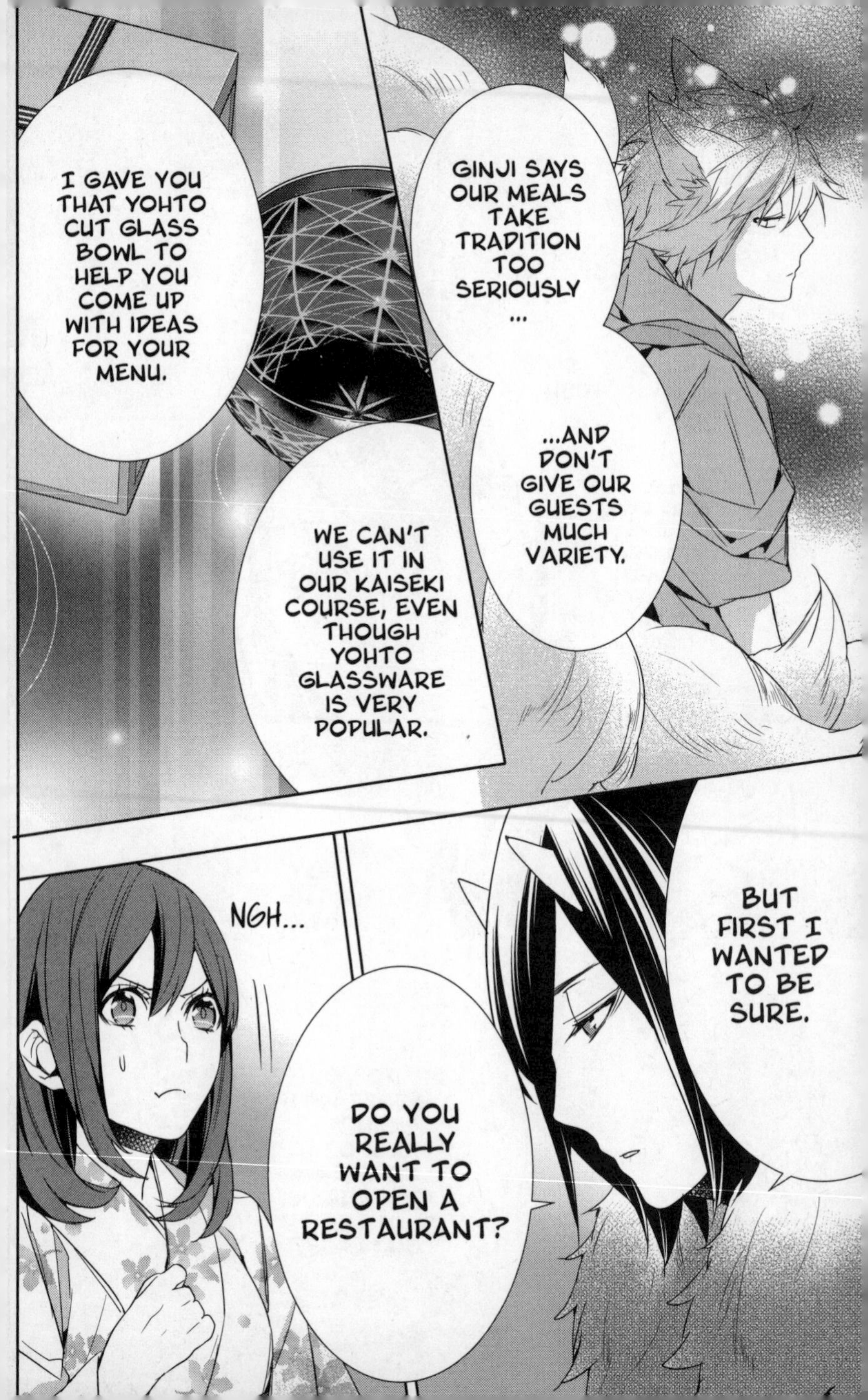
GINJI SAYS OUR MEALS TAKE TRADITION TOO SERIOUSLY ...
...AND DON'T GIVE OUR GUESTS MUCH VARIETY.
I GAVE YOU THAT YOHTO CUT GLASS BOWL TO HELP YOU COME UP WITH IDEAS FOR YOUR MENU.
WE CAN'T USE IT IN OUR KAISEKI COURSE, EVEN THOUGH YOHTO GLASSWARE IS VERY POPULAR.
BUT FIRST I WANTED TO BE SURE.
DO YOU REALLY WANT TO OPEN A RESTAURANT?
NGH...

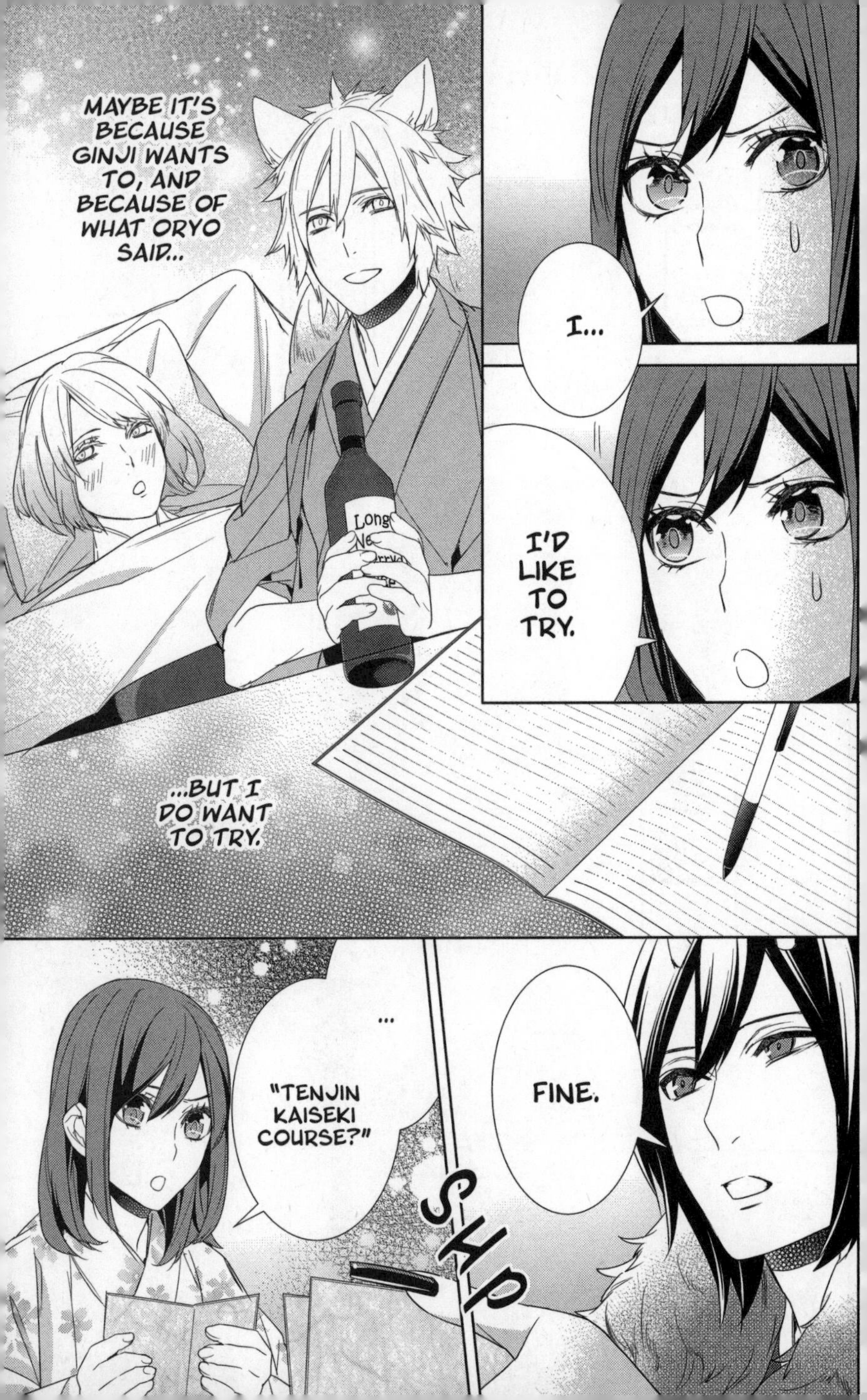
I...
I'D LIKE TO TRY.
MAYBE IT'S BECAUSE GINJI WANTS TO, AND BECAUSE OF WHAT ORYO SAID...
...BUT I DO WANT TO TRY.
FINE.
SHP
...
"TENJIN KAISEKI COURSE?"

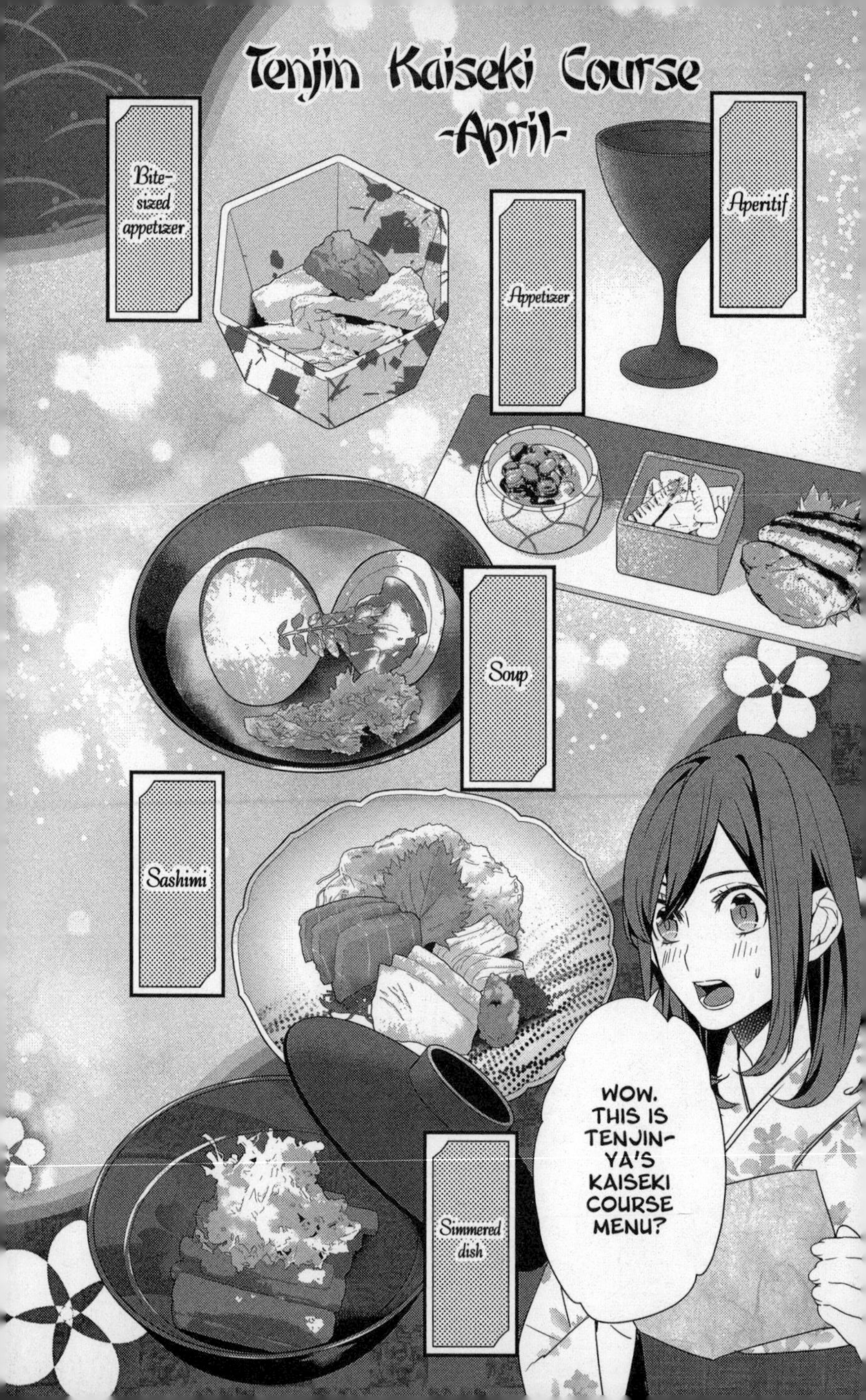
Tenjin Kaiseki Course
-April-
Aperitif
Appetizer
Bite-sized appetizer
Soup
Sashimi
WOW. THIS IS TENJIN-YA'S KAISEKI COURSE MENU?
Simmered dish

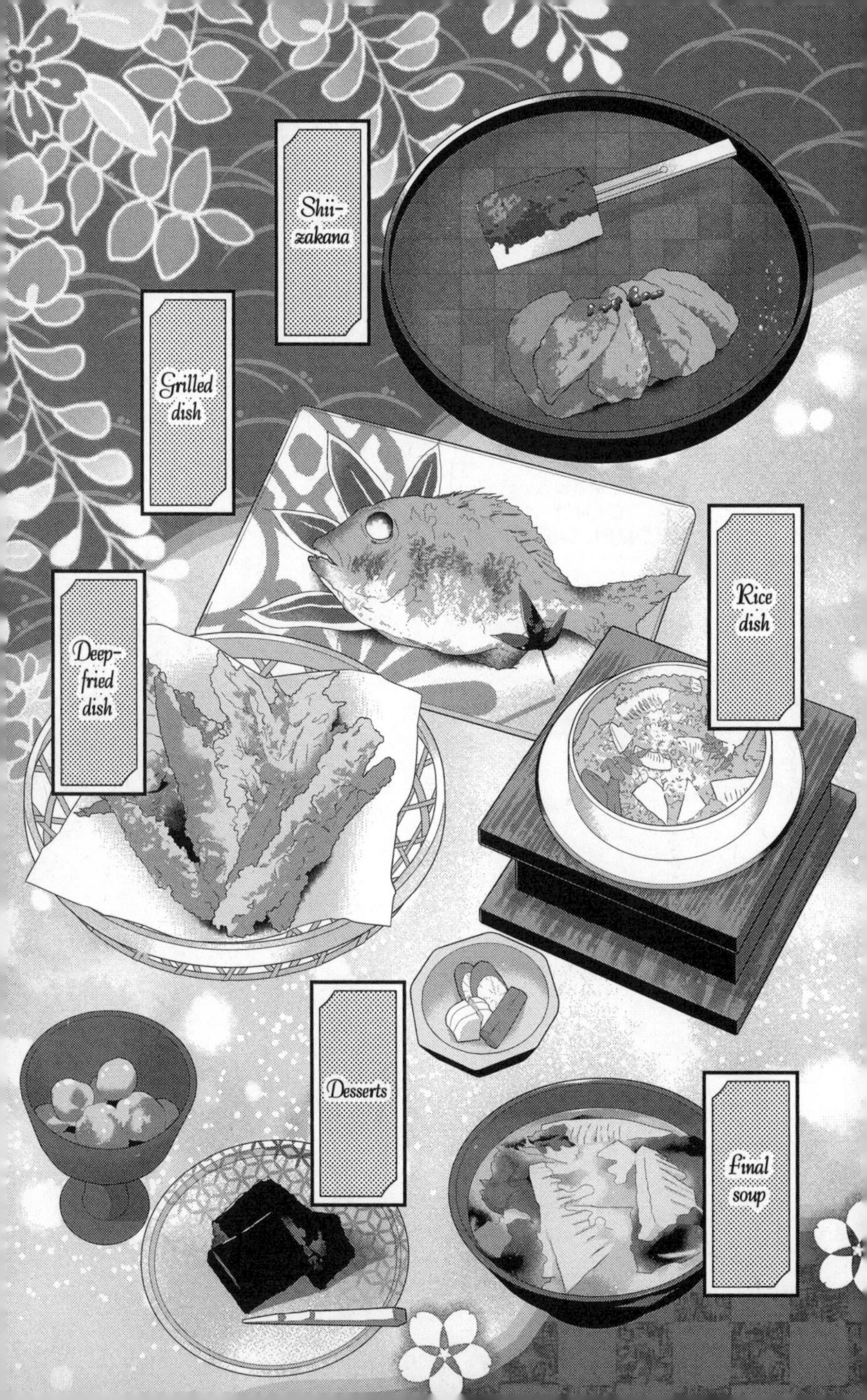
Shii-
zakana
Grilled
dish
Rice
dish
Deep-
fried
dish
Final
soup
Desserts

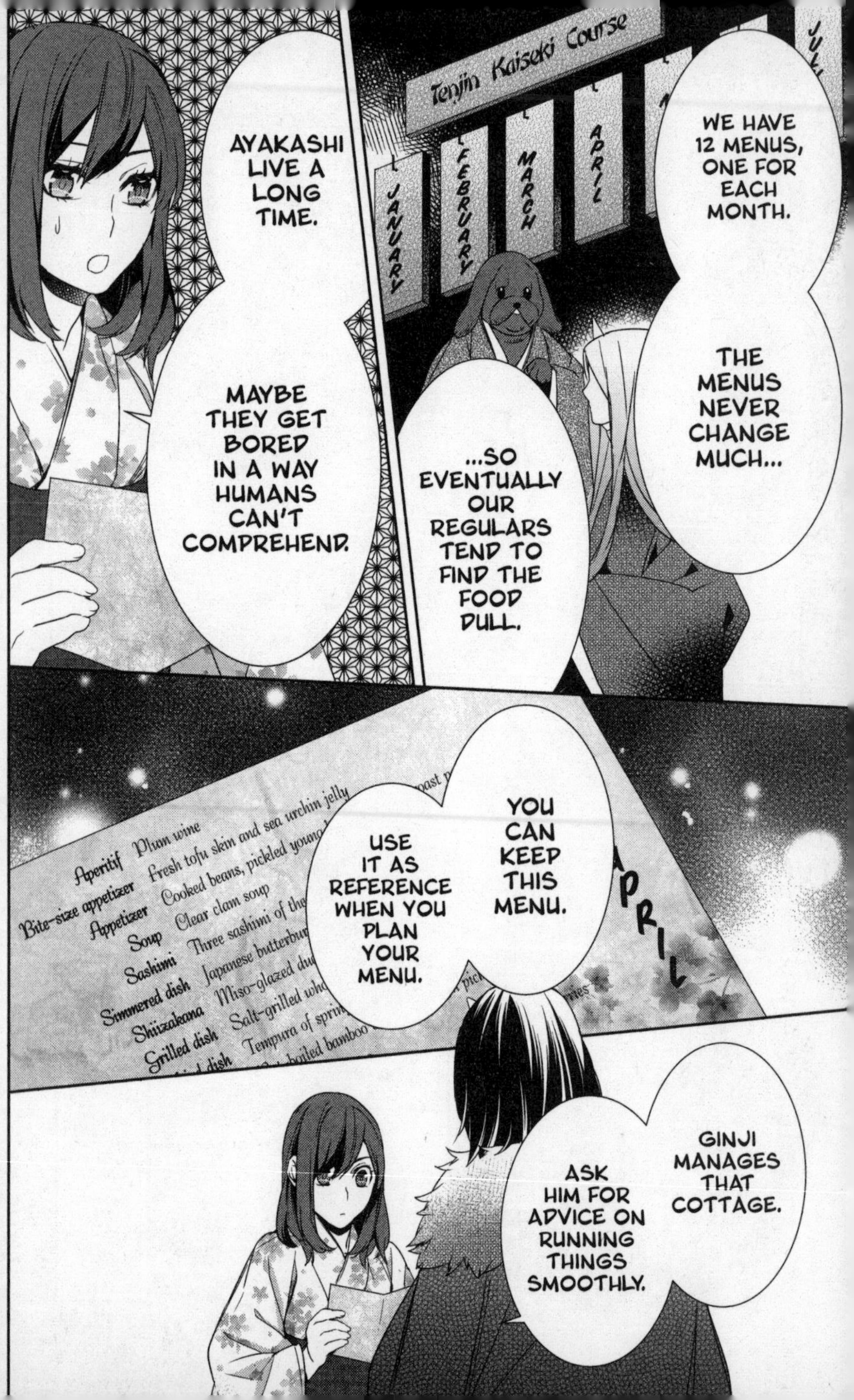
Tenjin Kaiseki Course
JANUARY
FEBRUARY
MARCH
APRIL
WE HAVE 12 MENUS, ONE FOR EACH MONTH.
THE MENUS NEVER CHANGE MUCH...
...SO EVENTUALLY OUR REGULARS TEND TO FIND THE FOOD DULL.
AYAKASHI LIVE A LONG TIME.
MAYBE THEY GET BORED IN A WAY HUMANS CAN'T COMPREHEND.
YOU CAN KEEP THIS MENU.
USE IT AS REFERENCE WHEN YOU PLAN YOUR MENU.
APRIL
Aperitif Plum wine
Bite-size appetizer Fresh tofu skin and sea urchin jelly
Appetizer Cooked beans, pickled
Soup Clear clam soup
Sashimi Three sashimi of the
Simmered dish Japanese
Shiizakana Miso-glazed
Grilled dish Salt-grilled
Tempura of
GINJI MANAGES THAT COTTAGE.
ASK HIM FOR ADVICE ON RUNNING THINGS SMOOTHLY.

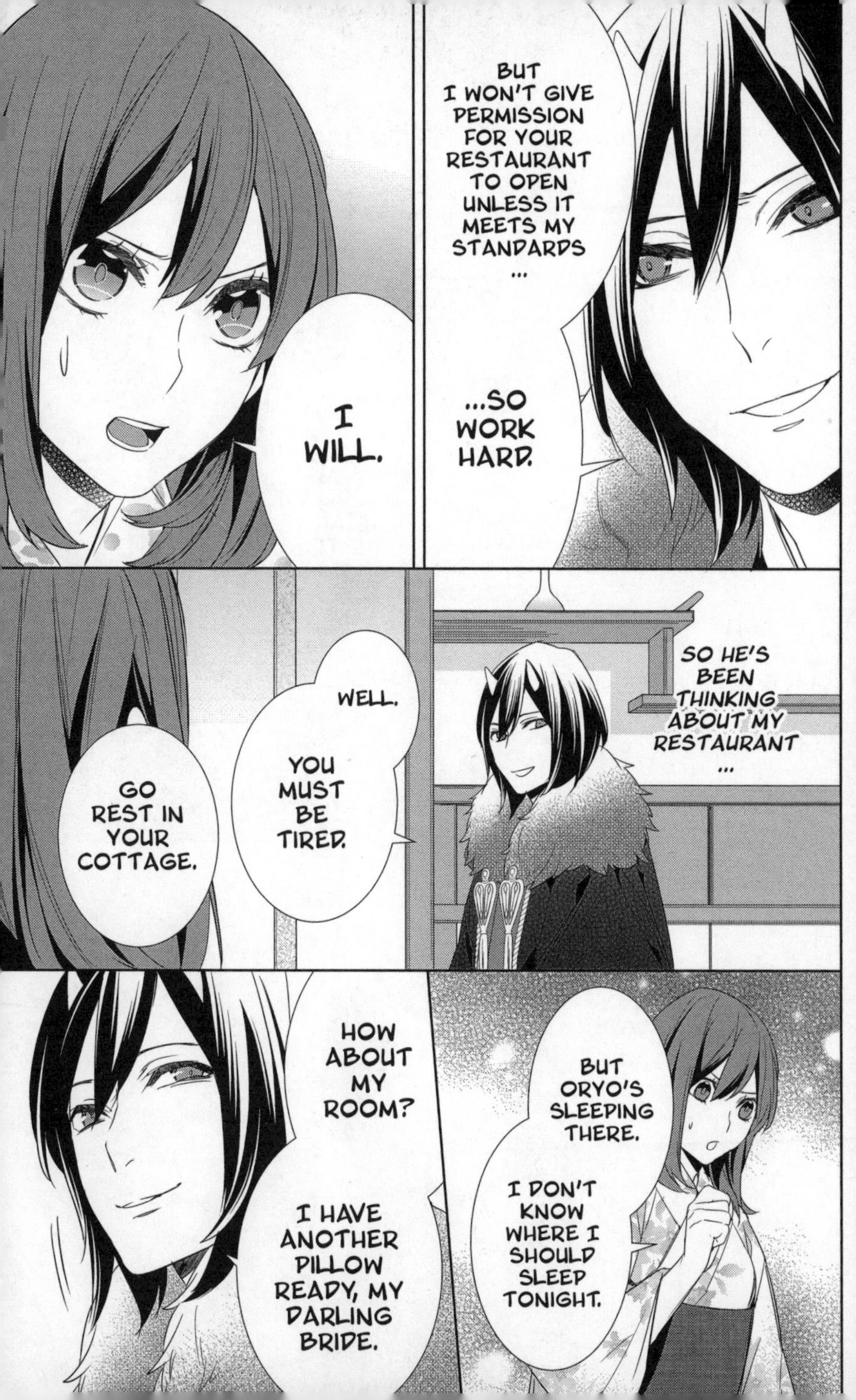

BUT I WON'T GIVE PERMISSION FOR YOUR RESTAURANT TO OPEN UNLESS IT MEETS MY STANDARDS...
...SO WORK HARD.
I WILL.
SO HE'S BEEN THINKING ABOUT MY RESTAURANT...
WELL.
YOU MUST BE TIRED.
GO REST IN YOUR COTTAGE.
BUT ORYO'S SLEEPING THERE.
I DON'T KNOW WHERE I SHOULD SLEEP TONIGHT.
HOW ABOUT MY ROOM?
I HAVE ANOTHER PILLOW READY, MY DARLING BRIDE.

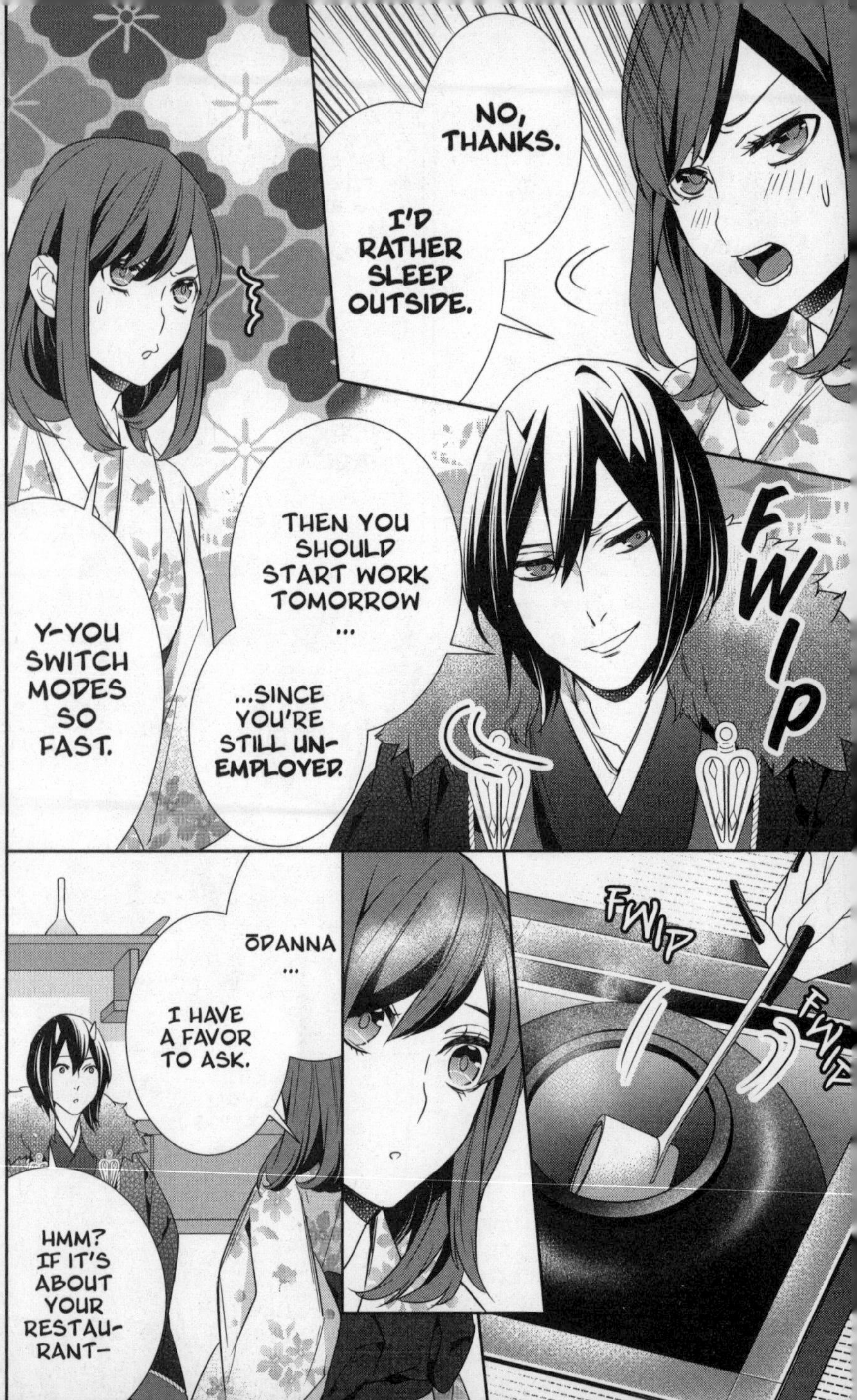
NO, THANKS.
I'D RATHER SLEEP OUTSIDE.
THEN YOU SHOULD START WORK TOMORROW...
...SINCE YOU'RE STILL UNEMPLOYED.
FWIP
Y-YOU SWITCH MODES SO FAST.
FWIP
FWIP
ŌDANNA...
I HAVE A FAVOR TO ASK.
HMM? IF IT'S ABOUT YOUR RESTAURANT-

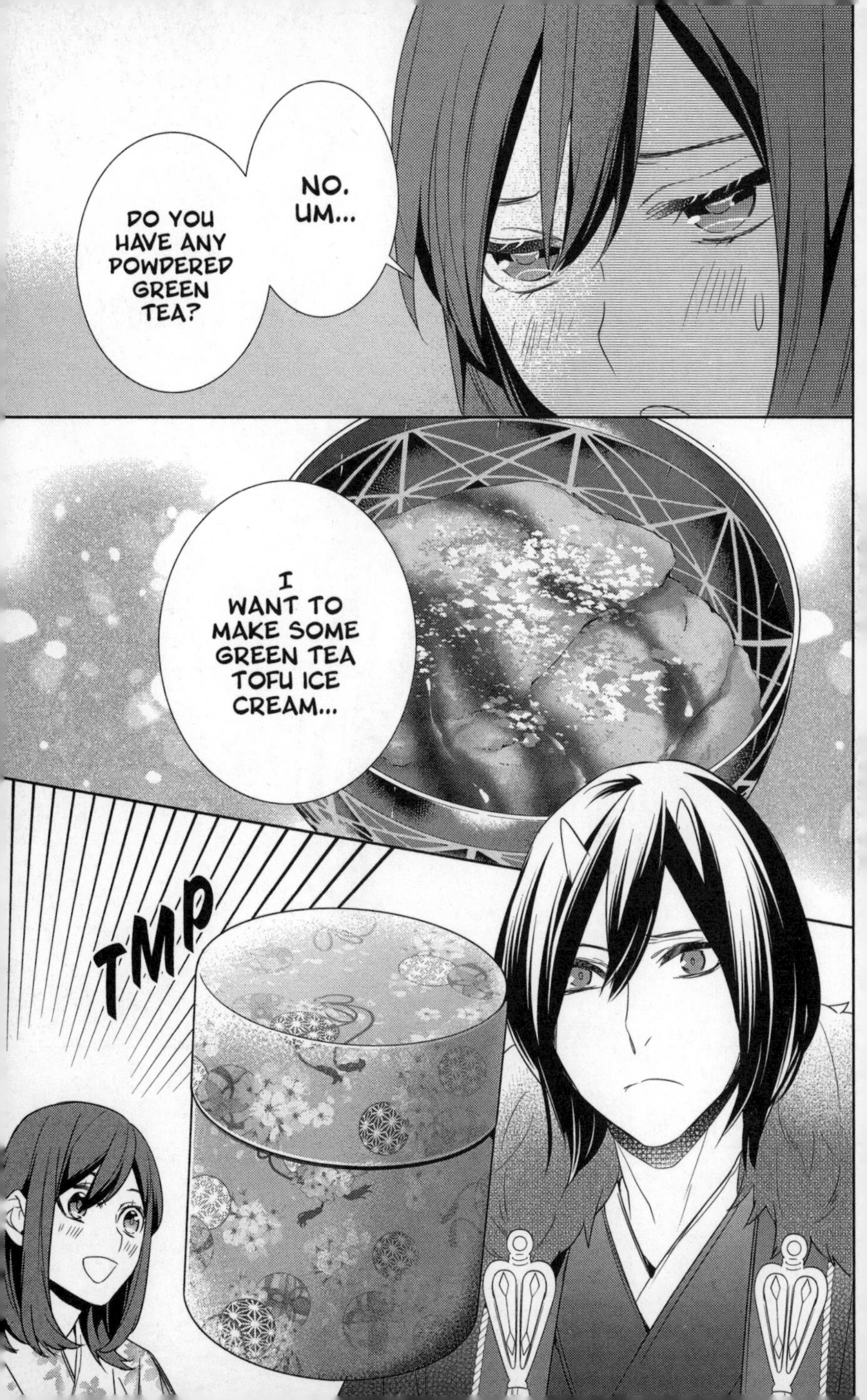
NO. UM...
DO YOU HAVE ANY POWDERED GREEN TEA?
I WANT TO MAKE SOME GREEN TEA TOFU ICE CREAM...
TMP

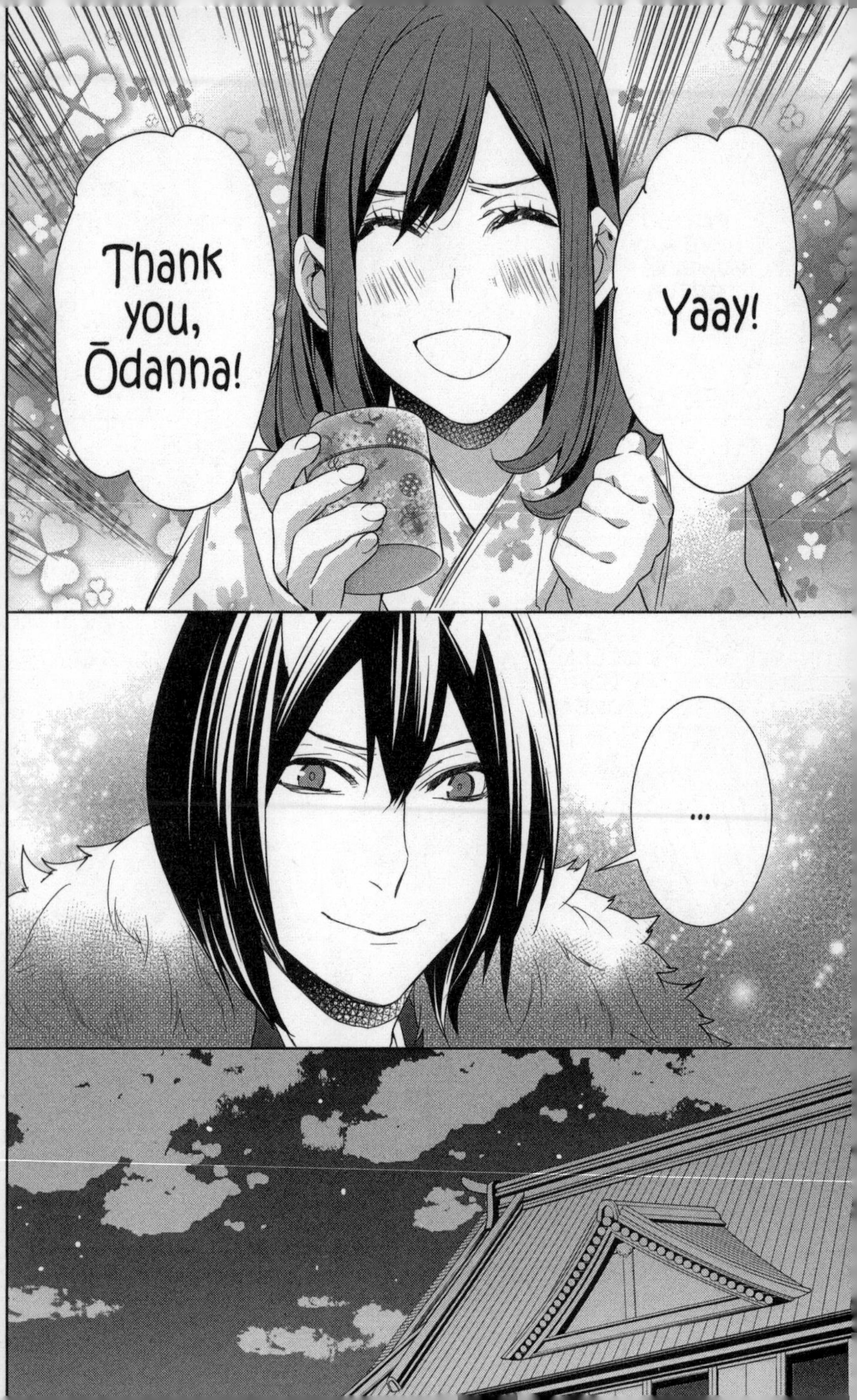
Yaay!
Thank you, Ōdanna!
...

Kakuriyo
Bed & Breakfast
for Spirits

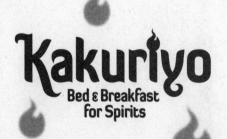

Kakuriyo

Bed & Breakfast
for Spirits

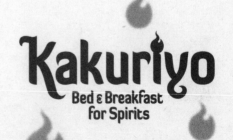

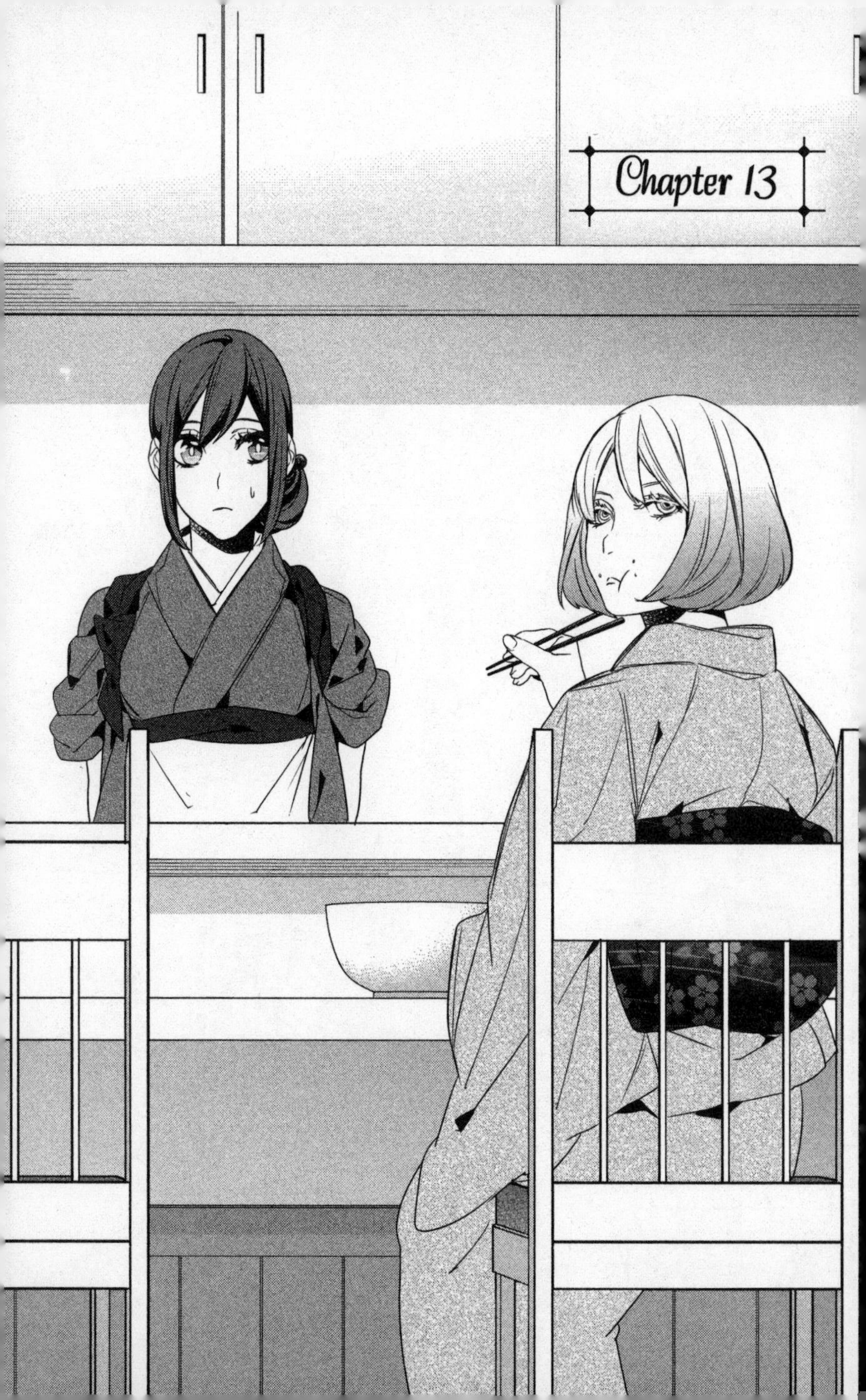
Chapter 13

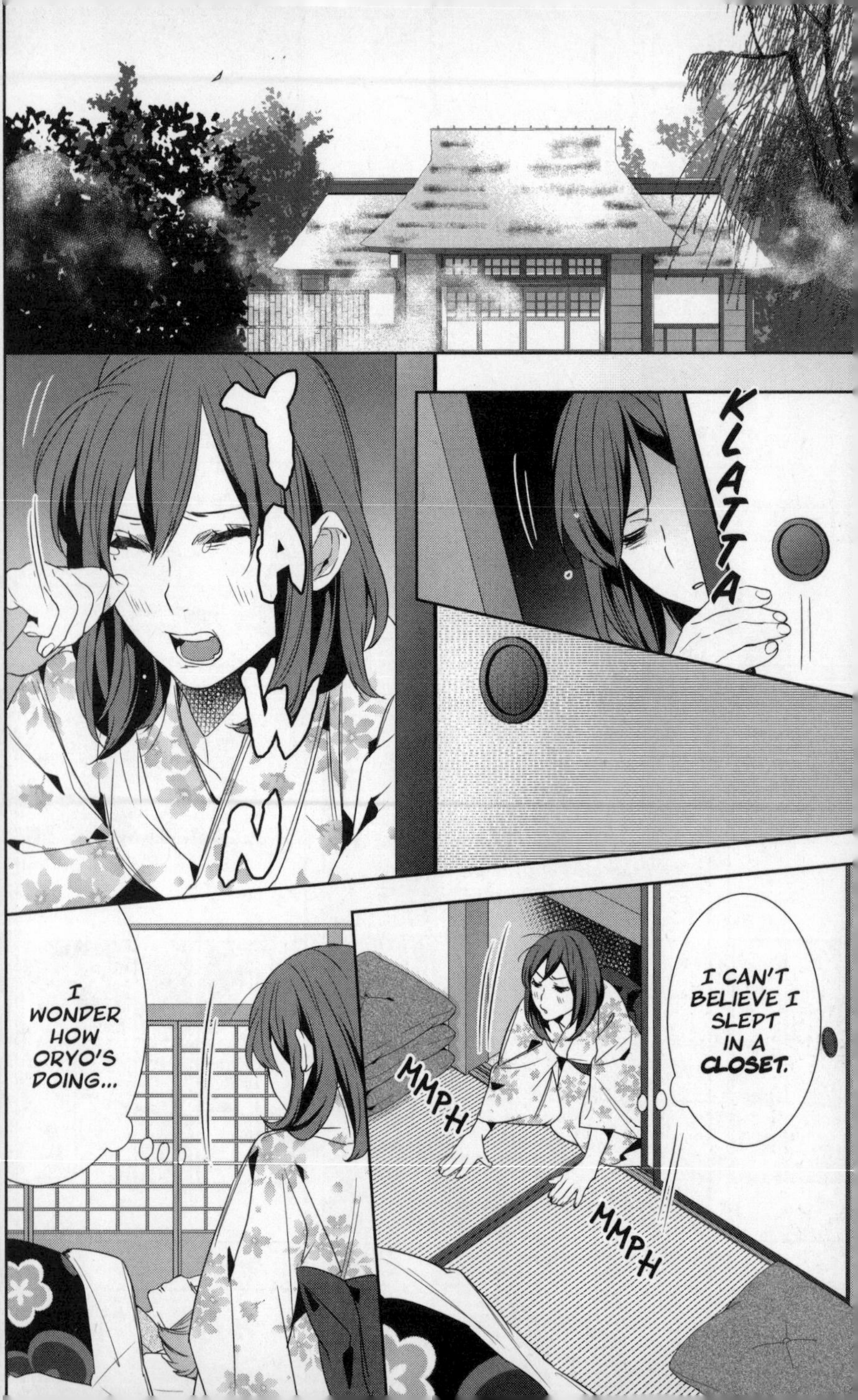
KLATTA
YAWN
I CAN'T BELIEVE I SLEPT IN A CLOSET.
MMPH
MMPH
I WONDER HOW ORYO'S DOING...

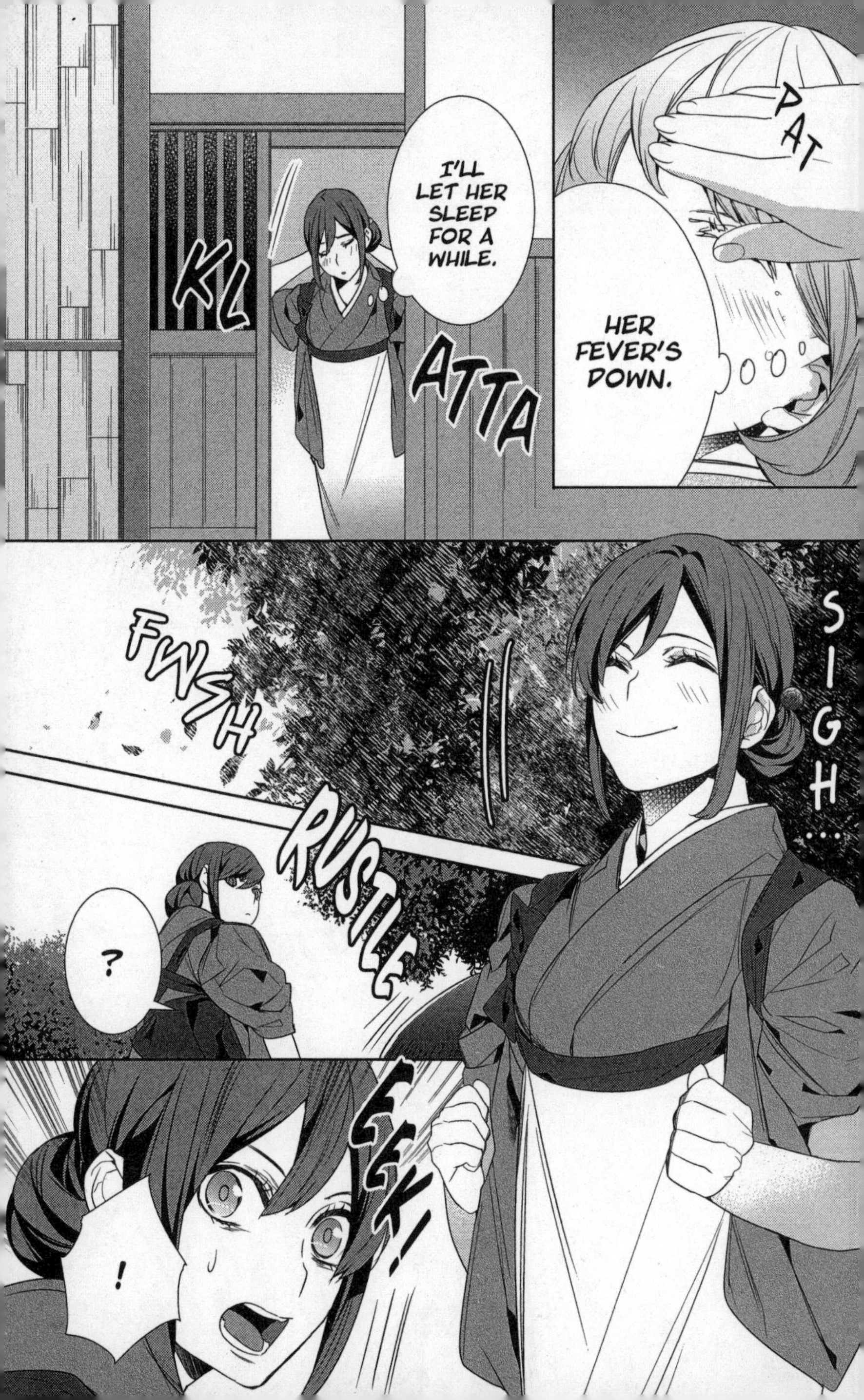
PAT
HER FEVER'S DOWN.
I'LL LET HER SLEEP FOR A WHILE.
KLATTA
SIGH...
FWSH
RUSTLE
?
EEK!
!

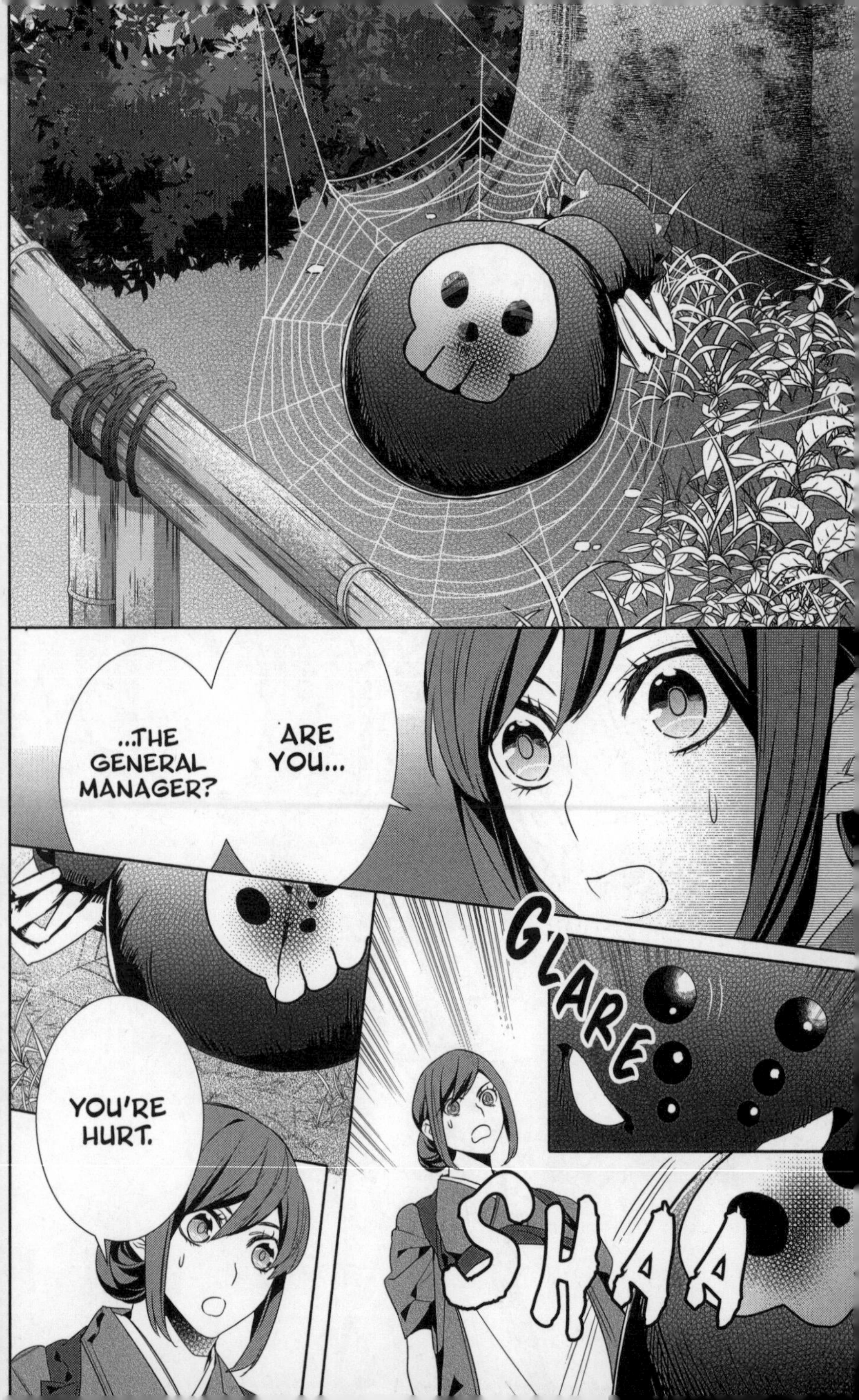
ARE YOU...
...THE GENERAL MANAGER?
GLARE
SHAA
YOU'RE HURT.

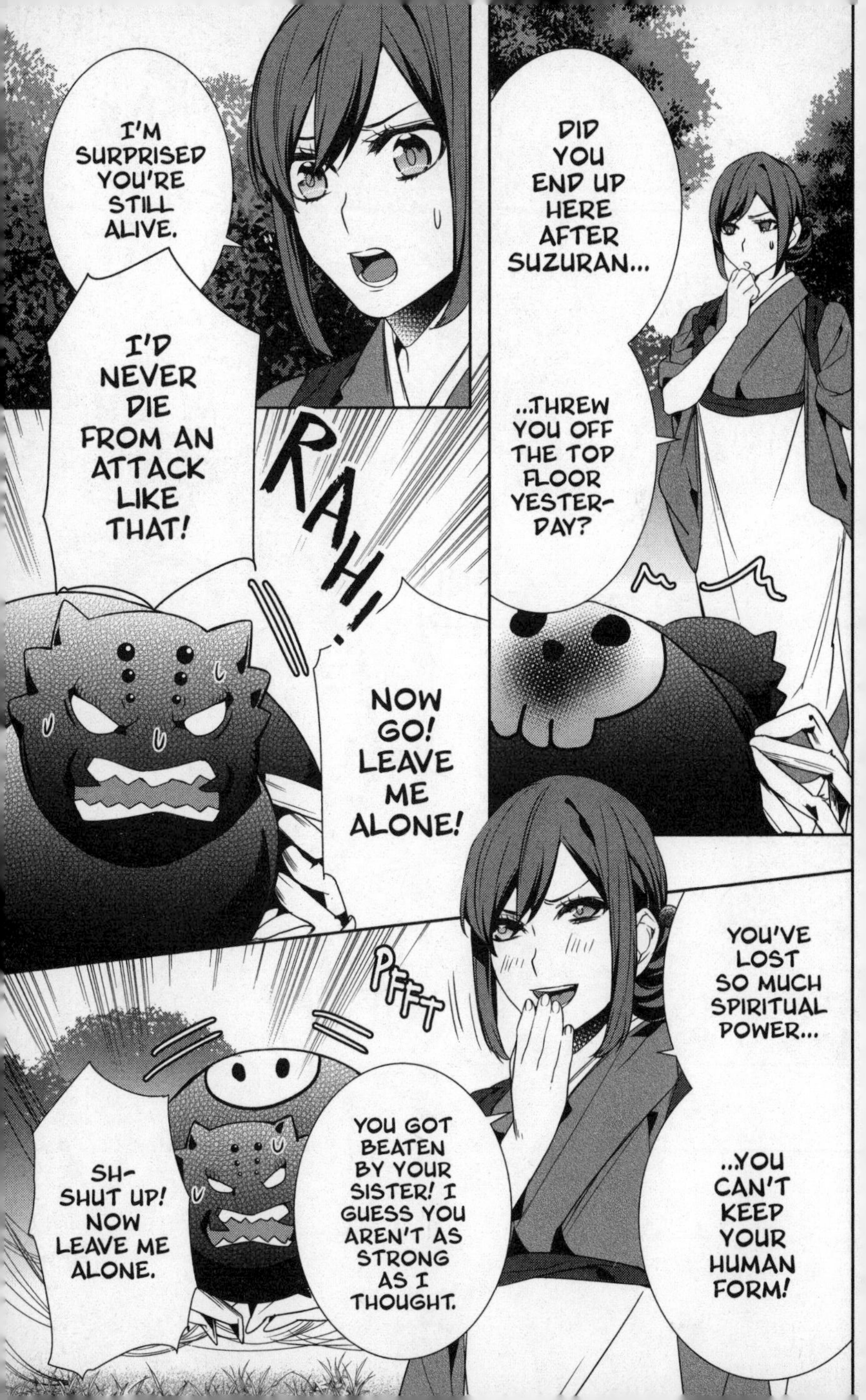

DID YOU END UP HERE AFTER SUZURAN...
...THREW YOU OFF THE TOP FLOOR YESTER-DAY?
I'M SURPRISED YOU'RE STILL ALIVE.
I'D NEVER DIE FROM AN ATTACK LIKE THAT!
RAH!!
NOW GO! LEAVE ME ALONE!
YOU'VE LOST SO MUCH SPIRITUAL POWER...
...YOU CAN'T KEEP YOUR HUMAN FORM!
PFFFT
YOU GOT BEATEN BY YOUR SISTER! I GUESS YOU AREN'T AS STRONG AS I THOUGHT.
SH-SHUT UP! NOW LEAVE ME ALONE.

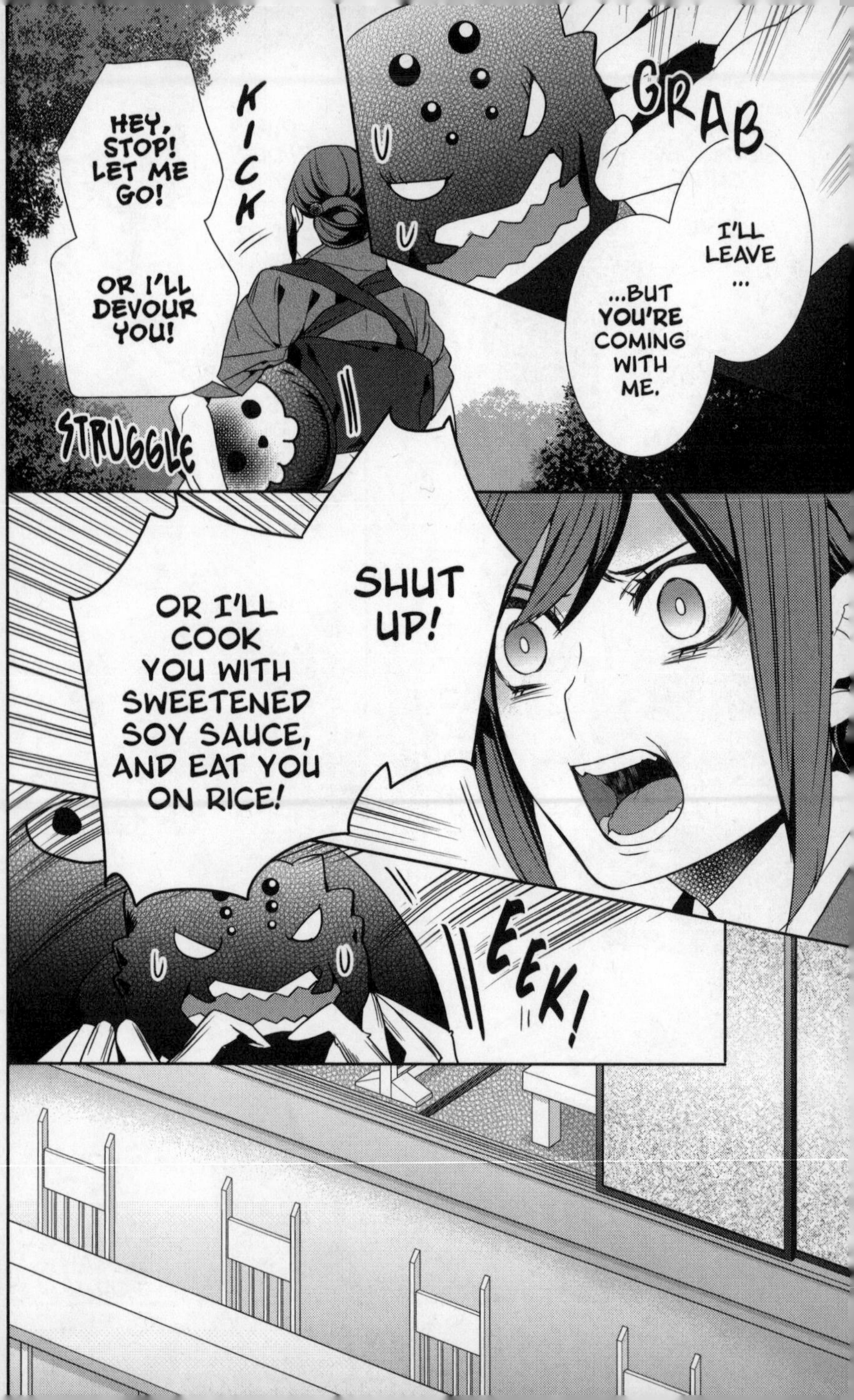
GRAB
I'LL LEAVE ...
...BUT YOU'RE COMING WITH ME.
KICK
HEY, STOP! LET ME GO!
OR I'LL DEVOUR YOU!
STRUGGLE
SHUT UP!
OR I'LL COOK YOU WITH SWEETENED SOY SAUCE, AND EAT YOU ON RICE!
EEK!

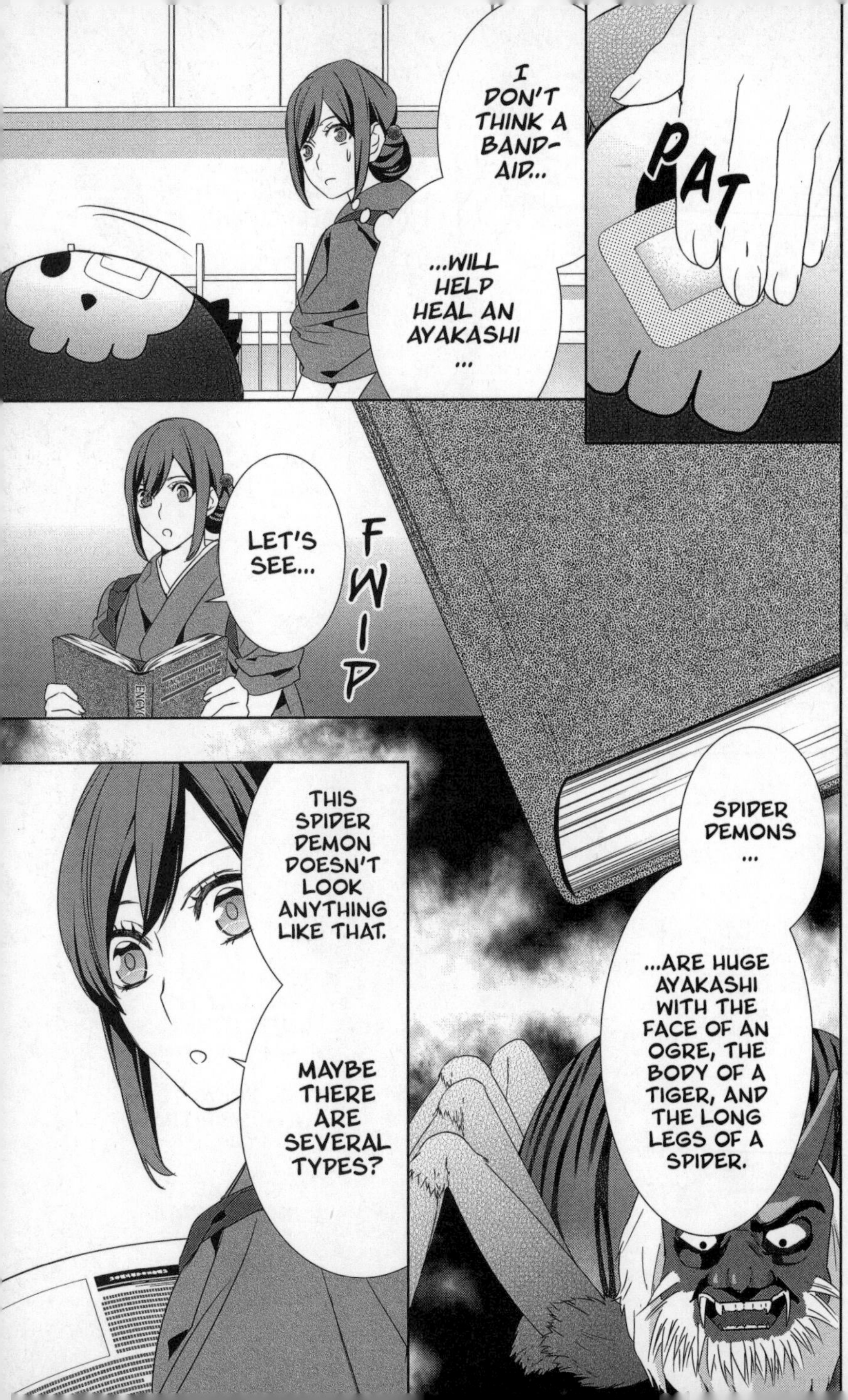
PAT
I DON'T THINK A BAND-AID...
...WILL HELP HEAL AN AYAKASHI ...
LET'S SEE...
FWIP
SPIDER DEMONS ...
...ARE HUGE AYAKASHI WITH THE FACE OF AN OGRE, THE BODY OF A TIGER, AND THE LONG LEGS OF A SPIDER.
THIS SPIDER DEMON DOESN'T LOOK ANYTHING LIKE THAT.
MAYBE THERE ARE SEVERAL TYPES?

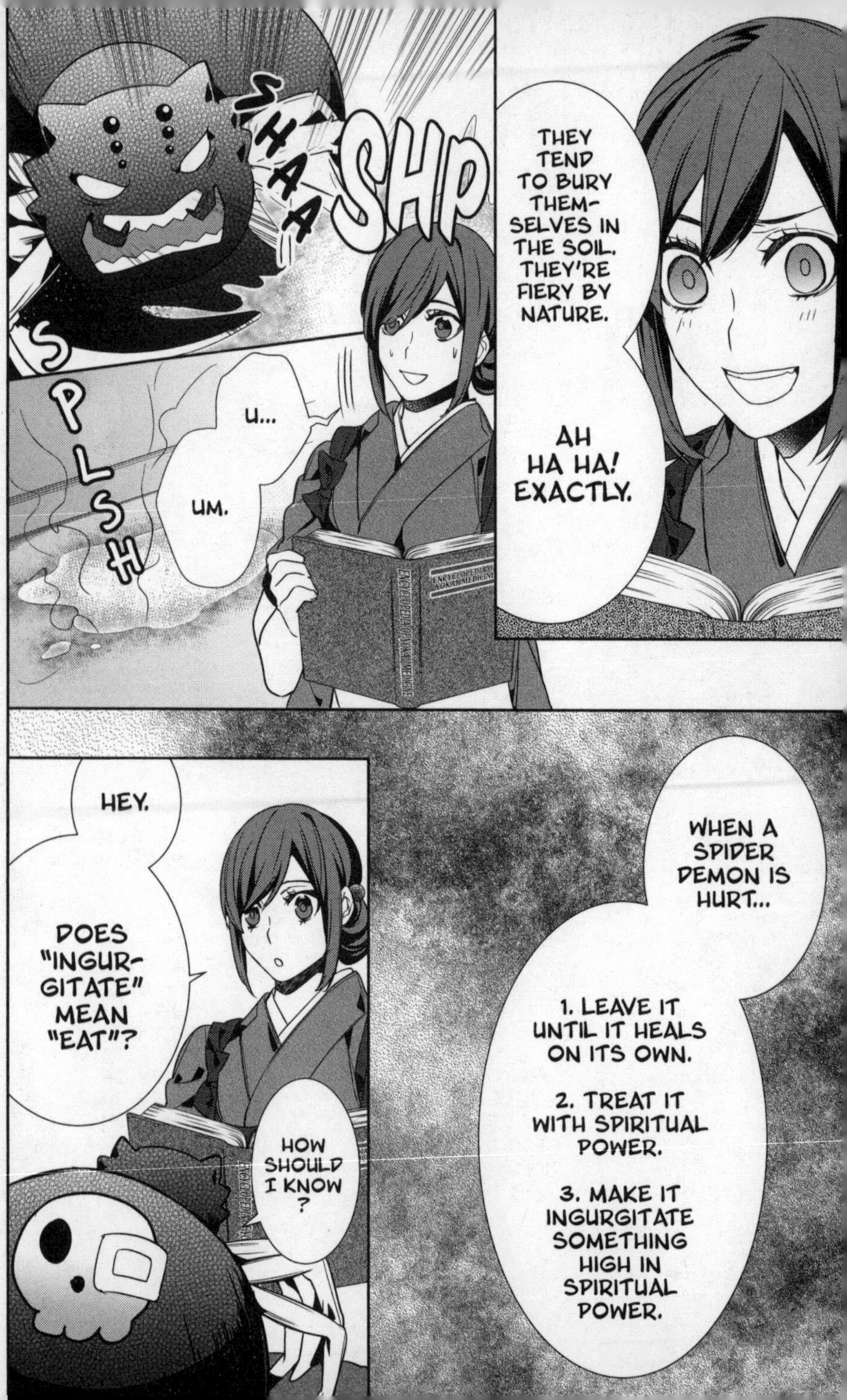
THEY TEND TO BURY THEM-SELVES IN THE SOIL. THEY'RE FIERY BY NATURE.
AH HA HA! EXACTLY.
SHAAA
SHP
SPLSH
U...
UM.
ENCYCLOPEDIA OF YOKAI MEDICINE
WHEN A SPIDER DEMON IS HURT...
1. LEAVE IT UNTIL IT HEALS ON ITS OWN.
2. TREAT IT WITH SPIRITUAL POWER.
3. MAKE IT INGURGITATE SOMETHING HIGH IN SPIRITUAL POWER.
HEY.
DOES "INGUR-GITATE" MEAN "EAT"?
HOW SHOULD I KNOW ?

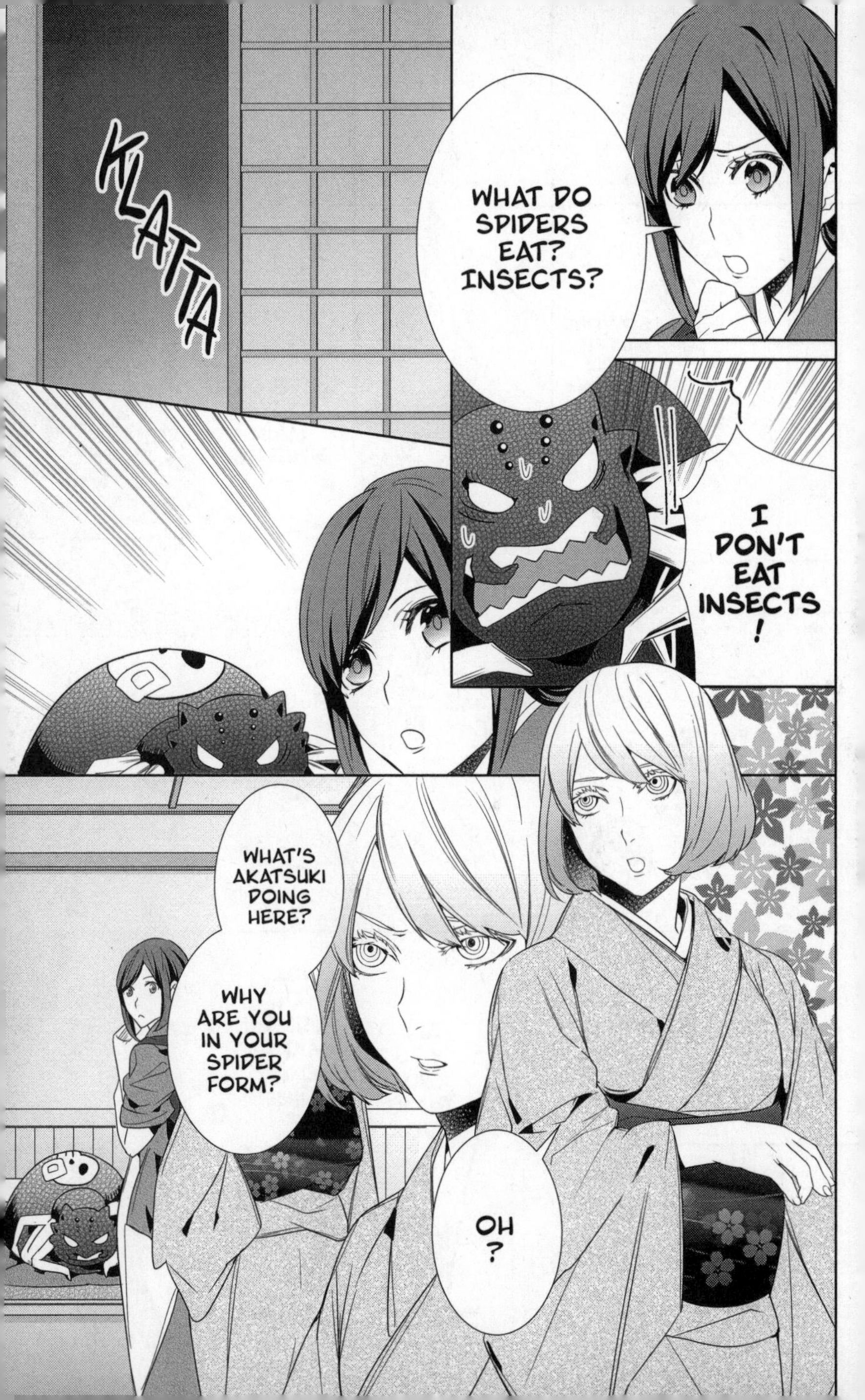
WHAT DO SPIDERS EAT? INSECTS?
KLATTA
I DON'T EAT INSECTS!
WHAT'S AKATSUKI DOING HERE?
WHY ARE YOU IN YOUR SPIDER FORM?
OH?

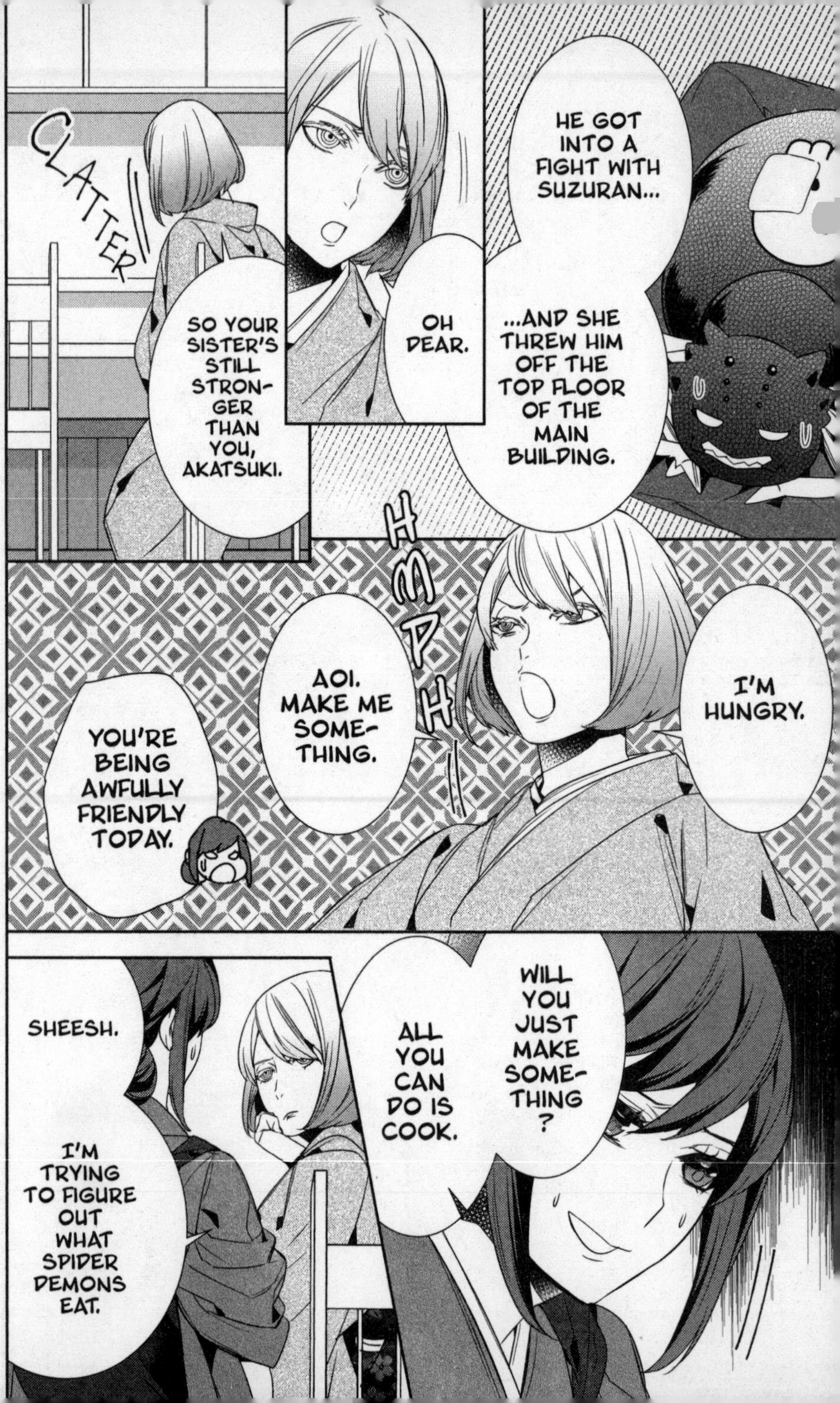
HE GOT INTO A FIGHT WITH SUZURAN...
...AND SHE THREW HIM OFF THE TOP FLOOR OF THE MAIN BUILDING.
OH DEAR.
CLATTER
SO YOUR SISTER'S STILL STRONGER THAN YOU, AKATSUKI.
I'M HUNGRY.
HMPH
AOI. MAKE ME SOMETHING.
YOU'RE BEING AWFULLY FRIENDLY TODAY.
WILL YOU JUST MAKE SOMETHING?
ALL YOU CAN DO IS COOK.
SHEESH.
I'M TRYING TO FIGURE OUT WHAT SPIDER DEMONS EAT.

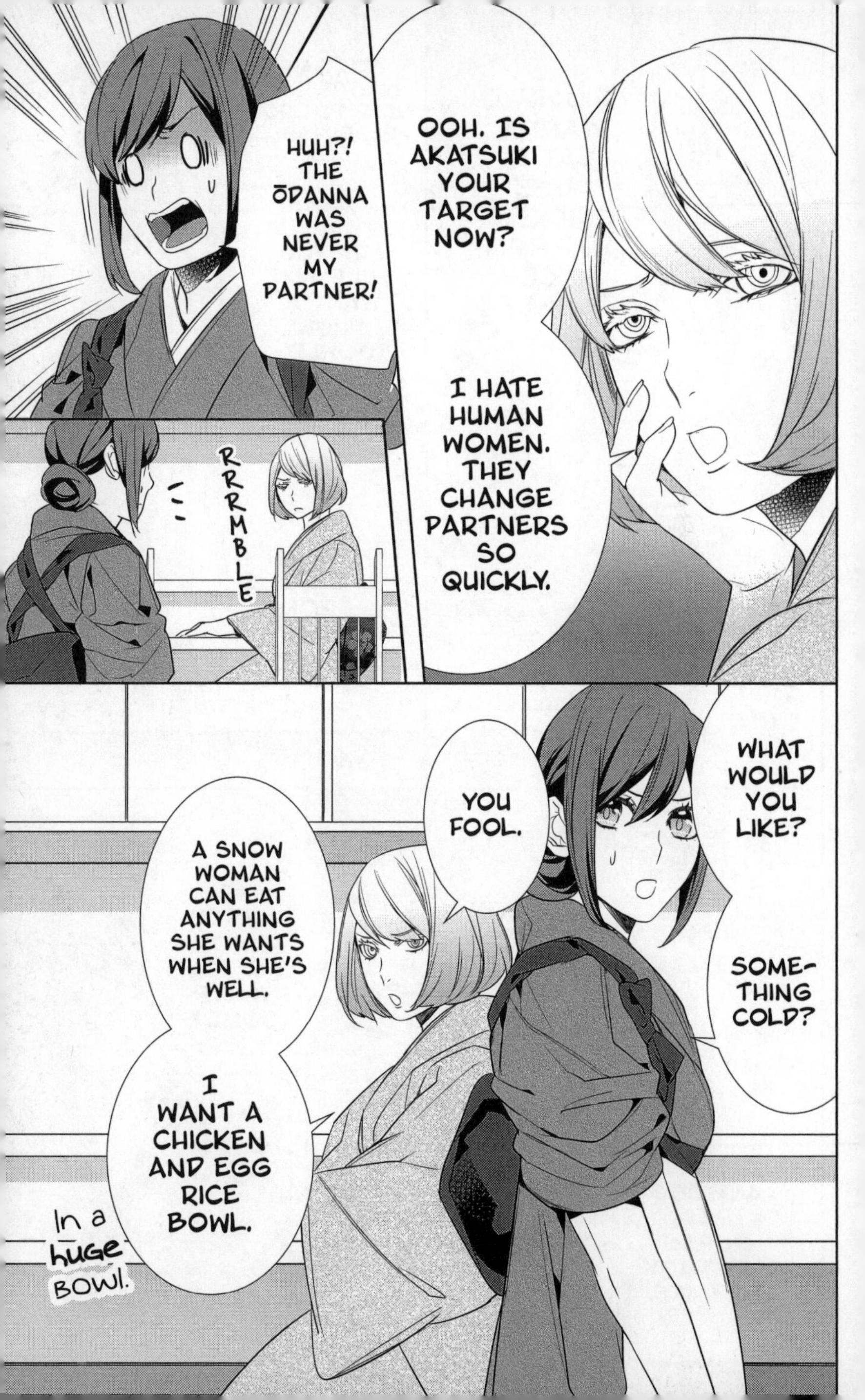
OOH. IS AKATSUKI YOUR TARGET NOW?
I HATE HUMAN WOMEN. THEY CHANGE PARTNERS SO QUICKLY.
HUH?! THE ŌDANNA WAS NEVER MY PARTNER!
RRRMBLE
WHAT WOULD YOU LIKE?
SOME-THING COLD?
YOU FOOL.
A SNOW WOMAN CAN EAT ANYTHING SHE WANTS WHEN SHE'S WELL.
I WANT A CHICKEN AND EGG RICE BOWL.
In a huge bowl.

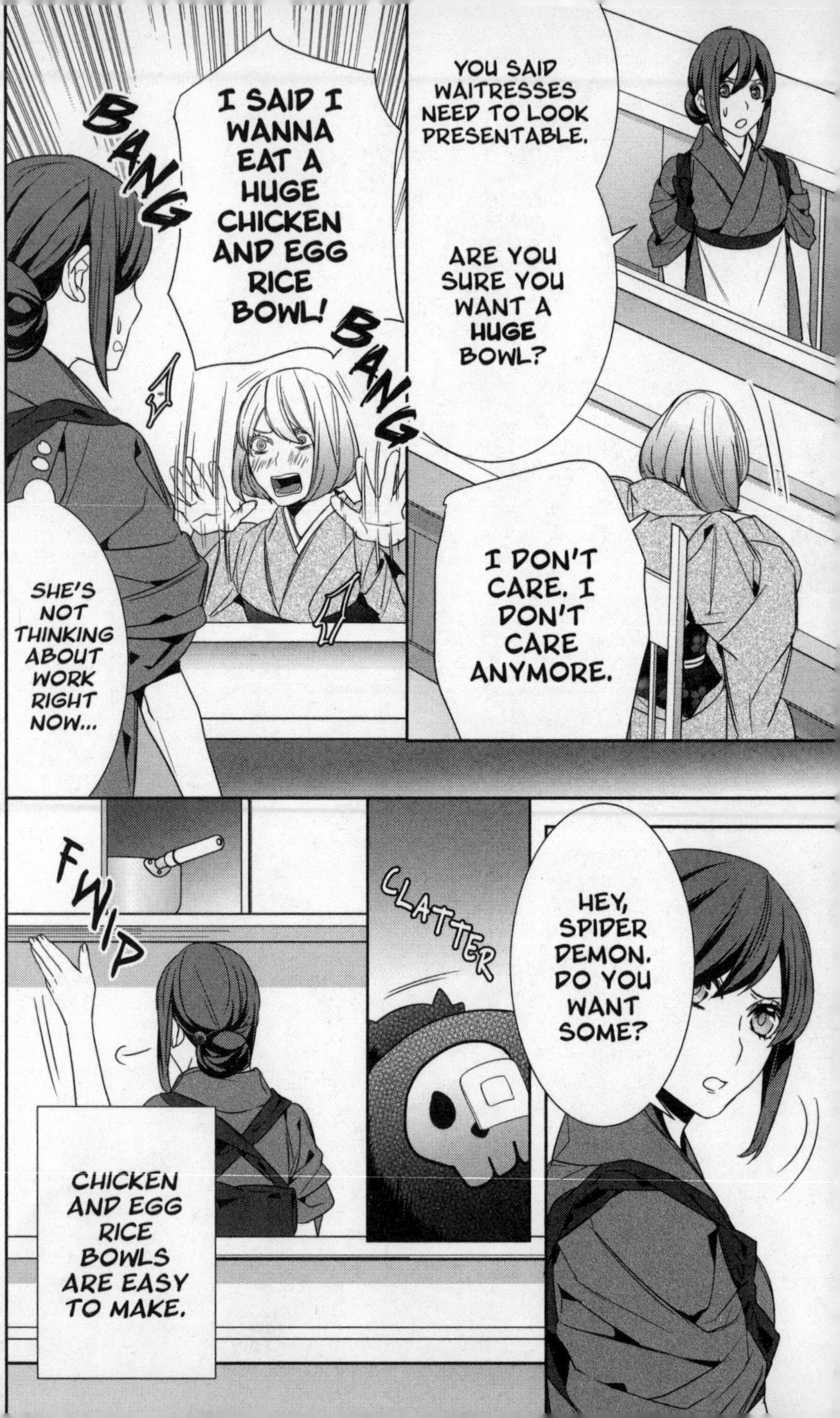
YOU SAID WAITRESSES NEED TO LOOK PRESENTABLE.
ARE YOU SURE YOU WANT A HUGE BOWL?
I DON'T CARE. I DON'T CARE ANYMORE.
BANG
I SAID I WANNA EAT A HUGE CHICKEN AND EGG RICE BOWL!
BANG
SHE'S NOT THINKING ABOUT WORK RIGHT NOW...
HEY, SPIDER DEMON. DO YOU WANT SOME?
CLATTER
FWIP
CHICKEN AND EGG RICE BOWLS ARE EASY TO MAKE.

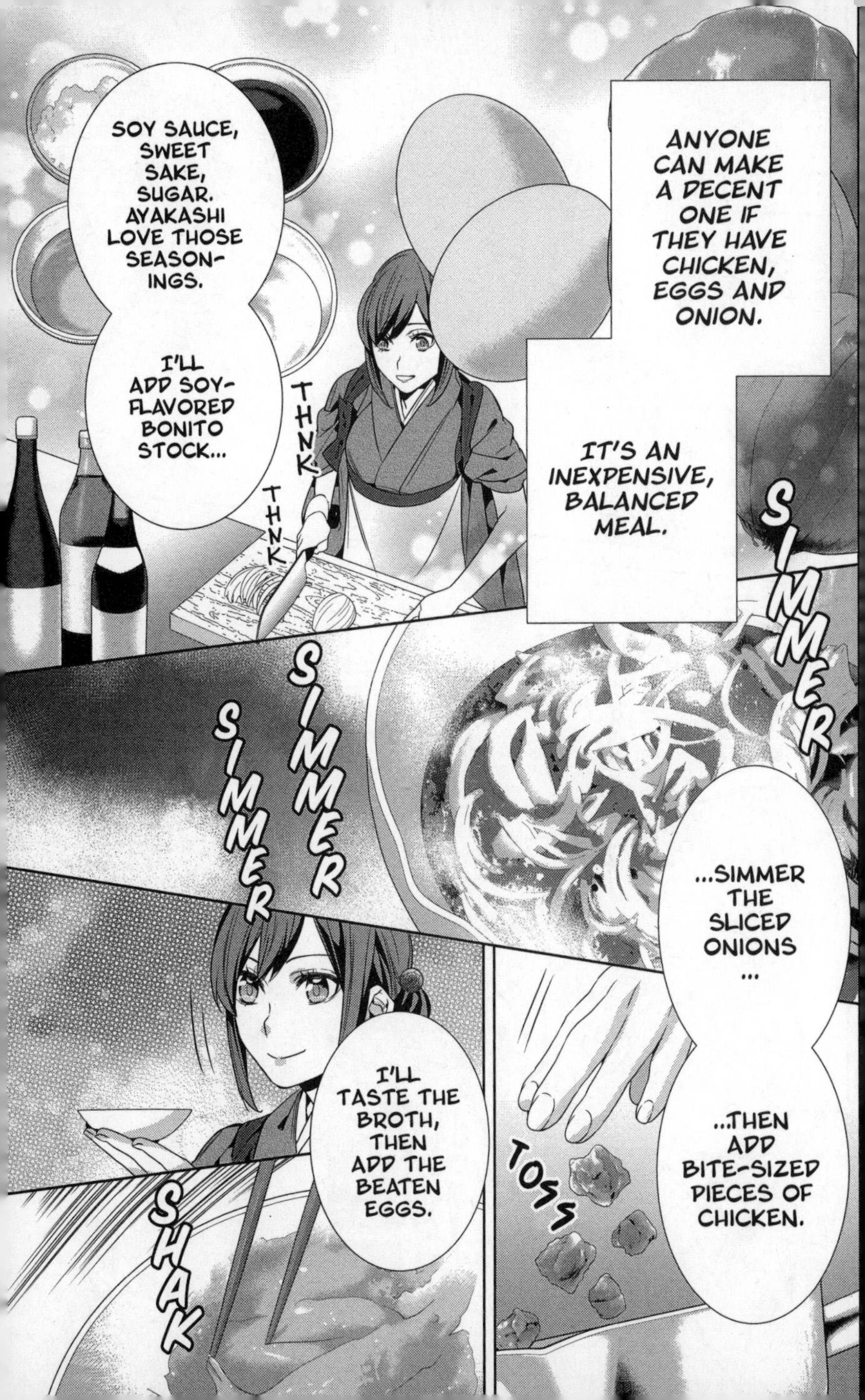
ANYONE CAN MAKE A DECENT ONE IF THEY HAVE CHICKEN, EGGS AND ONION.
IT'S AN INEXPENSIVE, BALANCED MEAL.
SOY SAUCE, SWEET SAKE, SUGAR. AYAKASHI LOVE THOSE SEASON-INGS.
I'LL ADD SOY-FLAVORED BONITO STOCK...
THNK
THNK
SIMMER
SIMMER
SIMMER
...SIMMER THE SLICED ONIONS ...
...THEN ADD BITE-SIZED PIECES OF CHICKEN.
TOSS
I'LL TASTE THE BROTH, THEN ADD THE BEATEN EGGS.
SHAK

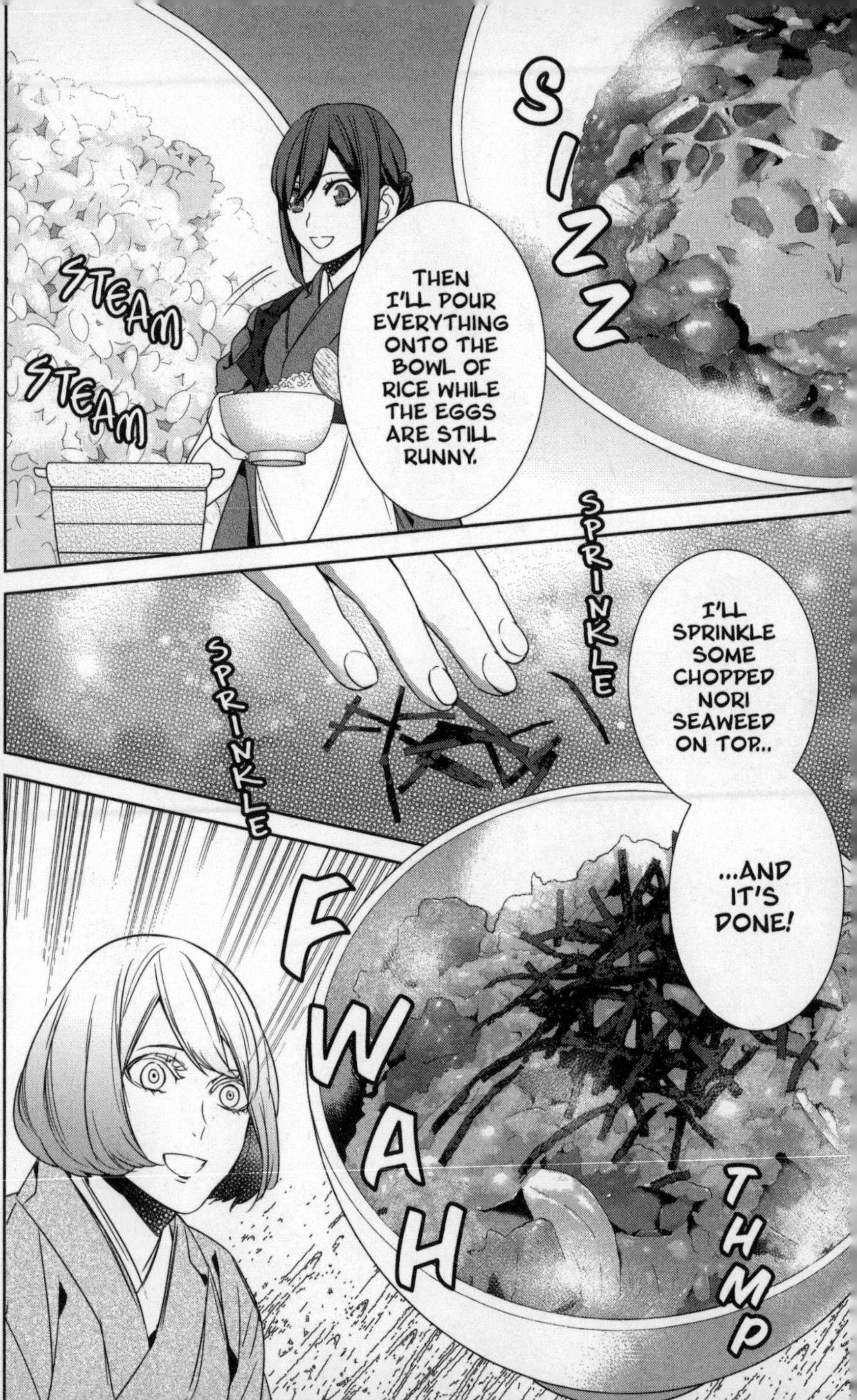
SIZZ
THEN I'LL POUR EVERYTHING ONTO THE BOWL OF RICE WHILE THE EGGS ARE STILL RUNNY.
STEAM
STEAM
I'LL SPRINKLE SOME CHOPPED NORI SEAWEED ON TOP..
SPRINKLE
SPRINKLE
...AND IT'S DONE!
THMP
FWAH

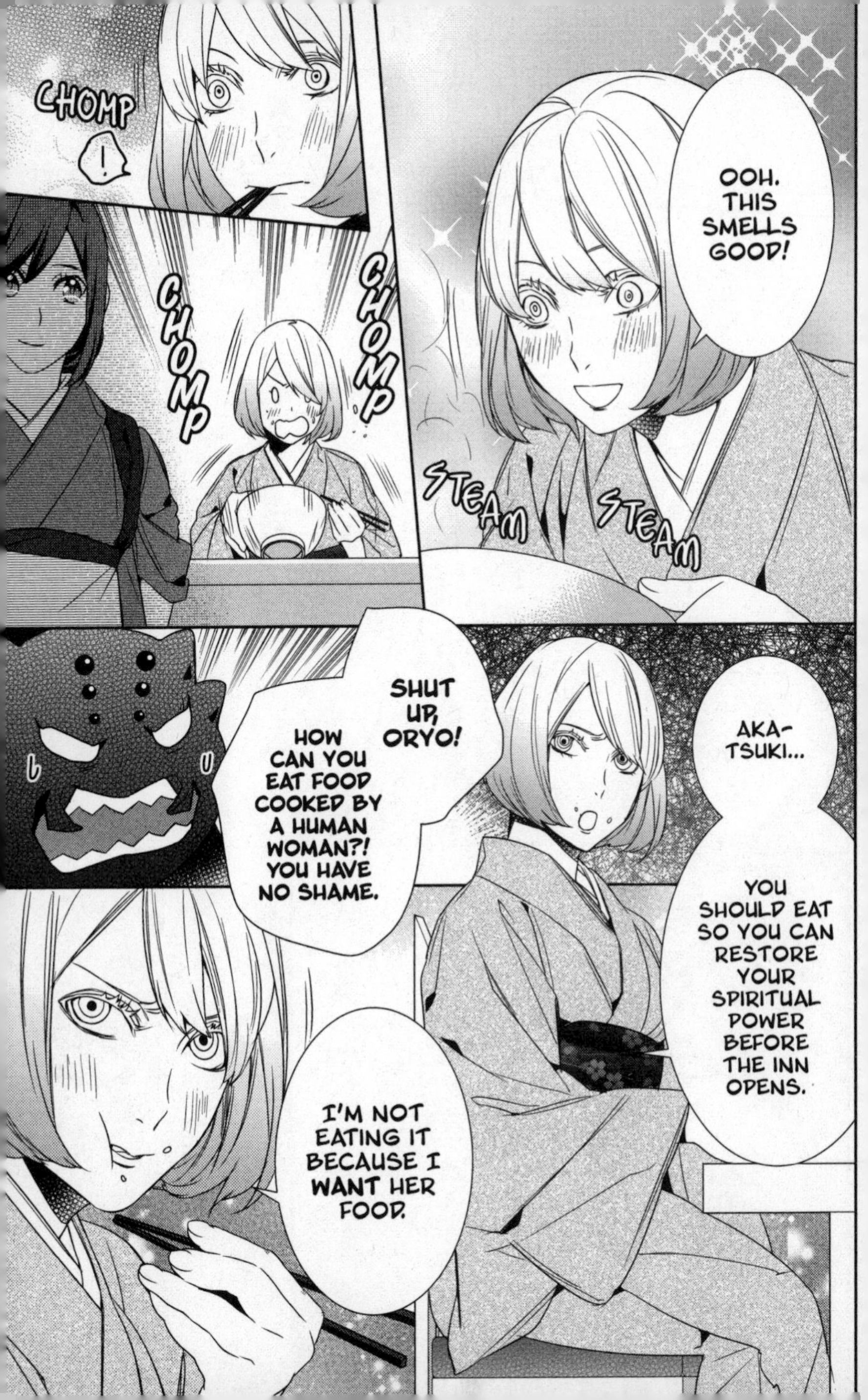
OOH. THIS SMELLS GOOD!
STEAM
STEAM
CHOMP
!
CHOMP
CHOMP
AKA-TSUKI...
YOU SHOULD EAT SO YOU CAN RESTORE YOUR SPIRITUAL POWER BEFORE THE INN OPENS.
SHUT UP, ORYO!
HOW CAN YOU EAT FOOD COOKED BY A HUMAN WOMAN?! YOU HAVE NO SHAME.
I'M NOT EATING IT BECAUSE I WANT HER FOOD.

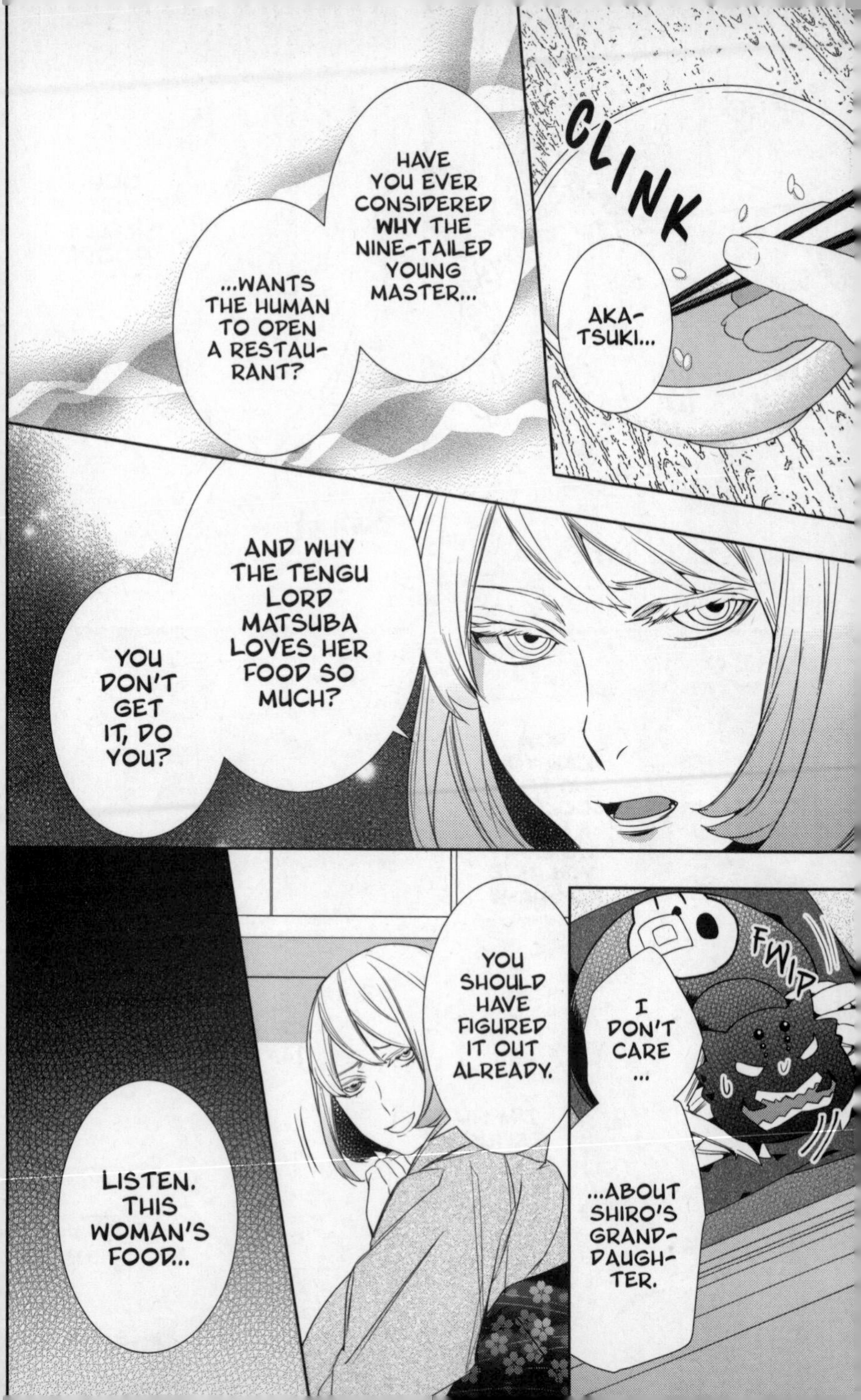
CLINK
AKA-TSUKI...
HAVE YOU EVER CONSIDERED WHY THE NINE-TAILED YOUNG MASTER...
...WANTS THE HUMAN TO OPEN A RESTAU-RANT?
AND WHY THE TENGU LORD MATSUBA LOVES HER FOOD SO MUCH?
YOU DON'T GET IT, DO YOU?
FWIP
I DON'T CARE ...
...ABOUT SHIRO'S GRAND-DAUGH-TER.
YOU SHOULD HAVE FIGURED IT OUT ALREADY.
LISTEN. THIS WOMAN'S FOOD...

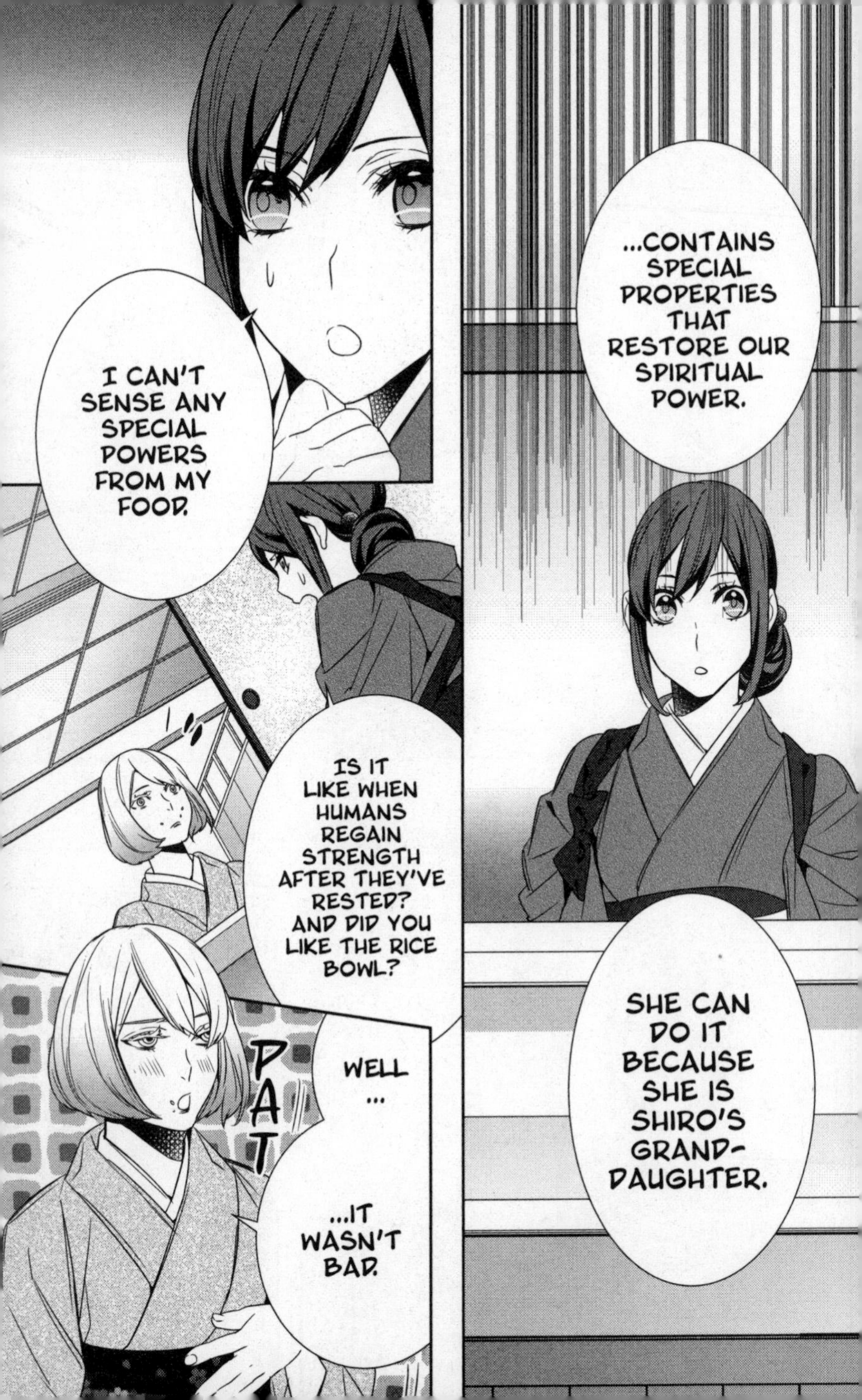
...CONTAINS SPECIAL PROPERTIES THAT RESTORE OUR SPIRITUAL POWER.
SHE CAN DO IT BECAUSE SHE IS SHIRO'S GRAND-DAUGHTER.
I CAN'T SENSE ANY SPECIAL POWERS FROM MY FOOD.
IS IT LIKE WHEN HUMANS REGAIN STRENGTH AFTER THEY'VE RESTED? AND DID YOU LIKE THE RICE BOWL?
WELL ...
PAT
...IT WASN'T BAD.

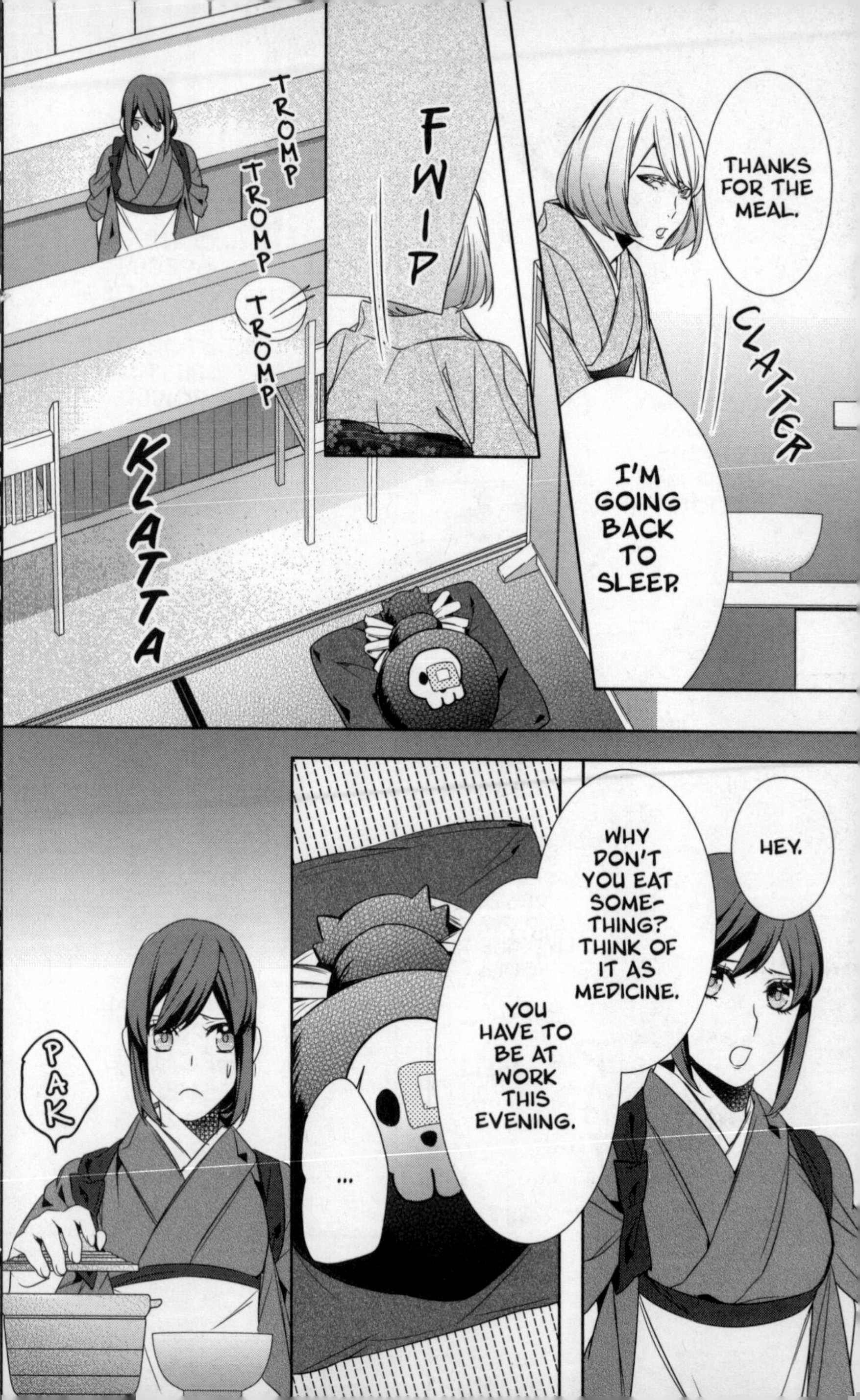
THANKS FOR THE MEAL.
CLATTER
I'M GOING BACK TO SLEEP.
FWIP
TROMP TROMP TROMP TROMP
KLATTA
HEY.
WHY DON'T YOU EAT SOME-THING? THINK OF IT AS MEDICINE.
YOU HAVE TO BE AT WORK THIS EVENING.
...
PAK

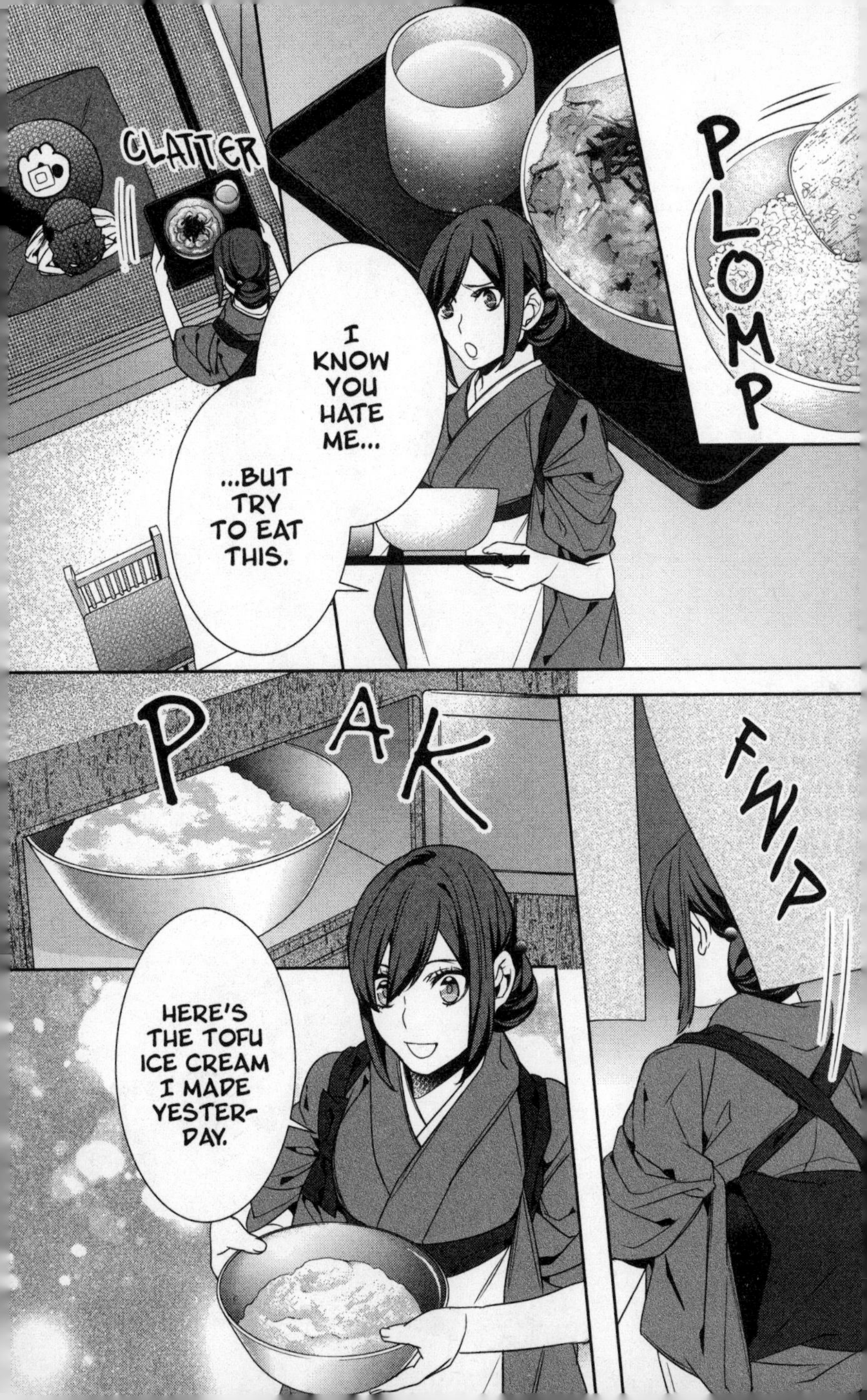
PLOMP
CLATTER
I KNOW YOU HATE ME...
...BUT TRY TO EAT THIS.
FWIP
PAK
HERE'S THE TOFU ICE CREAM I MADE YESTER-DAY.

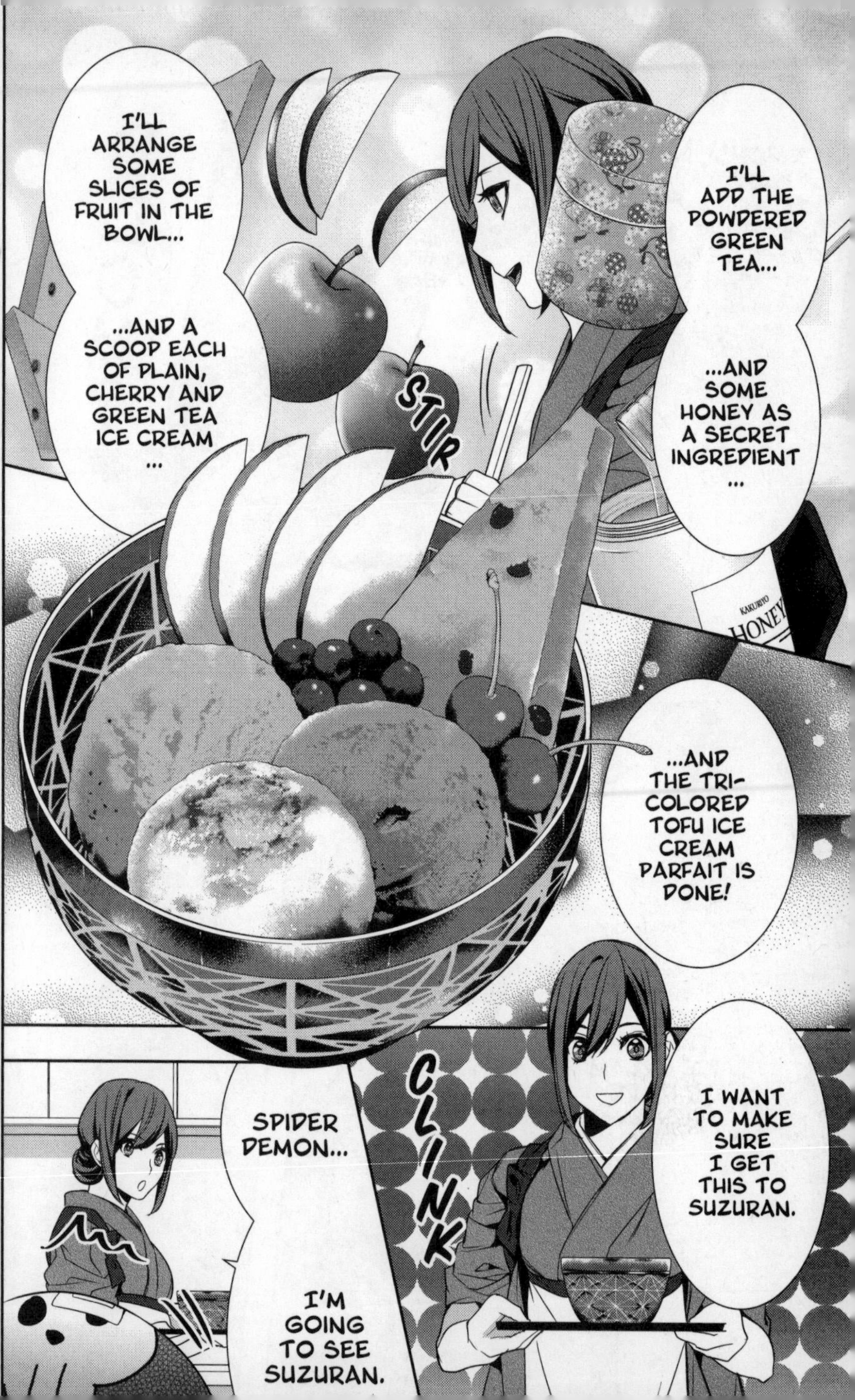
I'LL ADD THE POWDERED GREEN TEA...
...AND SOME HONEY AS A SECRET INGREDIENT...
I'LL ARRANGE SOME SLICES OF FRUIT IN THE BOWL...
...AND A SCOOP EACH OF PLAIN, CHERRY AND GREEN TEA ICE CREAM...
STIR
KAKURIYO HONEY
...AND THE TRI-COLORED TOFU ICE CREAM PARFAIT IS DONE!
I WANT TO MAKE SURE I GET THIS TO SUZURAN.
CLINK
SPIDER DEMON...
I'M GOING TO SEE SUZURAN.

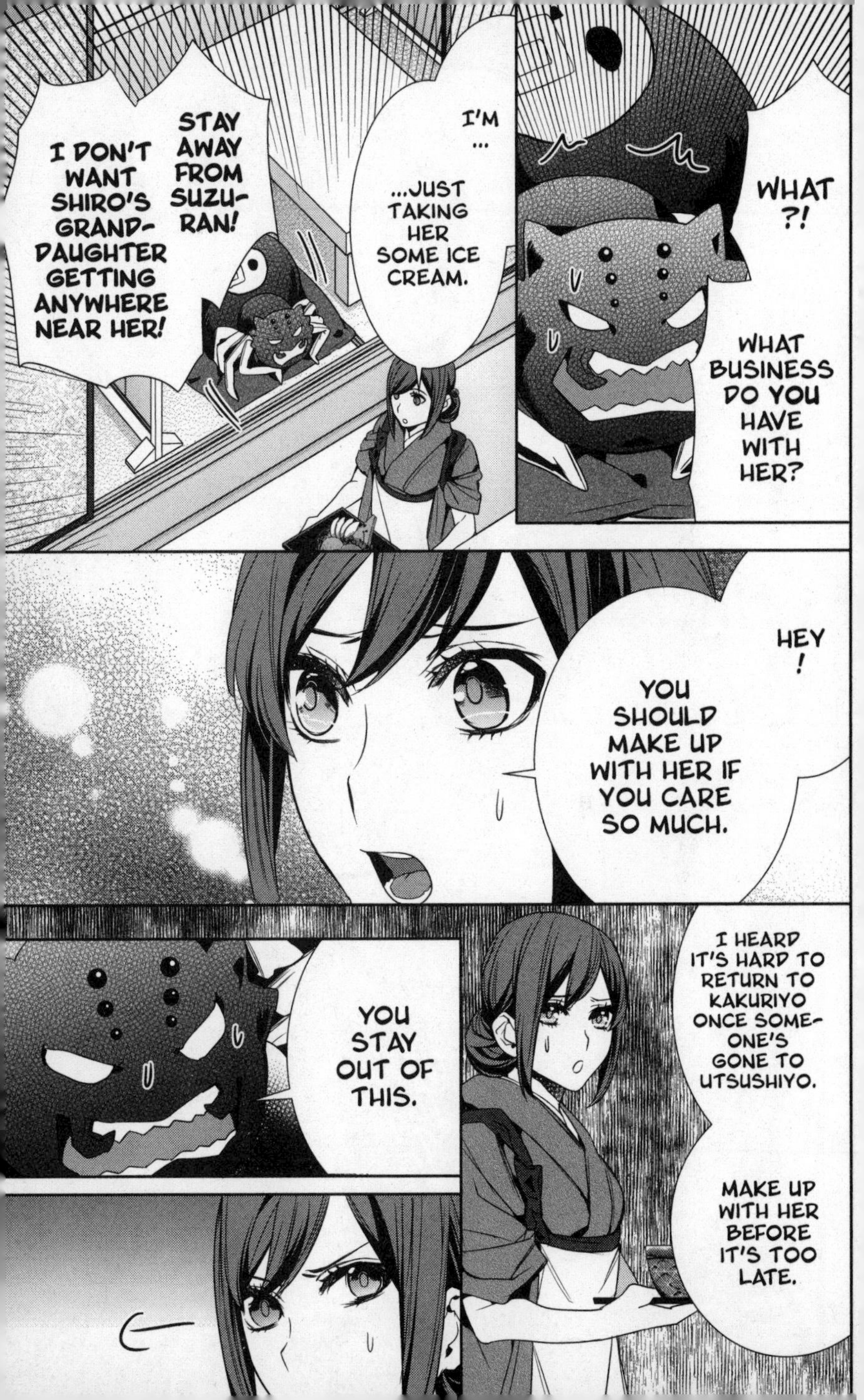
WHAT?!
WHAT BUSINESS DO YOU HAVE WITH HER?
I'M ...
...JUST TAKING HER SOME ICE CREAM.
STAY AWAY FROM SUZU-RAN!
I DON'T WANT SHIRO'S GRAND-DAUGHTER GETTING ANYWHERE NEAR HER!
HEY!
YOU SHOULD MAKE UP WITH HER IF YOU CARE SO MUCH.
I HEARD IT'S HARD TO RETURN TO KAKURIYO ONCE SOME-ONE'S GONE TO UTSUSHIYO.
MAKE UP WITH HER BEFORE IT'S TOO LATE.
YOU STAY OUT OF THIS.

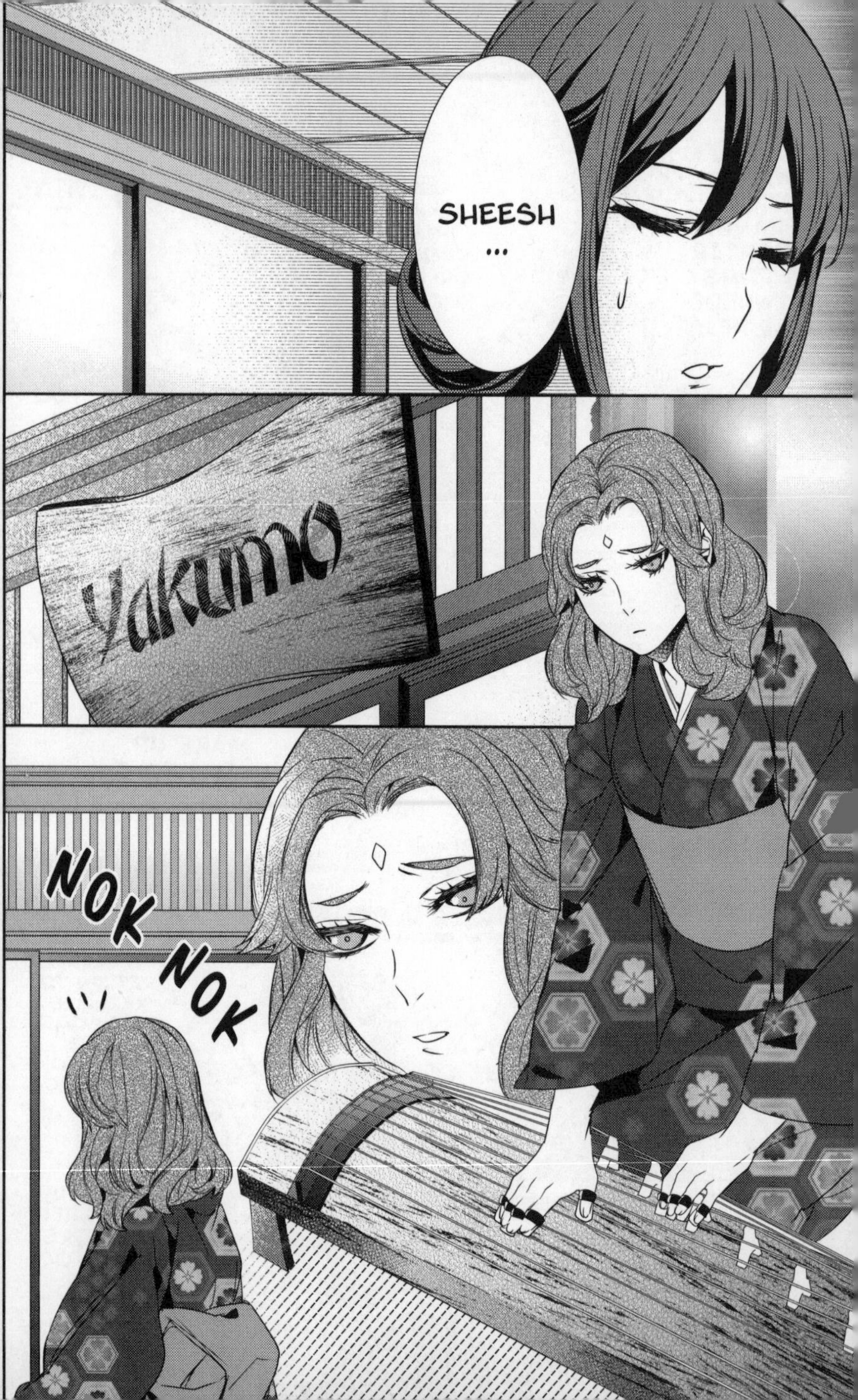
SHEESH ...
Yakumo
NOK NOK

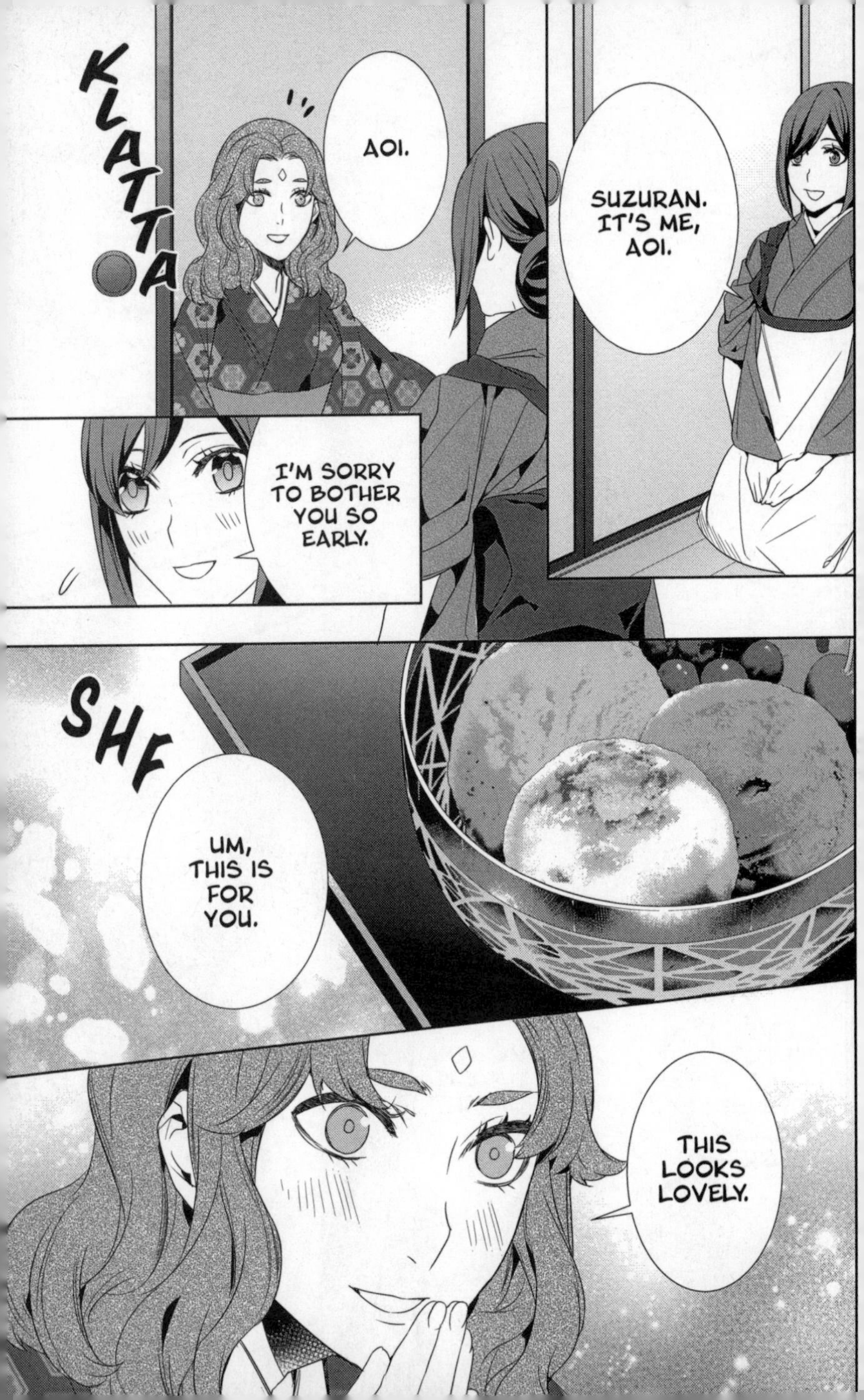
SUZURAN. IT'S ME, AOI.
KLATTA
AOI.
I'M SORRY TO BOTHER YOU SO EARLY.
SHF
UM, THIS IS FOR YOU.
THIS LOOKS LOVELY.

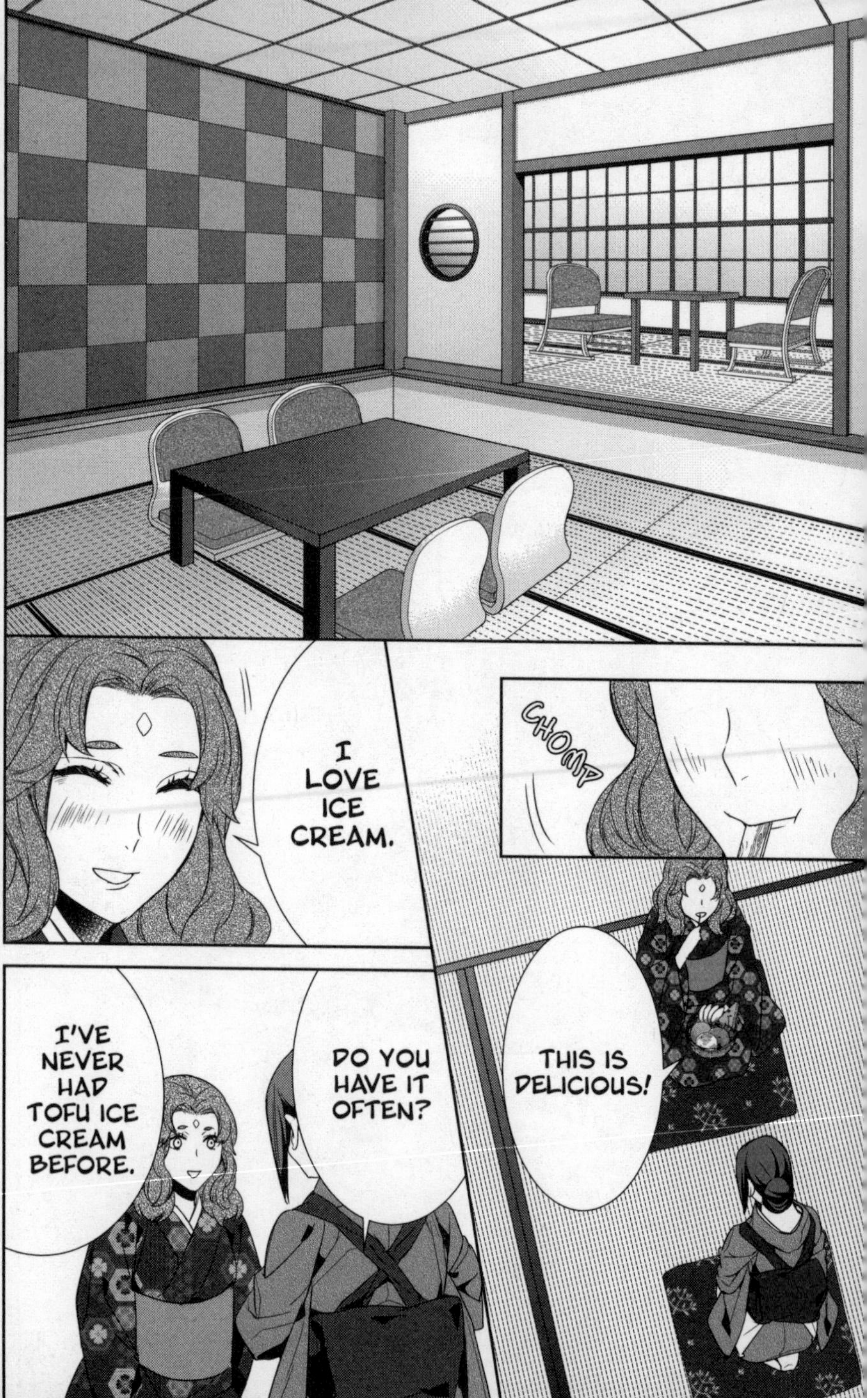
CHOMP
THIS IS DELICIOUS!
I LOVE ICE CREAM.
DO YOU HAVE IT OFTEN?
I'VE NEVER HAD TOFU ICE CREAM BEFORE.

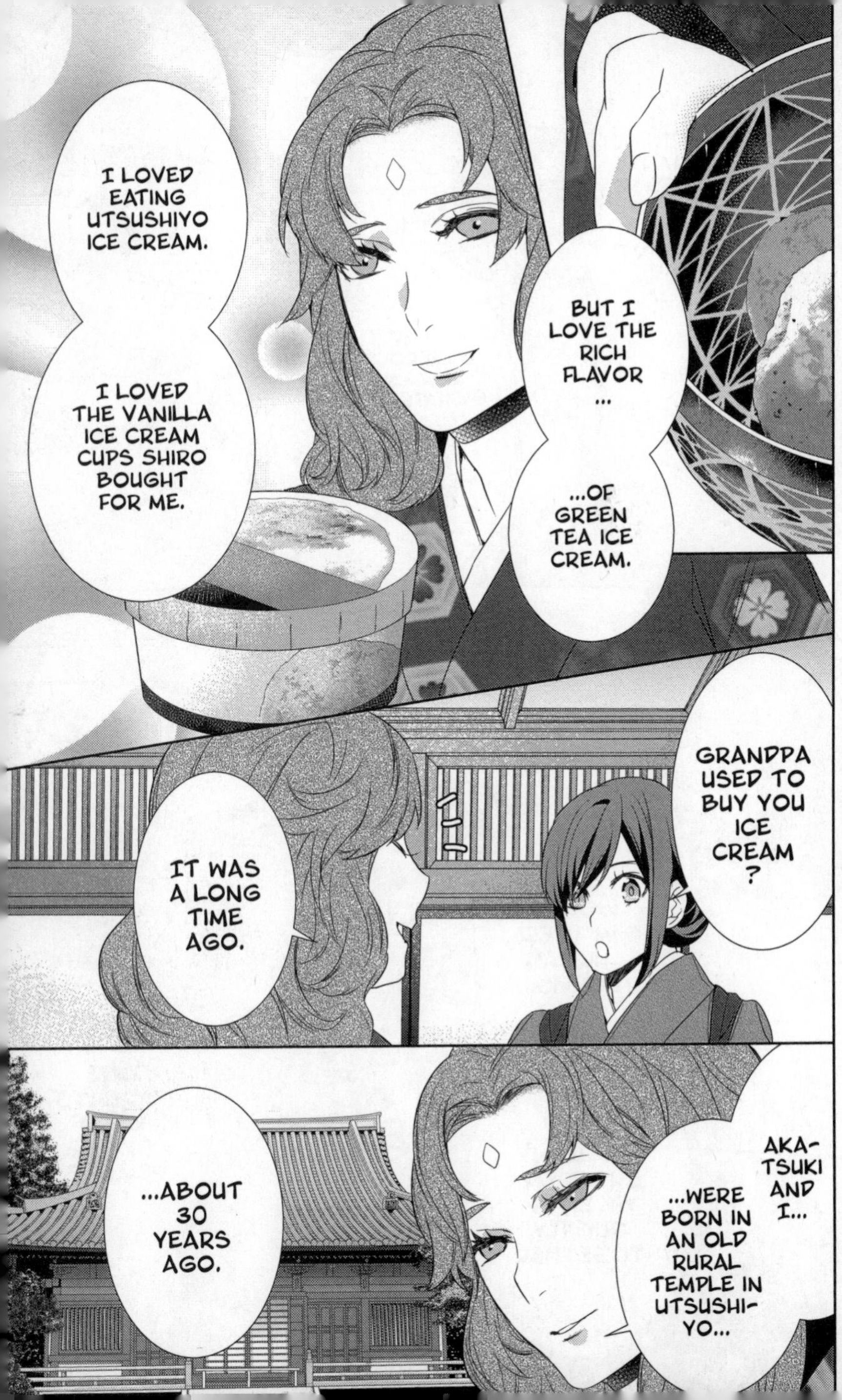
BUT I LOVE THE RICH FLAVOR...
...OF GREEN TEA ICE CREAM.
I LOVED EATING UTSUSHIYO ICE CREAM.
I LOVED THE VANILLA ICE CREAM CUPS SHIRO BOUGHT FOR ME.
GRANDPA USED TO BUY YOU ICE CREAM?
IT WAS A LONG TIME AGO.
AKATSUKI AND I...
...WERE BORN IN AN OLD RURAL TEMPLE IN UTSUSHIYO...
...ABOUT 30 YEARS AGO.

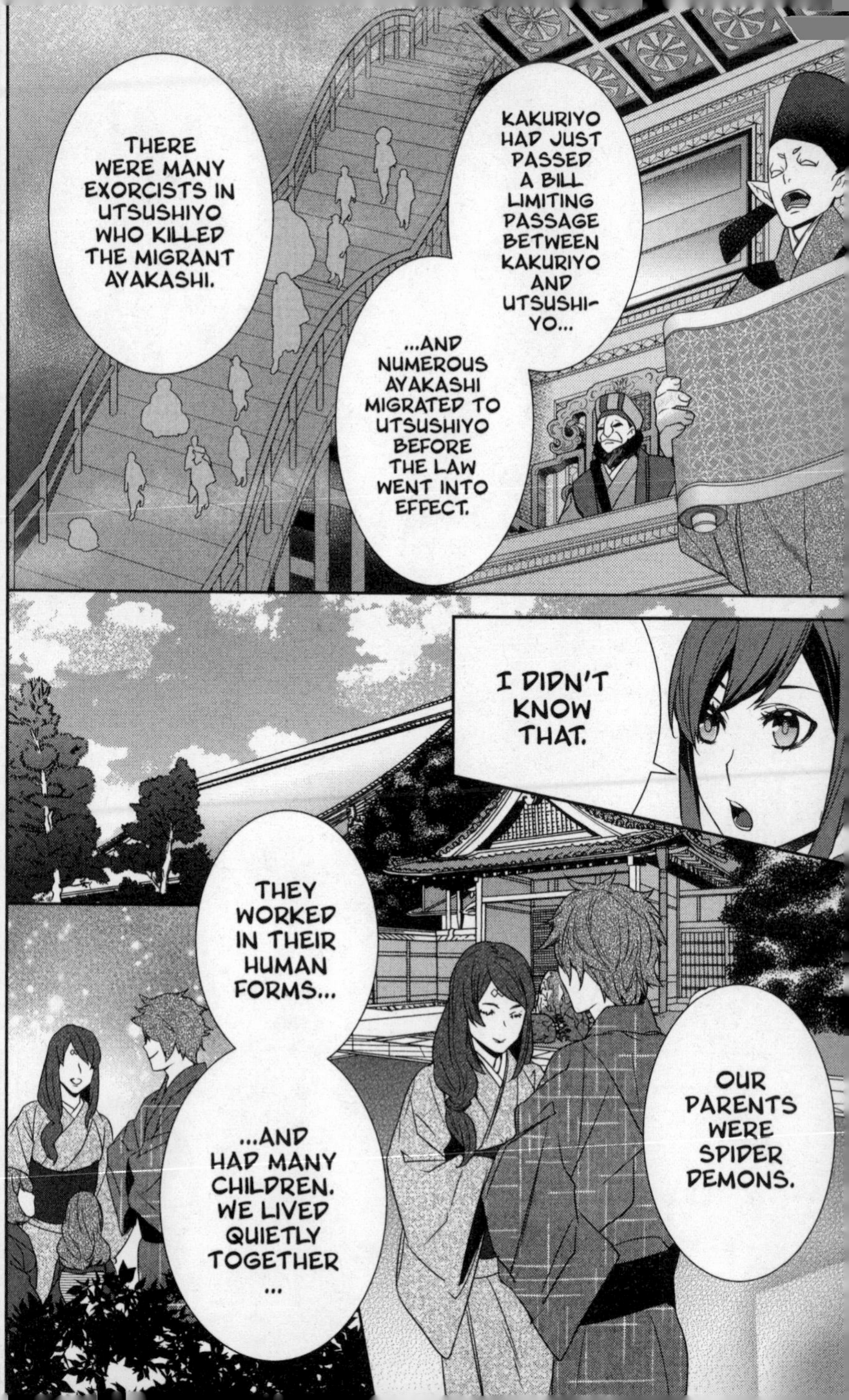
KAKURIYO HAD JUST PASSED A BILL LIMITING PASSAGE BETWEEN KAKURIYO AND UTSUSHI-YO...
...AND NUMEROUS AYAKASHI MIGRATED TO UTSUSHIYO BEFORE THE LAW WENT INTO EFFECT.
THERE WERE MANY EXORCISTS IN UTSUSHIYO WHO KILLED THE MIGRANT AYAKASHI.
I DIDN'T KNOW THAT.
OUR PARENTS WERE SPIDER DEMONS.
THEY WORKED IN THEIR HUMAN FORMS...
...AND HAD MANY CHILDREN. WE LIVED QUIETLY TOGETHER ...

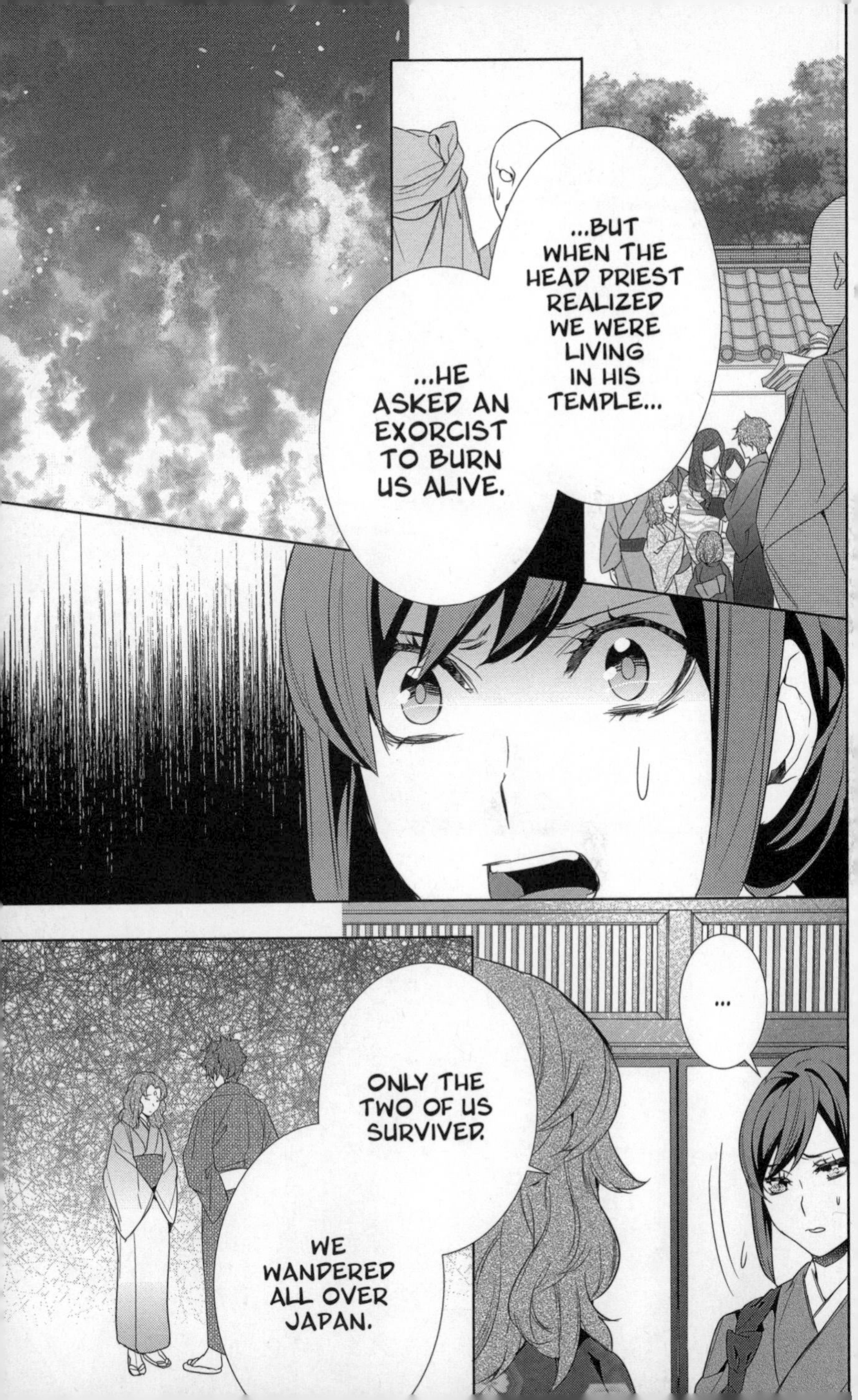
...BUT WHEN THE HEAD PRIEST REALIZED WE WERE LIVING IN HIS TEMPLE...
...HE ASKED AN EXORCIST TO BURN US ALIVE.
...
ONLY THE TWO OF US SURVIVED.
WE WANDERED ALL OVER JAPAN.

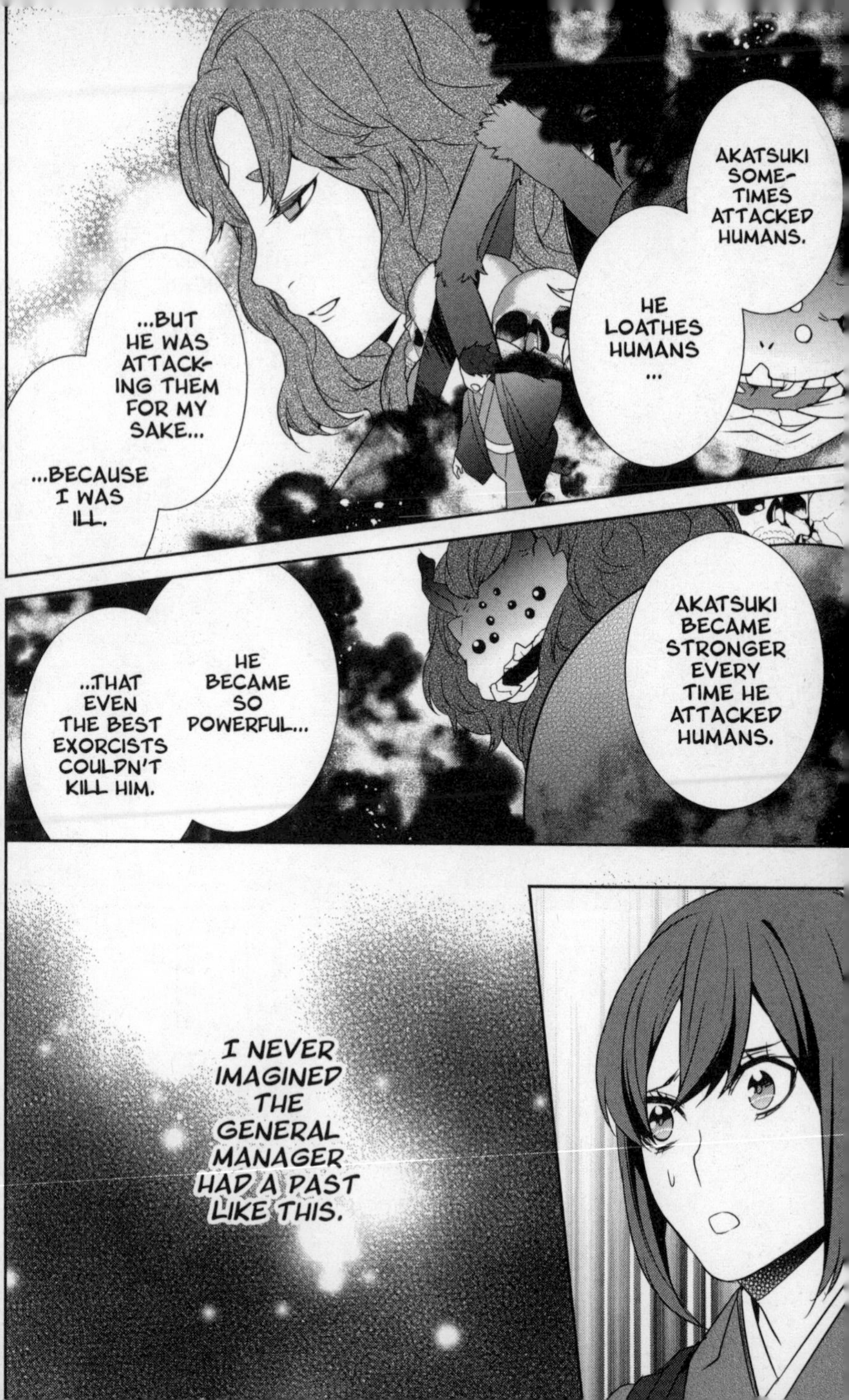
AKATSUKI SOMETIMES ATTACKED HUMANS.
HE LOATHES HUMANS...
...BUT HE WAS ATTACKING THEM FOR MY SAKE...
...BECAUSE I WAS ILL.
AKATSUKI BECAME STRONGER EVERY TIME HE ATTACKED HUMANS.
HE BECAME SO POWERFUL...
...THAT EVEN THE BEST EXORCISTS COULDN'T KILL HIM.
I NEVER IMAGINED THE GENERAL MANAGER HAD A PAST LIKE THIS.

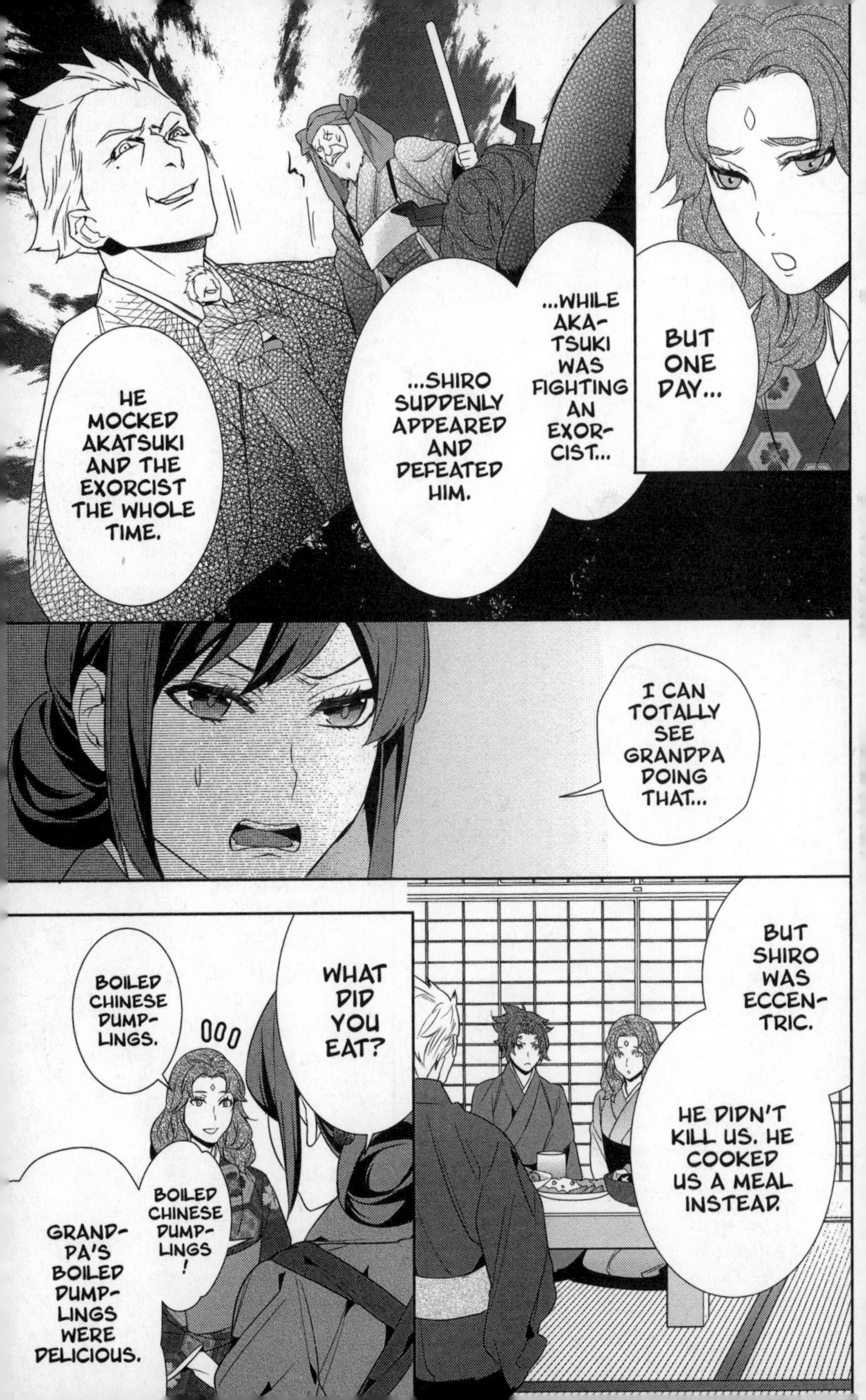
BUT ONE DAY...
...WHILE AKATSUKI WAS FIGHTING AN EXORCIST...
...SHIRO SUDDENLY APPEARED AND DEFEATED HIM.
HE MOCKED AKATSUKI AND THE EXORCIST THE WHOLE TIME.
I CAN TOTALLY SEE GRANDPA DOING THAT...
BUT SHIRO WAS ECCENTRIC.
HE DIDN'T KILL US. HE COOKED US A MEAL INSTEAD.
WHAT DID YOU EAT?
BOILED CHINESE DUMPLINGS.
OOO
BOILED CHINESE DUMPLINGS!
GRANDPA'S BOILED DUMPLINGS WERE DELICIOUS.

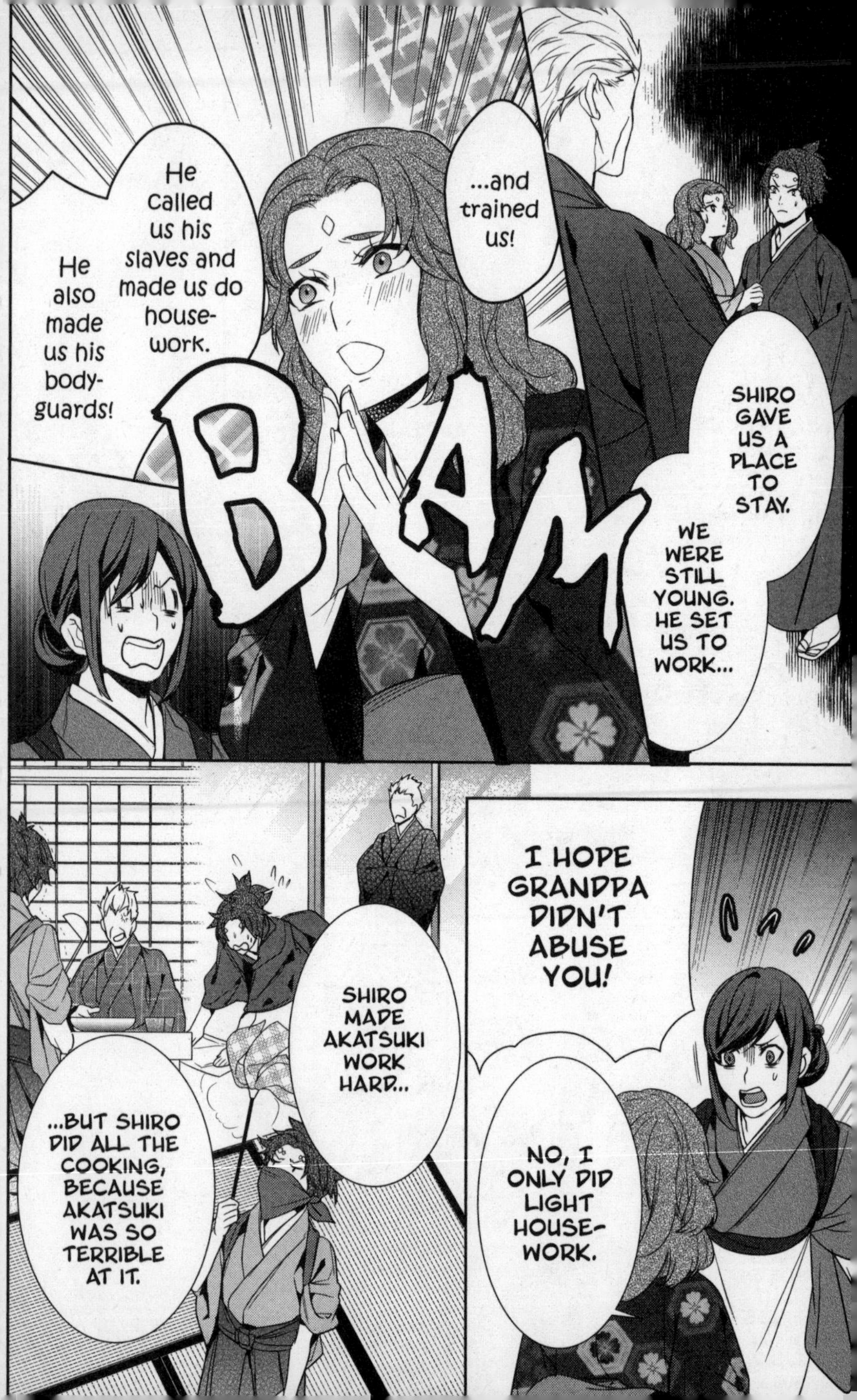
SHIRO GAVE US A PLACE TO STAY.
WE WERE STILL YOUNG. HE SET US TO WORK...
...and trained us!
He called us his slaves and made us do house-work.
He also made us his body-guards!
BAM
I HOPE GRANDPA DIDN'T ABUSE YOU!
NO, I ONLY DID LIGHT HOUSE-WORK.
SHIRO MADE AKATSUKI WORK HARD...
...BUT SHIRO DID ALL THE COOKING, BECAUSE AKATSUKI WAS SO TERRIBLE AT IT.

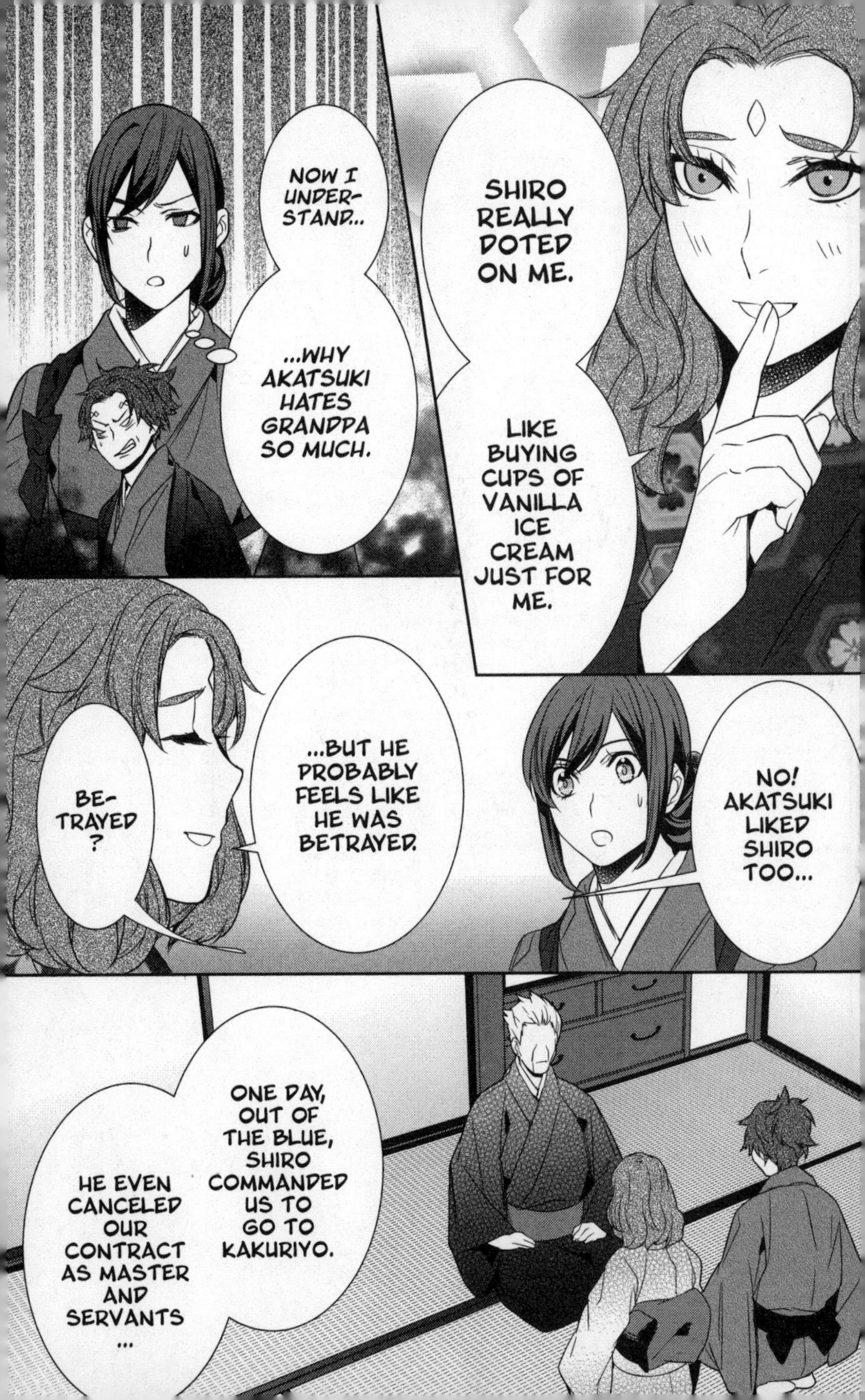

SHIRO REALLY DOTED ON ME.
LIKE BUYING CUPS OF VANILLA ICE CREAM JUST FOR ME.
NOW I UNDER-STAND...
...WHY AKATSUKI HATES GRANDPA SO MUCH.
NO! AKATSUKI LIKED SHIRO TOO...
...BUT HE PROBABLY FEELS LIKE HE WAS BETRAYED.
BE-TRAYED?
ONE DAY, OUT OF THE BLUE, SHIRO COMMANDED US TO GO TO KAKURIYO.
HE EVEN CANCELED OUR CONTRACT AS MASTER AND SERVANTS...

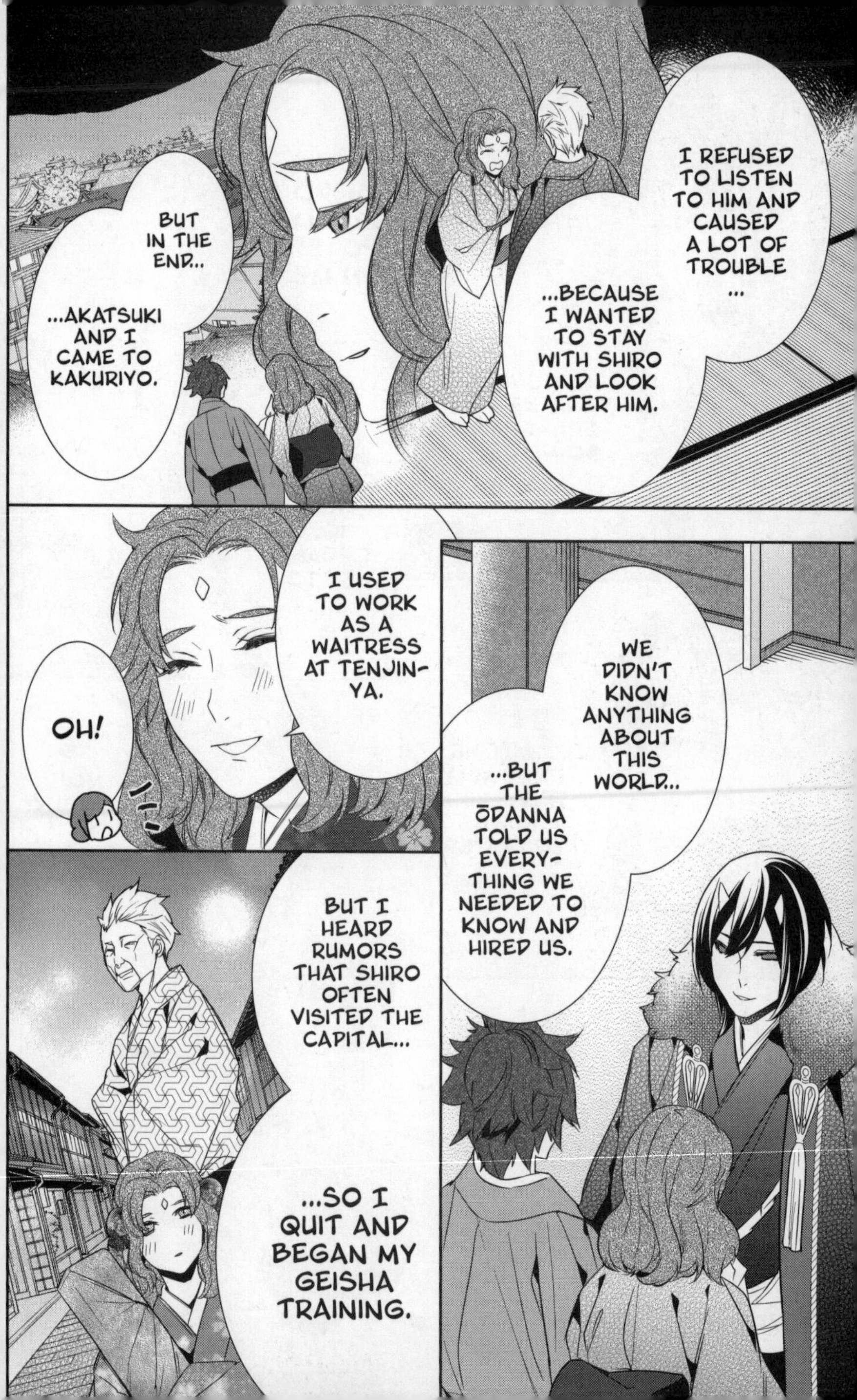
I REFUSED TO LISTEN TO HIM AND CAUSED A LOT OF TROUBLE...
...BECAUSE I WANTED TO STAY WITH SHIRO AND LOOK AFTER HIM.
BUT IN THE END...
...AKATSUKI AND I CAME TO KAKURIYO.
WE DIDN'T KNOW ANYTHING ABOUT THIS WORLD...
...BUT THE ŌDANNA TOLD US EVERY-THING WE NEEDED TO KNOW AND HIRED US.
I USED TO WORK AS A WAITRESS AT TENJIN-YA.
OH!
BUT I HEARD RUMORS THAT SHIRO OFTEN VISITED THE CAPITAL...
...SO I QUIT AND BEGAN MY GEISHA TRAINING.

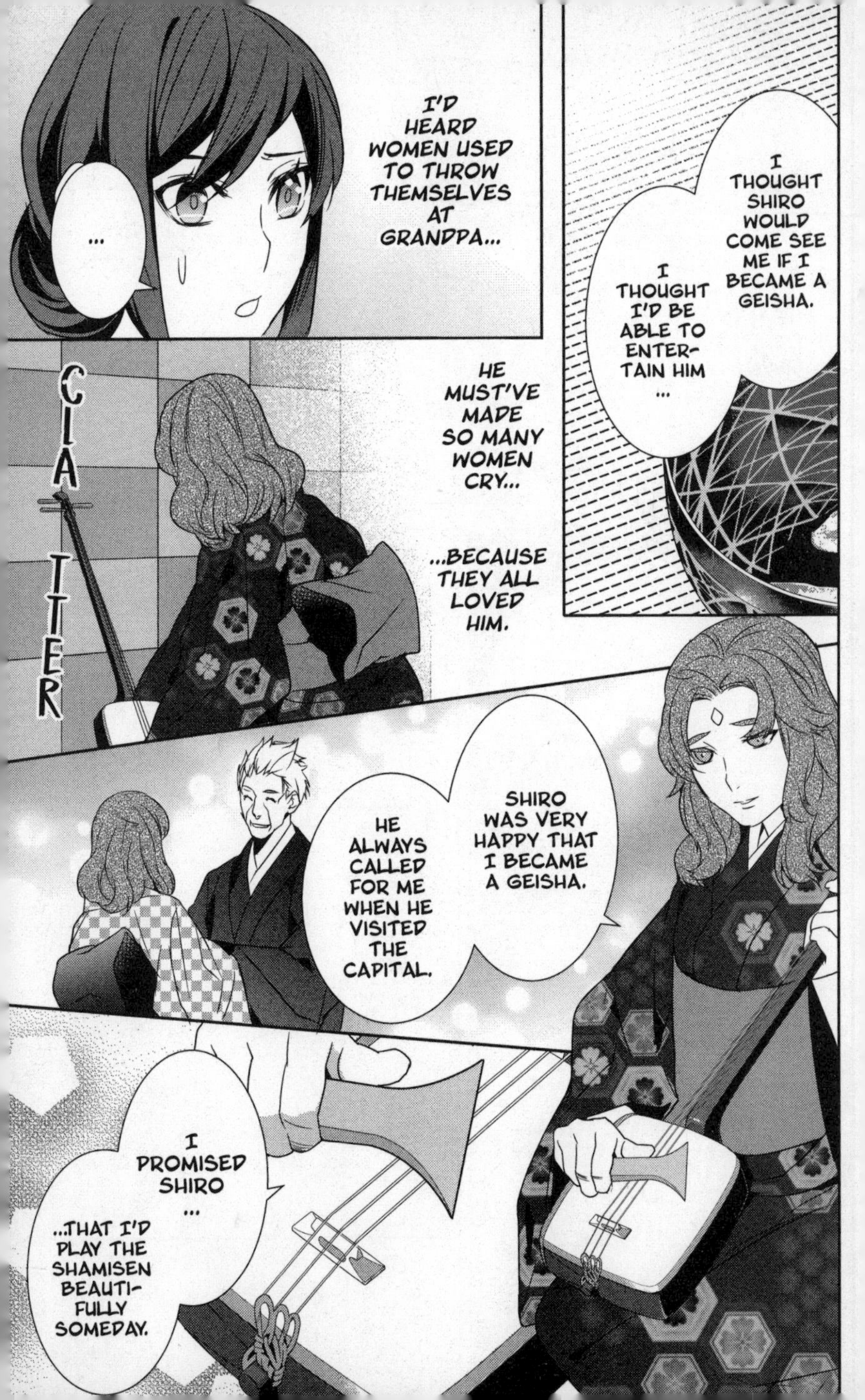
I THOUGHT SHIRO WOULD COME SEE ME IF I BECAME A GEISHA.
I THOUGHT I'D BE ABLE TO ENTERTAIN HIM...
I'D HEARD WOMEN USED TO THROW THEMSELVES AT GRANDPA...
...
HE MUST'VE MADE SO MANY WOMEN CRY...
...BECAUSE THEY ALL LOVED HIM.
CLATTER
SHIRO WAS VERY HAPPY THAT I BECAME A GEISHA.
HE ALWAYS CALLED FOR ME WHEN HE VISITED THE CAPITAL.
I PROMISED SHIRO...
...THAT I'D PLAY THE SHAMISEN BEAUTIFULLY SOMEDAY.

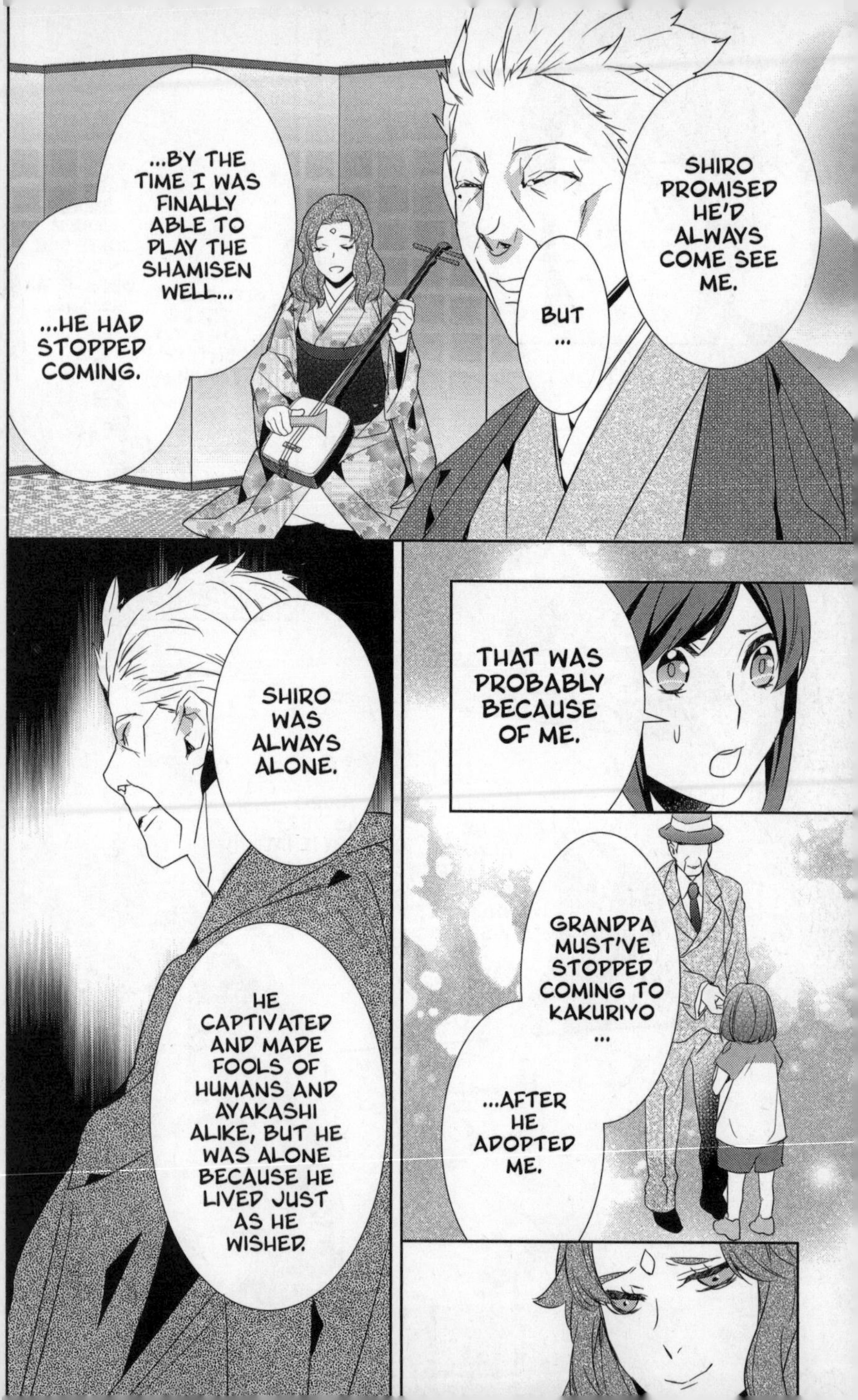
SHIRO PROMISED HE'D ALWAYS COME SEE ME.
BUT ...
...BY THE TIME I WAS FINALLY ABLE TO PLAY THE SHAMISEN WELL...
...HE HAD STOPPED COMING.
THAT WAS PROBABLY BECAUSE OF ME.
GRANDPA MUST'VE STOPPED COMING TO KAKURIYO ...
...AFTER HE ADOPTED ME.
SHIRO WAS ALWAYS ALONE.
HE CAPTIVATED AND MADE FOOLS OF HUMANS AND AYAKASHI ALIKE, BUT HE WAS ALONE BECAUSE HE LIVED JUST AS HE WISHED.

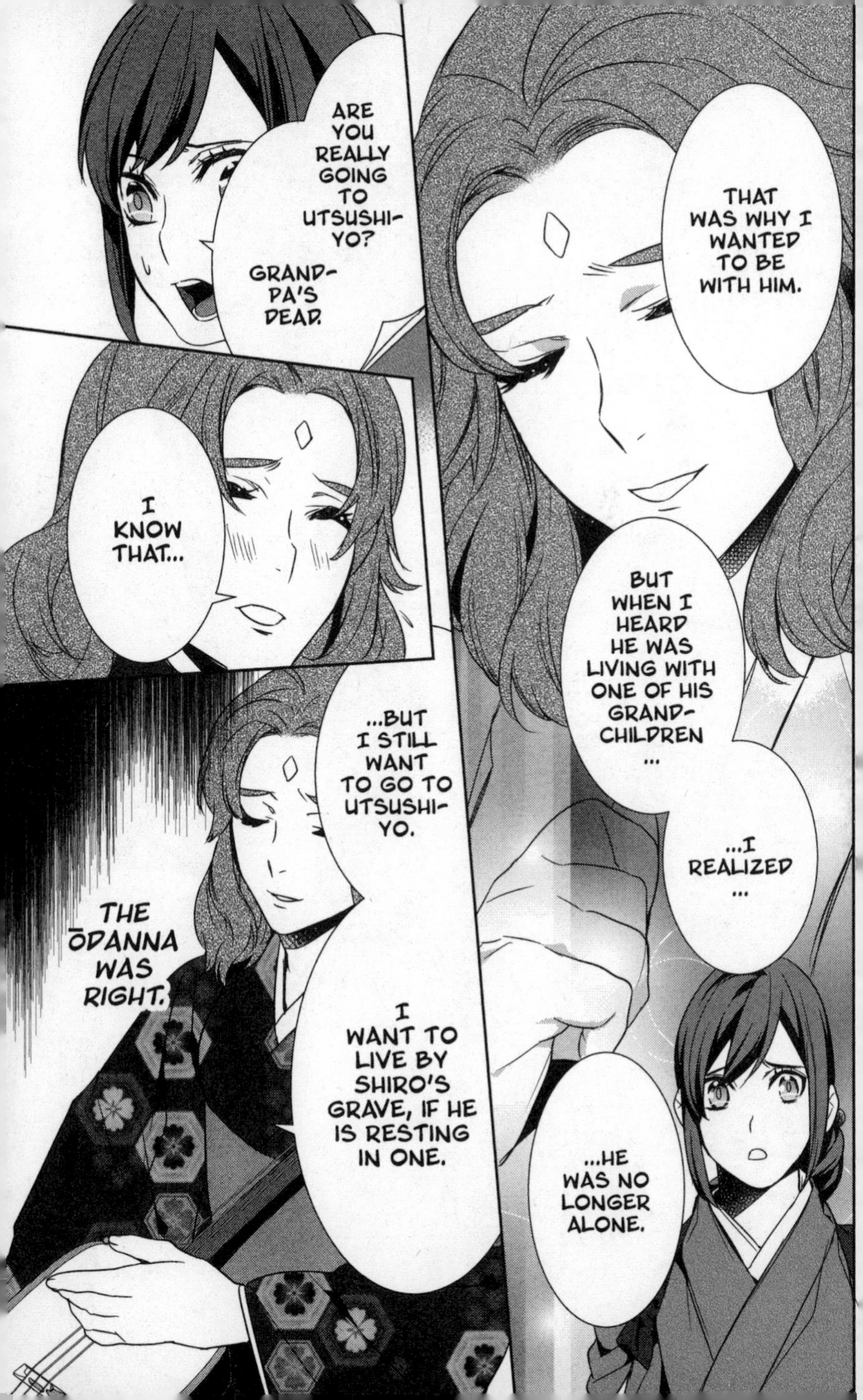
THAT WAS WHY I WANTED TO BE WITH HIM.
BUT WHEN I HEARD HE WAS LIVING WITH ONE OF HIS GRAND-CHILDREN ...
...I REALIZED ...
...HE WAS NO LONGER ALONE.
ARE YOU REALLY GOING TO UTSUSHI-YO?
GRAND-PA'S DEAD.
I KNOW THAT...
...BUT I STILL WANT TO GO TO UTSUSHI-YO.
I WANT TO LIVE BY SHIRO'S GRAVE, IF HE IS RESTING IN ONE.
THE ŌDANNA WAS RIGHT.

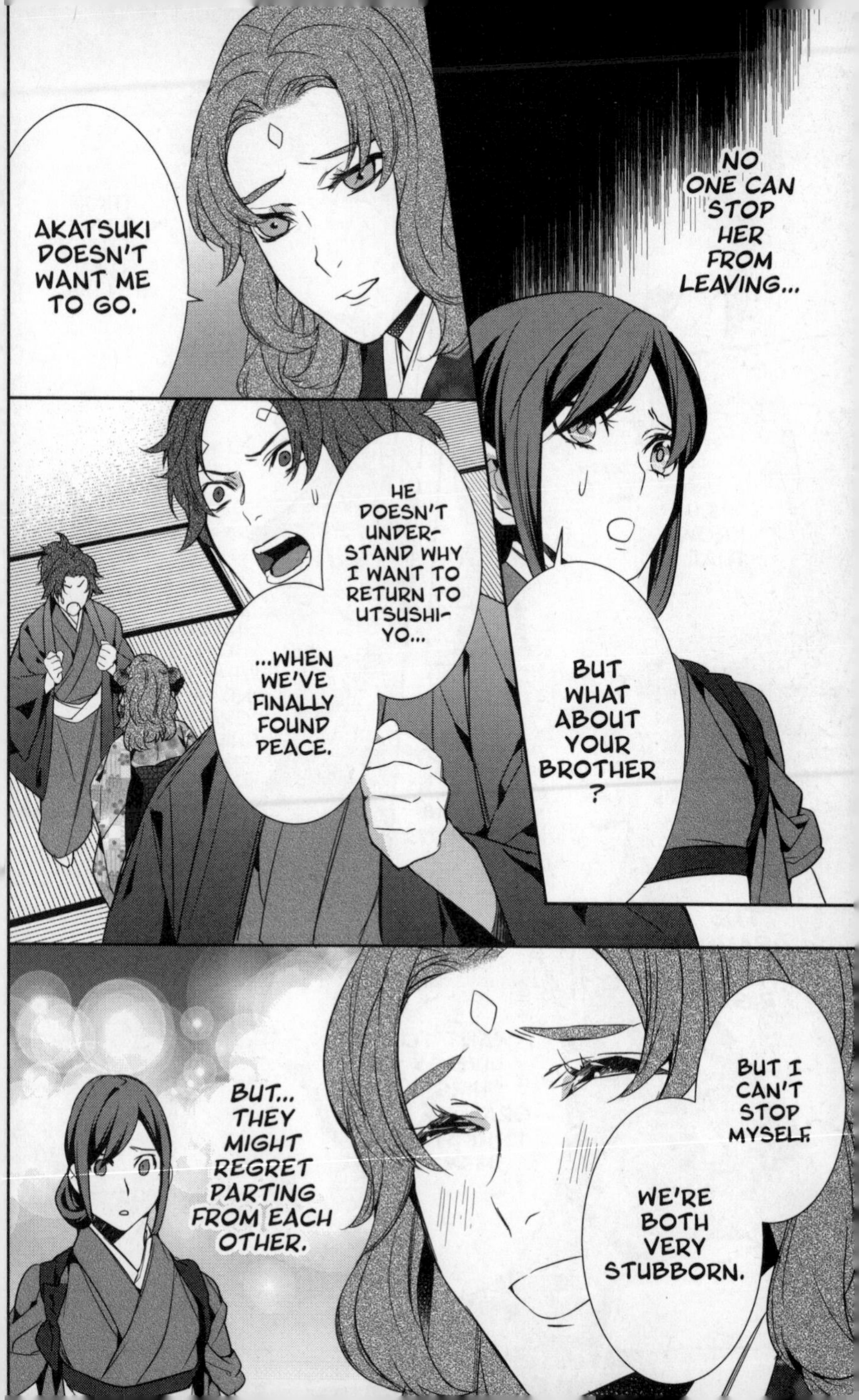
NO ONE CAN STOP HER FROM LEAVING...
BUT WHAT ABOUT YOUR BROTHER?
AKATSUKI DOESN'T WANT ME TO GO.
HE DOESN'T UNDER-STAND WHY I WANT TO RETURN TO UTSUSHI-YO...
...WHEN WE'VE FINALLY FOUND PEACE.
BUT I CAN'T STOP MYSELF.
WE'RE BOTH VERY STUBBORN.
BUT... THEY MIGHT REGRET PARTING FROM EACH OTHER.

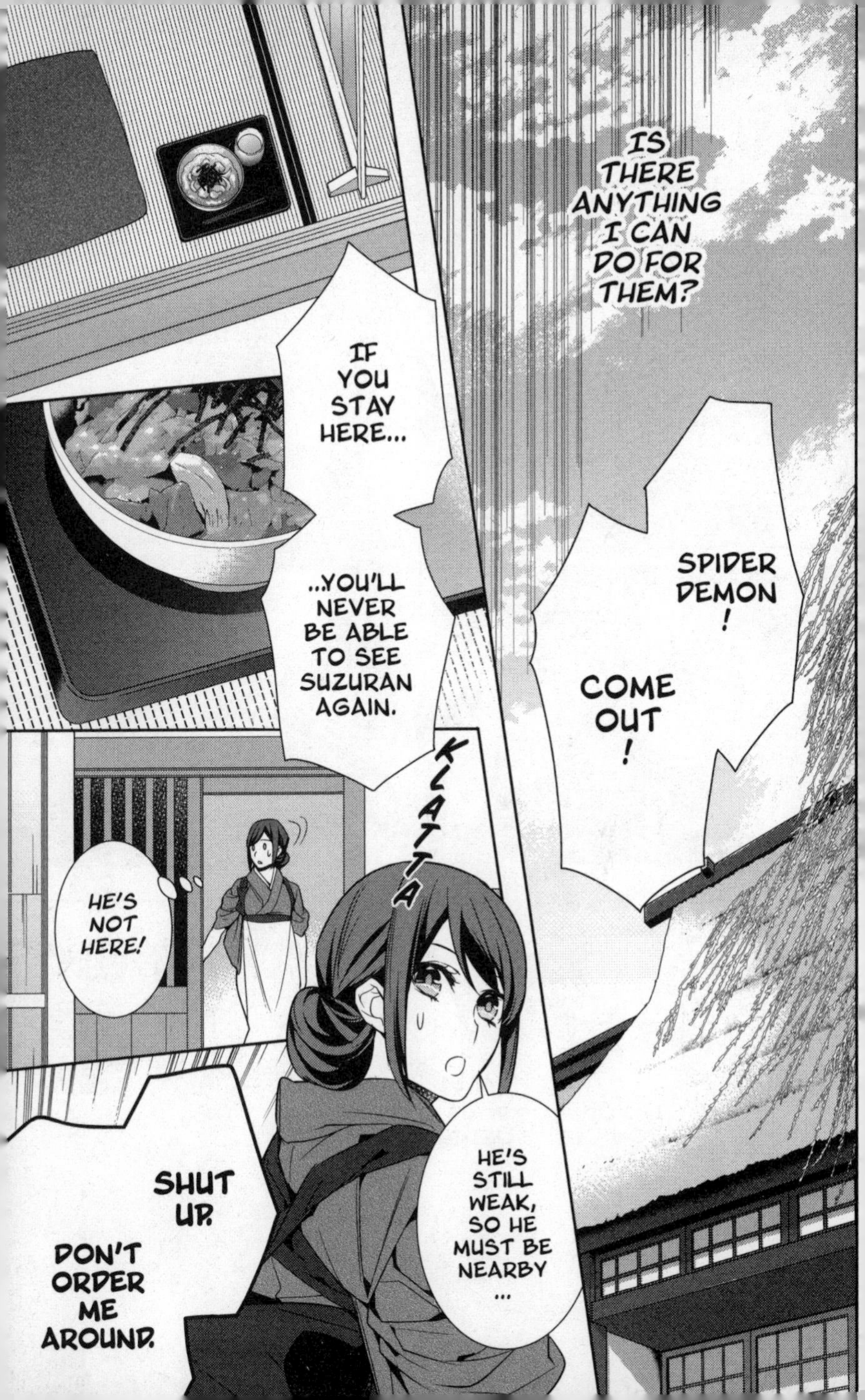
IS THERE ANYTHING I CAN DO FOR THEM?
SPIDER DEMON!
COME OUT!
IF YOU STAY HERE...
...YOU'LL NEVER BE ABLE TO SEE SUZURAN AGAIN.
KLATTA
HE'S NOT HERE!
HE'S STILL WEAK, SO HE MUST BE NEARBY...
SHUT UP.
DON'T ORDER ME AROUND.

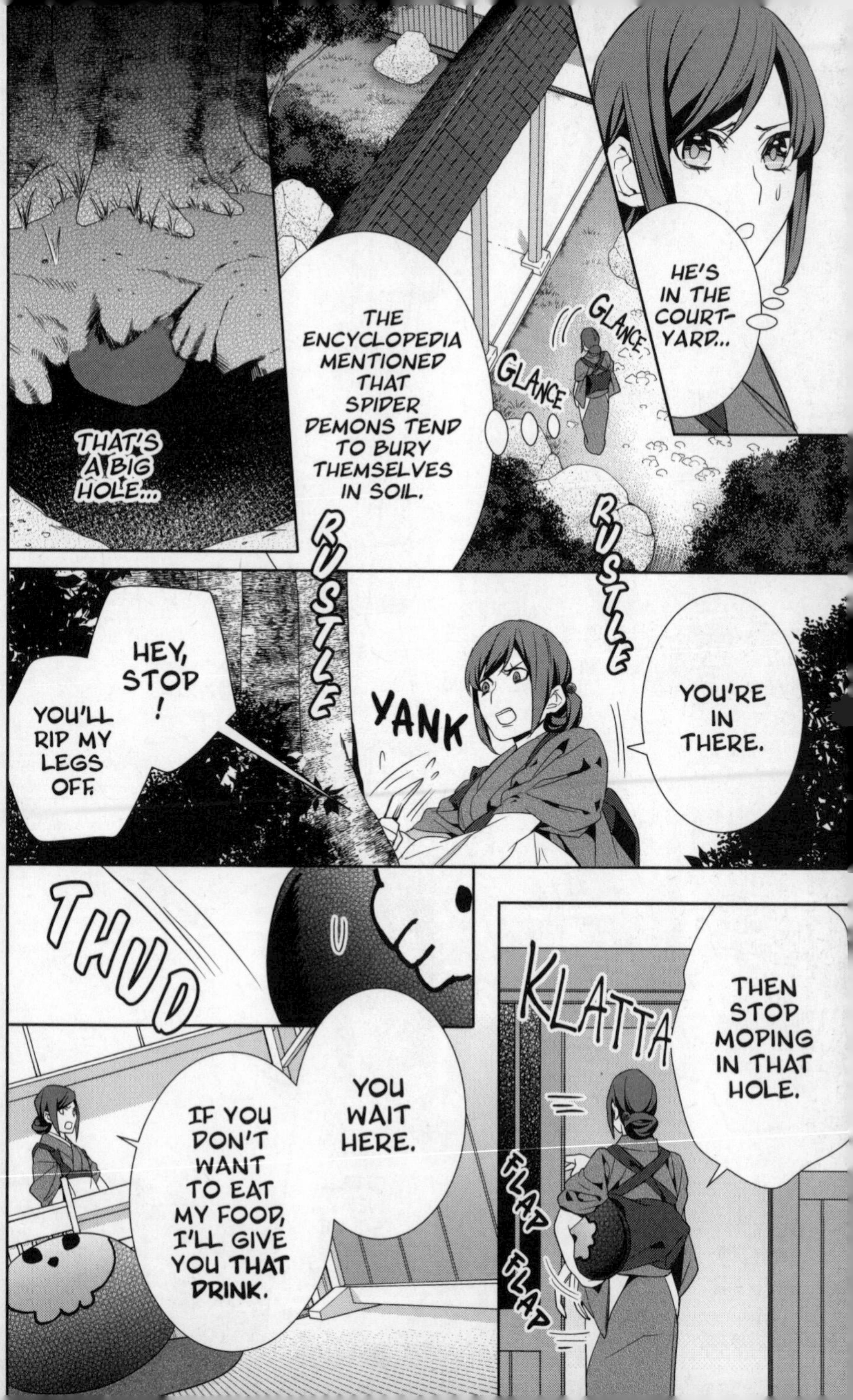
HE'S IN THE COURT-YARD...
GLANCE
GLANCE
THE ENCYCLOPEDIA MENTIONED THAT SPIDER DEMONS TEND TO BURY THEMSELVES IN SOIL.
RUSTLE
RUSTLE
THAT'S A BIG HOLE...
YOU'RE IN THERE.
YANK
HEY, STOP!
YOU'LL RIP MY LEGS OFF.
KLATTA
THEN STOP MOPING IN THAT HOLE.
FLAP
FLAP
THUD
YOU WAIT HERE.
IF YOU DON'T WANT TO EAT MY FOOD, I'LL GIVE YOU THAT DRINK.

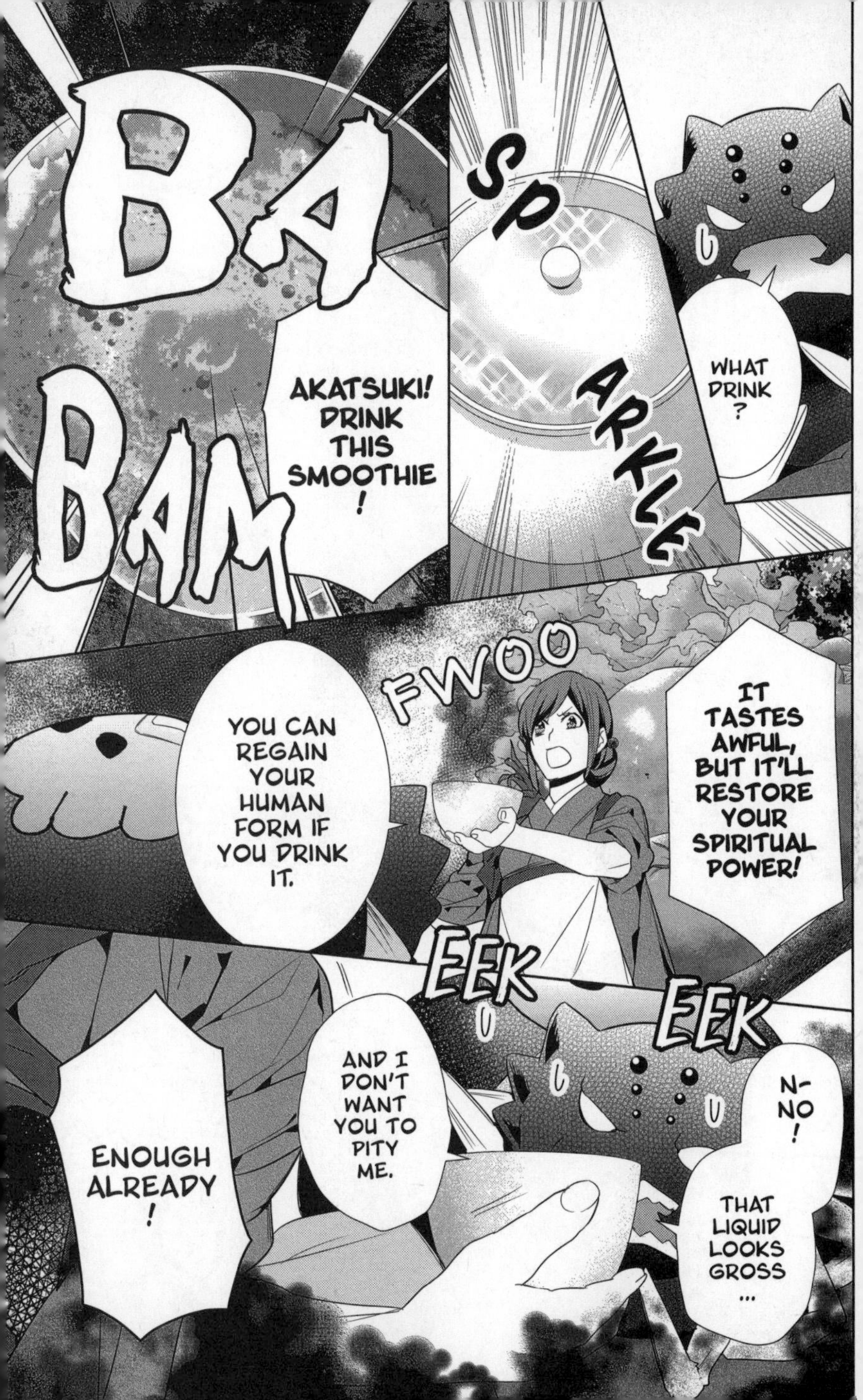
SPARKLE
WHAT DRINK?
BA BAM
AKATSUKI! DRINK THIS SMOOTHIE!
IT TASTES AWFUL, BUT IT'LL RESTORE YOUR SPIRITUAL POWER!
FWOO
YOU CAN REGAIN YOUR HUMAN FORM IF YOU DRINK IT.
EEK EEK
N-NO!
THAT LIQUID LOOKS GROSS...
AND I DON'T WANT YOU TO PITY ME.
ENOUGH ALREADY!

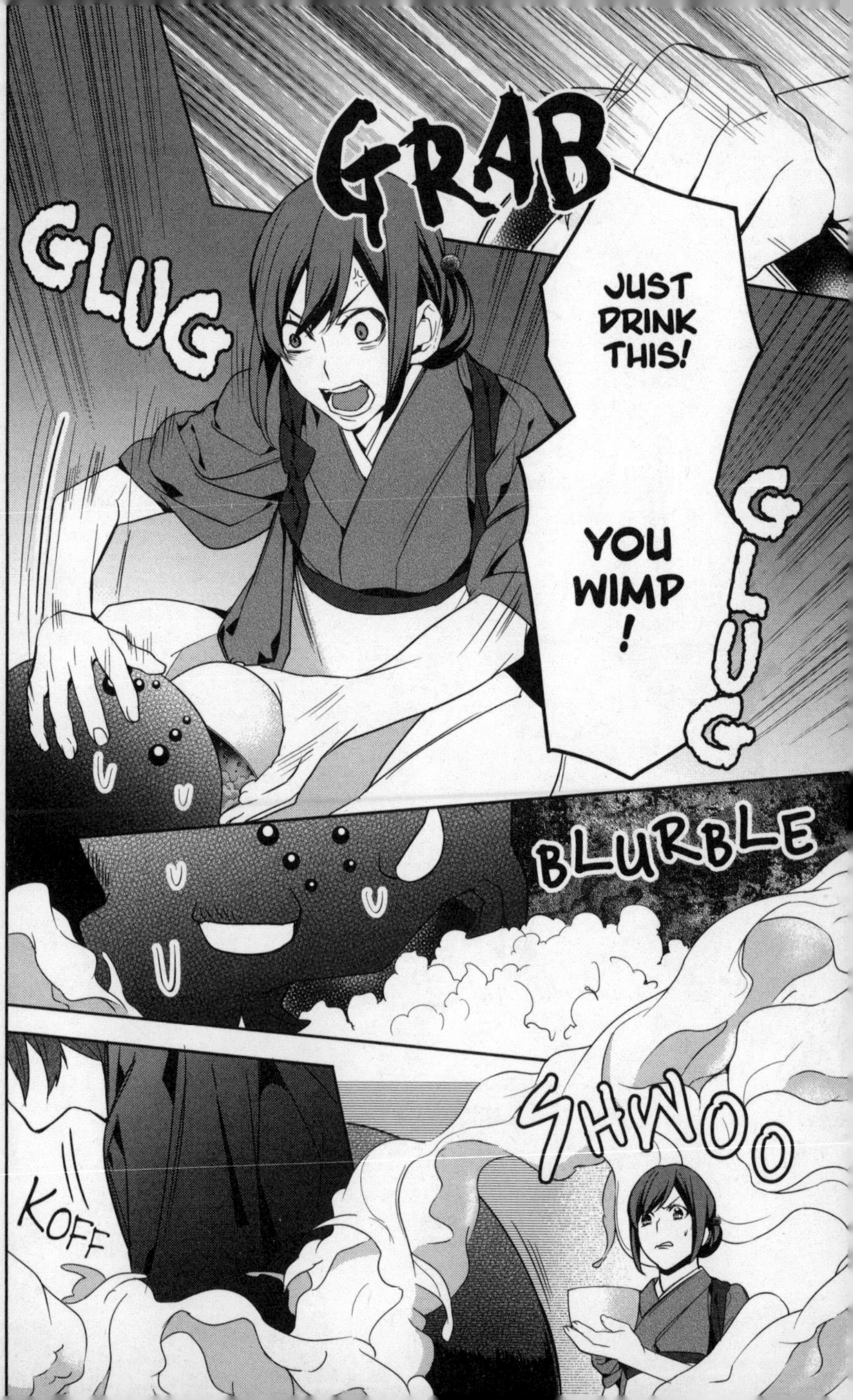
GRAB
JUST DRINK THIS!
YOU WIMP!
GLUG
GLUG
BLURBLE
SHWOO
KOFF

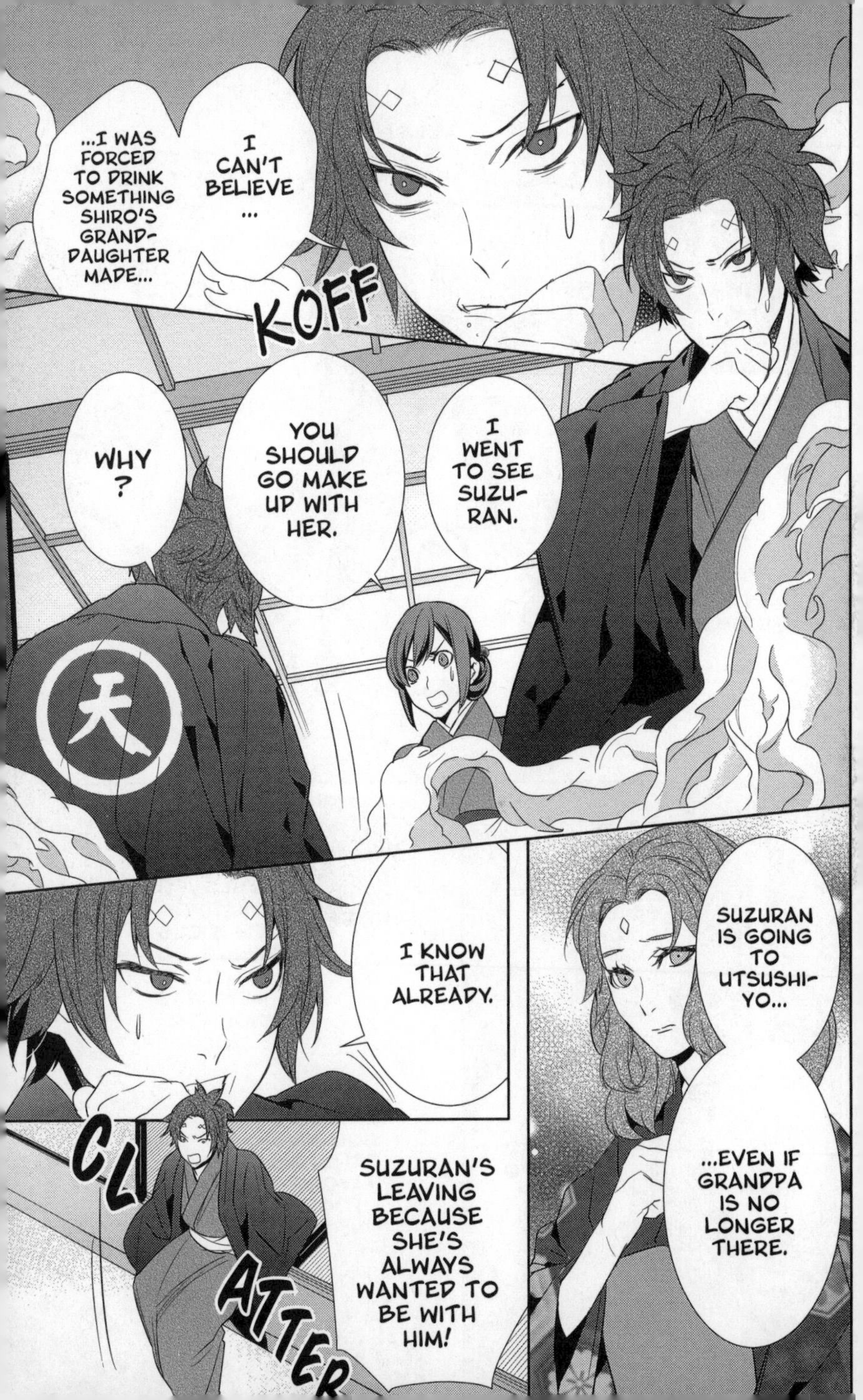

I CAN'T BELIEVE ...
...I WAS FORCED TO DRINK SOMETHING SHIRO'S GRAND-DAUGHTER MADE...
KOFF
I WENT TO SEE SUZU-RAN.
YOU SHOULD GO MAKE UP WITH HER.
WHY?
SUZURAN IS GOING TO UTSUSHI-YO...
...EVEN IF GRANDPA IS NO LONGER THERE.
I KNOW THAT ALREADY.
SUZURAN'S LEAVING BECAUSE SHE'S ALWAYS WANTED TO BE WITH HIM!
CLATTER

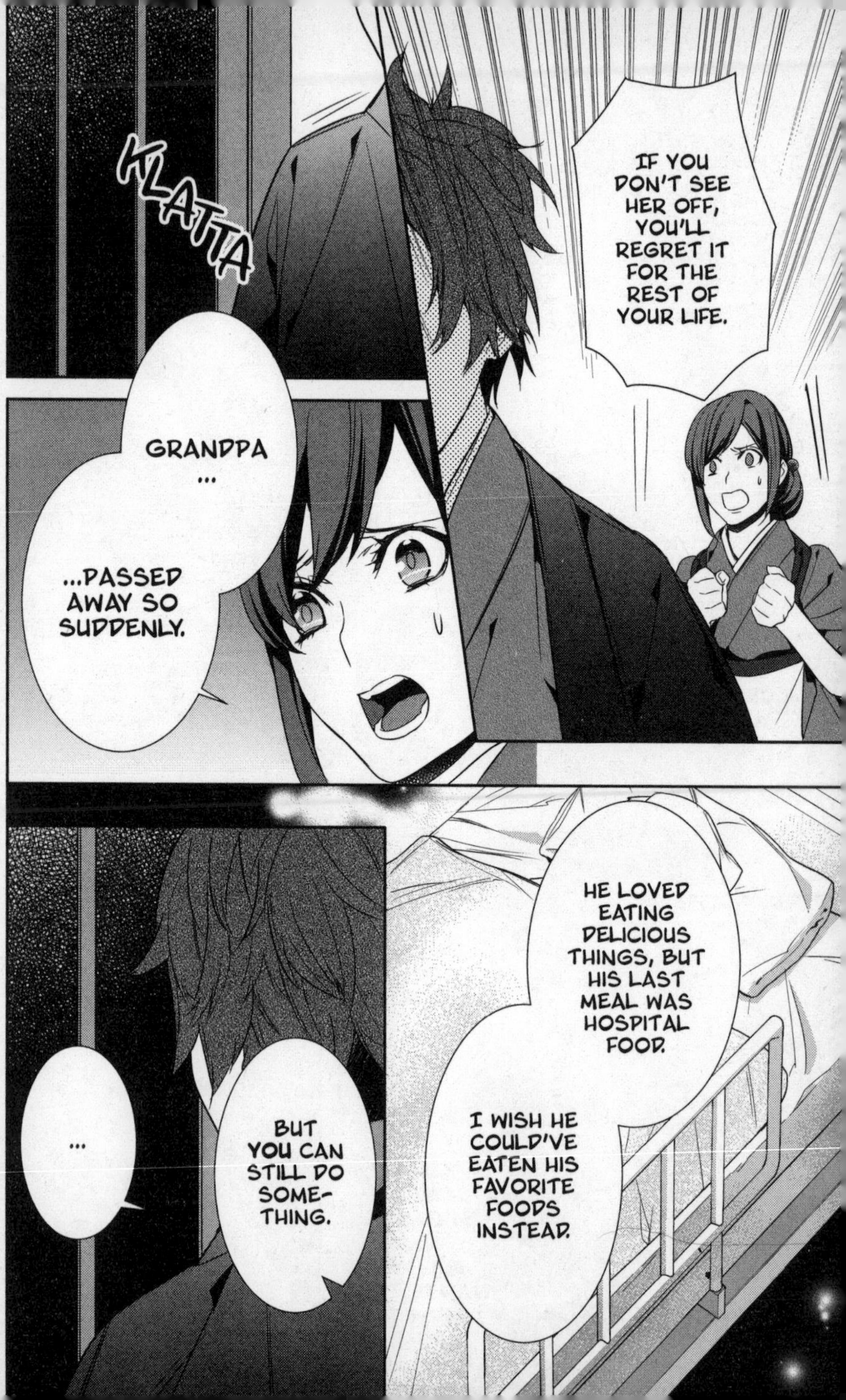
IF YOU DON'T SEE HER OFF, YOU'LL REGRET IT FOR THE REST OF YOUR LIFE.
KLATTA
GRANDPA ...
...PASSED AWAY SO SUDDENLY.
HE LOVED EATING DELICIOUS THINGS, BUT HIS LAST MEAL WAS HOSPITAL FOOD.
I WISH HE COULD'VE EATEN HIS FAVORITE FOODS INSTEAD.
BUT YOU CAN STILL DO SOME-THING.
...

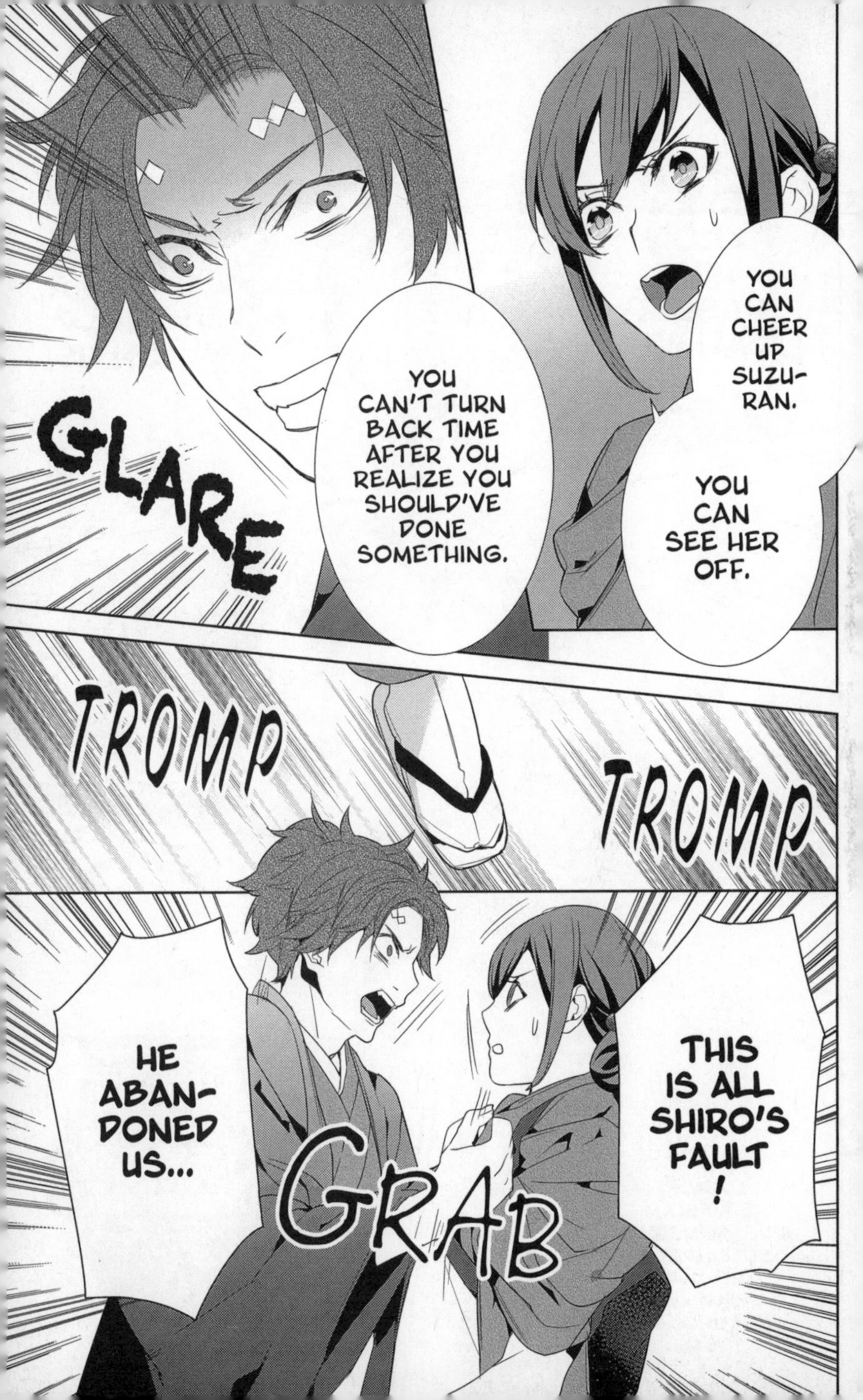
YOU CAN CHEER UP SUZU-RAN.
YOU CAN SEE HER OFF.
YOU CAN'T TURN BACK TIME AFTER YOU REALIZE YOU SHOULD'VE DONE SOMETHING.
GLARE
TROMP
TROMP
THIS IS ALL SHIRO'S FAULT!
GRAB
HE ABAN-DONED US...

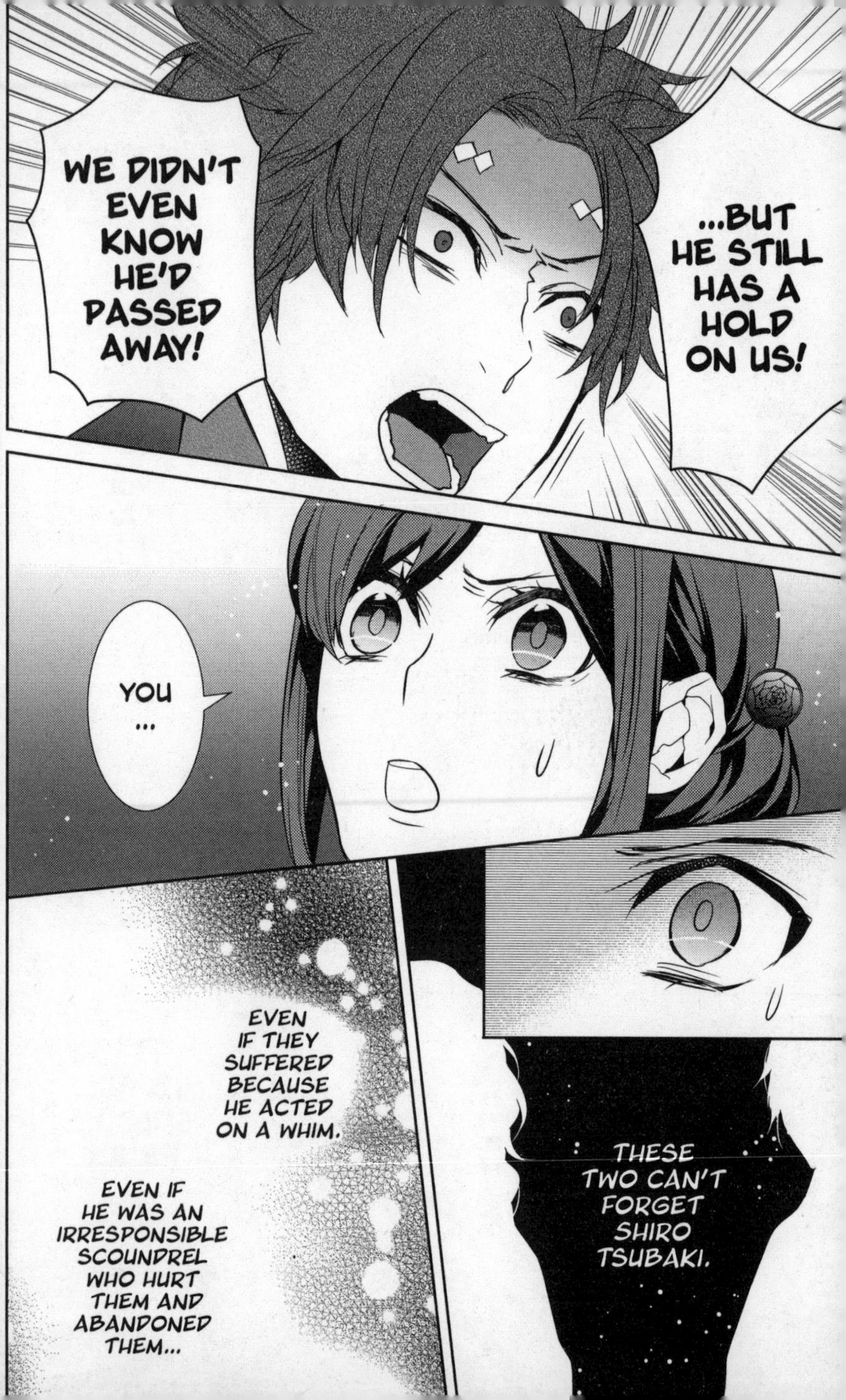
...BUT HE STILL HAS A HOLD ON US!
WE DIDN'T EVEN KNOW HE'D PASSED AWAY!
YOU ...
THESE TWO CAN'T FORGET SHIRO TSUBAKI.
EVEN IF THEY SUFFERED BECAUSE HE ACTED ON A WHIM.
EVEN IF HE WAS AN IRRESPONSIBLE SCOUNDREL WHO HURT THEM AND ABANDONED THEM...

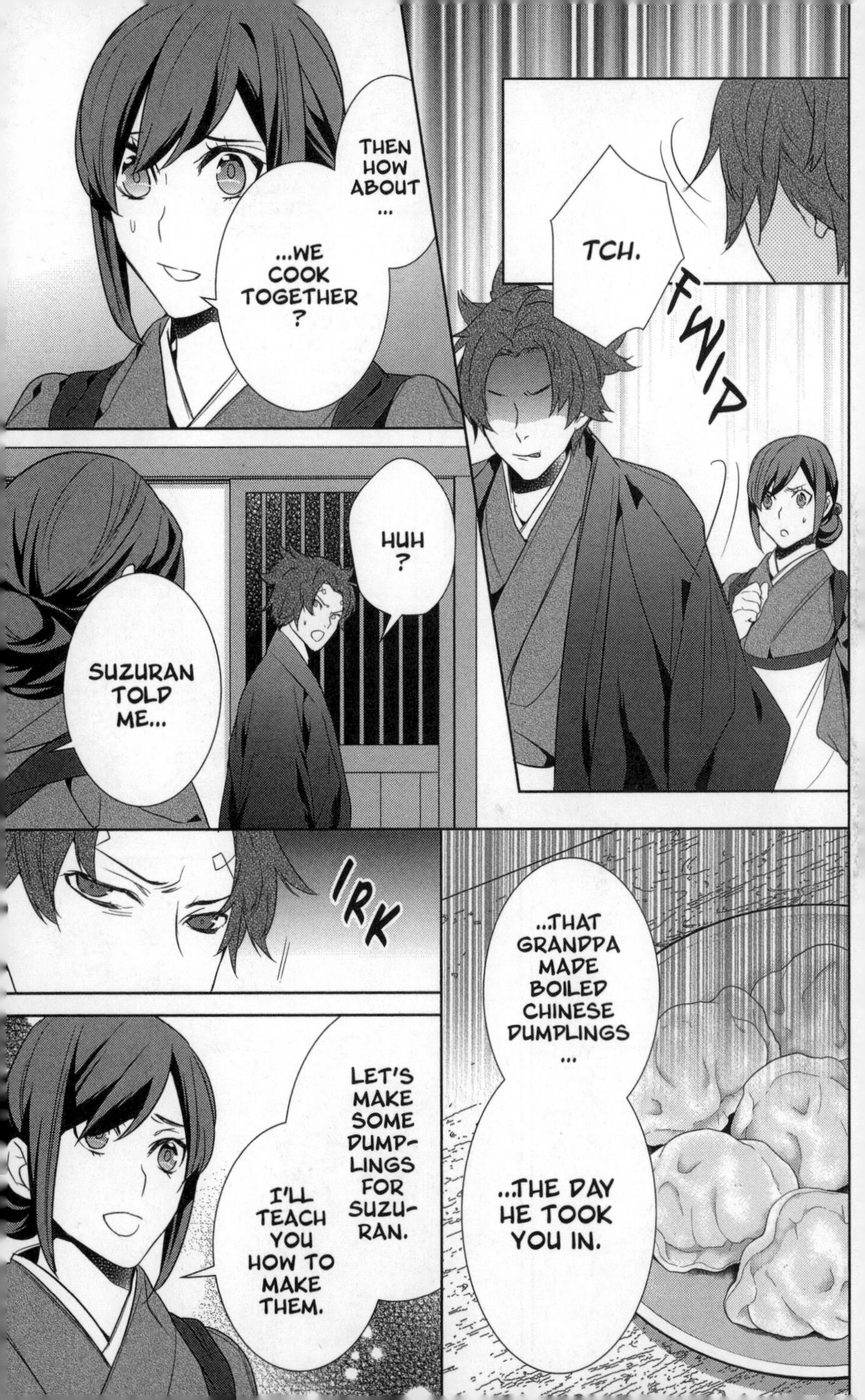
TCH.
FWIP
THEN HOW ABOUT ...
...WE COOK TOGETHER ?
HUH ?
SUZURAN TOLD ME...
...THAT GRANDPA MADE BOILED CHINESE DUMPLINGS ...
...THE DAY HE TOOK YOU IN.
IRK
LET'S MAKE SOME DUMP-LINGS FOR SUZU-RAN.
I'LL TEACH YOU HOW TO MAKE THEM.

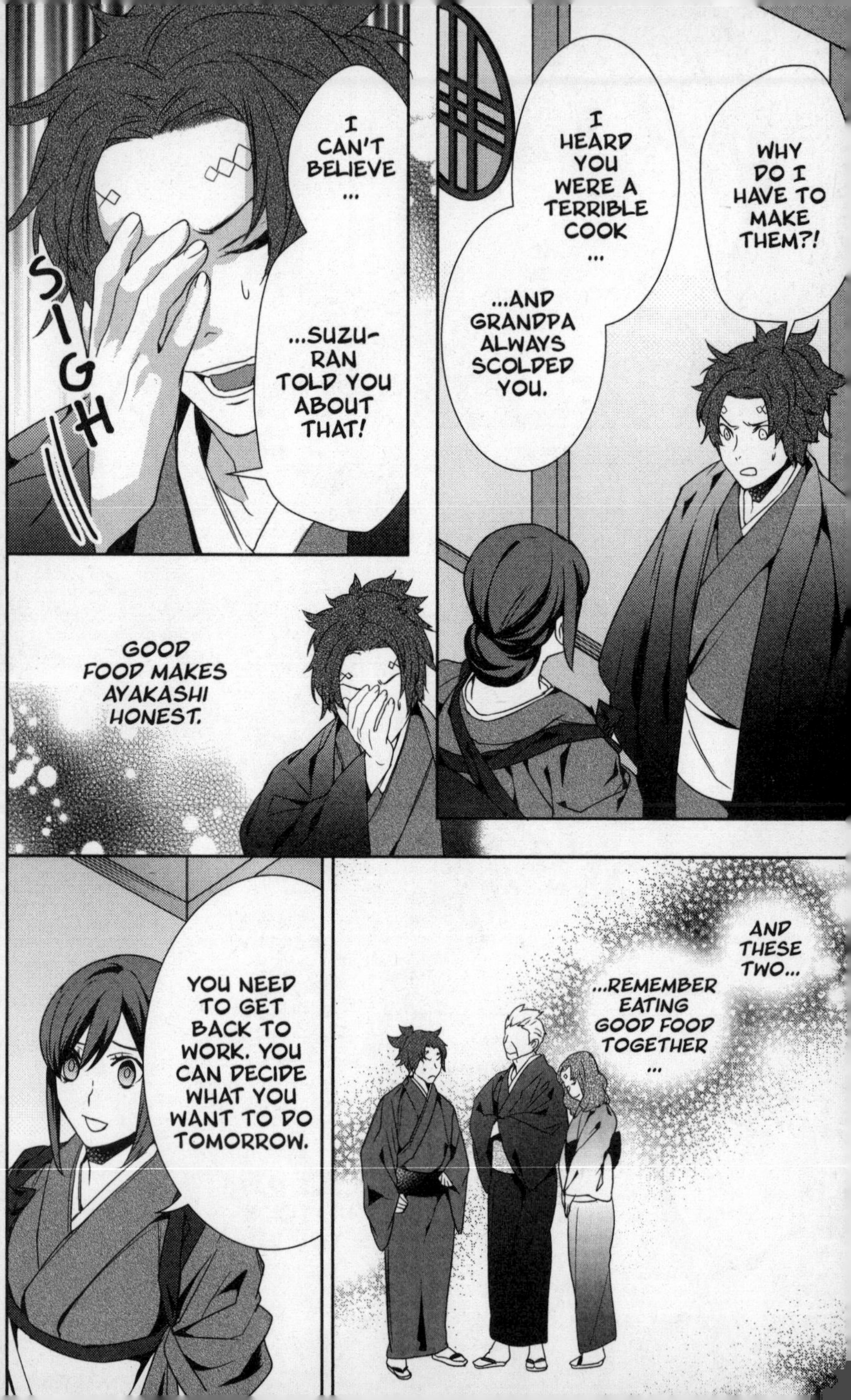
WHY DO I HAVE TO MAKE THEM?!
I HEARD YOU WERE A TERRIBLE COOK...
...AND GRANDPA ALWAYS SCOLDED YOU.
I CAN'T BELIEVE...
...SUZURAN TOLD YOU ABOUT THAT!
SIGH
GOOD FOOD MAKES AYAKASHI HONEST.
AND THESE TWO...
...REMEMBER EATING GOOD FOOD TOGETHER...
YOU NEED TO GET BACK TO WORK. YOU CAN DECIDE WHAT YOU WANT TO DO TOMORROW.

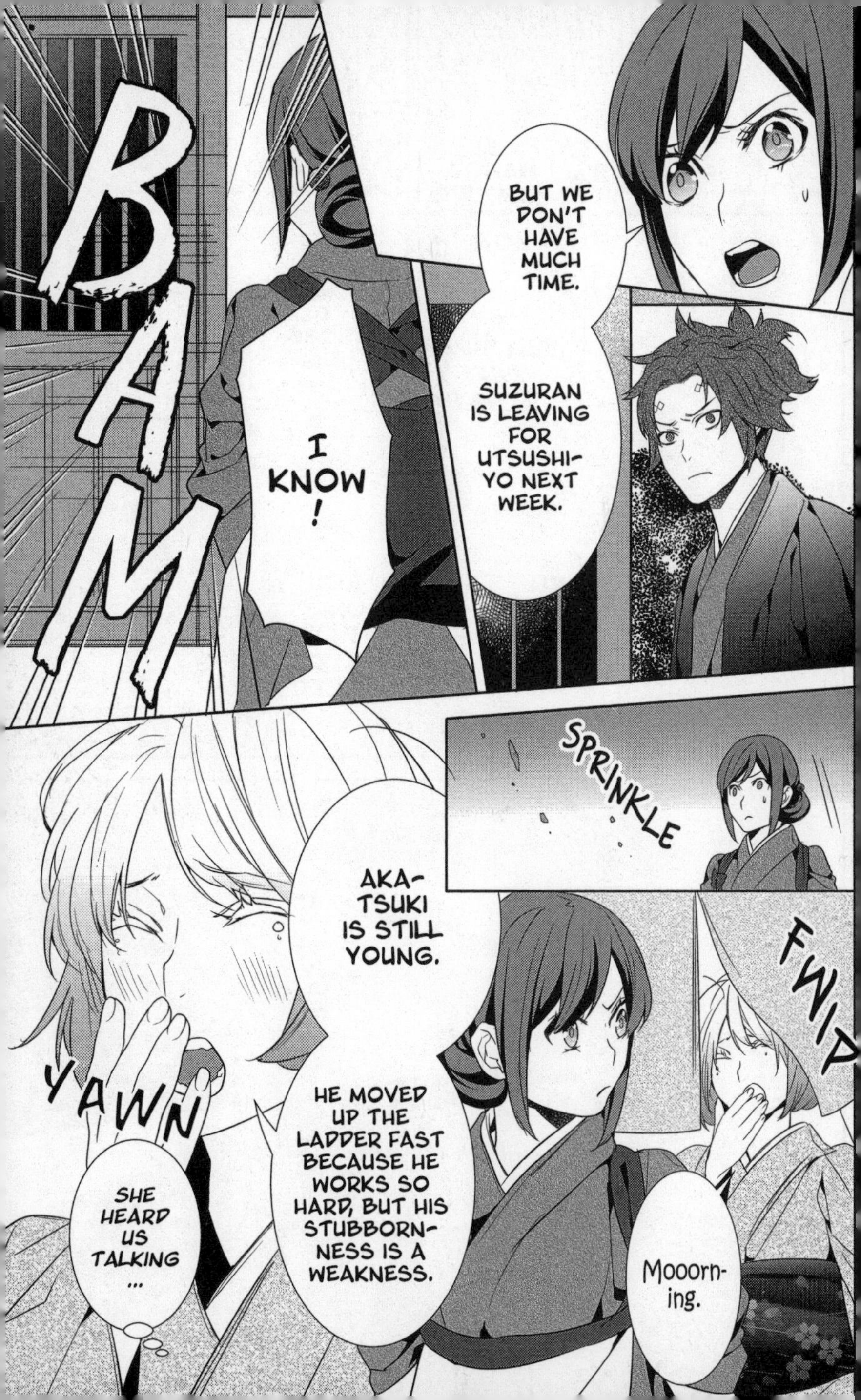
BUT WE DON'T HAVE MUCH TIME.
SUZURAN IS LEAVING FOR UTSUSHIYO NEXT WEEK.
BAM
I KNOW!
SPRINKLE
FWIP
Mooorning.
AKATSUKI IS STILL YOUNG.
HE MOVED UP THE LADDER FAST BECAUSE HE WORKS SO HARD, BUT HIS STUBBORNNESS IS A WEAKNESS.
YAWN
SHE HEARD US TALKING...

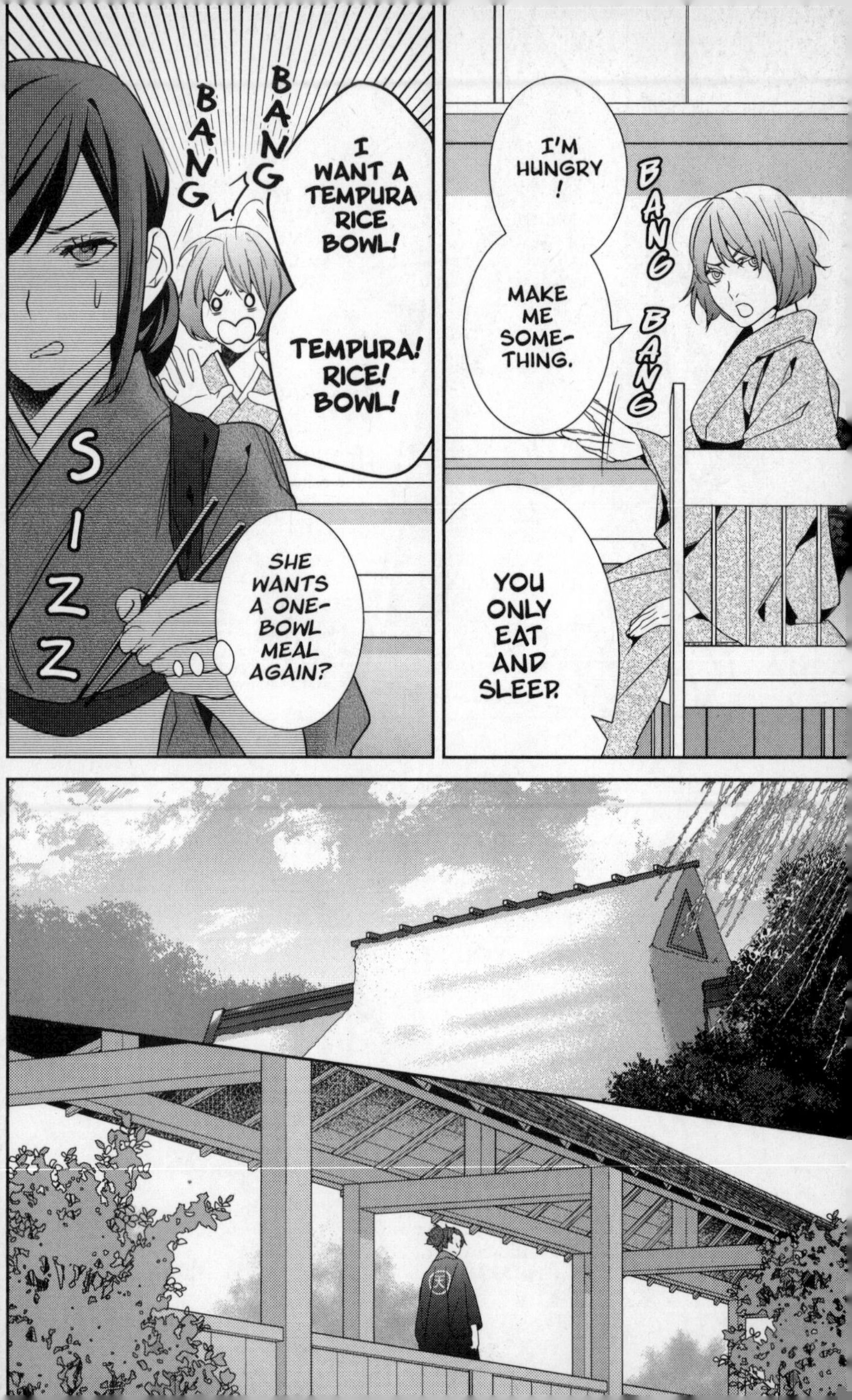
I'M HUNGRY!
MAKE ME SOMETHING.
BANG BANG
BANG BANG
YOU ONLY EAT AND SLEEP.
BANG
BANG
I WANT A TEMPURA RICE BOWL!
TEMPURA! RICE! BOWL!
SIZZ
SHE WANTS A ONE-BOWL MEAL AGAIN?

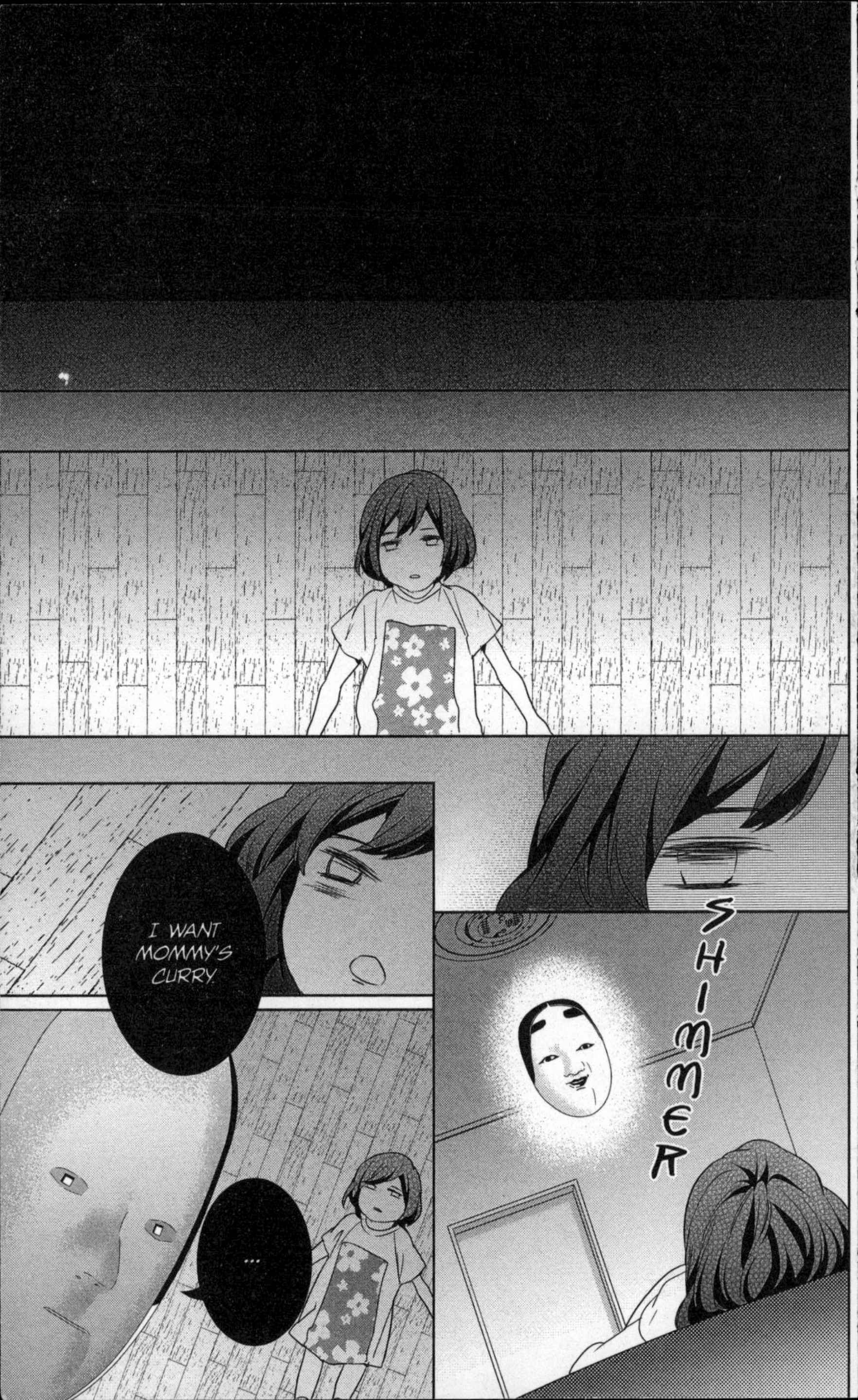
I WANT MOMMY'S CURRY.
SHIMMER
...

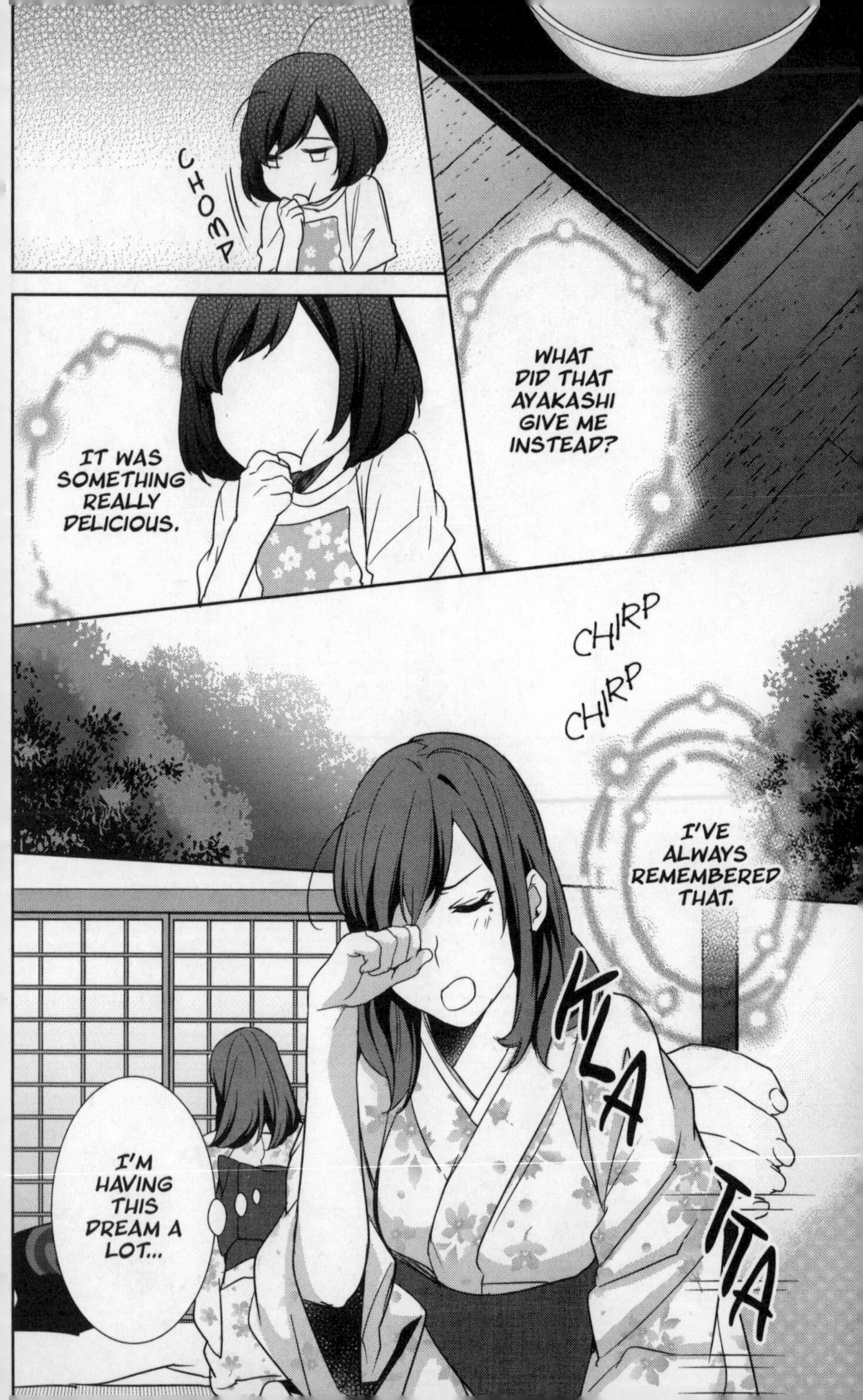
WHAT DID THAT AYAKASHI GIVE ME INSTEAD?
CHOMP
IT WAS SOMETHING REALLY DELICIOUS.
CHIRP
CHIRP
I'VE ALWAYS REMEMBERED THAT.
KLATTA
I'M HAVING THIS DREAM A LOT...

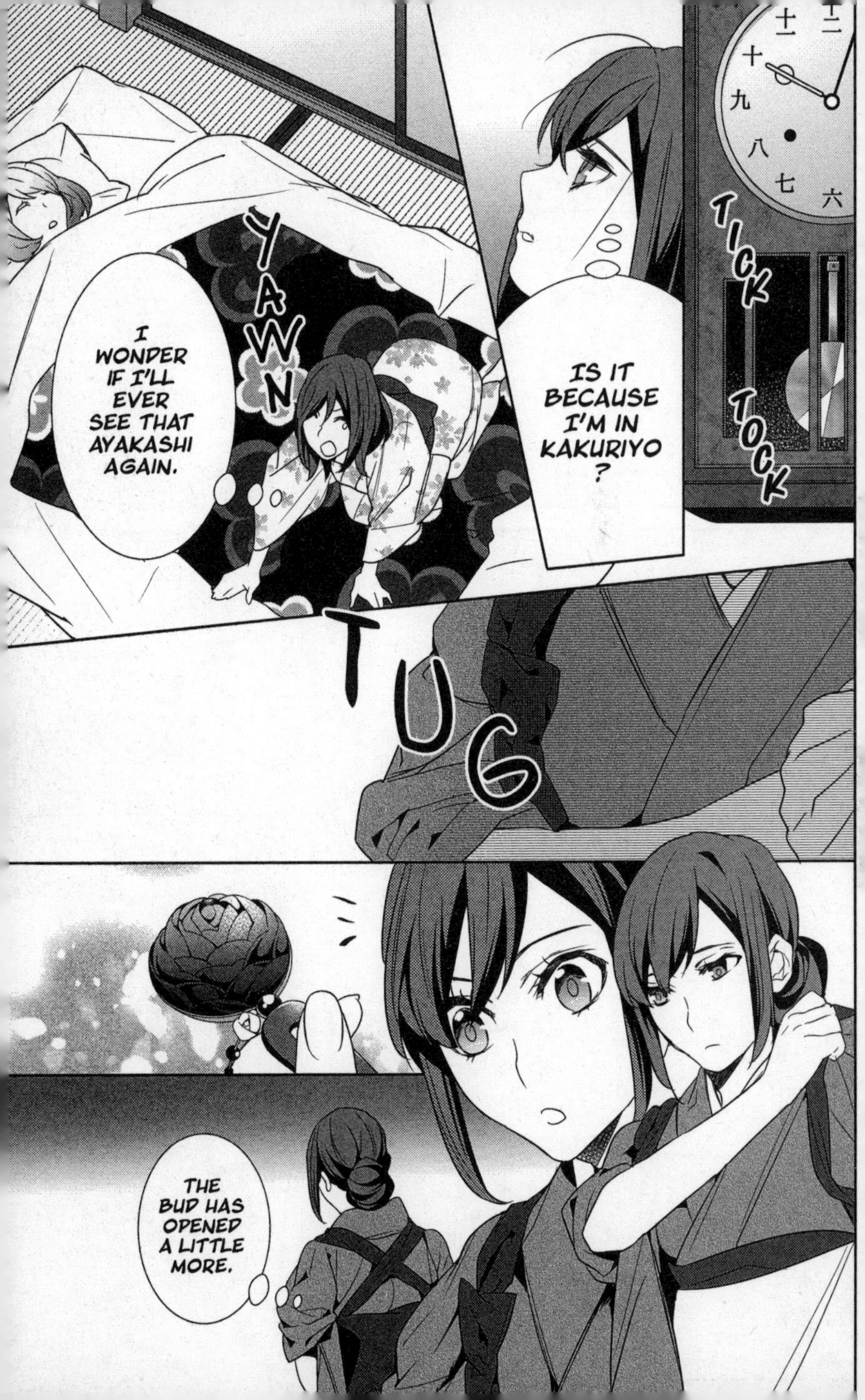
TICK TOCK
IS IT BECAUSE I'M IN KAKURIYO?
YAWN
I WONDER IF I'LL EVER SEE THAT AYAKASHI AGAIN.
TUG
THE BUD HAS OPENED A LITTLE MORE.

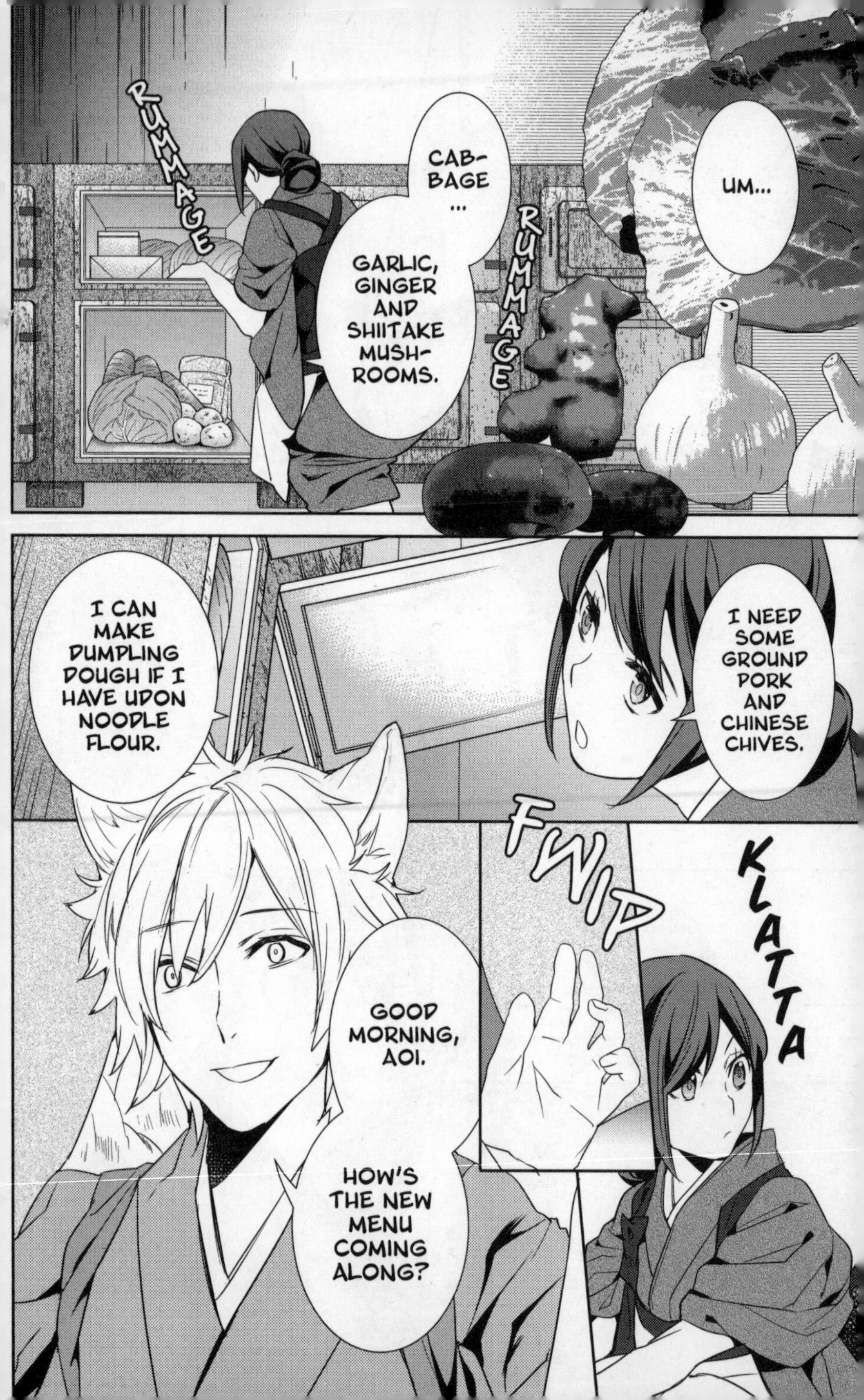
UM...
RUMMAGE
CAB-BAGE ...
GARLIC, GINGER AND SHIITAKE MUSH-ROOMS.
RUMMAGE
I NEED SOME GROUND PORK AND CHINESE CHIVES.
I CAN MAKE DUMPLING DOUGH IF I HAVE UDON NOODLE FLOUR.
KLATTA
FWIP
GOOD MORNING, AOI.
HOW'S THE NEW MENU COMING ALONG?

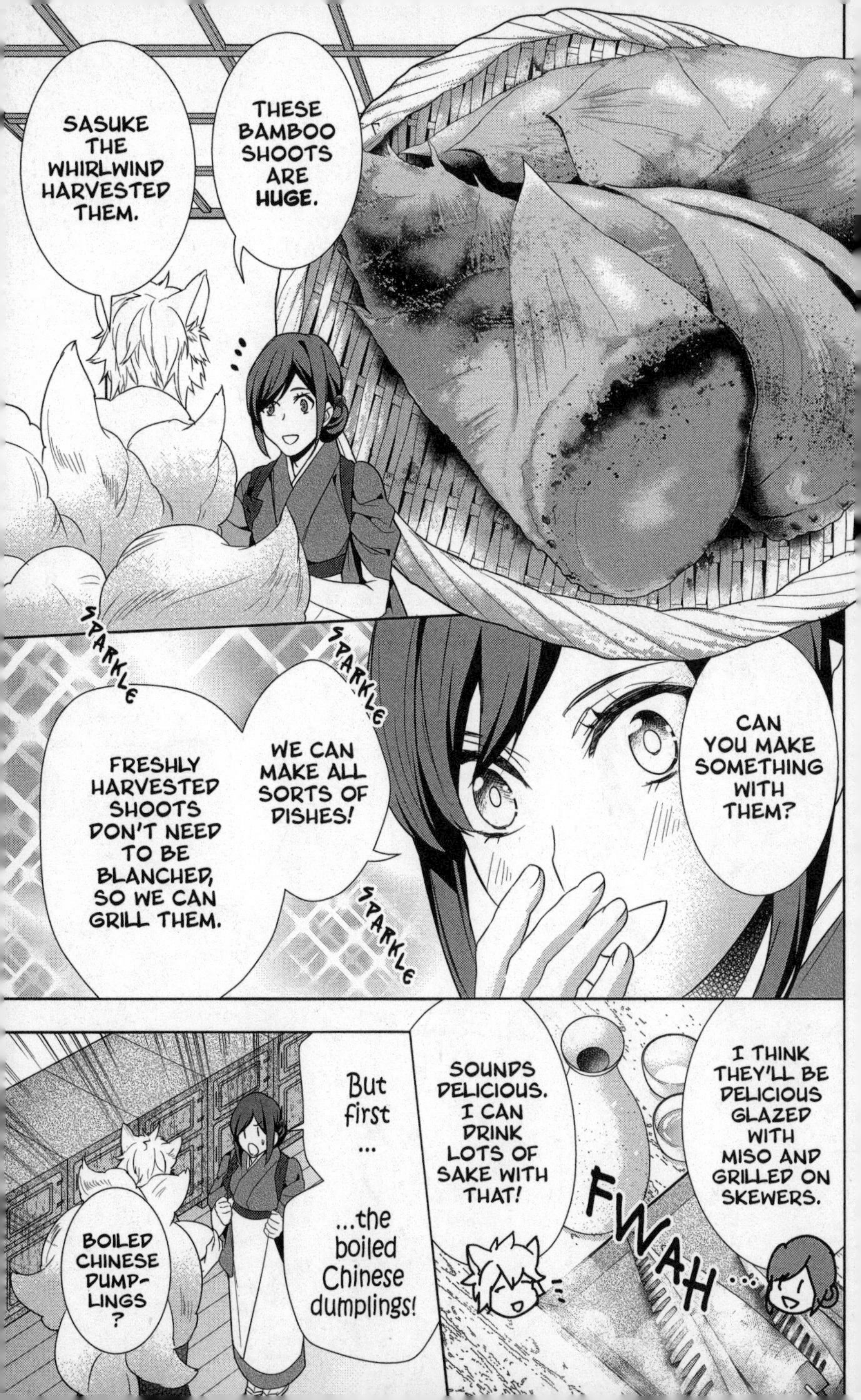
THESE BAMBOO SHOOTS ARE HUGE.
SASUKE THE WHIRLWIND HARVESTED THEM.
...
SPARKLE
SPARKLE
CAN YOU MAKE SOMETHING WITH THEM?
WE CAN MAKE ALL SORTS OF DISHES!
FRESHLY HARVESTED SHOOTS DON'T NEED TO BE BLANCHED, SO WE CAN GRILL THEM.
SPARKLE
I THINK THEY'LL BE DELICIOUS GLAZED WITH MISO AND GRILLED ON SKEWERS.
SOUNDS DELICIOUS. I CAN DRINK LOTS OF SAKE WITH THAT!
FWAH
But first ...
...the boiled Chinese dumplings!
BOILED CHINESE DUMP-LINGS?

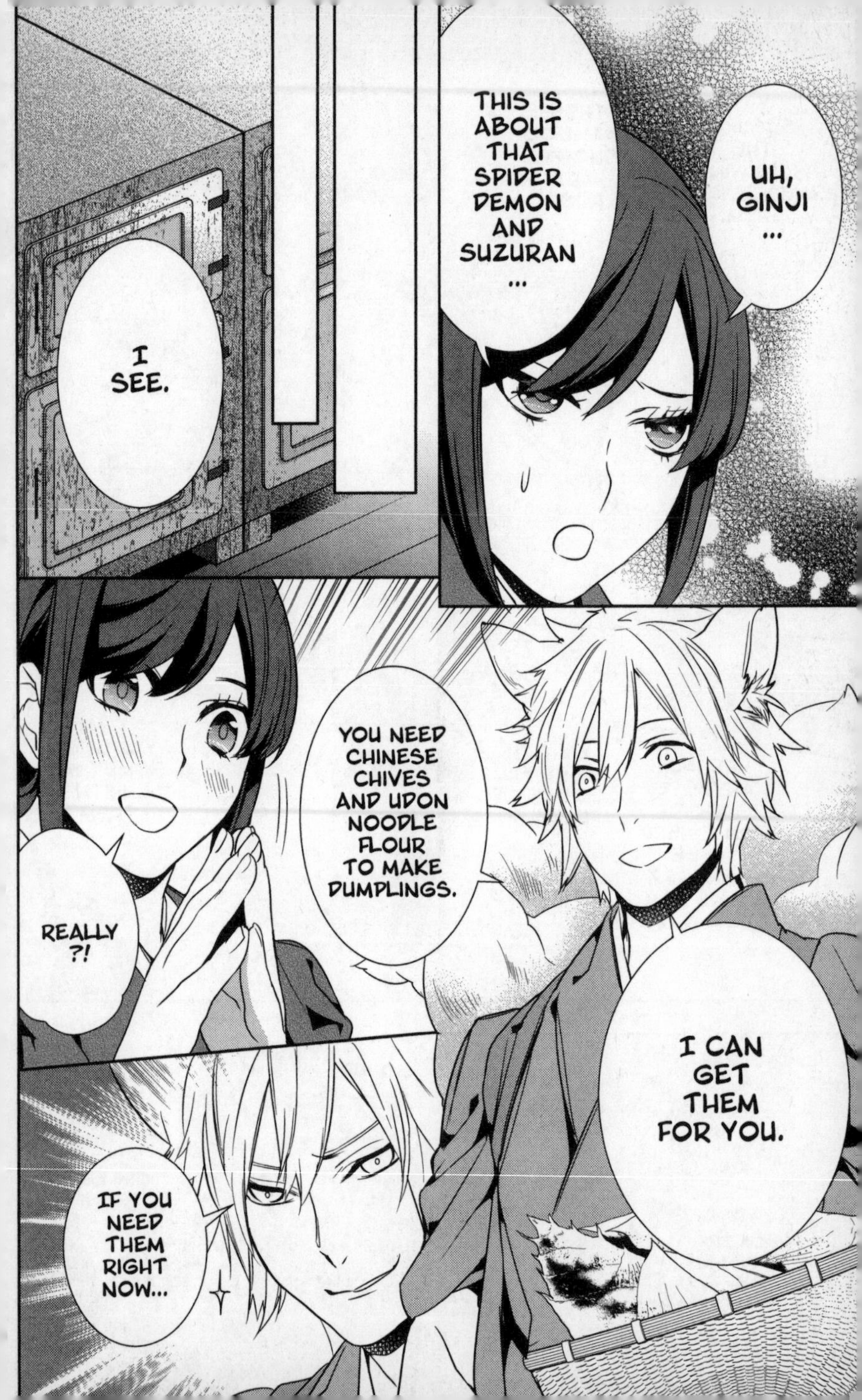
UH, GINJI ...
THIS IS ABOUT THAT SPIDER DEMON AND SUZURAN ...
I SEE.
YOU NEED CHINESE CHIVES AND UDON NOODLE FLOUR TO MAKE DUMPLINGS.
I CAN GET THEM FOR YOU.
REALLY ?!
IF YOU NEED THEM RIGHT NOW...

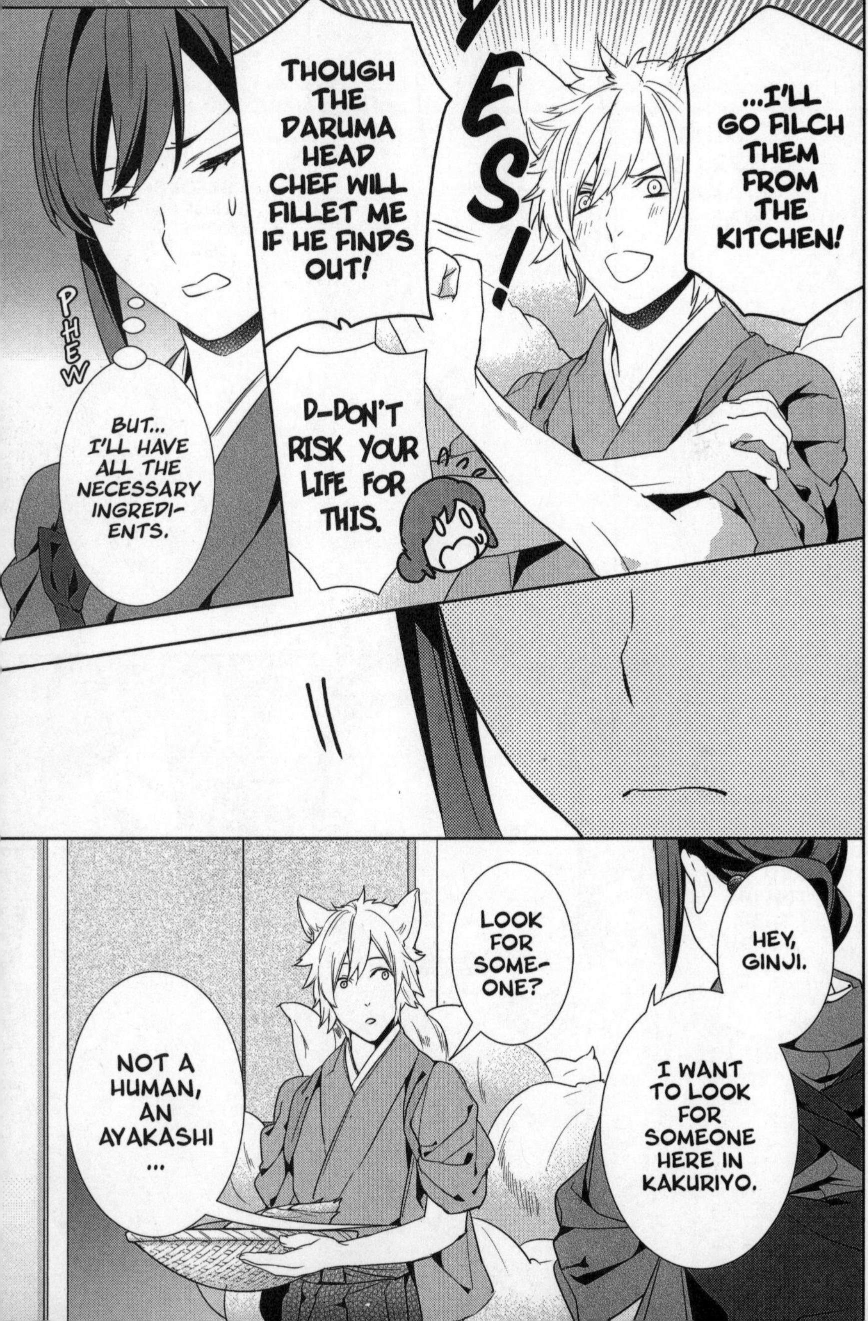
...I'LL GO FILCH THEM FROM THE KITCHEN!
YES!
THOUGH THE DARUMA HEAD CHEF WILL FILLET ME IF HE FINDS OUT!
D-DON'T RISK YOUR LIFE FOR THIS.
PHEW
BUT... I'LL HAVE ALL THE NECESSARY INGREDI-ENTS.
HEY, GINJI.
I WANT TO LOOK FOR SOMEONE HERE IN KAKURIYO.
LOOK FOR SOME-ONE?
NOT A HUMAN, AN AYAKASHI ...

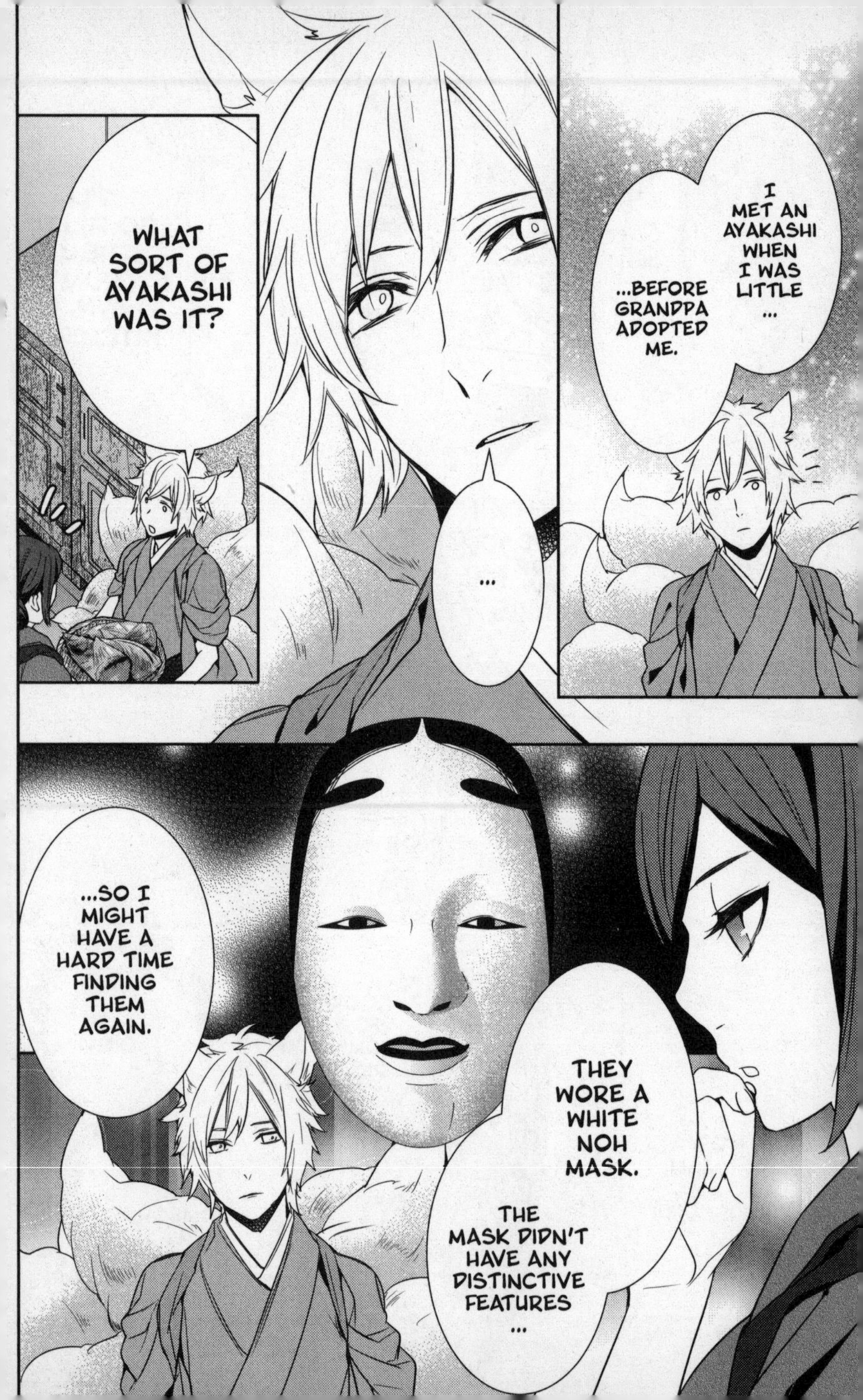
I MET AN AYAKASHI WHEN I WAS LITTLE ...
...BEFORE GRANDPA ADOPTED ME.
...
WHAT SORT OF AYAKASHI WAS IT?
THEY WORE A WHITE NOH MASK.
THE MASK DIDN'T HAVE ANY DISTINCTIVE FEATURES ...
...SO I MIGHT HAVE A HARD TIME FINDING THEM AGAIN.

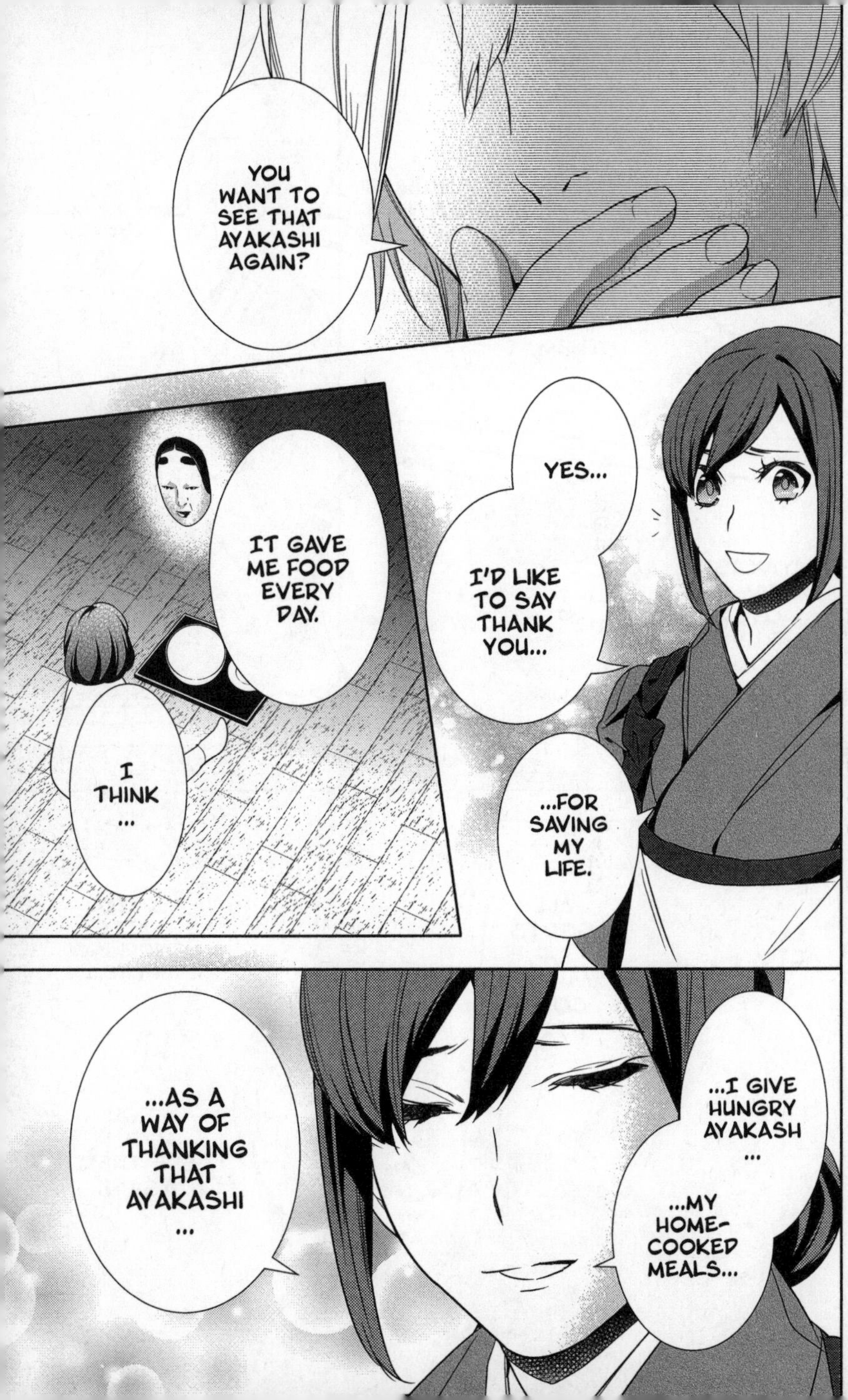
YOU WANT TO SEE THAT AYAKASHI AGAIN?
YES...
I'D LIKE TO SAY THANK YOU...
...FOR SAVING MY LIFE.
IT GAVE ME FOOD EVERY DAY.
I THINK...
...I GIVE HUNGRY AYAKASH...
...MY HOME-COOKED MEALS...
...AS A WAY OF THANKING THAT AYAKASHI...

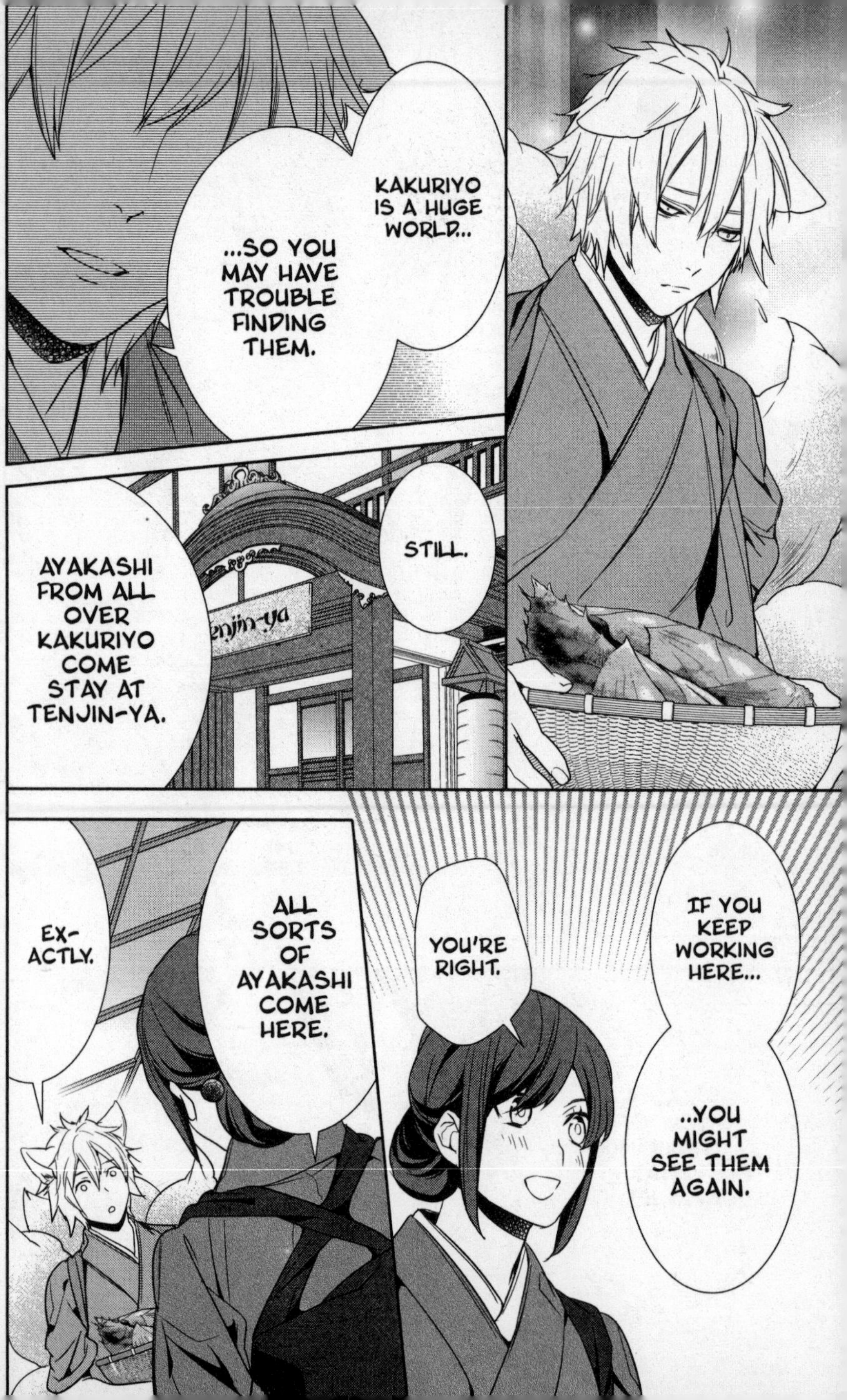
KAKURIYO IS A HUGE WORLD...
...SO YOU MAY HAVE TROUBLE FINDING THEM.
STILL.
AYAKASHI FROM ALL OVER KAKURIYO COME STAY AT TENJIN-YA.
Tenjin-ya
IF YOU KEEP WORKING HERE...
...YOU MIGHT SEE THEM AGAIN.
YOU'RE RIGHT.
ALL SORTS OF AYAKASHI COME HERE.
EX-ACTLY.

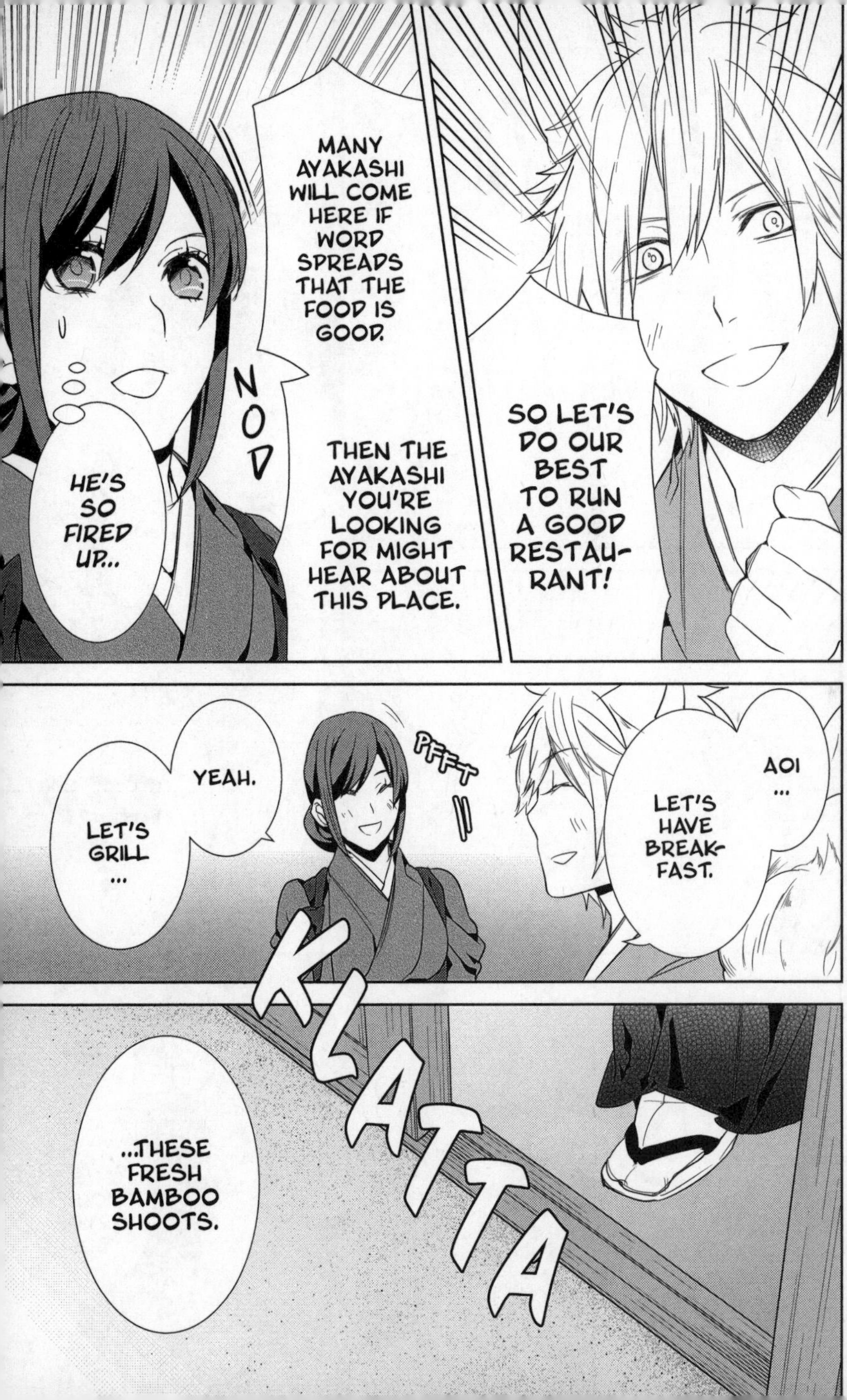
MANY AYAKASHI WILL COME HERE IF WORD SPREADS THAT THE FOOD IS GOOD.
THEN THE AYAKASHI YOU'RE LOOKING FOR MIGHT HEAR ABOUT THIS PLACE.
SO LET'S DO OUR BEST TO RUN A GOOD RESTAU-RANT!
NOD
HE'S SO FIRED UP...
AOI...
LET'S HAVE BREAK-FAST.
PFFFT
YEAH.
LET'S GRILL...
KLATTA
...THESE FRESH BAMBOO SHOOTS.

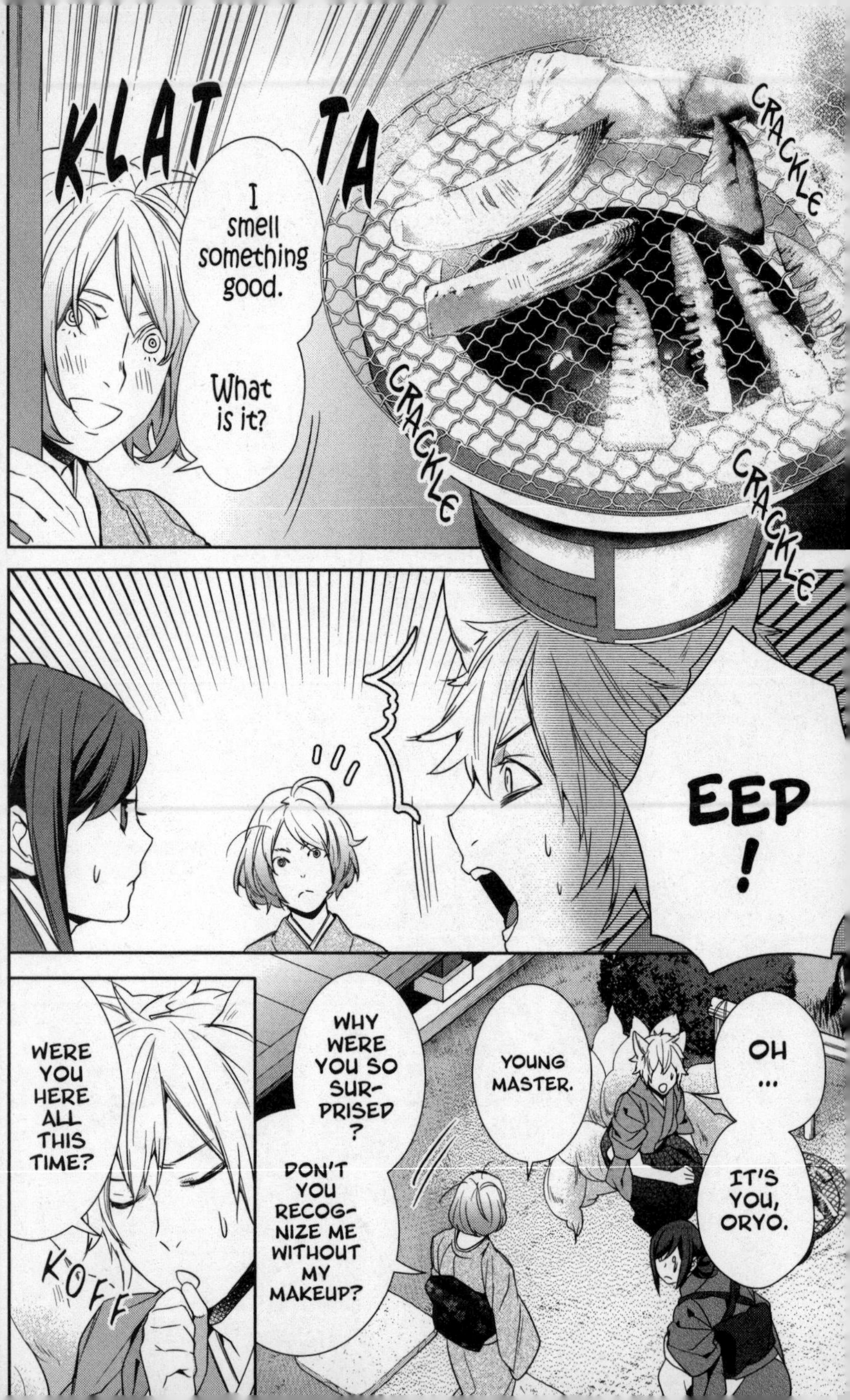
CRACKLE
CRACKLE
CRACKLE
KLAT TA
I smell something good.
What is it?
EEP!
OH ...
IT'S YOU, ORYO.
YOUNG MASTER.
WHY WERE YOU SO SUR-PRISED?
DON'T YOU RECOG-NIZE ME WITHOUT MY MAKEUP?
WERE YOU HERE ALL THIS TIME?
KOFF

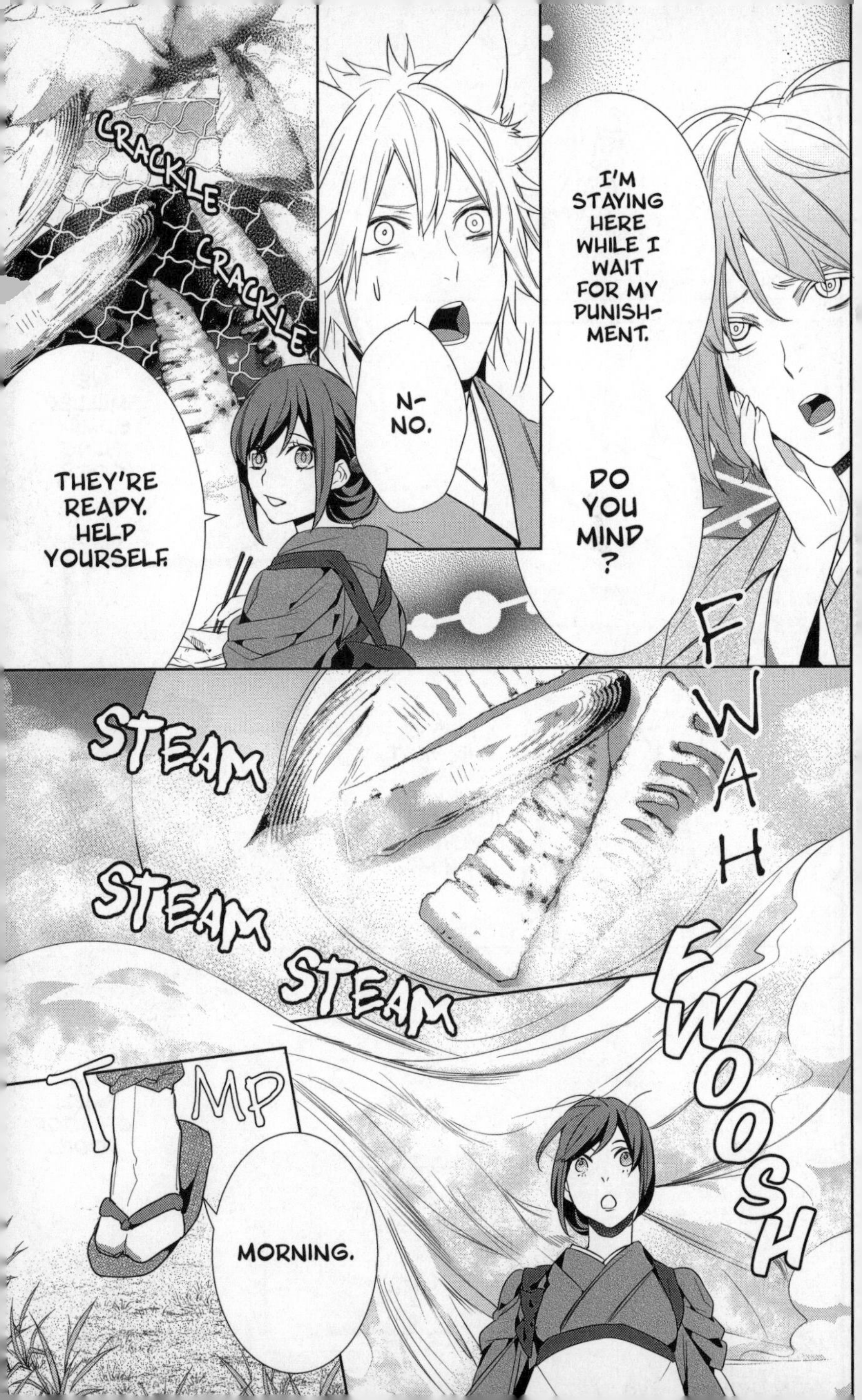
I'M STAYING HERE WHILE I WAIT FOR MY PUNISHMENT.
DO YOU MIND?
N-NO.
CRACKLE
CRACKLE
THEY'RE READY. HELP YOURSELF.
FWAH
STEAM
STEAM
STEAM
FWOOSH
TMP
MORNING.

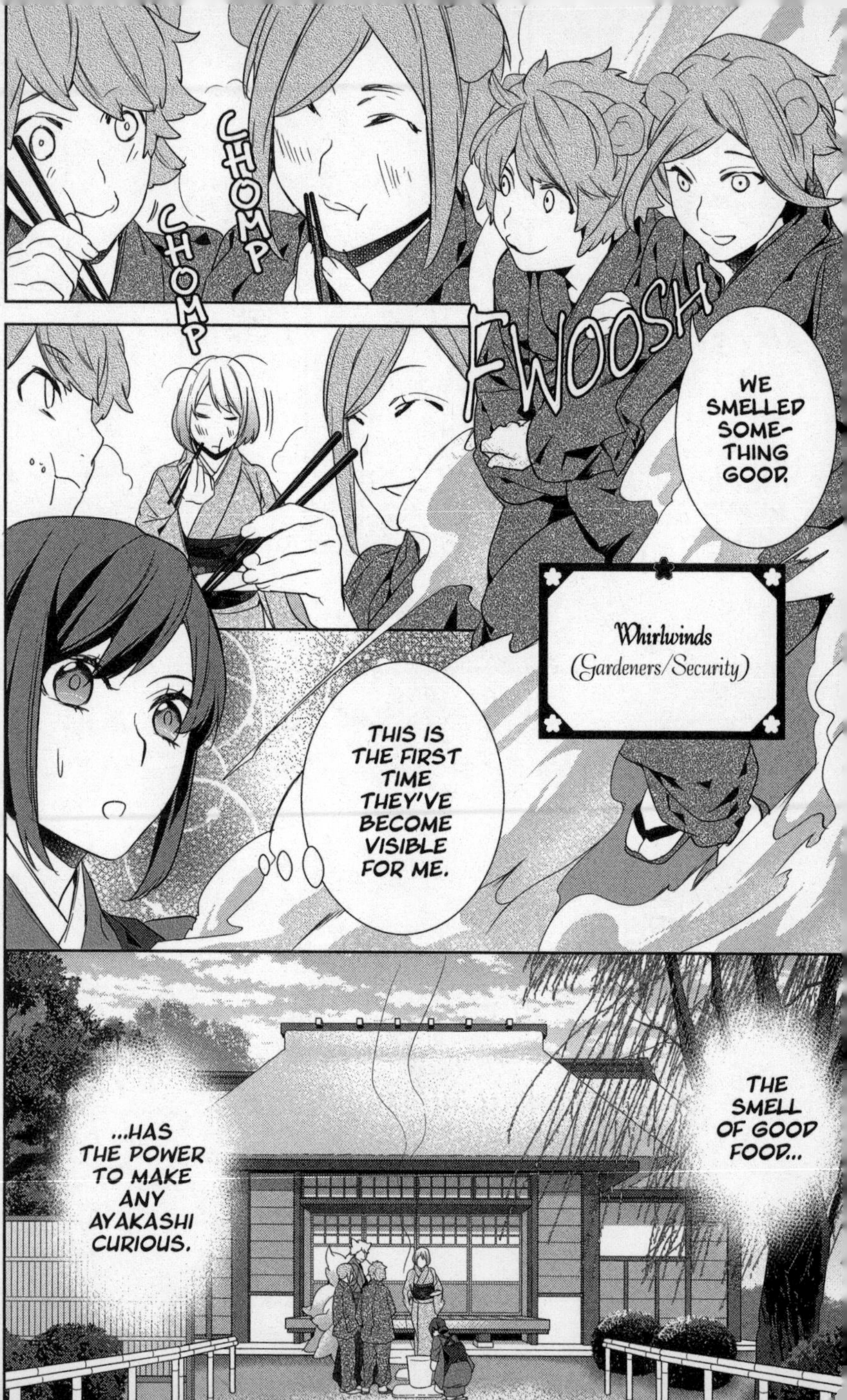
FWOOSH
WE SMELLED SOME-THING GOOD.
Whirlwinds (Gardeners/Security)
CHOMP CHOMP
CHOMP
THIS IS THE FIRST TIME THEY'VE BECOME VISIBLE FOR ME.
THE SMELL OF GOOD FOOD...
...HAS THE POWER TO MAKE ANY AYAKASHI CURIOUS.

Kakuriyo
Bed & Breakfast for Spirits

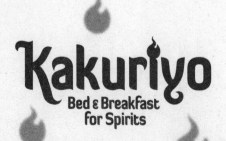

Kakuriyo
Bed & Breakfast
for Spirits

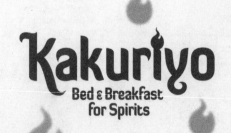

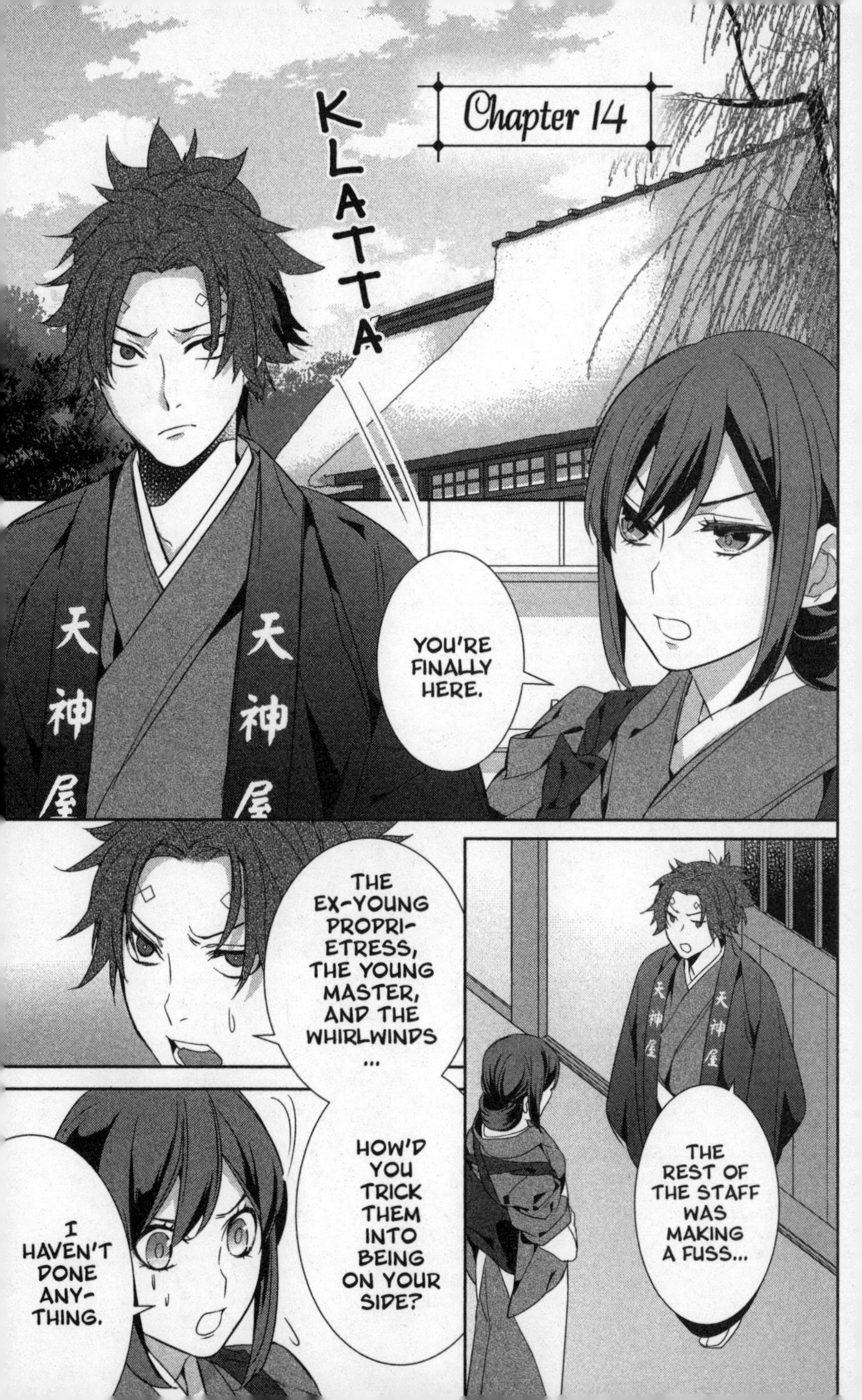
Chapter 14
KLATTA
YOU'RE FINALLY HERE.
THE REST OF THE STAFF WAS MAKING A FUSS...
THE EX-YOUNG PROPRIETRESS, THE YOUNG MASTER, AND THE WHIRLWINDS ...
HOW'D YOU TRICK THEM INTO BEING ON YOUR SIDE?
I HAVEN'T DONE ANYTHING.

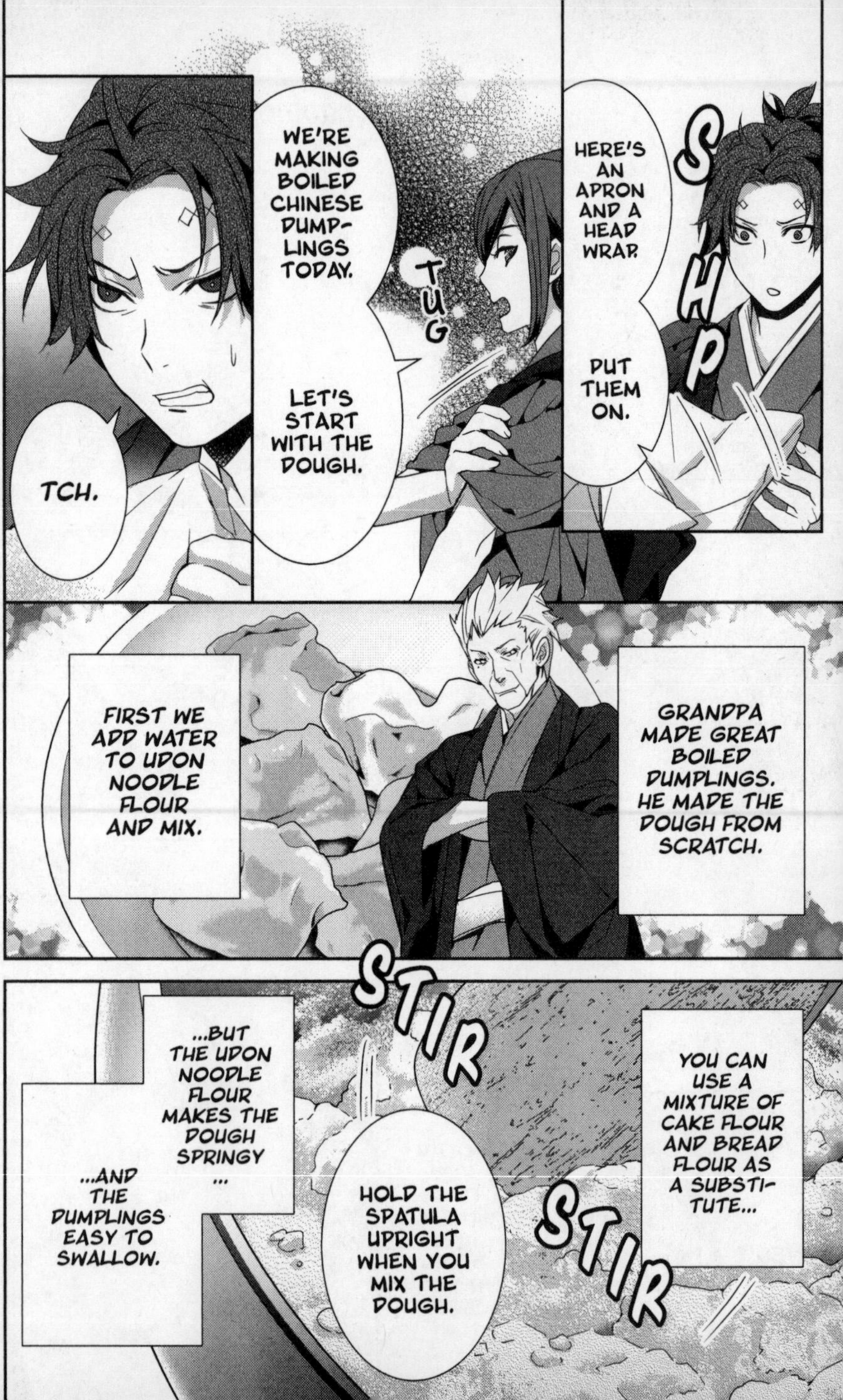
SHP
HERE'S AN APRON AND A HEAD WRAP.
PUT THEM ON.
WE'RE MAKING BOILED CHINESE DUMPLINGS TODAY.
LET'S START WITH THE DOUGH.
TUG
TCH.
GRANDPA MADE GREAT BOILED DUMPLINGS. HE MADE THE DOUGH FROM SCRATCH.
FIRST WE ADD WATER TO UDON NOODLE FLOUR AND MIX.
STIR
YOU CAN USE A MIXTURE OF CAKE FLOUR AND BREAD FLOUR AS A SUBSTITUTE...
STIR
HOLD THE SPATULA UPRIGHT WHEN YOU MIX THE DOUGH.
...BUT THE UDON NOODLE FLOUR MAKES THE DOUGH SPRINGY...
...AND THE DUMPLINGS EASY TO SWALLOW.

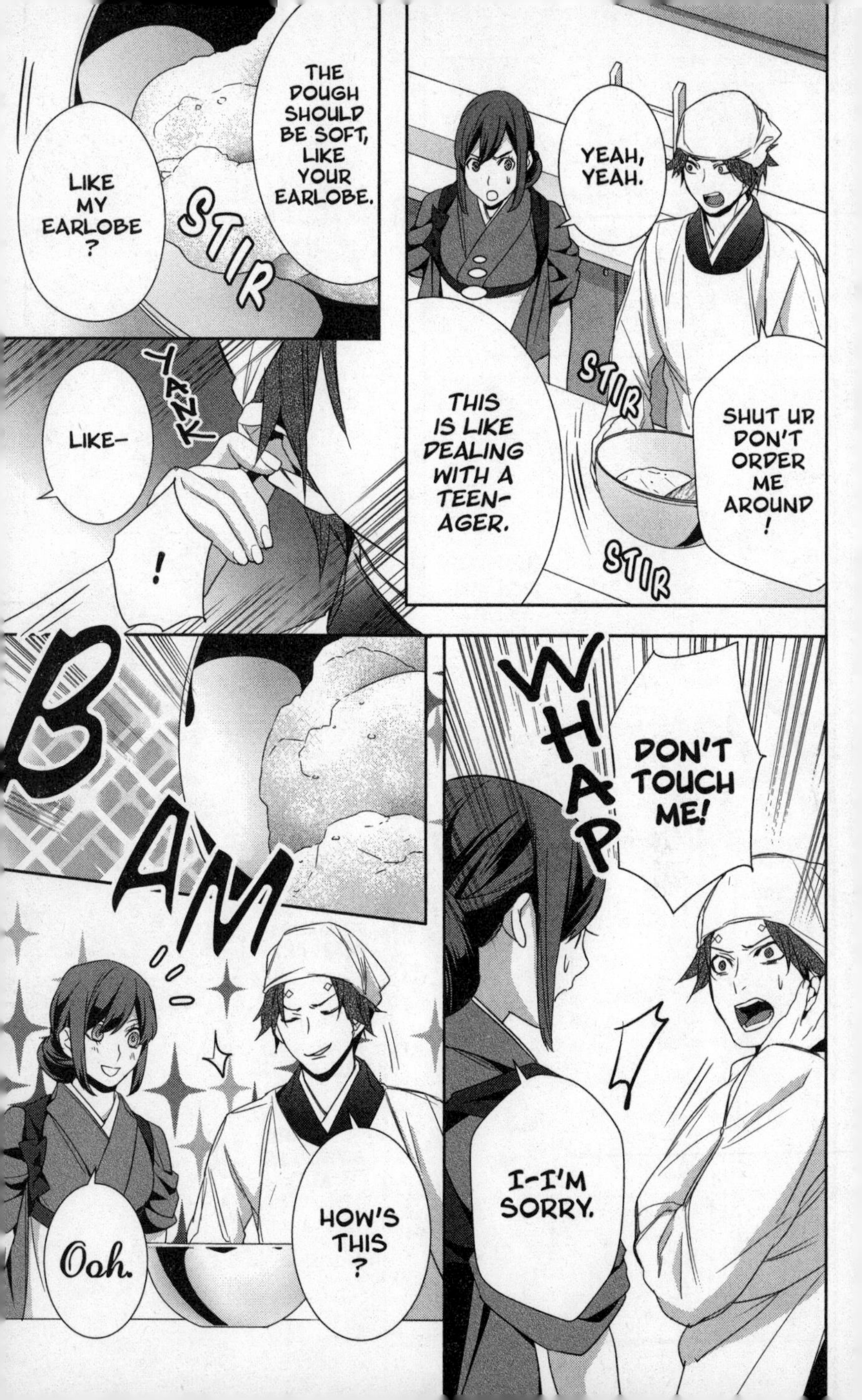
YEAH, YEAH.
STIR
THIS IS LIKE DEALING WITH A TEEN-AGER.
SHUT UP. DON'T ORDER ME AROUND!
STIR
THE DOUGH SHOULD BE SOFT, LIKE YOUR EARLOBE.
STIR
LIKE MY EARLOBE?
YANK
LIKE-
!
WHAP
DON'T TOUCH ME!
I-I'M SORRY.
BAM
HOW'S THIS?
Ooh.

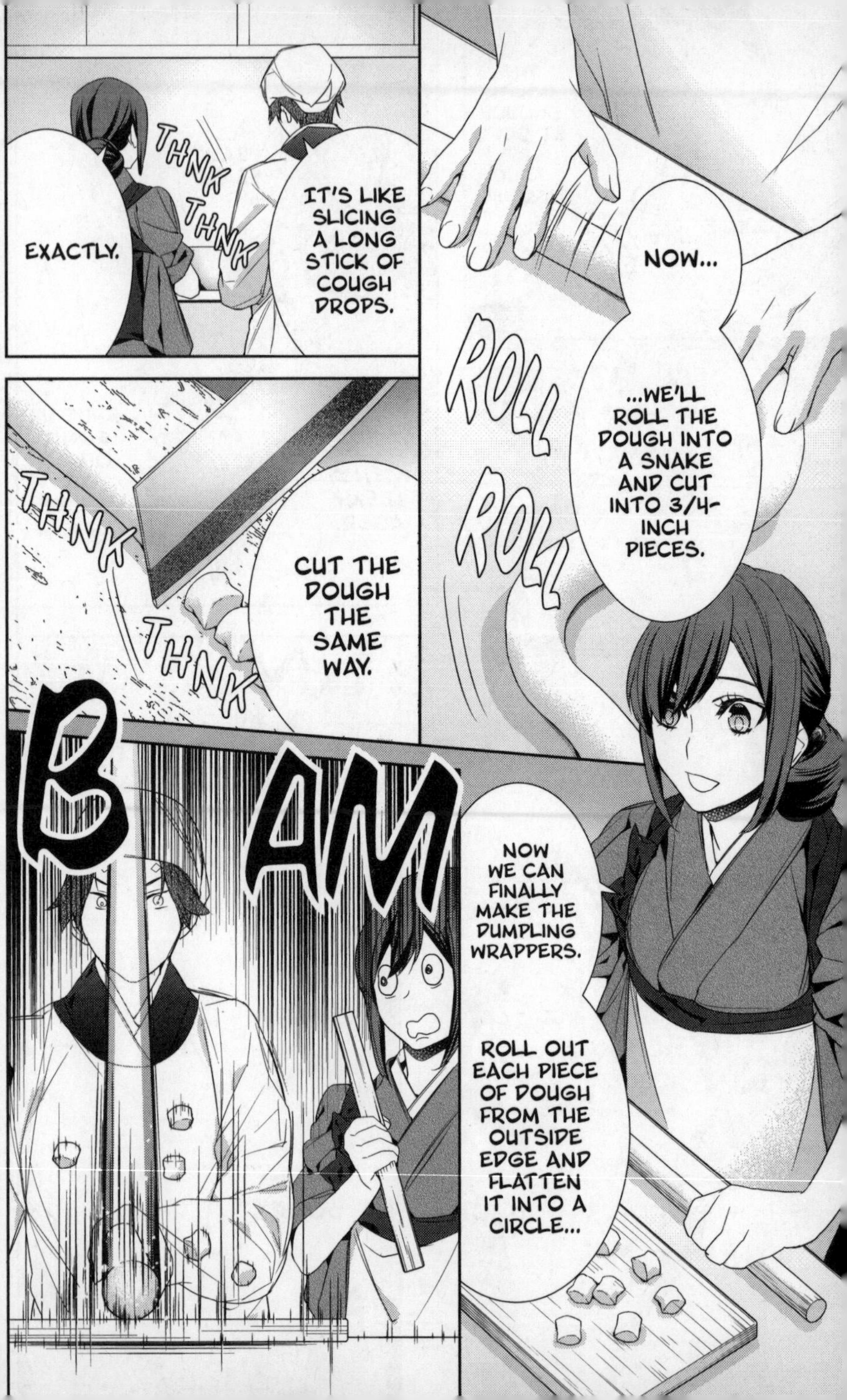
NOW...
...WE'LL ROLL THE DOUGH INTO A SNAKE AND CUT INTO 3/4-INCH PIECES.
ROLL
ROLL
THNK
THNK
IT'S LIKE SLICING A LONG STICK OF COUGH DROPS.
EXACTLY.
THNK
THNK
CUT THE DOUGH THE SAME WAY.
NOW WE CAN FINALLY MAKE THE DUMPLING WRAPPERS.
ROLL OUT EACH PIECE OF DOUGH FROM THE OUTSIDE EDGE AND FLATTEN IT INTO A CIRCLE...
BAM

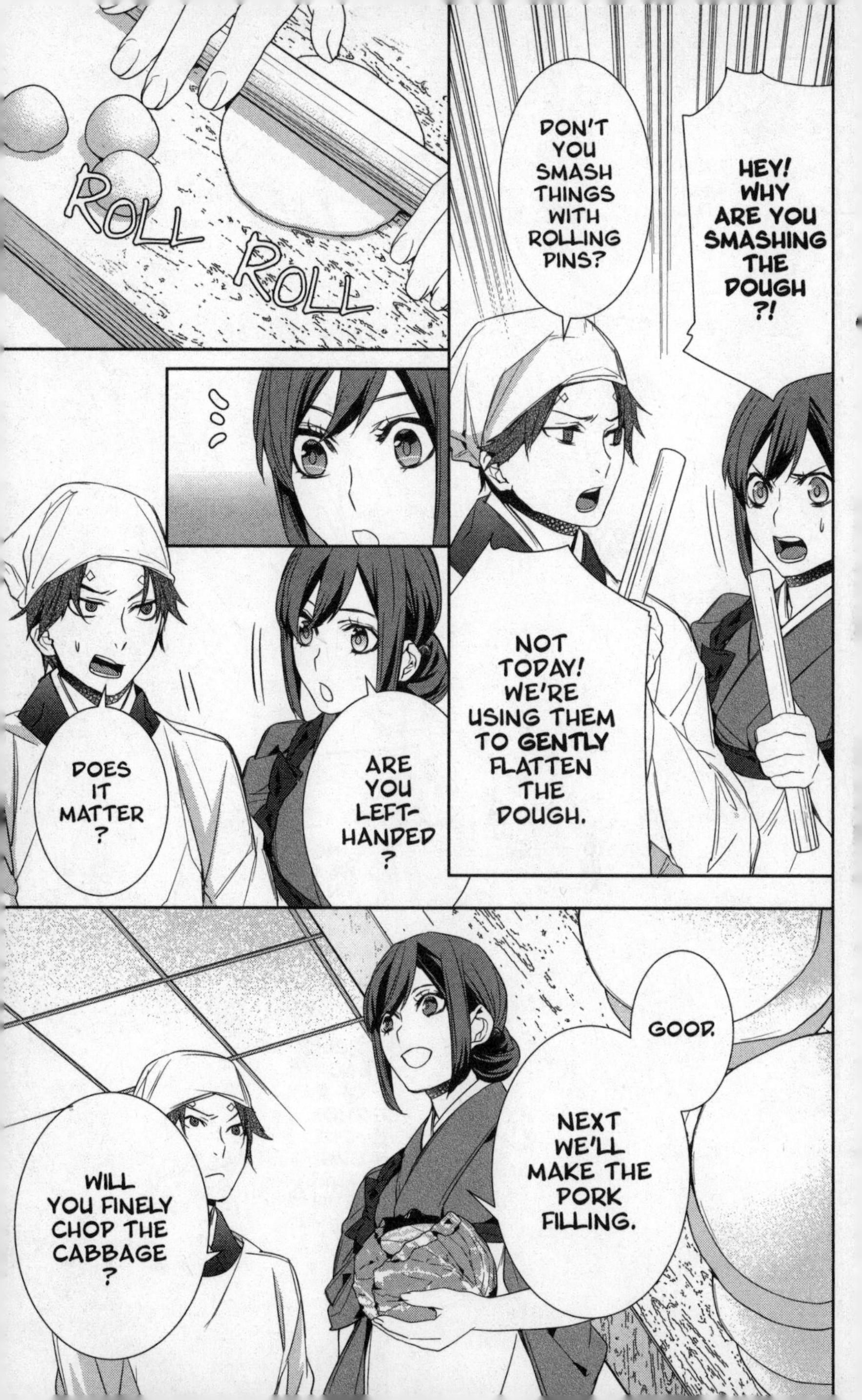
HEY! WHY ARE YOU SMASHING THE DOUGH ?!
DON'T YOU SMASH THINGS WITH ROLLING PINS?
NOT TODAY! WE'RE USING THEM TO GENTLY FLATTEN THE DOUGH.
ROLL
ROLL
...
ARE YOU LEFT-HANDED ?
DOES IT MATTER ?
GOOD.
NEXT WE'LL MAKE THE PORK FILLING.
WILL YOU FINELY CHOP THE CABBAGE ?

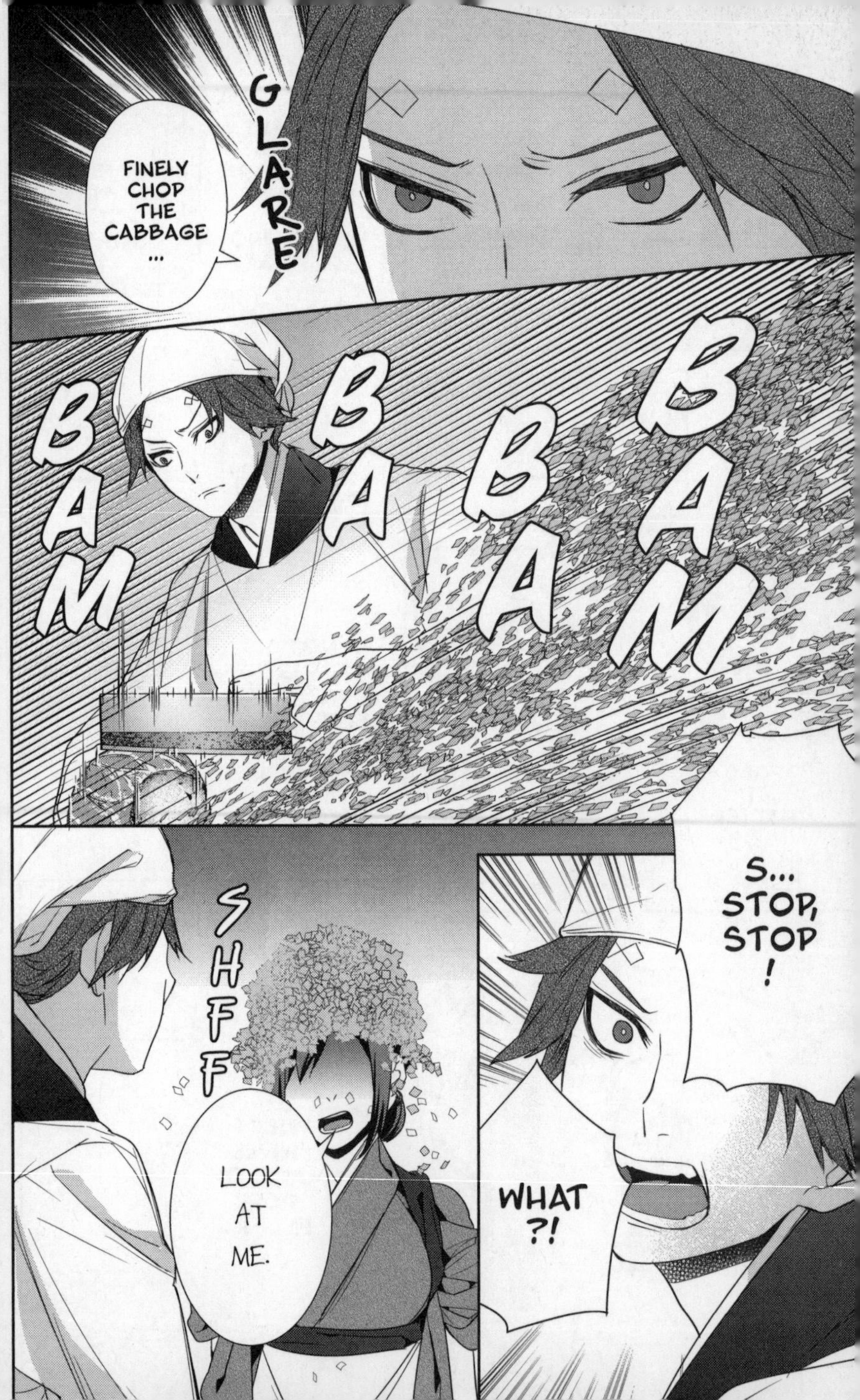
GLARE
FINELY CHOP THE CABBAGE ...
BAM
BA
BA
BAM
S... STOP, STOP!
WHAT?!
SHFF
LOOK AT ME.

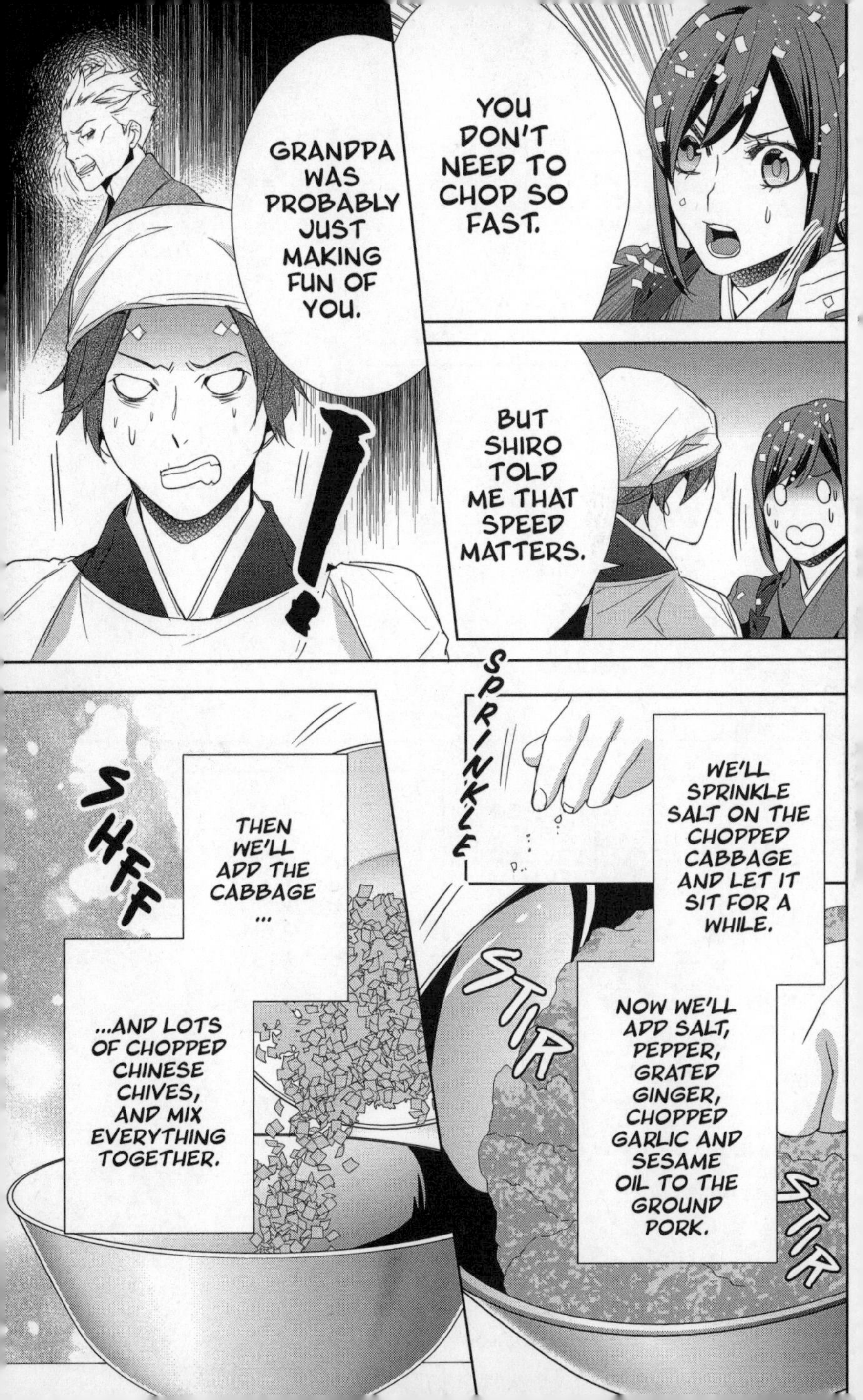
YOU DON'T NEED TO CHOP SO FAST.
BUT SHIRO TOLD ME THAT SPEED MATTERS.
GRANDPA WAS PROBABLY JUST MAKING FUN OF YOU.
!
SPRINKLE
WE'LL SPRINKLE SALT ON THE CHOPPED CABBAGE AND LET IT SIT FOR A WHILE.
NOW WE'LL ADD SALT, PEPPER, GRATED GINGER, CHOPPED GARLIC AND SESAME OIL TO THE GROUND PORK.
STIR
STIR
THEN WE'LL ADD THE CABBAGE ...
SHFF
...AND LOTS OF CHOPPED CHINESE CHIVES, AND MIX EVERYTHING TOGETHER.

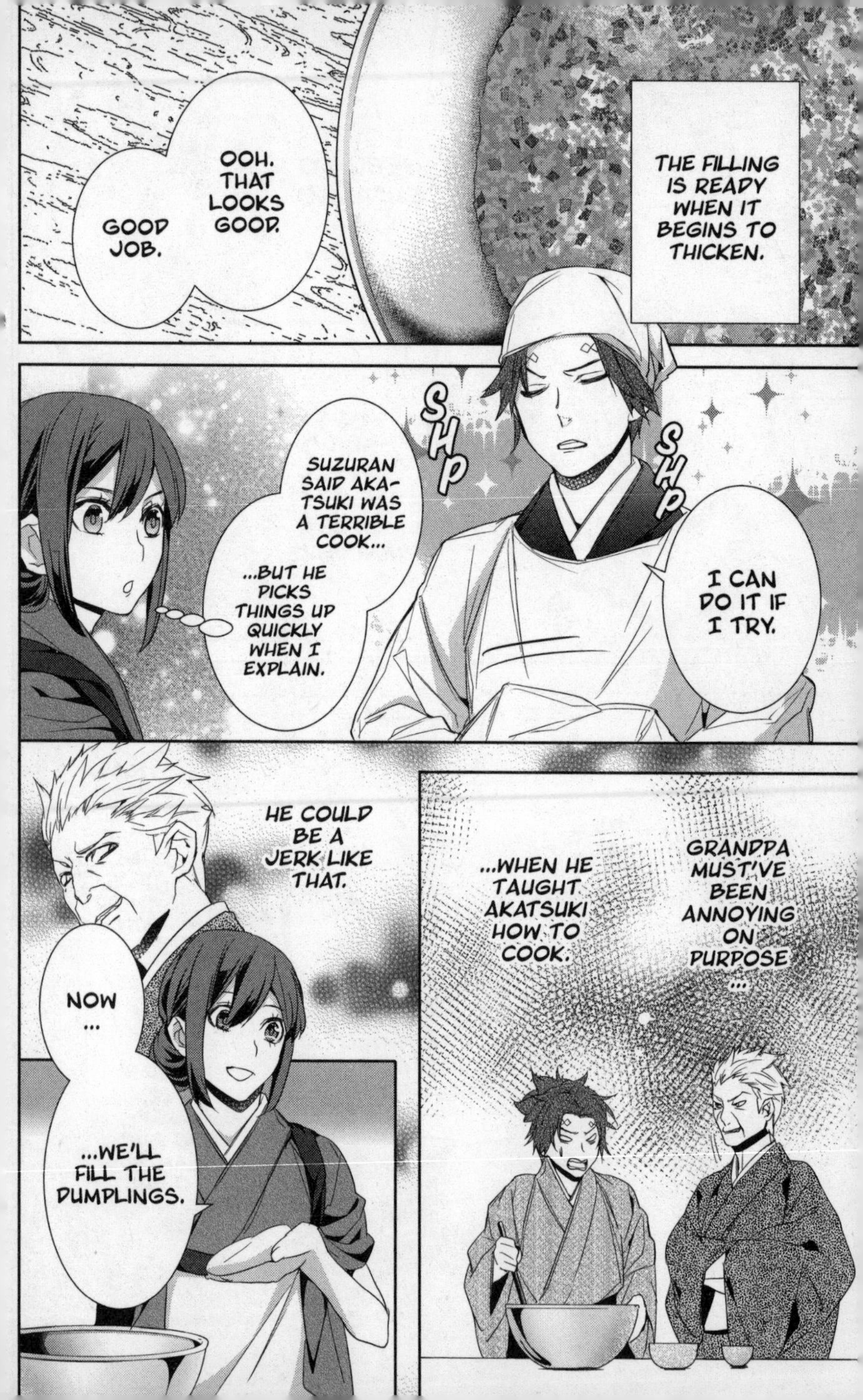
THE FILLING IS READY WHEN IT BEGINS TO THICKEN.
OOH. THAT LOOKS GOOD.
GOOD JOB.
SHP
SHP
I CAN DO IT IF I TRY.
SUZURAN SAID AKA-TSUKI WAS A TERRIBLE COOK...
...BUT HE PICKS THINGS UP QUICKLY WHEN I EXPLAIN.
GRANDPA MUST'VE BEEN ANNOYING ON PURPOSE...
...WHEN HE TAUGHT AKATSUKI HOW TO COOK.
HE COULD BE A JERK LIKE THAT.
NOW...
...WE'LL FILL THE DUMPLINGS.

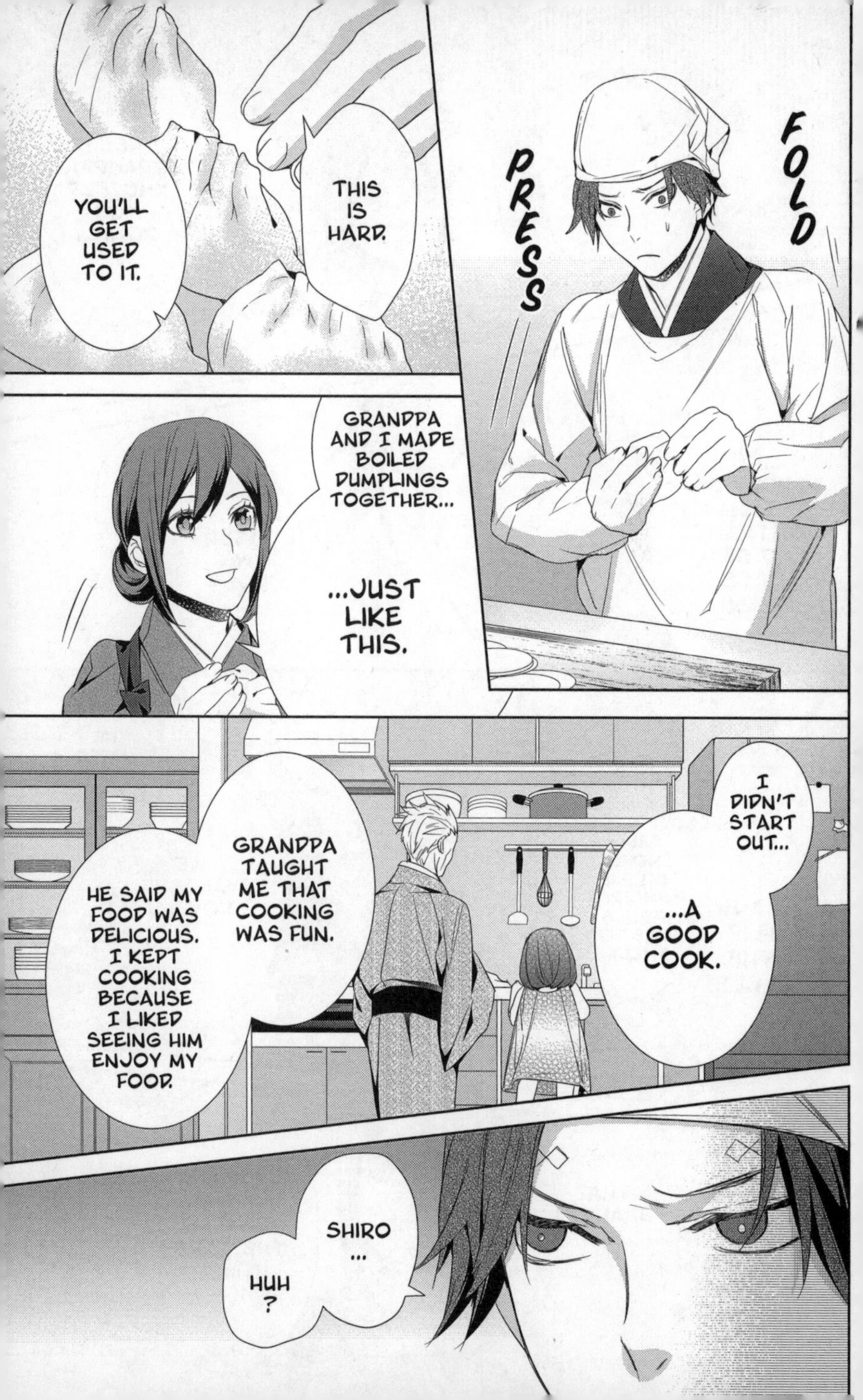
FOLD
PRESS
THIS IS HARD.
YOU'LL GET USED TO IT.
GRANDPA AND I MADE BOILED DUMPLINGS TOGETHER...
...JUST LIKE THIS.
I DIDN'T START OUT...
...A GOOD COOK.
GRANDPA TAUGHT ME THAT COOKING WAS FUN.
HE SAID MY FOOD WAS DELICIOUS. I KEPT COOKING BECAUSE I LIKED SEEING HIM ENJOY MY FOOD.
SHIRO...
HUH?

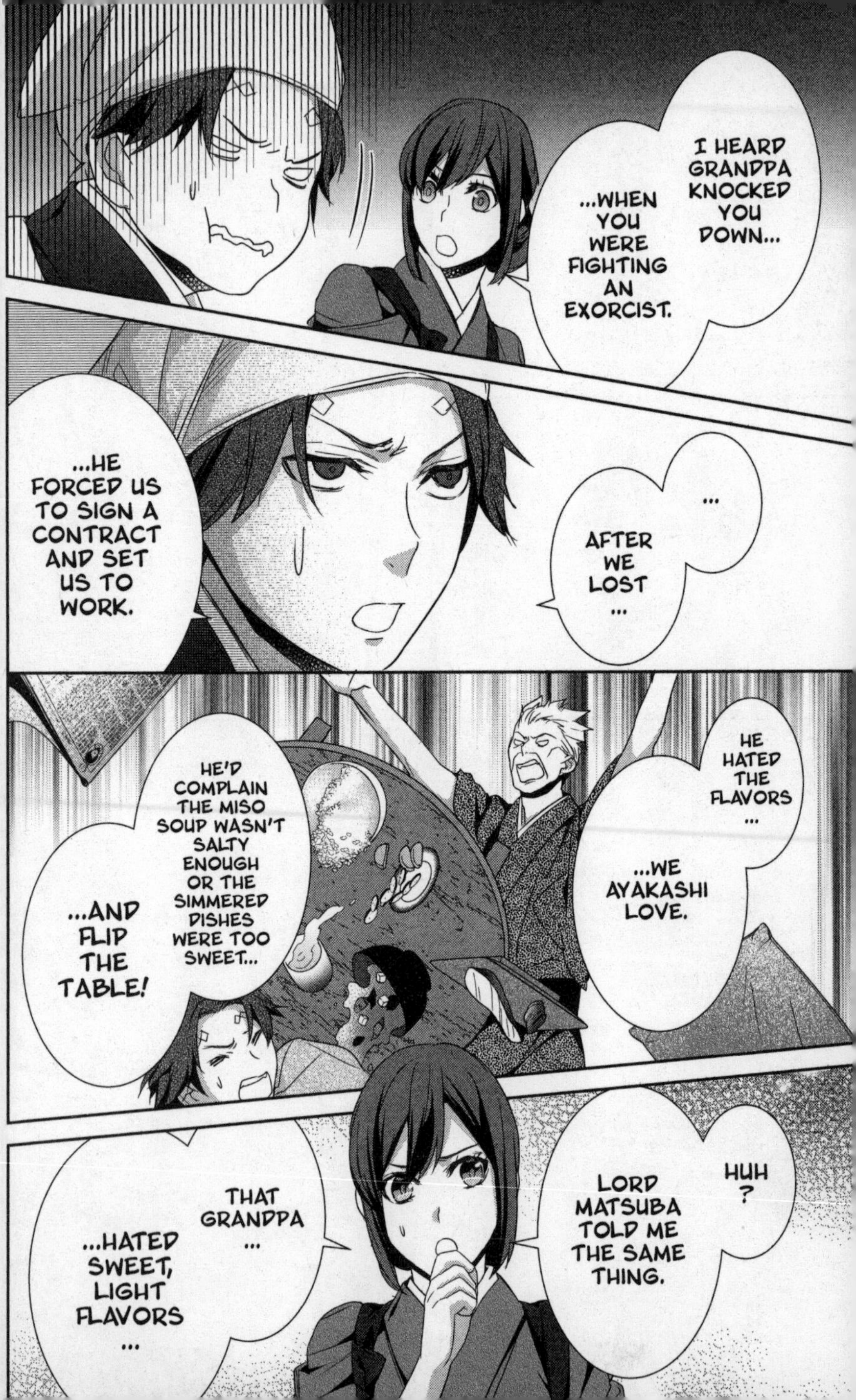
I HEARD GRANDPA KNOCKED YOU DOWN...
...WHEN YOU WERE FIGHTING AN EXORCIST.
...
AFTER WE LOST ...
...HE FORCED US TO SIGN A CONTRACT AND SET US TO WORK.
HE HATED THE FLAVORS ...
...WE AYAKASHI LOVE.
HE'D COMPLAIN THE MISO SOUP WASN'T SALTY ENOUGH OR THE SIMMERED DISHES WERE TOO SWEET...
...AND FLIP THE TABLE!
HUH ?
LORD MATSUBA TOLD ME THE SAME THING.
THAT GRANDPA ...
...HATED SWEET, LIGHT FLAVORS ...

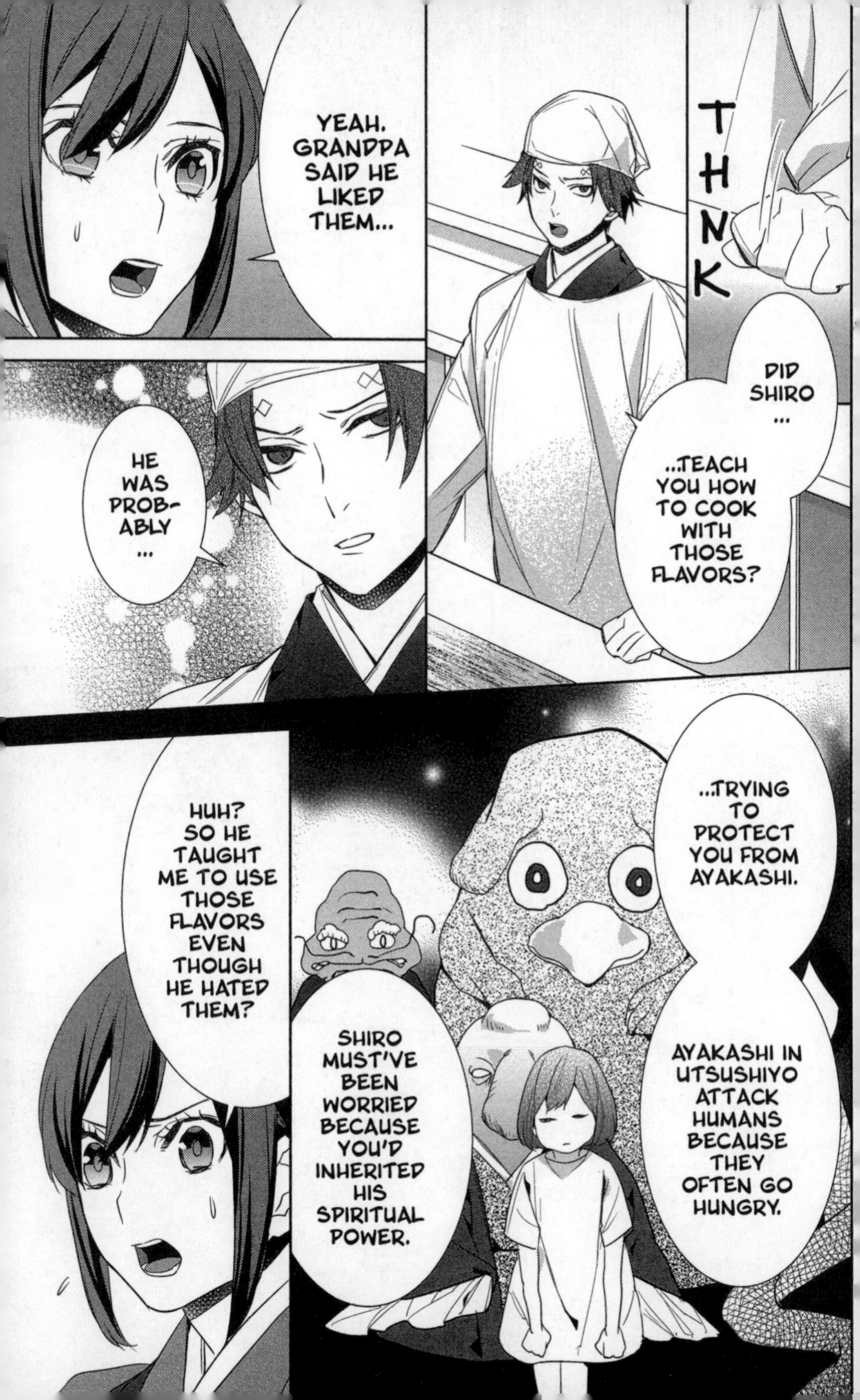
THNK
DID SHIRO ...
...TEACH YOU HOW TO COOK WITH THOSE FLAVORS?
YEAH. GRANDPA SAID HE LIKED THEM...
HE WAS PROBABLY ...
...TRYING TO PROTECT YOU FROM AYAKASHI.
AYAKASHI IN UTSUSHIYO ATTACK HUMANS BECAUSE THEY OFTEN GO HUNGRY.
SHIRO MUST'VE BEEN WORRIED BECAUSE YOU'D INHERITED HIS SPIRITUAL POWER.
HUH? SO HE TAUGHT ME TO USE THOSE FLAVORS EVEN THOUGH HE HATED THEM?

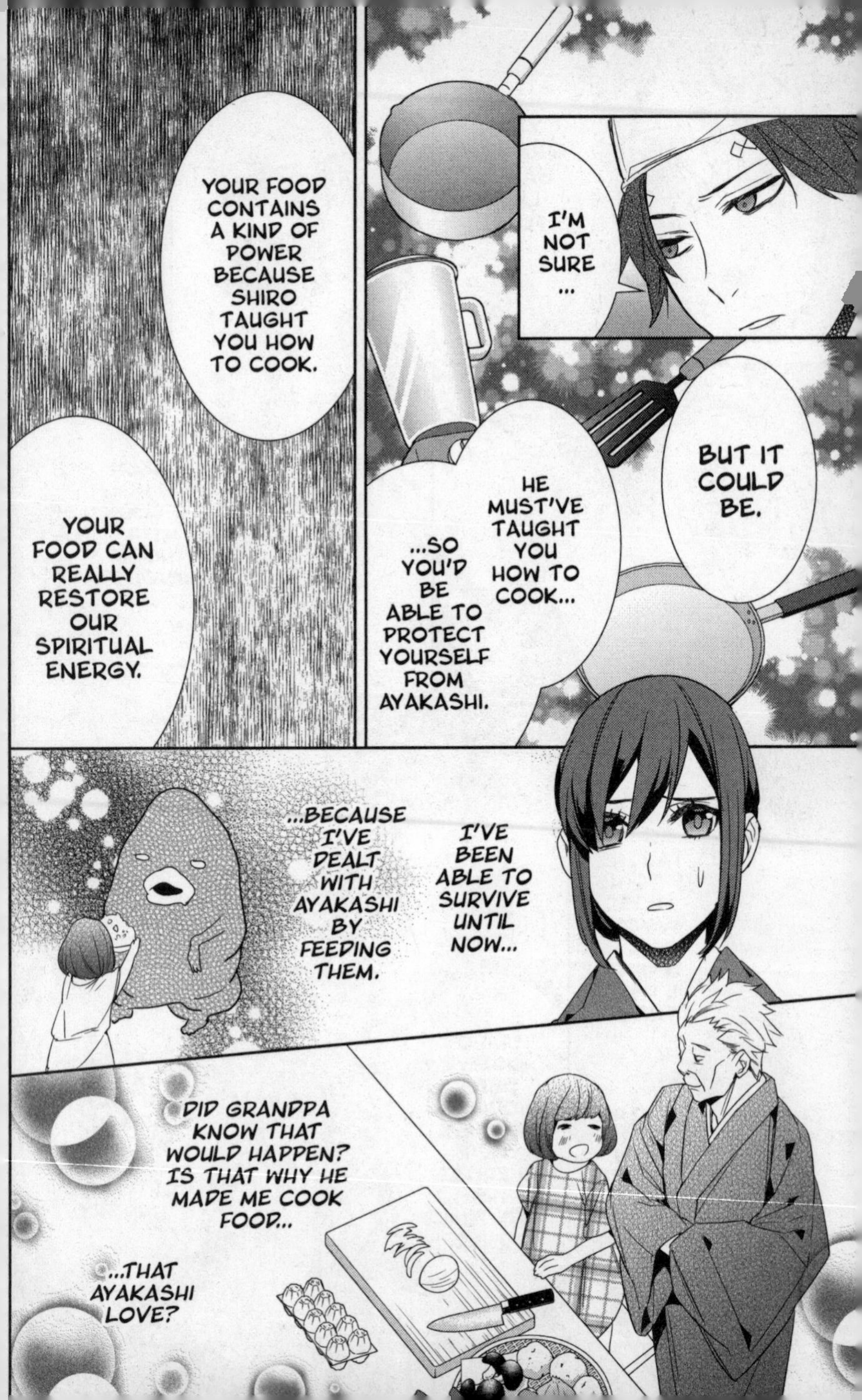
I'M NOT SURE ...
BUT IT COULD BE.
HE MUST'VE TAUGHT YOU HOW TO COOK...
...SO YOU'D BE ABLE TO PROTECT YOURSELF FROM AYAKASHI.
YOUR FOOD CONTAINS A KIND OF POWER BECAUSE SHIRO TAUGHT YOU HOW TO COOK.
YOUR FOOD CAN REALLY RESTORE OUR SPIRITUAL ENERGY.
I'VE BEEN ABLE TO SURVIVE UNTIL NOW...
...BECAUSE I'VE DEALT WITH AYAKASHI BY FEEDING THEM.
DID GRANDPA KNOW THAT WOULD HAPPEN? IS THAT WHY HE MADE ME COOK FOOD...
...THAT AYAKASHI LOVE?

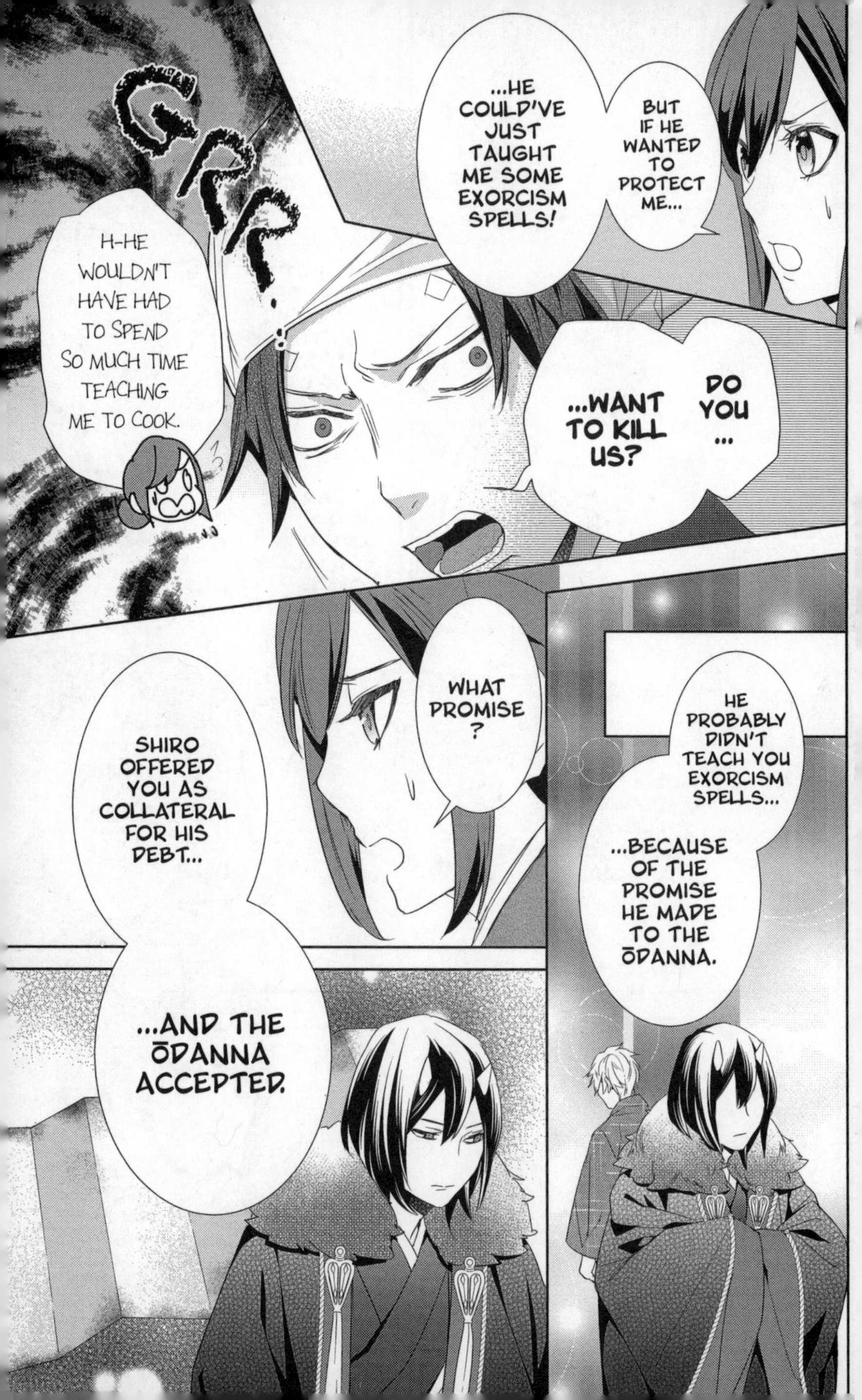
BUT IF HE WANTED TO PROTECT ME...
...HE COULD'VE JUST TAUGHT ME SOME EXORCISM SPELLS!
DO YOU ...
...WANT TO KILL US?
GRR
H-HE WOULDN'T HAVE HAD TO SPEND SO MUCH TIME TEACHING ME TO COOK.
HE PROBABLY DIDN'T TEACH YOU EXORCISM SPELLS...
...BECAUSE OF THE PROMISE HE MADE TO THE ŌDANNA.
WHAT PROMISE?
SHIRO OFFERED YOU AS COLLATERAL FOR HIS DEBT...
...AND THE ŌDANNA ACCEPTED.

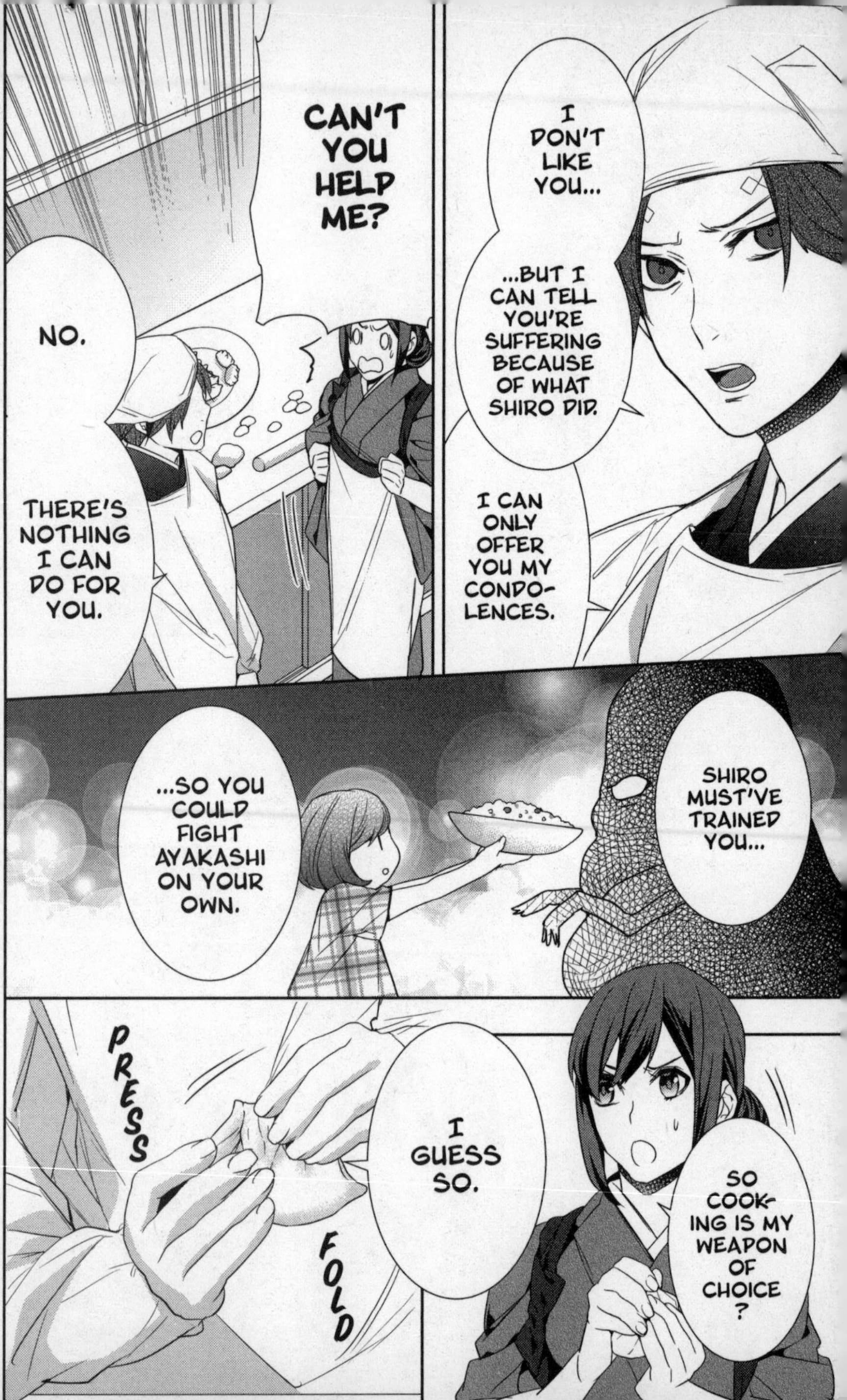
I DON'T LIKE YOU...
...BUT I CAN TELL YOU'RE SUFFERING BECAUSE OF WHAT SHIRO DID.
I CAN ONLY OFFER YOU MY CONDOLENCES.
CAN'T YOU HELP ME?
NO.
THERE'S NOTHING I CAN DO FOR YOU.
SHIRO MUST'VE TRAINED YOU...
...SO YOU COULD FIGHT AYAKASHI ON YOUR OWN.
SO COOKING IS MY WEAPON OF CHOICE?
I GUESS SO.
PRESS
FOLD

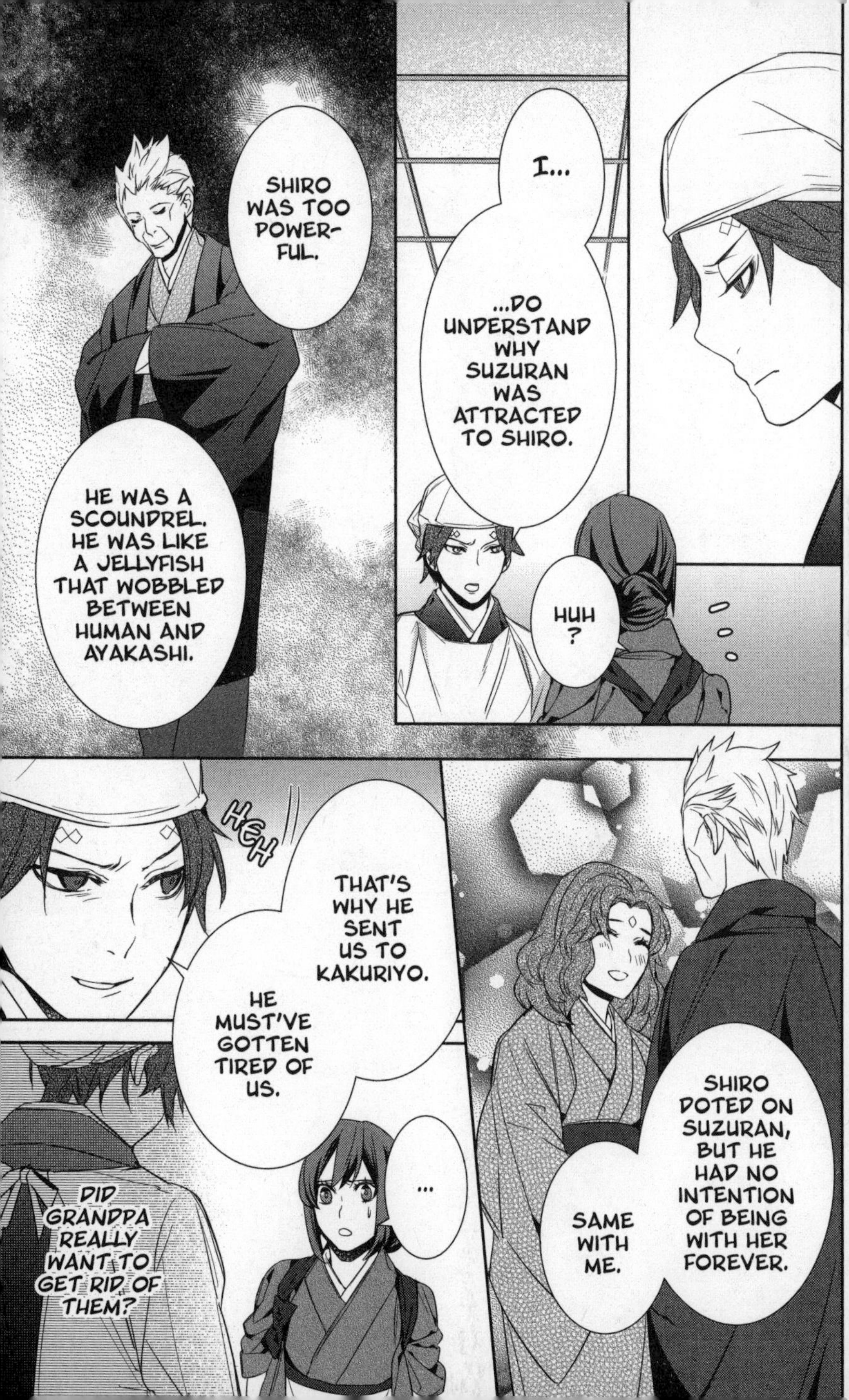
I...
...DO UNDERSTAND WHY SUZURAN WAS ATTRACTED TO SHIRO.
HUH?
SHIRO WAS TOO POWER-FUL.
HE WAS A SCOUNDREL. HE WAS LIKE A JELLYFISH THAT WOBBLED BETWEEN HUMAN AND AYAKASHI.
SHIRO DOTED ON SUZURAN, BUT HE HAD NO INTENTION OF BEING WITH HER FOREVER.
SAME WITH ME.
HEH
THAT'S WHY HE SENT US TO KAKURIYO.
HE MUST'VE GOTTEN TIRED OF US.
...
DID GRANDPA REALLY WANT TO GET RID OF THEM?

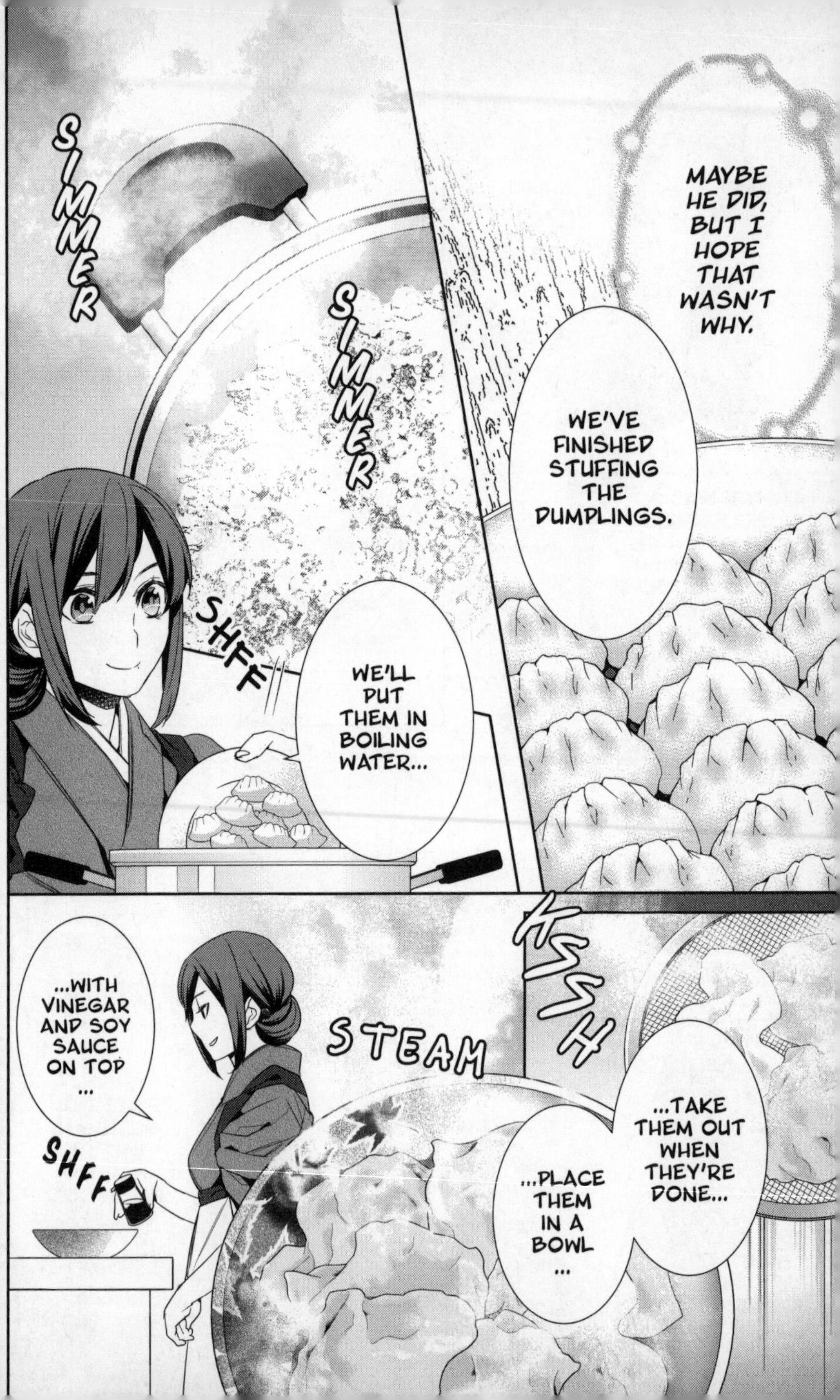
MAYBE HE DID, BUT I HOPE THAT WASN'T WHY.
WE'VE FINISHED STUFFING THE DUMPLINGS.
SIMMER
SIMMER
SHFF
WE'LL PUT THEM IN BOILING WATER...
KSSH
...TAKE THEM OUT WHEN THEY'RE DONE...
...PLACE THEM IN A BOWL ...
STEAM
...WITH VINEGAR AND SOY SAUCE ON TOP ...
SHFF

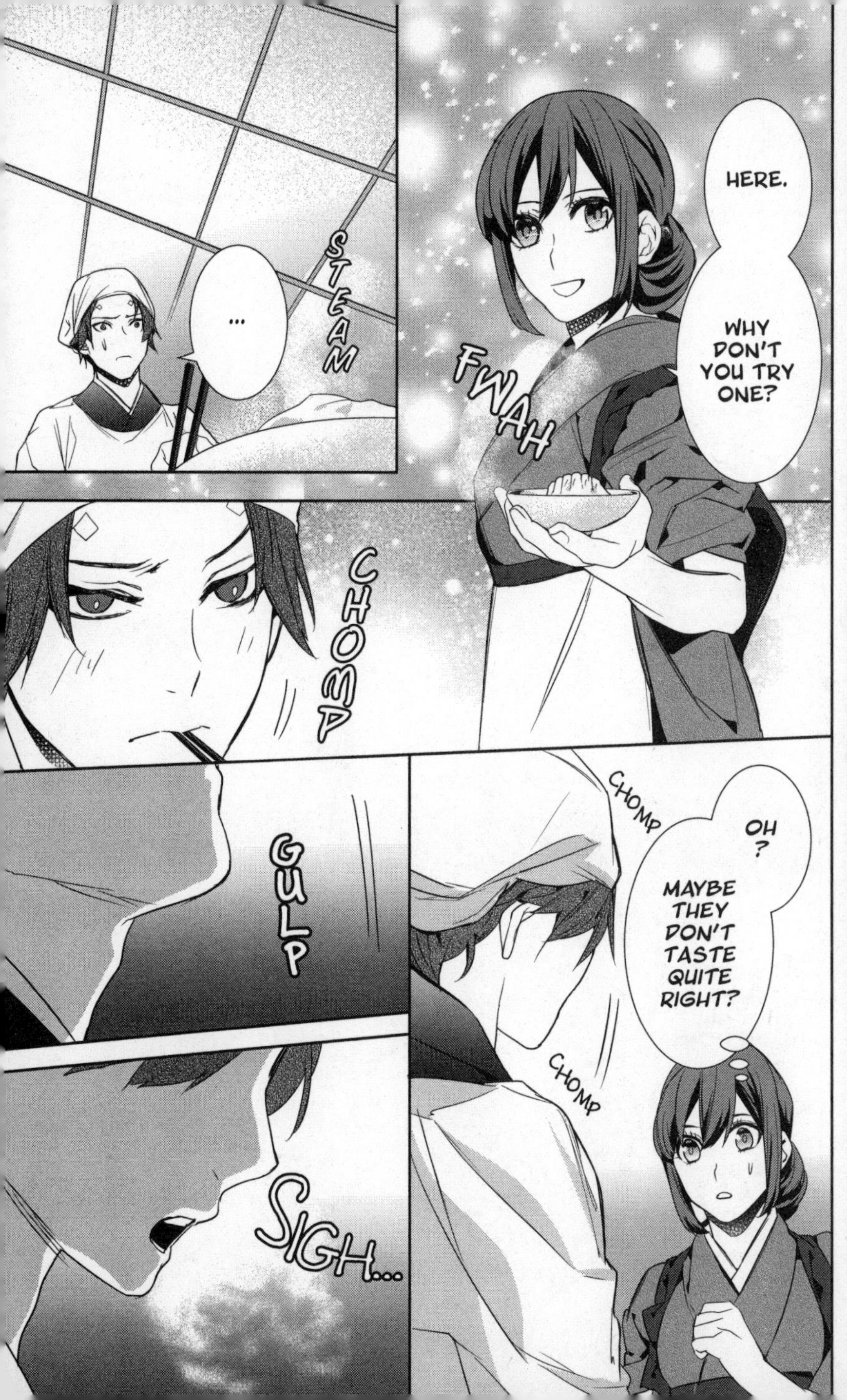

HERE.
WHY DON'T YOU TRY ONE?
FWAH
STEAM
...
CHOMP
CHOMP
OH?
MAYBE THEY DON'T TASTE QUITE RIGHT?
CHOMP
GULP
SIGH...

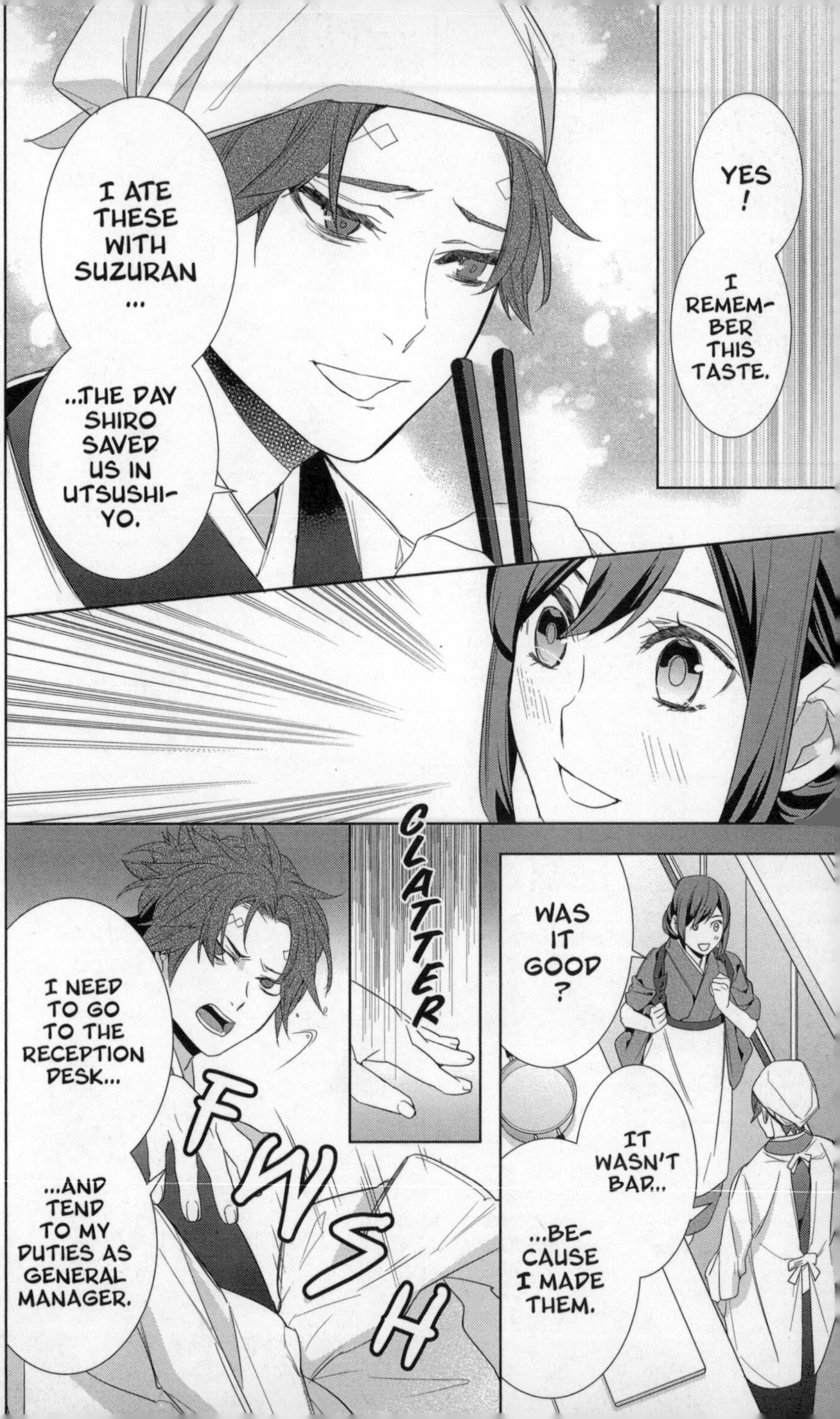
YES! I REMEMBER THIS TASTE.
I ATE THESE WITH SUZURAN...
...THE DAY SHIRO SAVED US IN UTSUSHIYO.
WAS IT GOOD?
IT WASN'T BAD...
...BECAUSE I MADE THEM.
CLATTER
I NEED TO GO TO THE RECEPTION DESK...
...AND TEND TO MY DUTIES AS GENERAL MANAGER.
FWSH

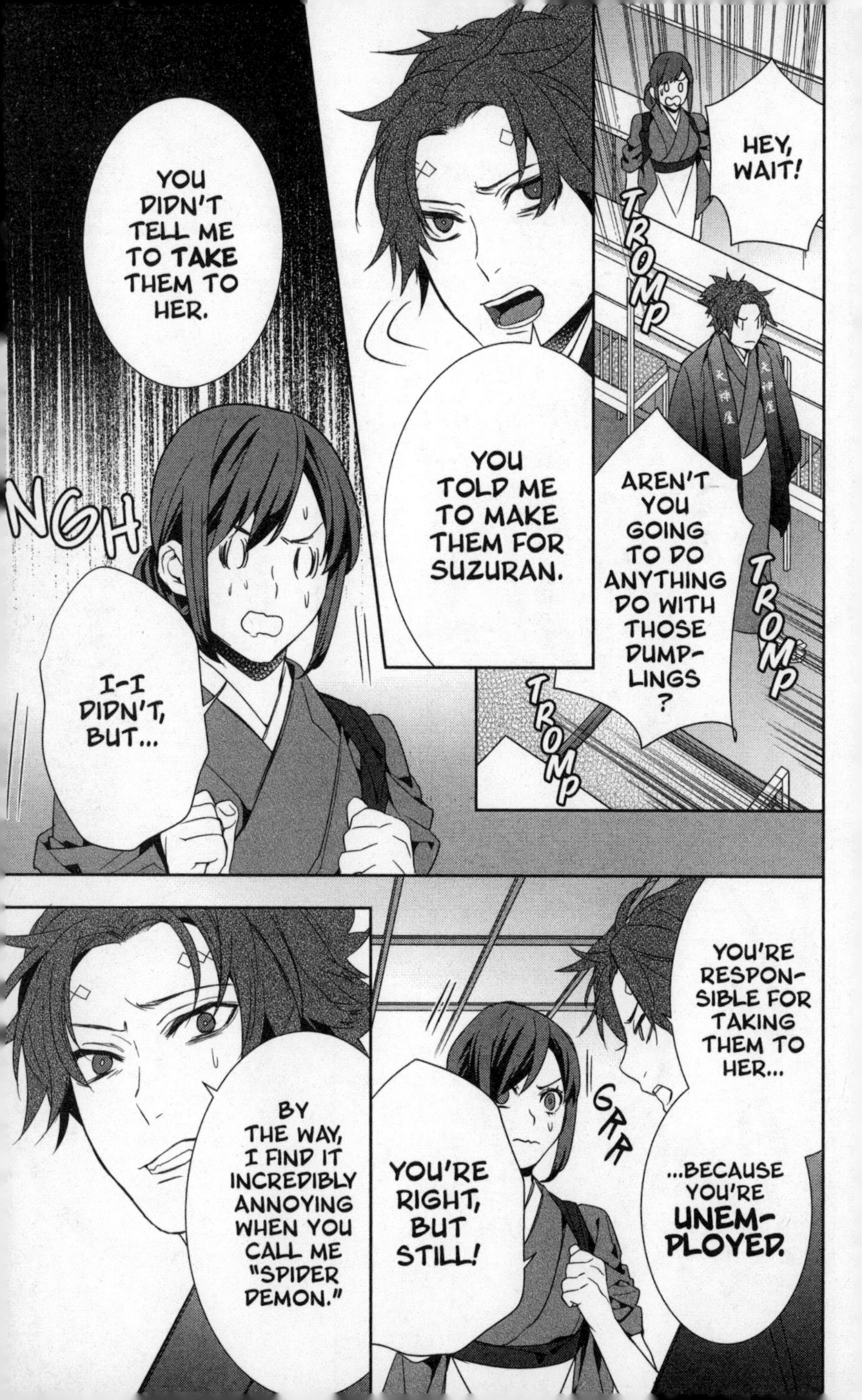
HEY, WAIT!
TROMP
AREN'T YOU GOING TO DO ANYTHING DO WITH THOSE DUMPLINGS?
TROMP
TROMP
YOU TOLD ME TO MAKE THEM FOR SUZURAN.
YOU DIDN'T TELL ME TO TAKE THEM TO HER.
NGH
I-I DIDN'T, BUT...
YOU'RE RESPONSIBLE FOR TAKING THEM TO HER...
...BECAUSE YOU'RE UNEMPLOYED.
GRR
YOU'RE RIGHT, BUT STILL!
BY THE WAY, I FIND IT INCREDIBLY ANNOYING WHEN YOU CALL ME "SPIDER DEMON."

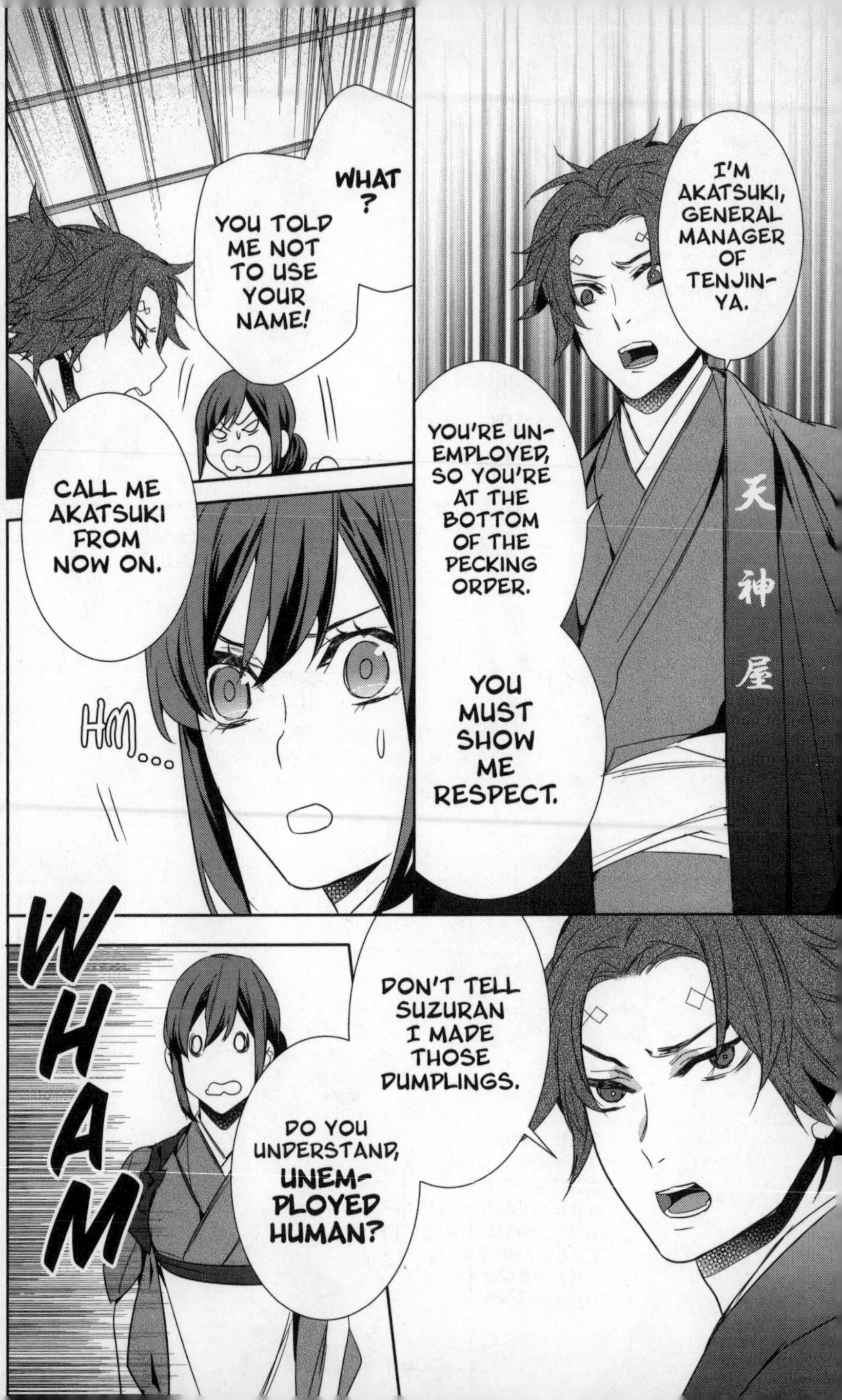
I'M AKATSUKI, GENERAL MANAGER OF TENJIN-YA.
YOU'RE UN-EMPLOYED, SO YOU'RE AT THE BOTTOM OF THE PECKING ORDER.
YOU MUST SHOW ME RESPECT.
天神屋
WHAT?
YOU TOLD ME NOT TO USE YOUR NAME!
CALL ME AKATSUKI FROM NOW ON.
HM...
DON'T TELL SUZURAN I MADE THOSE DUMPLINGS.
DO YOU UNDERSTAND, **UNEMPLOYED HUMAN?**
WHAM

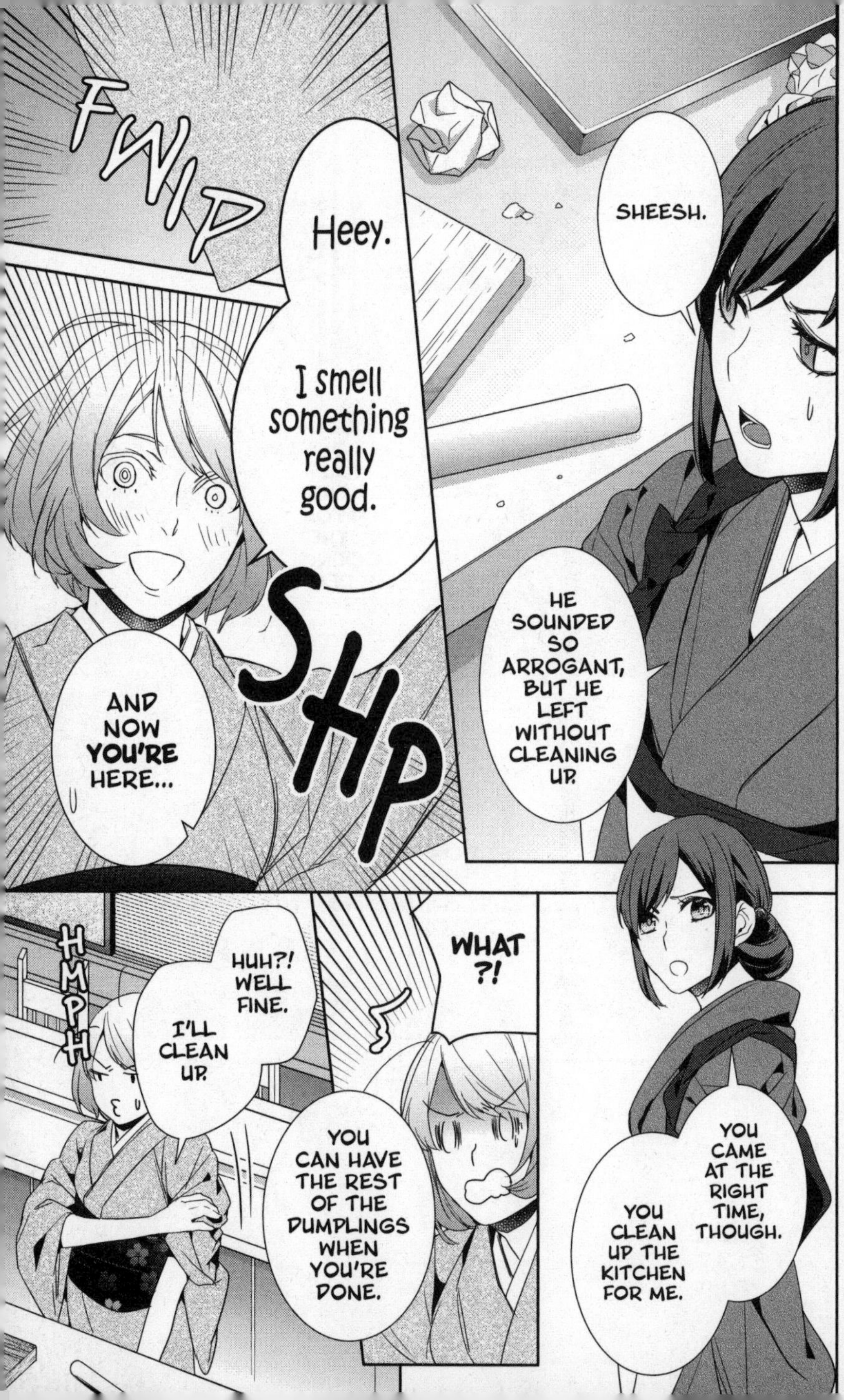
SHEESH.
HE SOUNDED SO ARROGANT, BUT HE LEFT WITHOUT CLEANING UP.
Heey.
FWIP
I smell something really good.
SHP
AND NOW YOU'RE HERE...
YOU CAME AT THE RIGHT TIME, THOUGH.
YOU CLEAN UP THE KITCHEN FOR ME.
WHAT?!
YOU CAN HAVE THE REST OF THE DUMPLINGS WHEN YOU'RE DONE.
HUH?! WELL FINE.
HMPH
I'LL CLEAN UP.

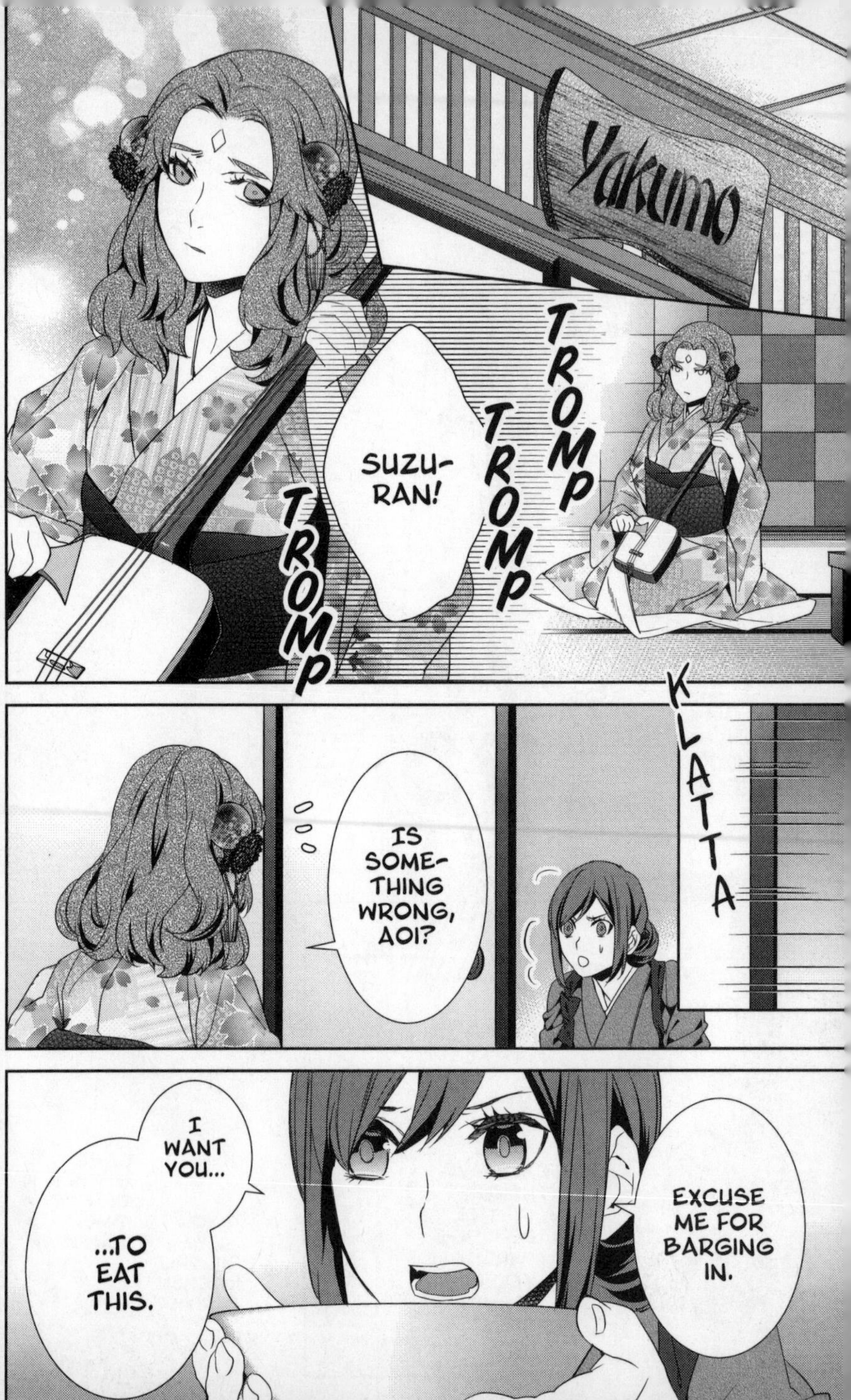
Yakumo
TROMP
TROMP
SUZU-RAN!
TROMP
KLATTA
IS SOMETHING WRONG, AOI?
EXCUSE ME FOR BARGING IN.
I WANT YOU...
...TO EAT THIS.

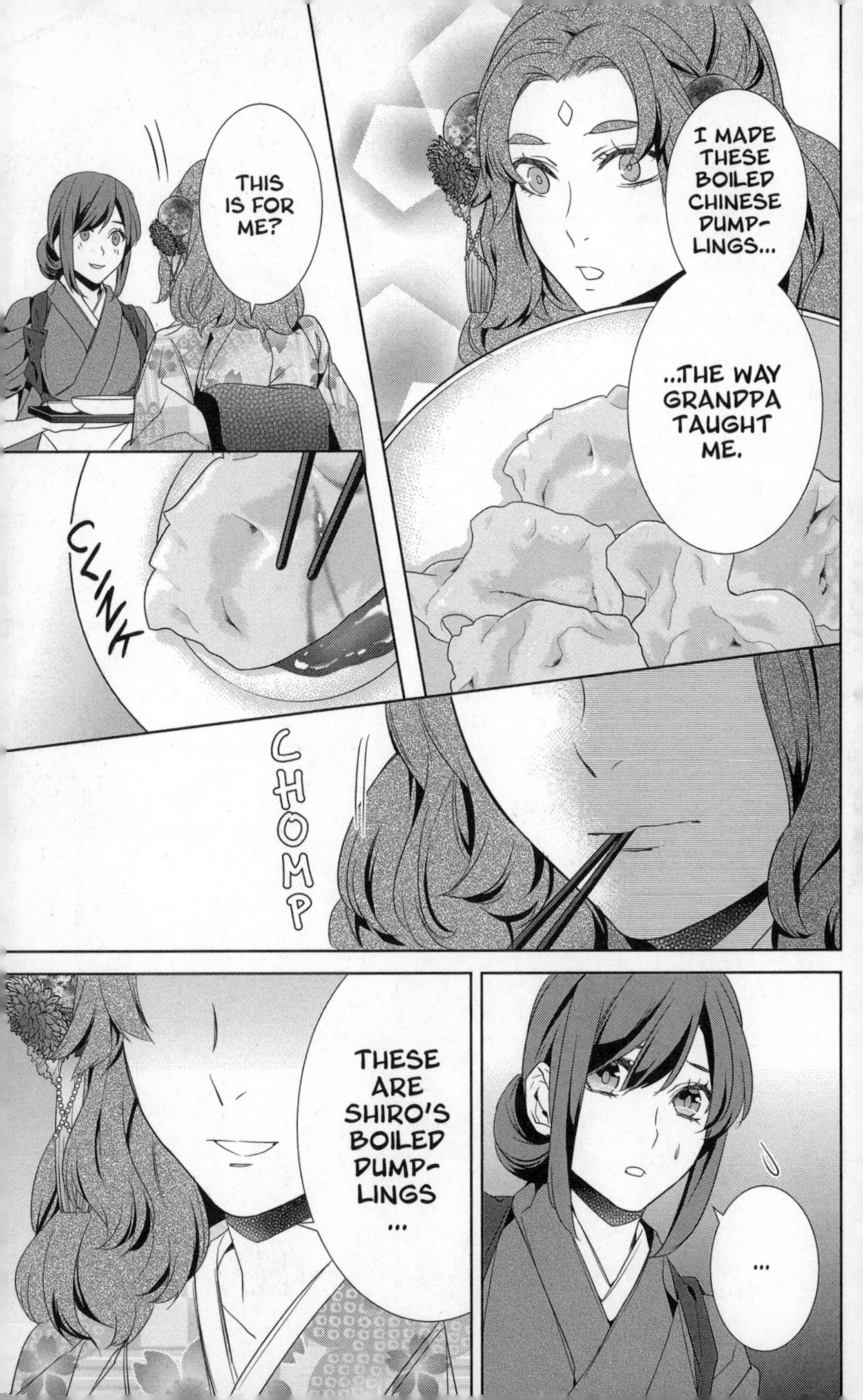
I MADE THESE BOILED CHINESE DUMPLINGS...
...THE WAY GRANDPA TAUGHT ME.
THIS IS FOR ME?
CLINK
CHOMP
...
THESE ARE SHIRO'S BOILED DUMPLINGS ...

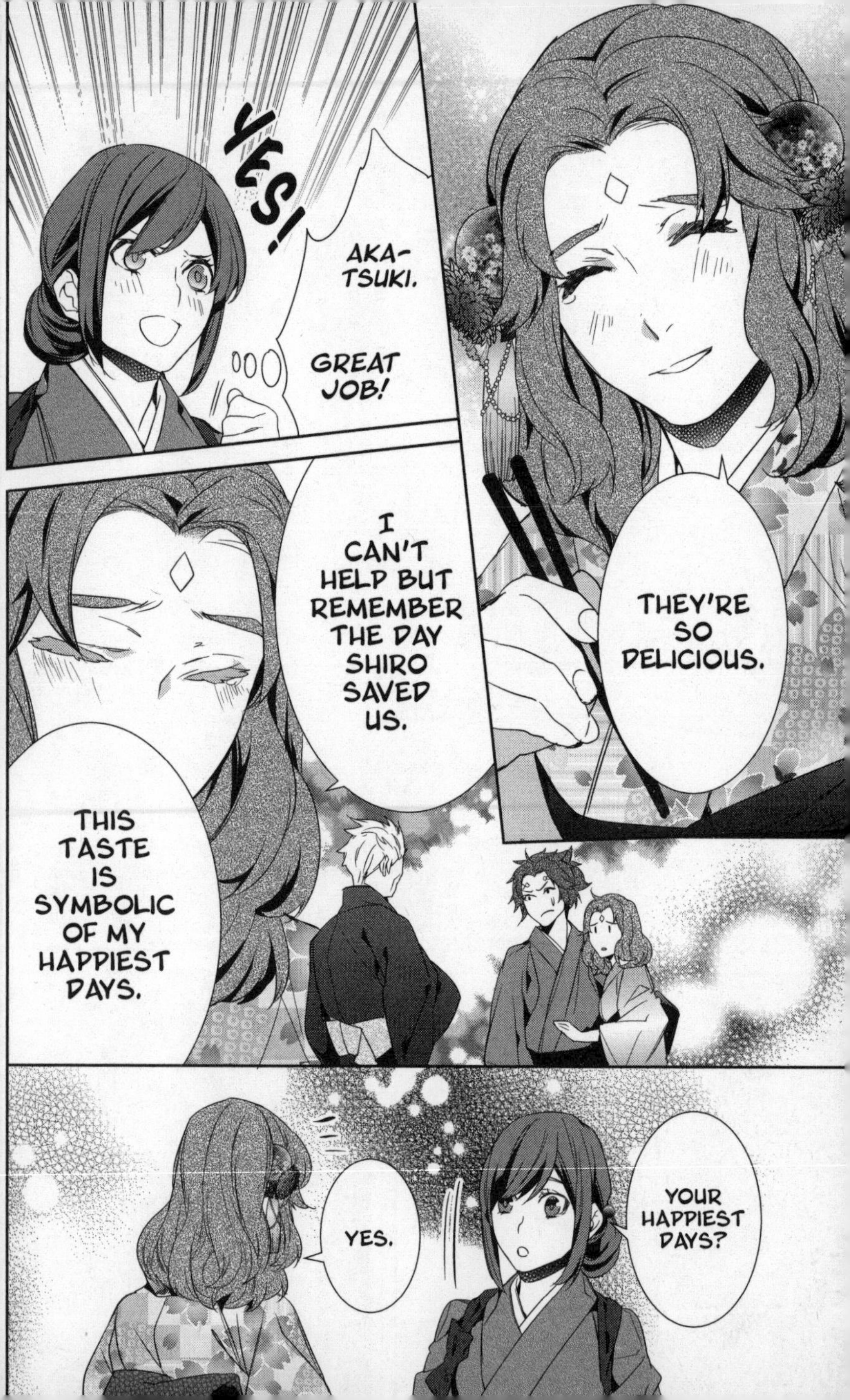
THEY'RE SO DELICIOUS.
YES!
AKA-TSUKI.
GREAT JOB!
I CAN'T HELP BUT REMEMBER THE DAY SHIRO SAVED US.
THIS TASTE IS SYMBOLIC OF MY HAPPIEST DAYS.
YOUR HAPPIEST DAYS?
YES.

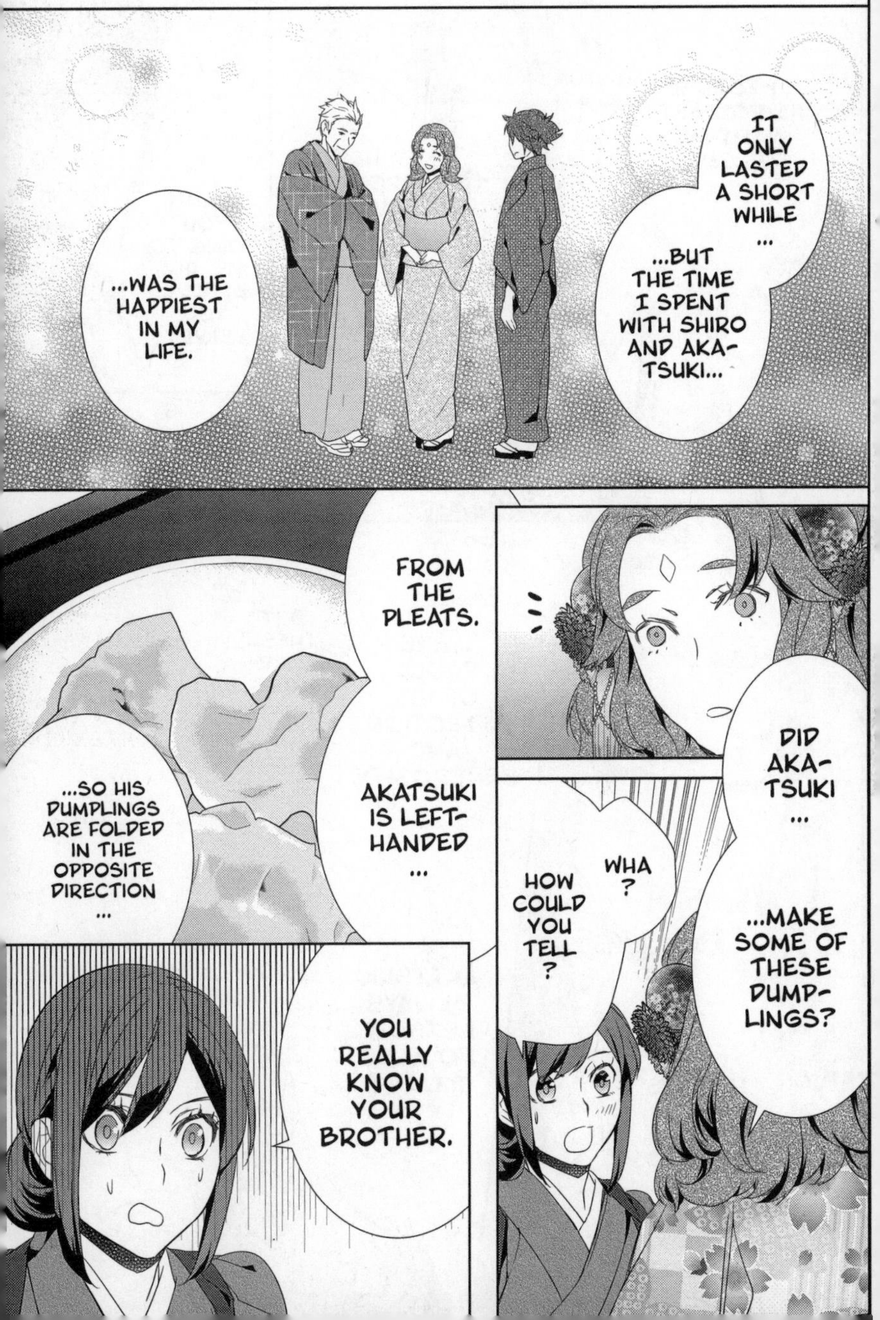
IT ONLY LASTED A SHORT WHILE ...
...BUT THE TIME I SPENT WITH SHIRO AND AKA-TSUKI...
...WAS THE HAPPIEST IN MY LIFE.
DID AKA-TSUKI ...
...MAKE SOME OF THESE DUMP-LINGS?
WHA?
HOW COULD YOU TELL?
FROM THE PLEATS.
AKATSUKI IS LEFT-HANDED ...
...SO HIS DUMPLINGS ARE FOLDED IN THE OPPOSITE DIRECTION ...
YOU REALLY KNOW YOUR BROTHER.

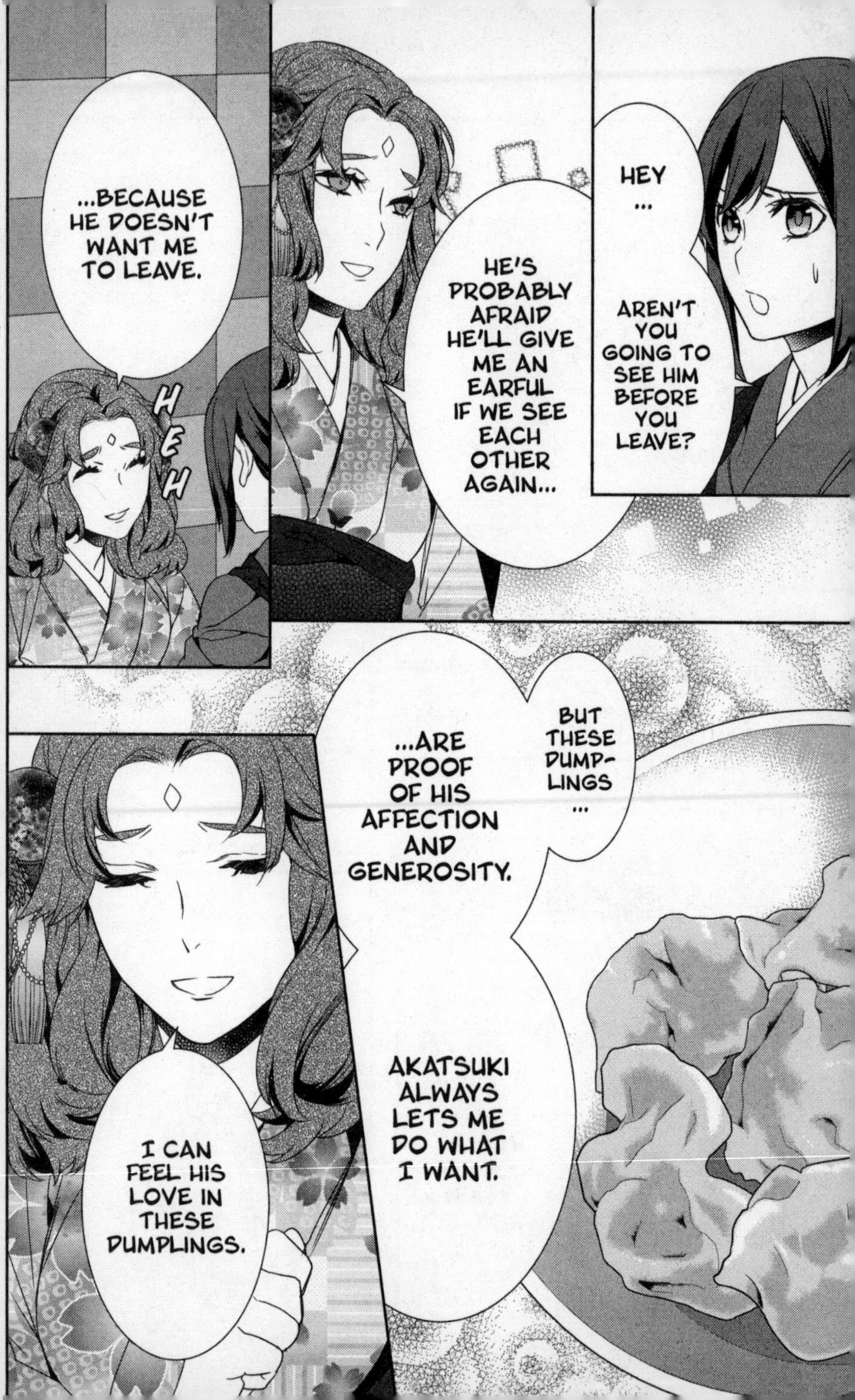
HEY ...
AREN'T YOU GOING TO SEE HIM BEFORE YOU LEAVE?
HE'S PROBABLY AFRAID HE'LL GIVE ME AN EARFUL IF WE SEE EACH OTHER AGAIN...
...BECAUSE HE DOESN'T WANT ME TO LEAVE.
HEH
AKATSUKI ALWAYS LETS ME DO WHAT I WANT.
BUT THESE DUMPLINGS ...
...ARE PROOF OF HIS AFFECTION AND GENEROSITY.
I CAN FEEL HIS LOVE IN THESE DUMPLINGS.

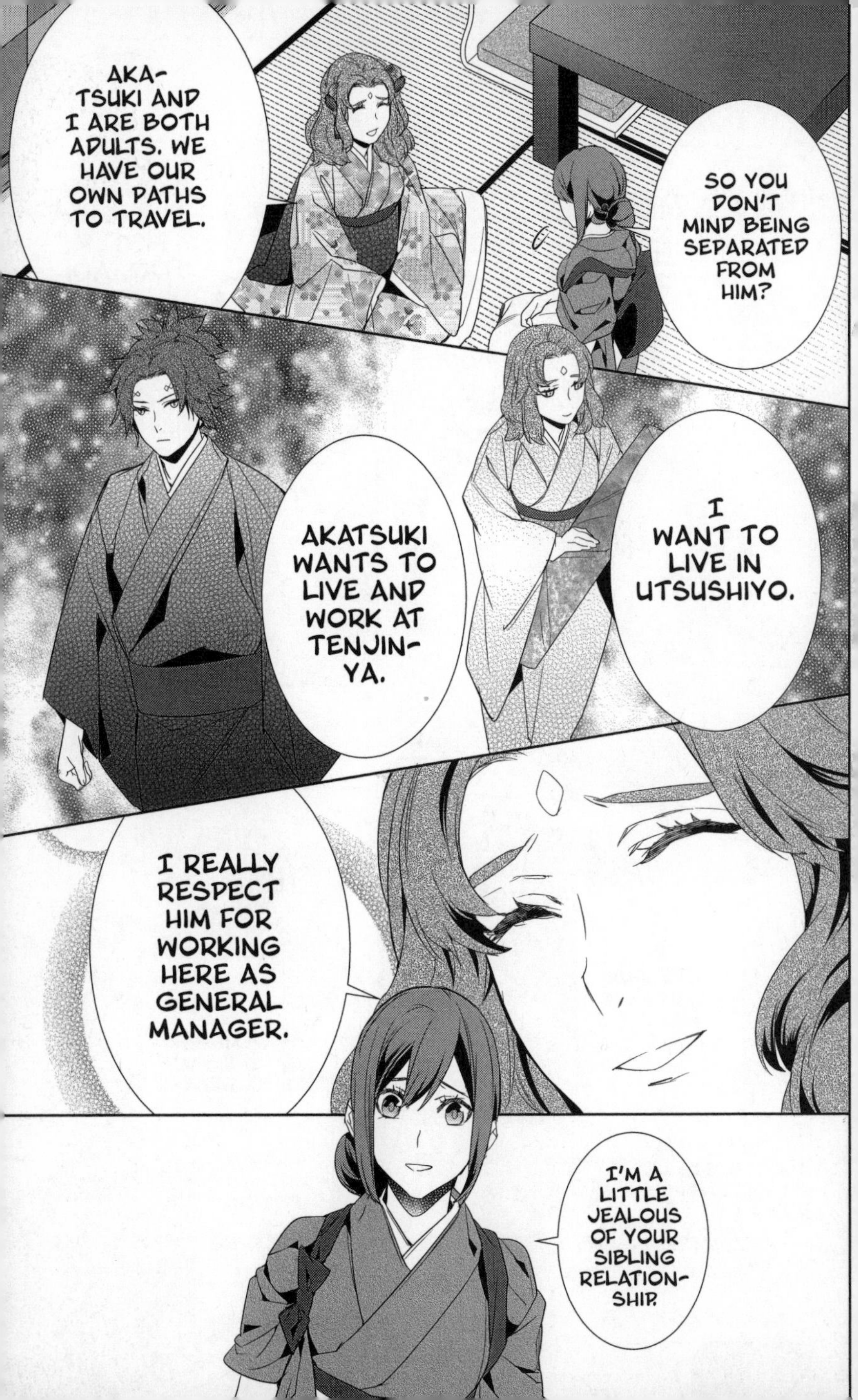
SO YOU DON'T MIND BEING SEPARATED FROM HIM?
AKA-TSUKI AND I ARE BOTH ADULTS. WE HAVE OUR OWN PATHS TO TRAVEL.
I WANT TO LIVE IN UTSUSHIYO.
AKATSUKI WANTS TO LIVE AND WORK AT TENJIN-YA.
I REALLY RESPECT HIM FOR WORKING HERE AS GENERAL MANAGER.
I'M A LITTLE JEALOUS OF YOUR SIBLING RELATION-SHIP.

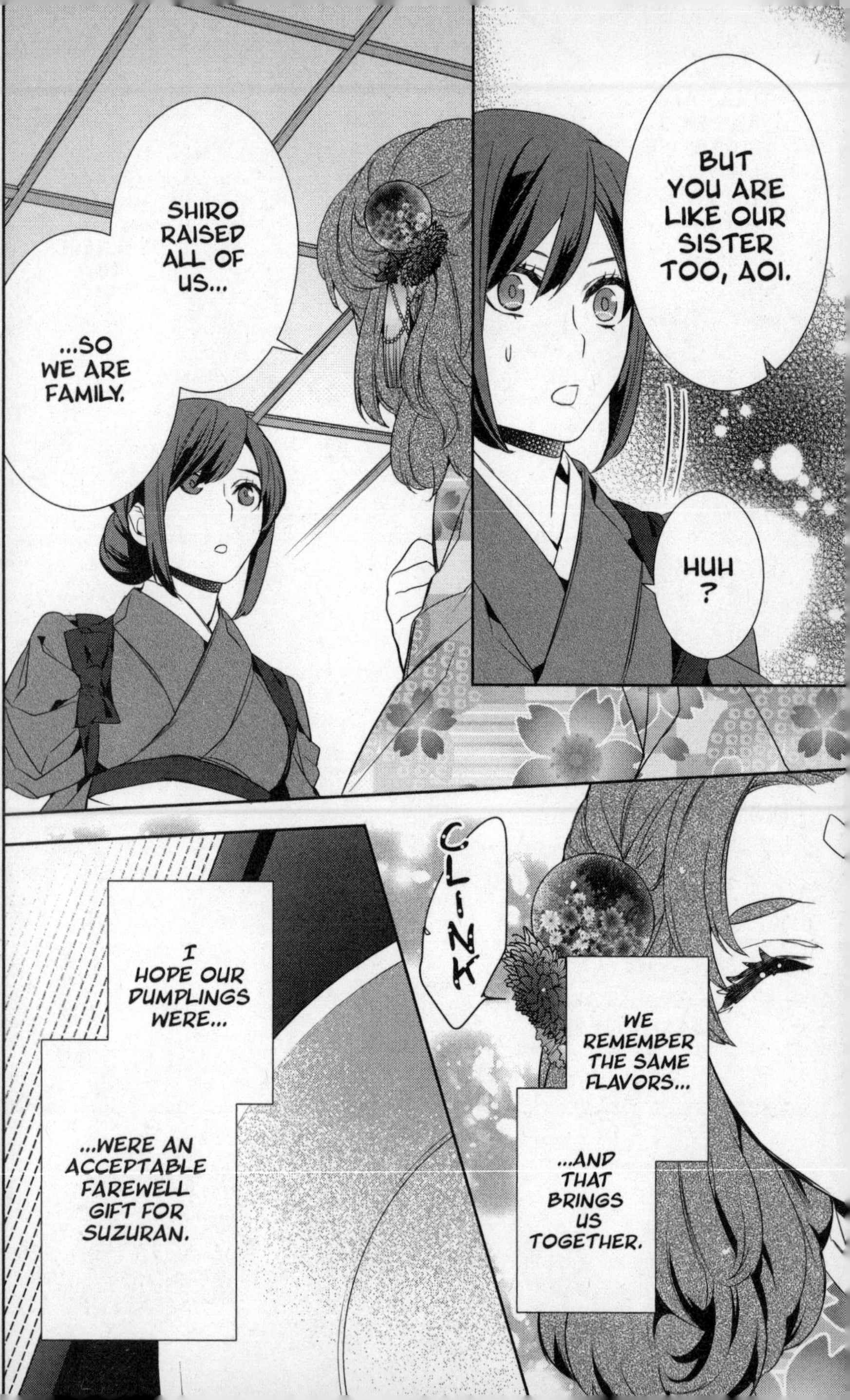
BUT YOU ARE LIKE OUR SISTER TOO, AOI.
HUH?
SHIRO RAISED ALL OF US...
...SO WE ARE FAMILY.
WE REMEMBER THE SAME FLAVORS...
...AND THAT BRINGS US TOGETHER.
CLINK
I HOPE OUR DUMPLINGS WERE...
...WERE AN ACCEPTABLE FAREWELL GIFT FOR SUZURAN.

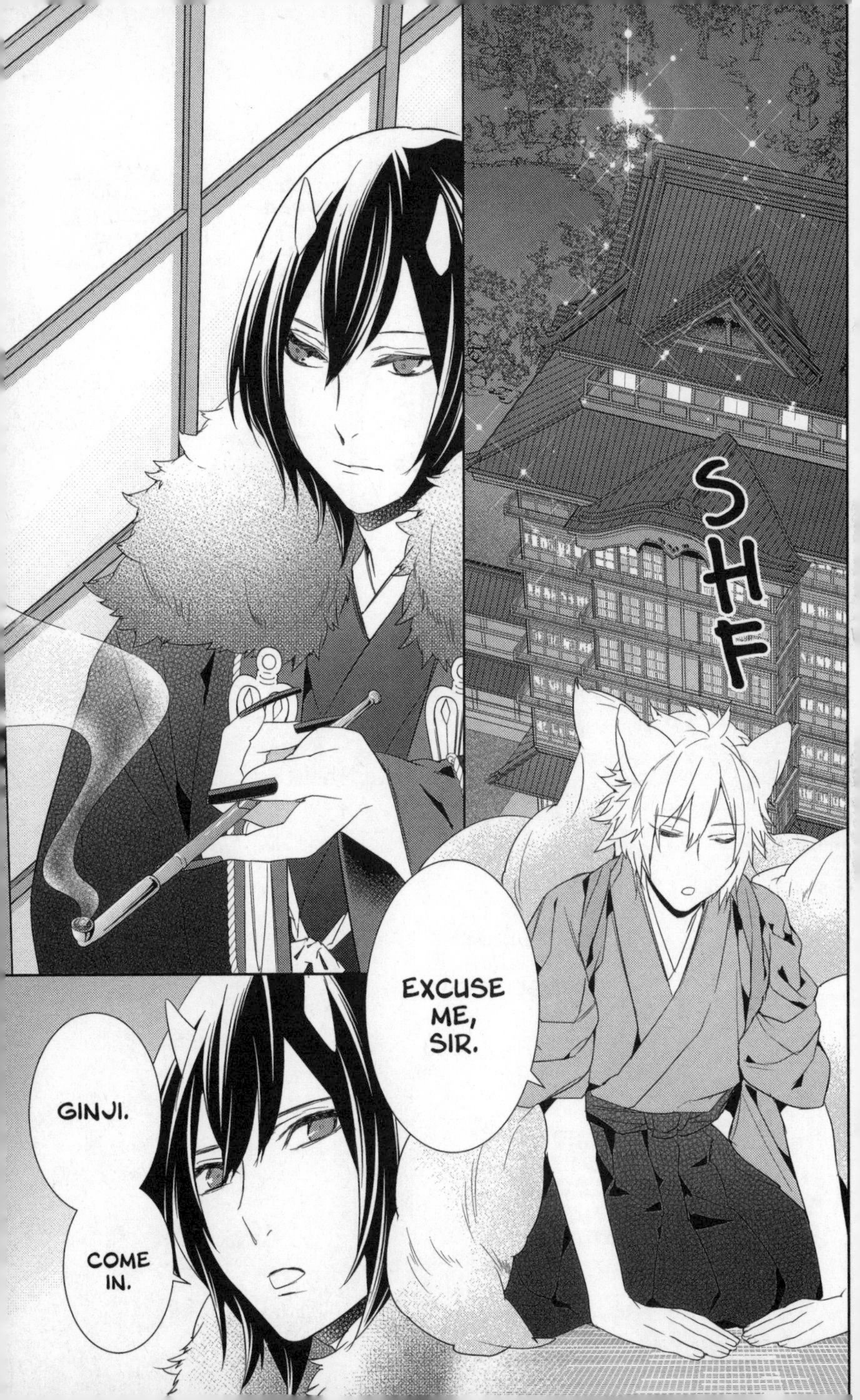
SHF
EXCUSE ME, SIR.
GINJI.
COME IN.

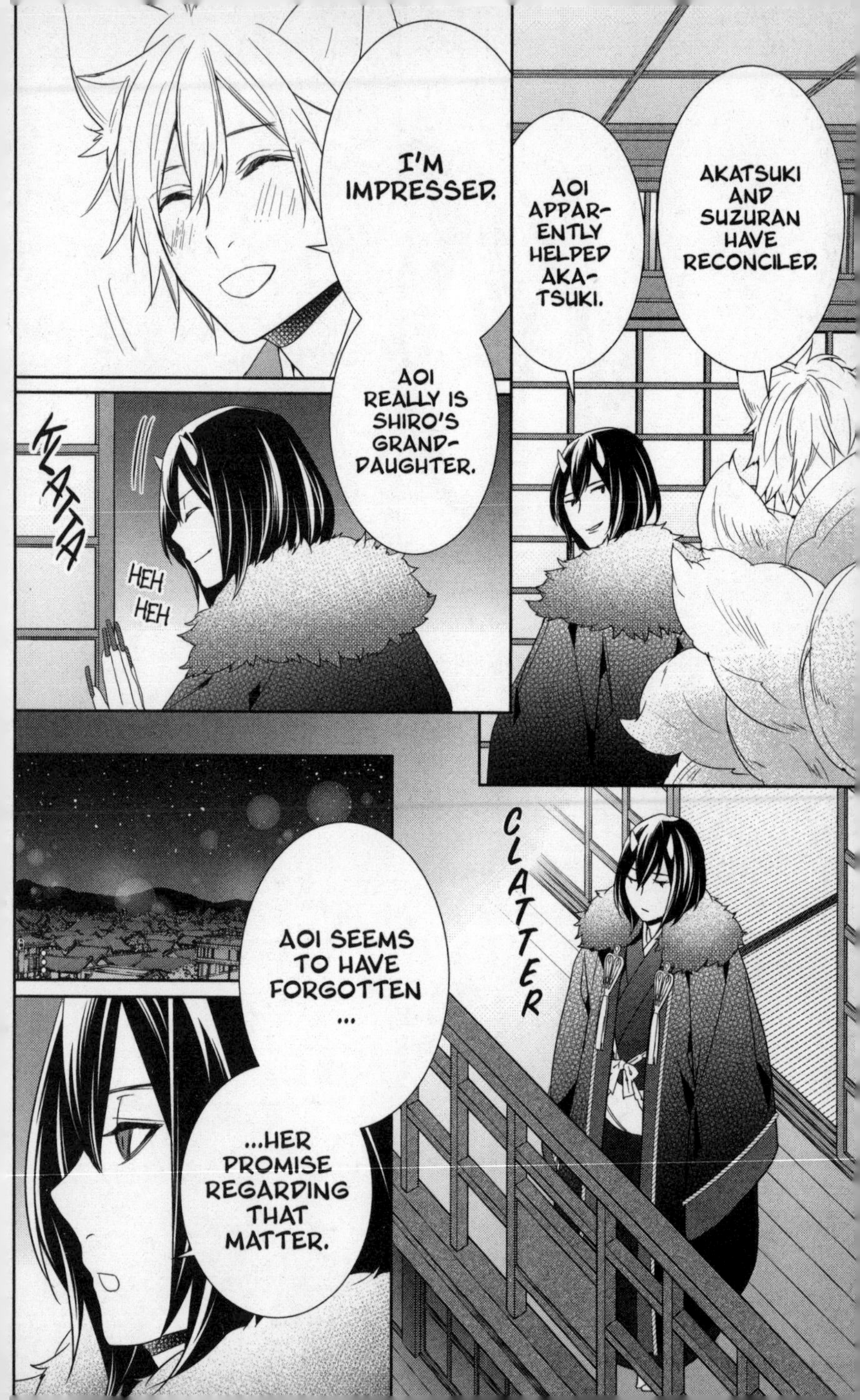
AKATSUKI AND SUZURAN HAVE RECONCILED.
AOI APPARENTLY HELPED AKATSUKI.
I'M IMPRESSED.
AOI REALLY IS SHIRO'S GRANDDAUGHTER.
KLATTA
HEH HEH
CLATTER
AOI SEEMS TO HAVE FORGOTTEN...
...HER PROMISE REGARDING THAT MATTER.

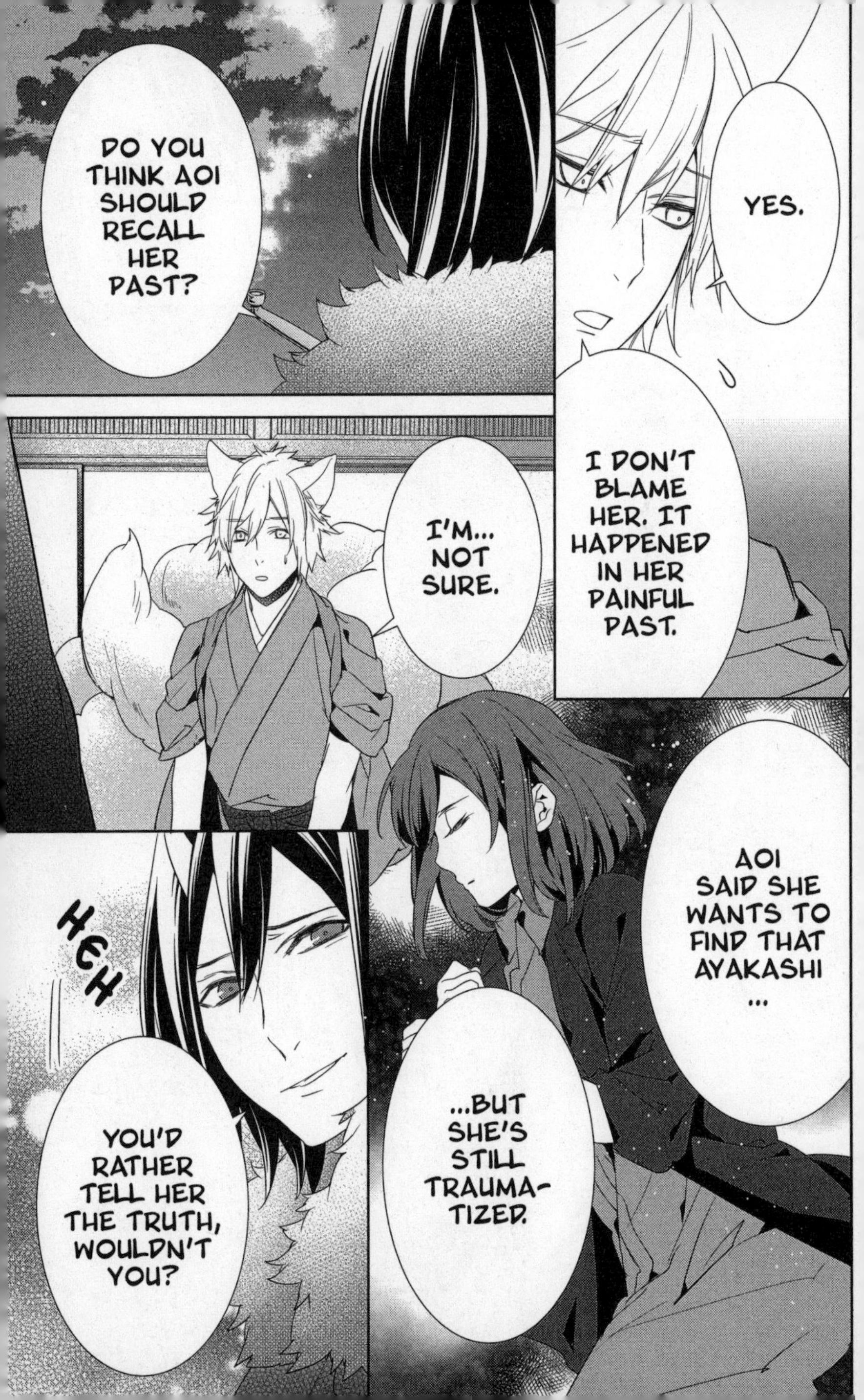
YES.
I DON'T BLAME HER. IT HAPPENED IN HER PAINFUL PAST.
DO YOU THINK AOI SHOULD RECALL HER PAST?
I'M... NOT SURE.
AOI SAID SHE WANTS TO FIND THAT AYAKASHI ...
...BUT SHE'S STILL TRAUMATIZED.
HEH
YOU'D RATHER TELL HER THE TRUTH, WOULDN'T YOU?

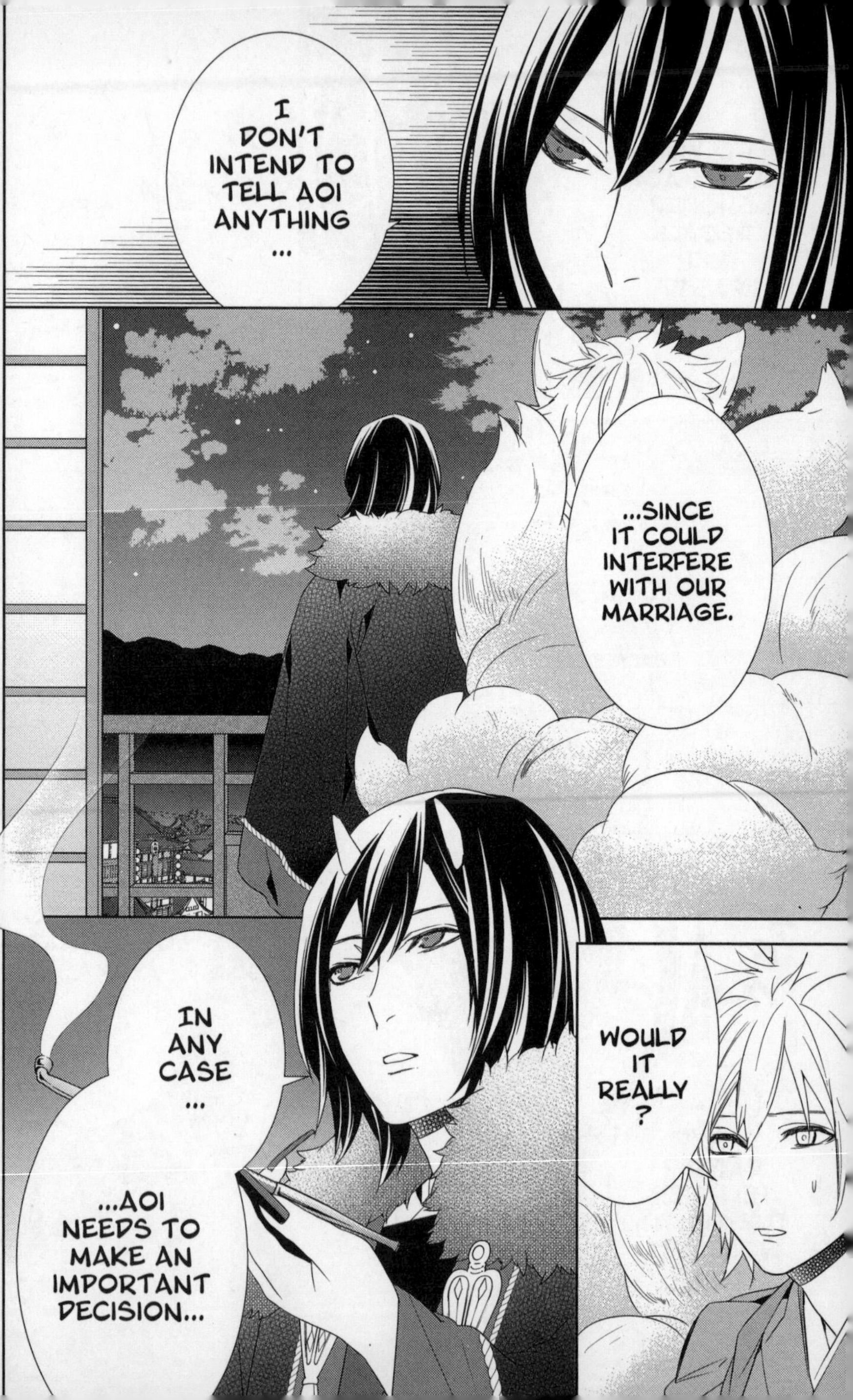
I DON'T INTEND TO TELL AOI ANYTHING...
...SINCE IT COULD INTERFERE WITH OUR MARRIAGE.
WOULD IT REALLY?
IN ANY CASE...
...AOI NEEDS TO MAKE AN IMPORTANT DECISION...

Kakuriyo

Bed & Breakfast for Spirits

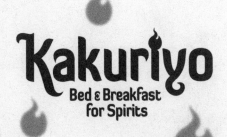

Kakuriyo
Bed & Breakfast
for Spirits

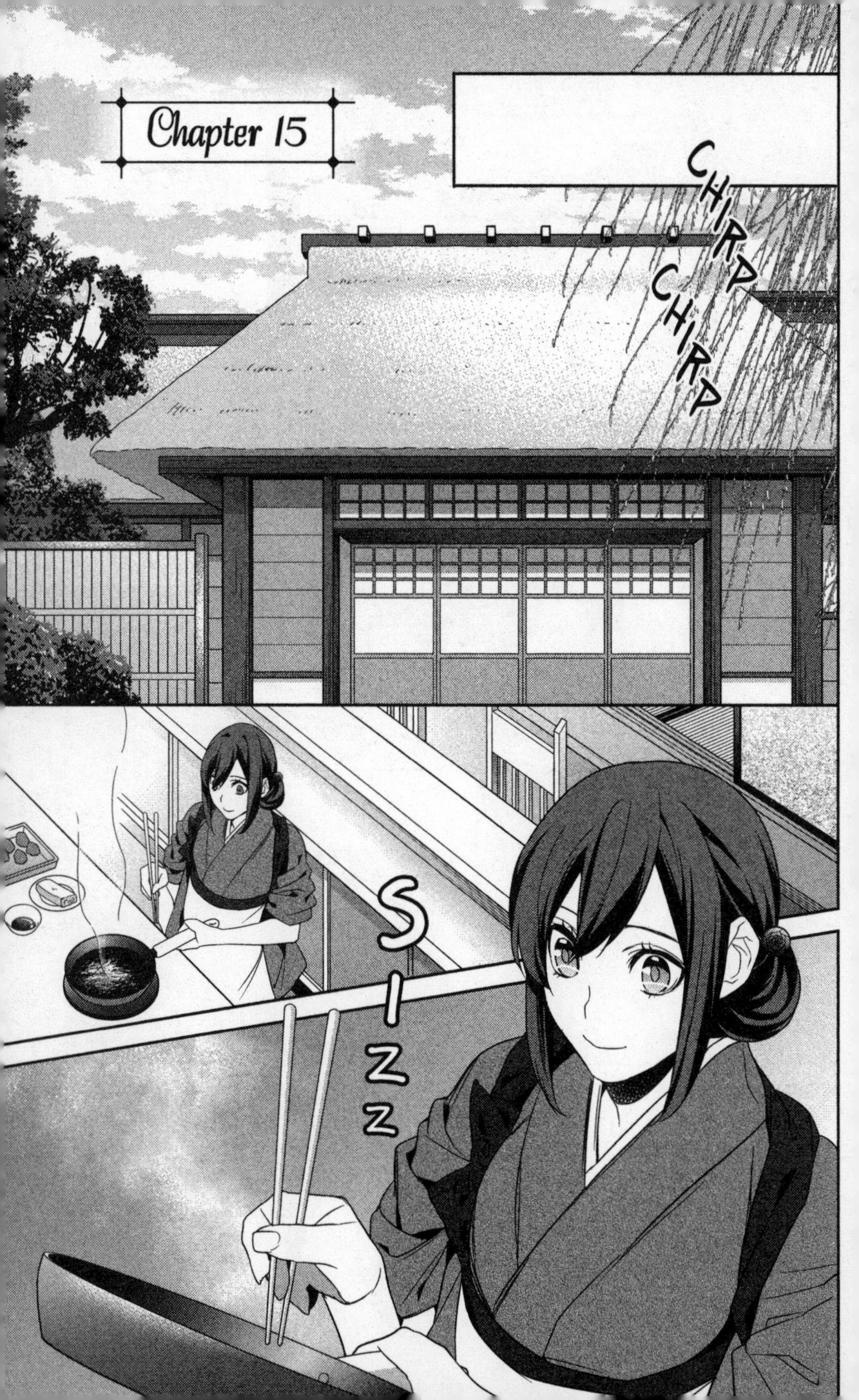
Chapter 15
CHIRP CHIRP
CHIRP
SIZZ
SIZZZ

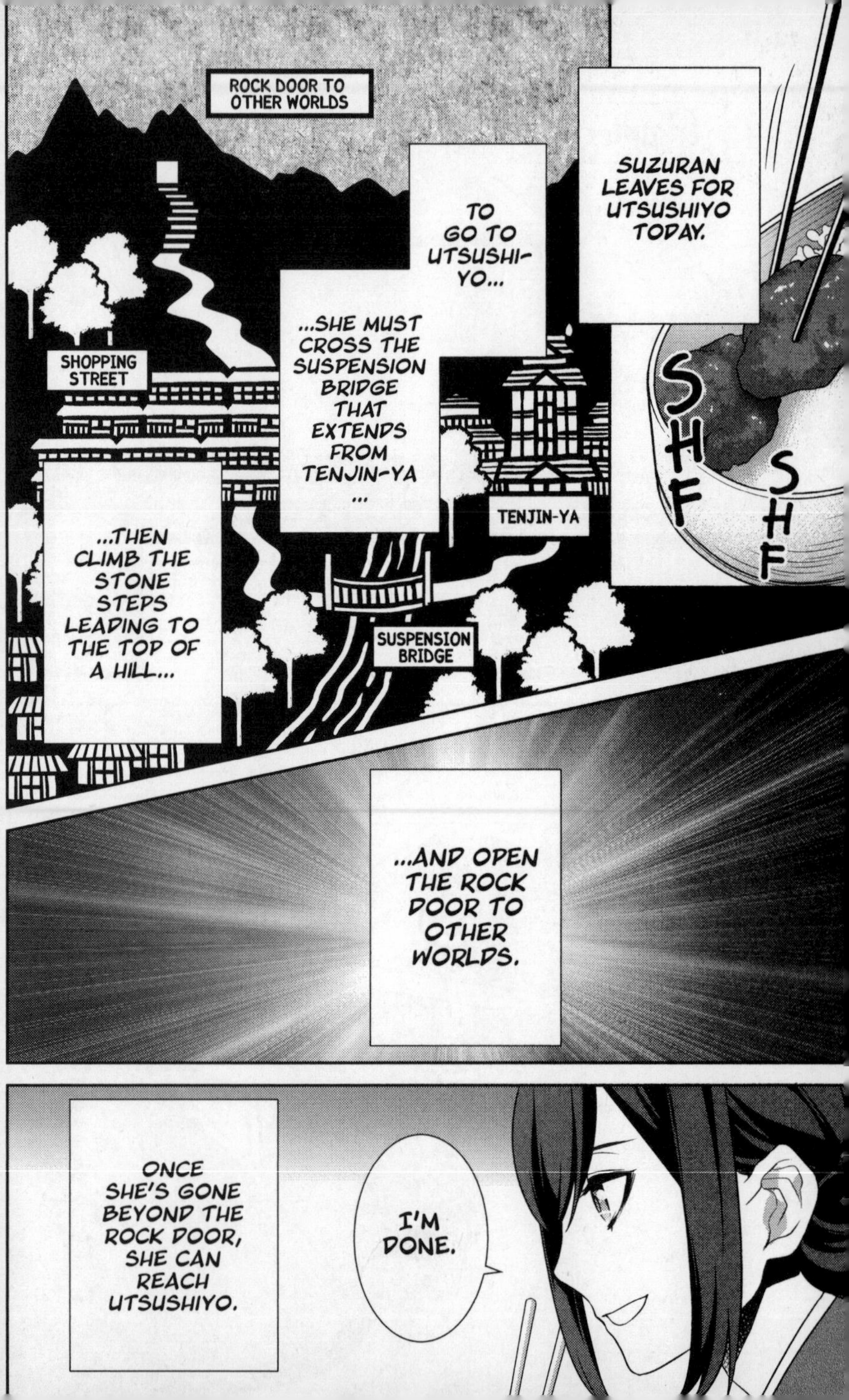
SUZURAN LEAVES FOR UTSUSHIYO TODAY.
SHF SHF
TO GO TO UTSUSHI-YO...
ROCK DOOR TO OTHER WORLDS
...SHE MUST CROSS THE SUSPENSION BRIDGE THAT EXTENDS FROM TENJIN-YA...
TENJIN-YA
SHOPPING STREET
...THEN CLIMB THE STONE STEPS LEADING TO THE TOP OF A HILL...
SUSPENSION BRIDGE
...AND OPEN THE ROCK DOOR TO OTHER WORLDS.
I'M DONE.
ONCE SHE'S GONE BEYOND THE ROCK DOOR, SHE CAN REACH UTSUSHIYO.

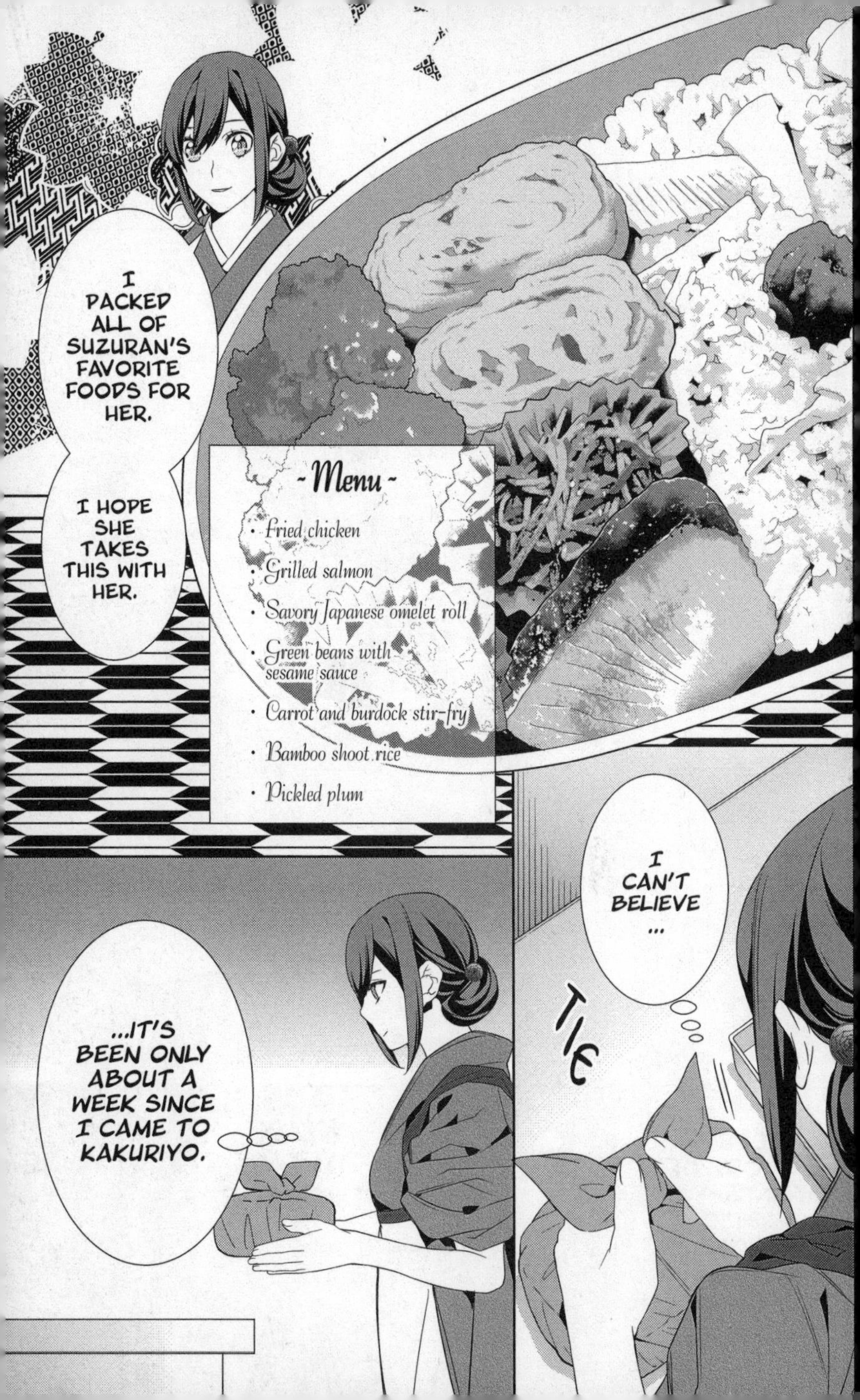
I PACKED ALL OF SUZURAN'S FAVORITE FOODS FOR HER.
I HOPE SHE TAKES THIS WITH HER.
~Menu~
· Fried chicken
· Grilled salmon
· Savory Japanese omelet roll
· Green beans with sesame sauce
· Carrot and burdock stir-fry
· Bamboo shoot rice
· Pickled plum
I CAN'T BELIEVE ...
TIE
...IT'S BEEN ONLY ABOUT A WEEK SINCE I CAME TO KAKURIYO.

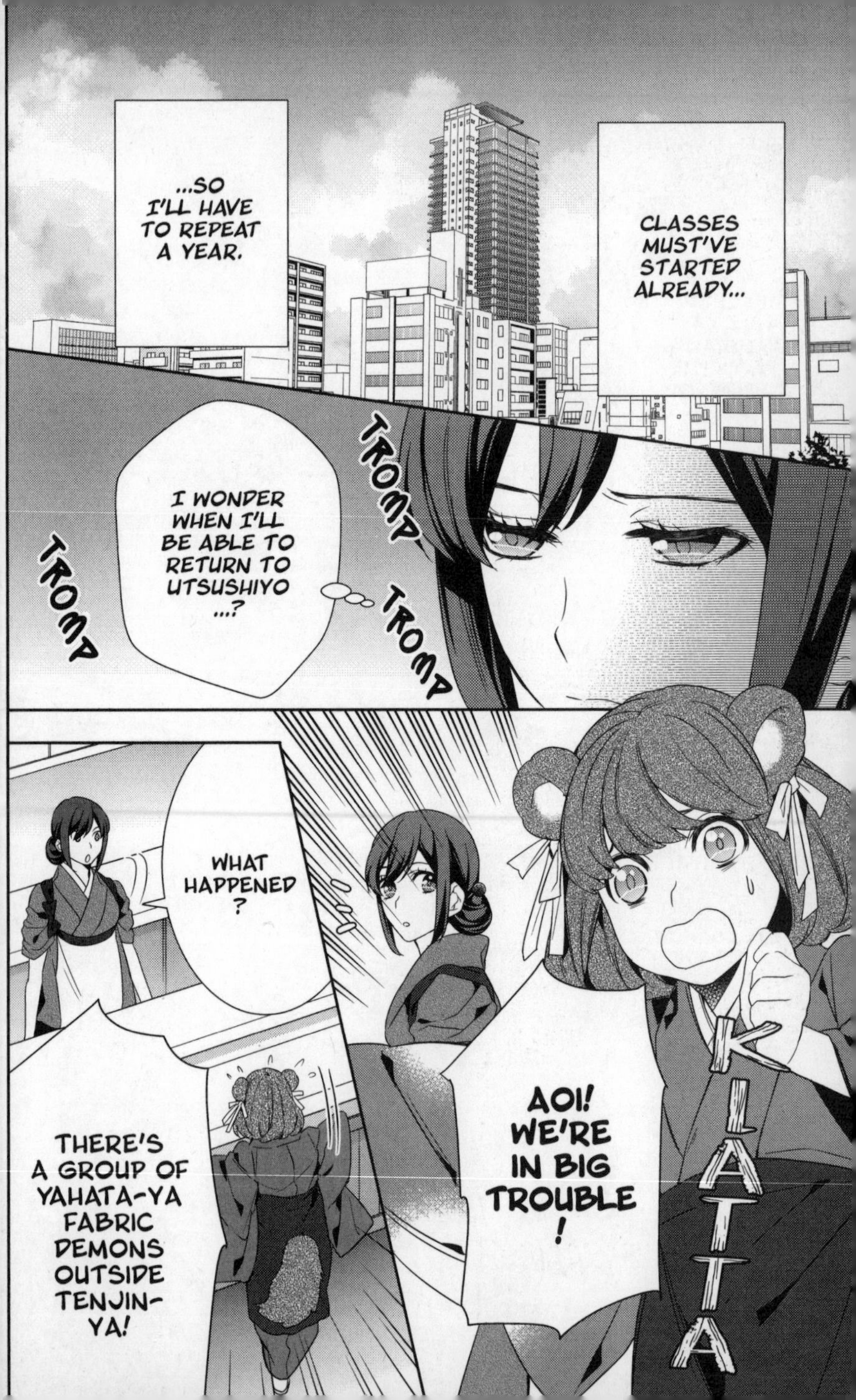
CLASSES MUST'VE STARTED ALREADY...
...SO I'LL HAVE TO REPEAT A YEAR.
TROMP
TROMP
I WONDER WHEN I'LL BE ABLE TO RETURN TO UTSUSHIYO ...?
TROMP
KLATTA
AOI! WE'RE IN BIG TROUBLE!
WHAT HAPPENED?
THERE'S A GROUP OF YAHATA-YA FABRIC DEMONS OUTSIDE TENJIN-YA!

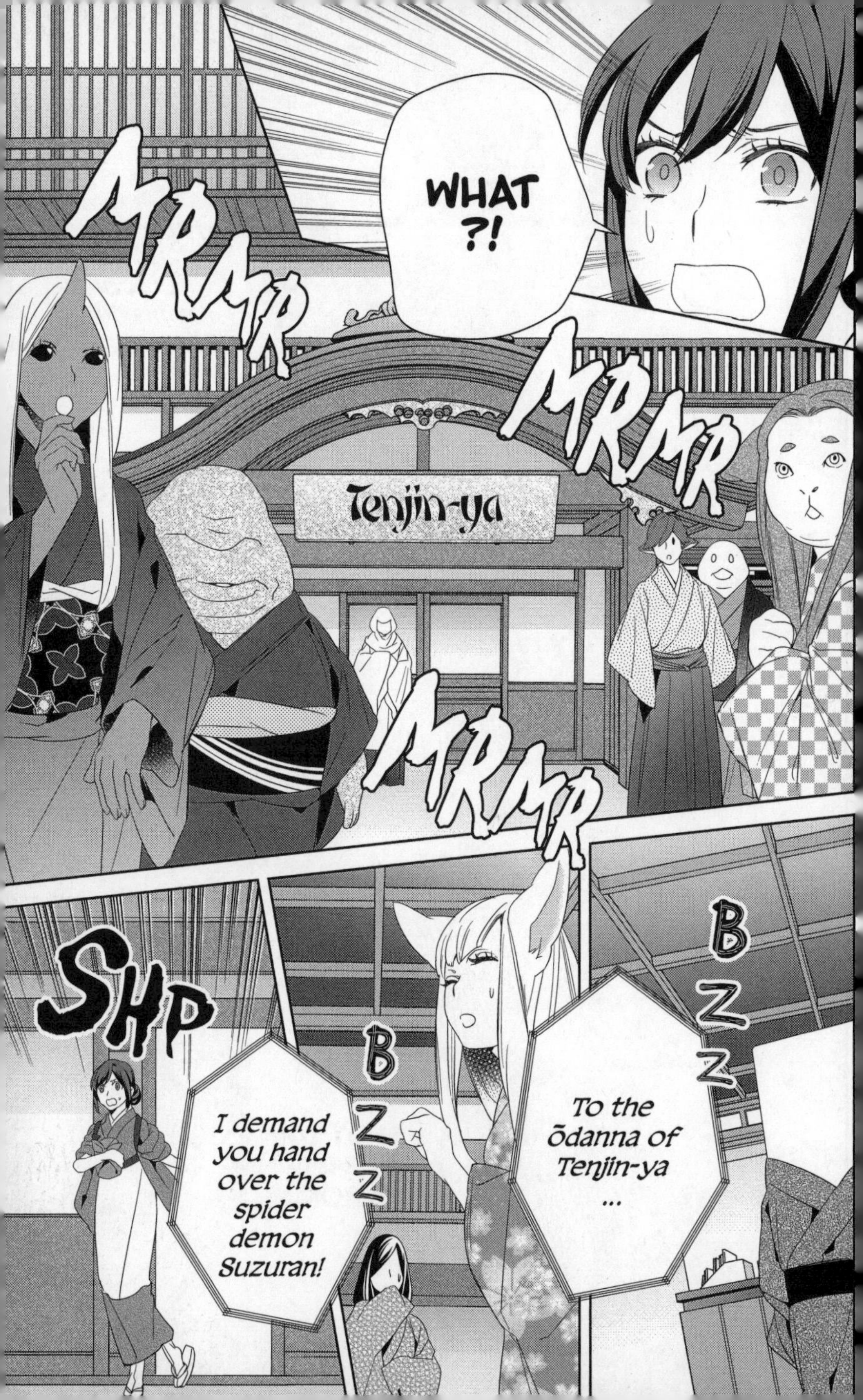
WHAT ?!
MRMR
MRMR
Tenjin-ya
MRMR
BZZ
To the ōdanna of Tenjin-ya ...
BZZ
I demand you hand over the spider demon Suzuran!
SHP

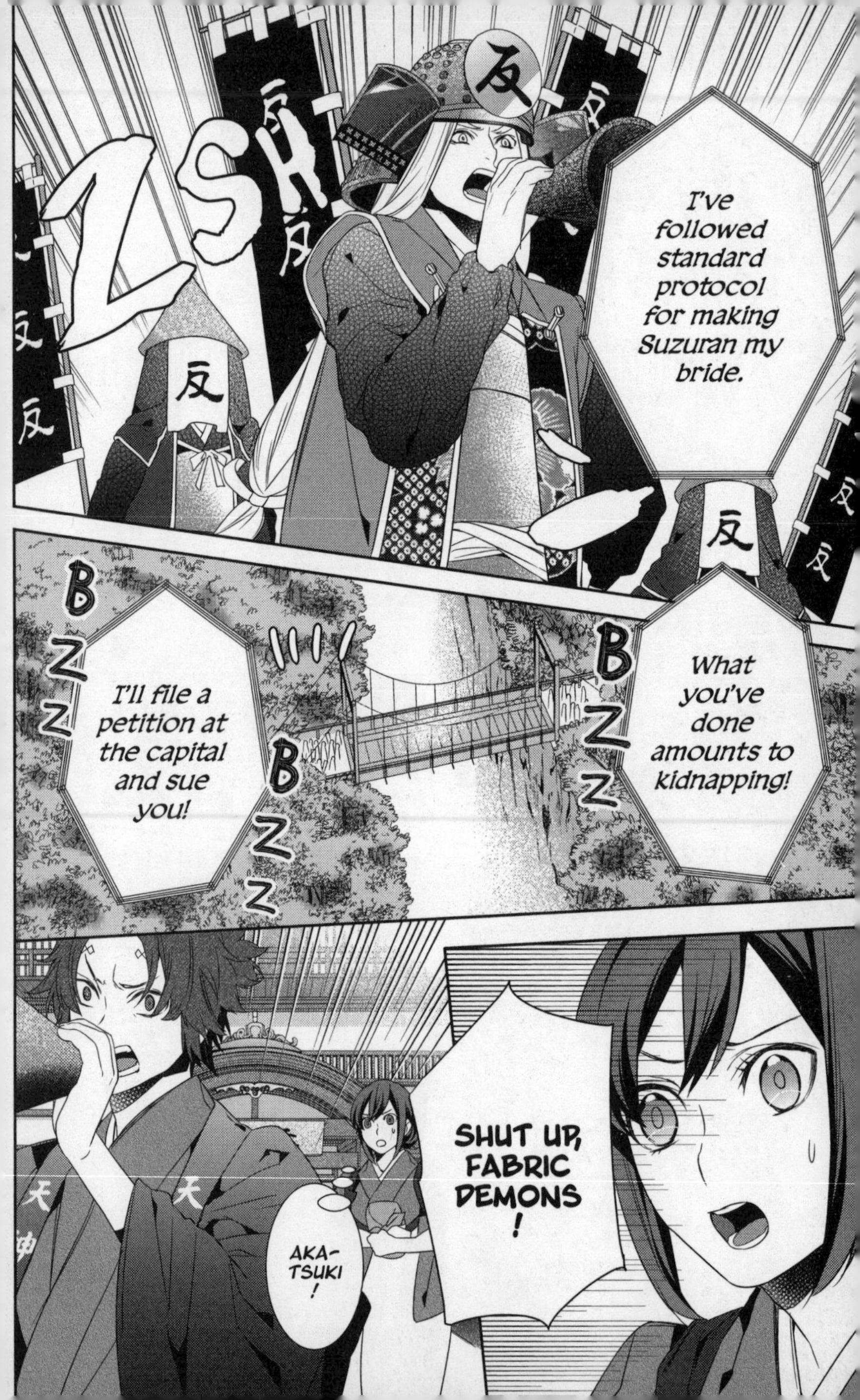
ZSH
I've followed standard protocol for making Suzuran my bride.
What you've done amounts to kidnapping!
BZZ
I'll file a petition at the capital and sue you!
BZZ
BZZ
SHUT UP, FABRIC DEMONS!
AKA-TSUKI!

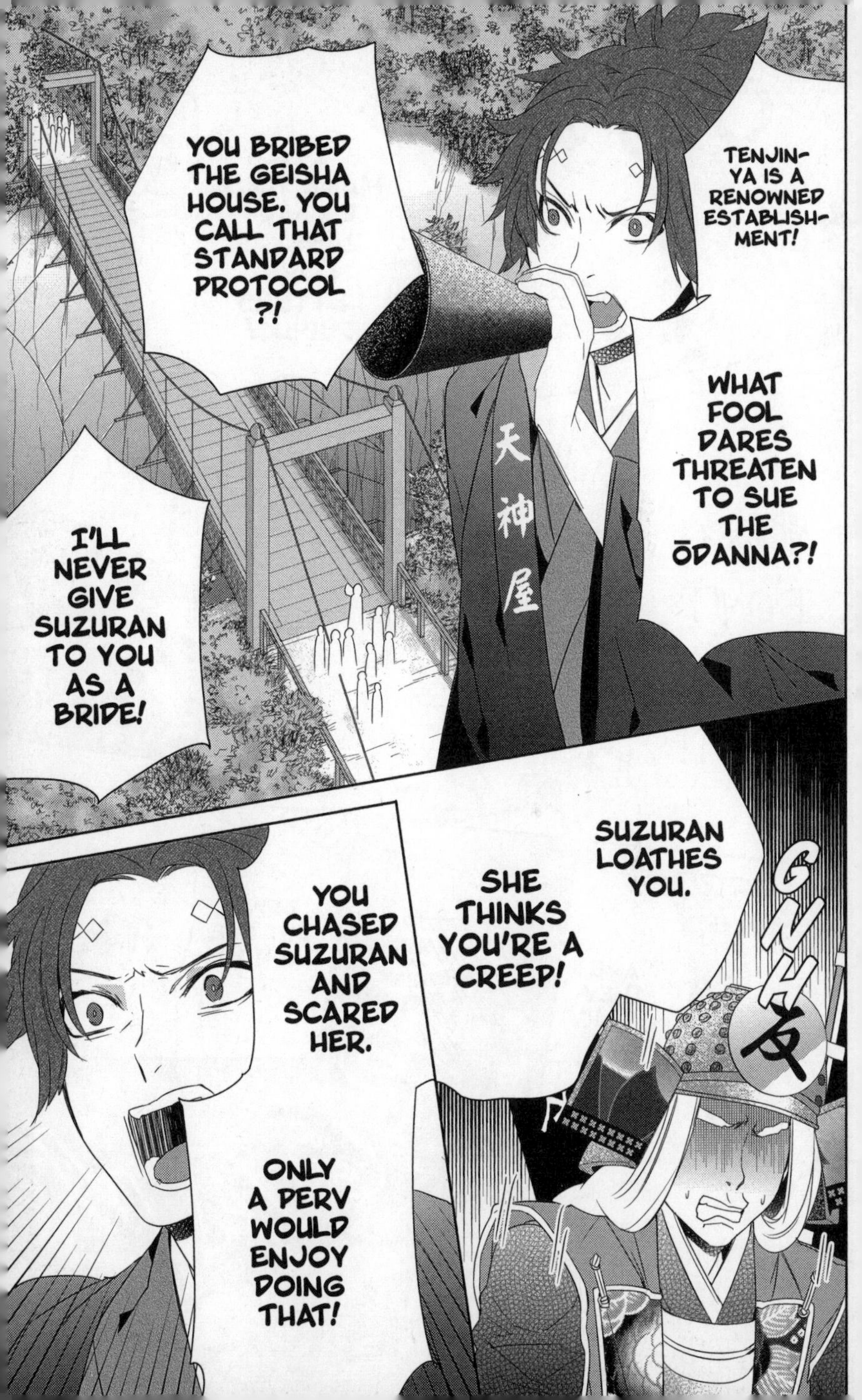
TENJIN-YA IS A RENOWNED ESTABLISHMENT!
WHAT FOOL DARES THREATEN TO SUE THE ŌDANNA?!
YOU BRIBED THE GEISHA HOUSE. YOU CALL THAT STANDARD PROTOCOL?!
I'LL NEVER GIVE SUZURAN TO YOU AS A BRIDE!
天神屋
GNH
SUZURAN LOATHES YOU.
SHE THINKS YOU'RE A CREEP!
YOU CHASED SUZURAN AND SCARED HER.
ONLY A PERV WOULD ENJOY DOING THAT!

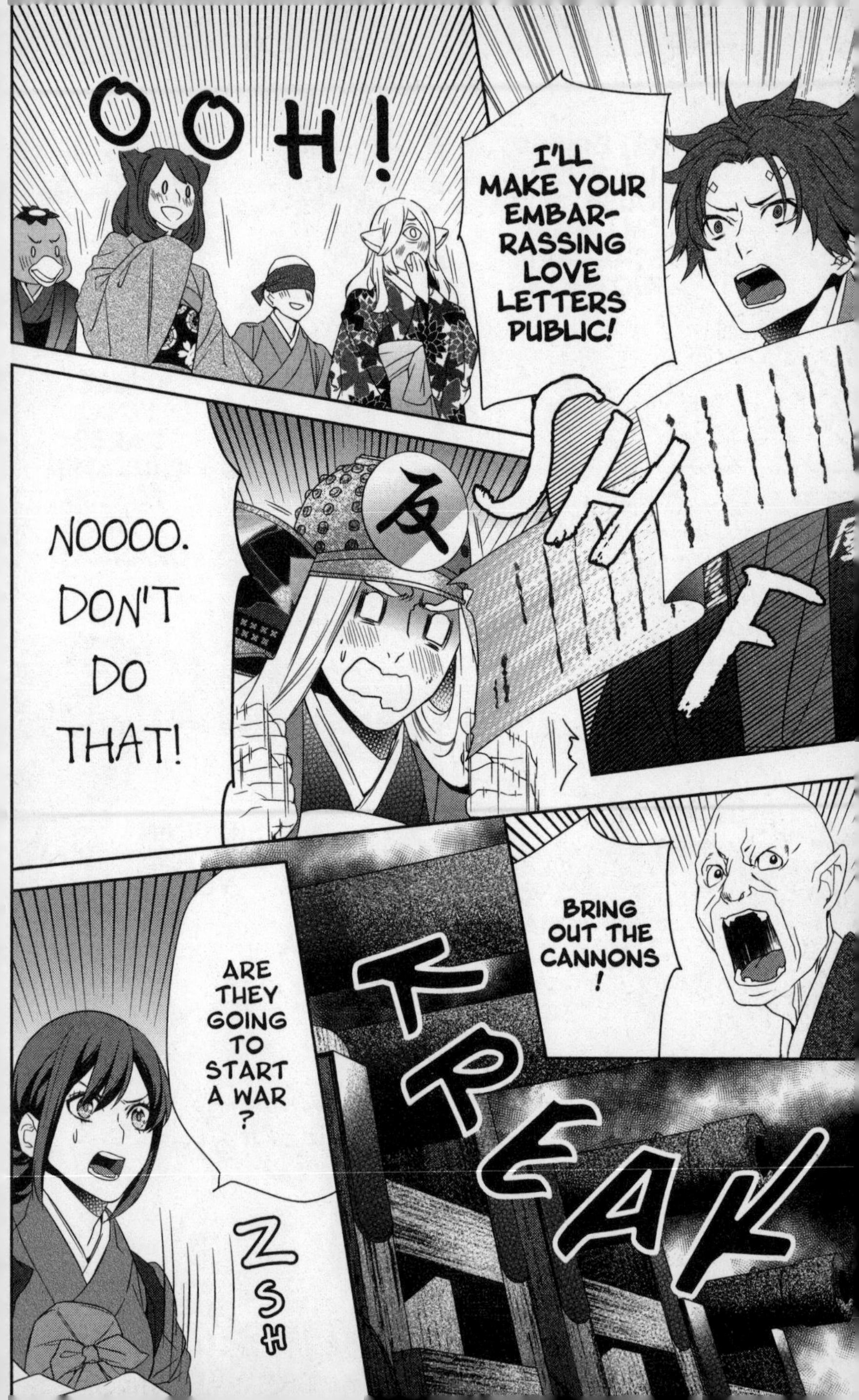
I'LL MAKE YOUR EMBARRASSING LOVE LETTERS PUBLIC!
OOH!
SHFF
NOOOO. DON'T DO THAT!
BRING OUT THE CANNONS!
KREAK
ARE THEY GOING TO START A WAR?
ZSH

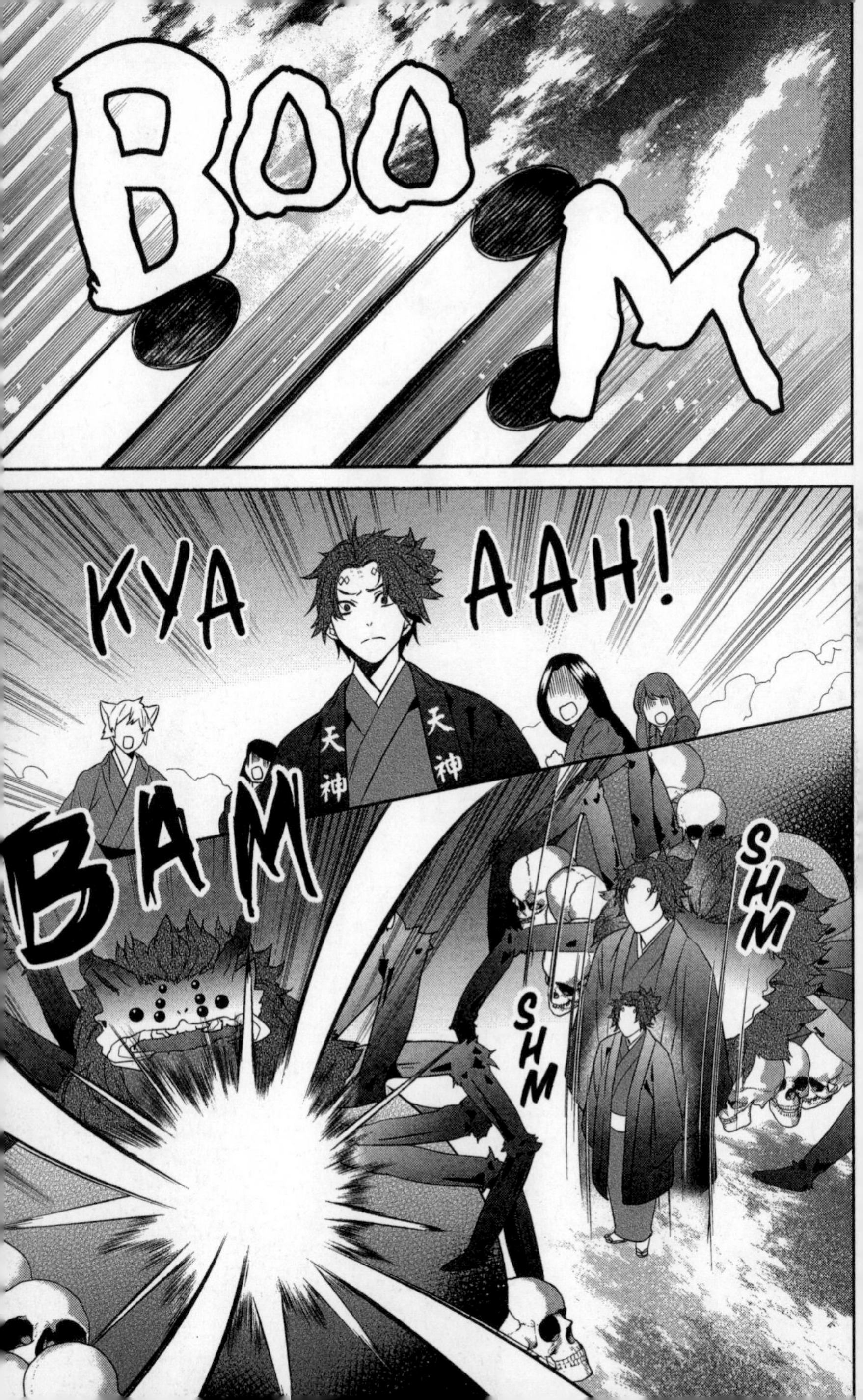
BOOM
KYA AAH!
天神
天神
SHM SHM
SHM SHM
BAM

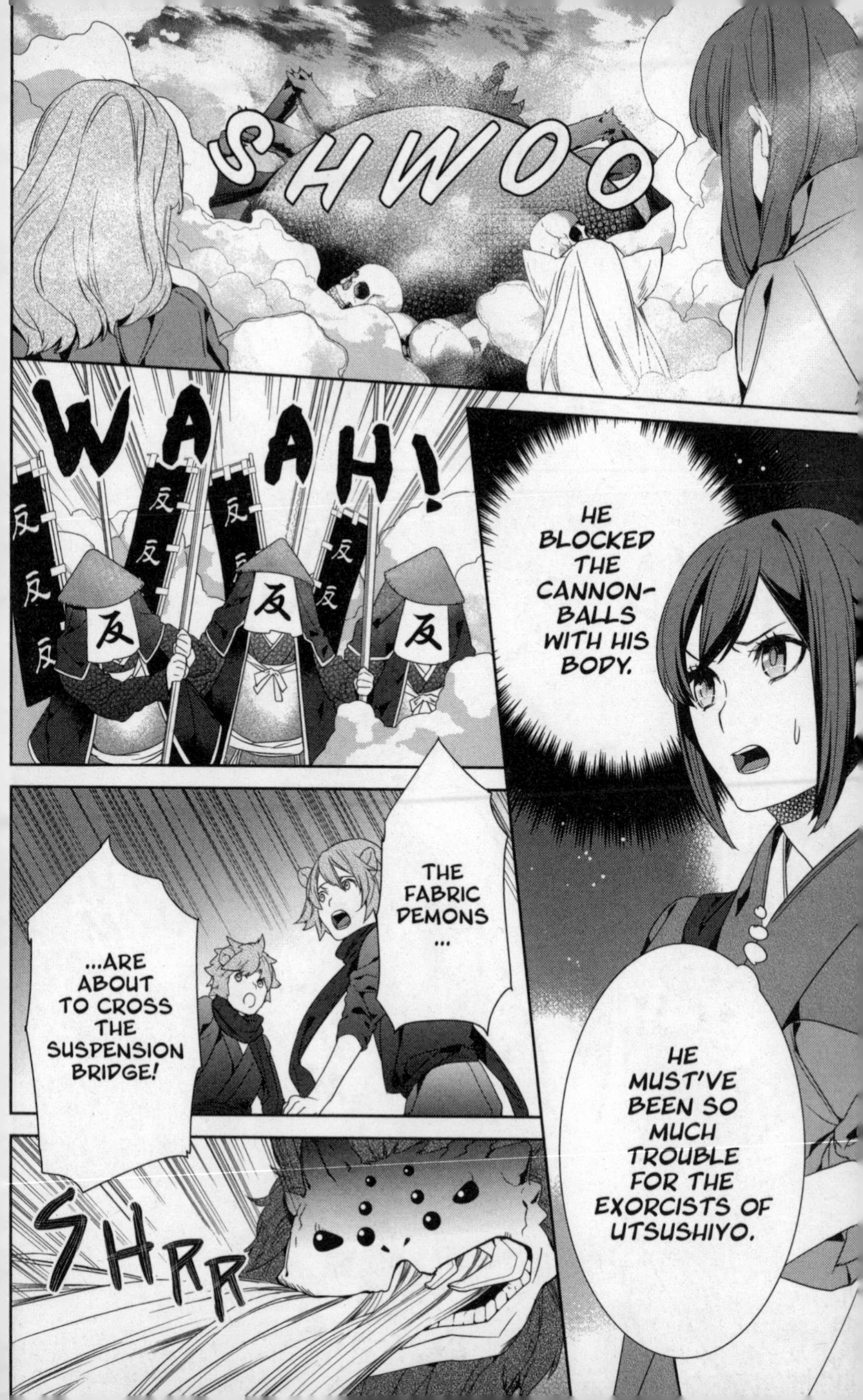
SHWOO
HE BLOCKED THE CANNON-BALLS WITH HIS BODY.
HE MUST'VE BEEN SO MUCH TROUBLE FOR THE EXORCISTS OF UTSUSHIYO.
WAAH!
THE FABRIC DEMONS...
...ARE ABOUT TO CROSS THE SUSPENSION BRIDGE!
SHRR

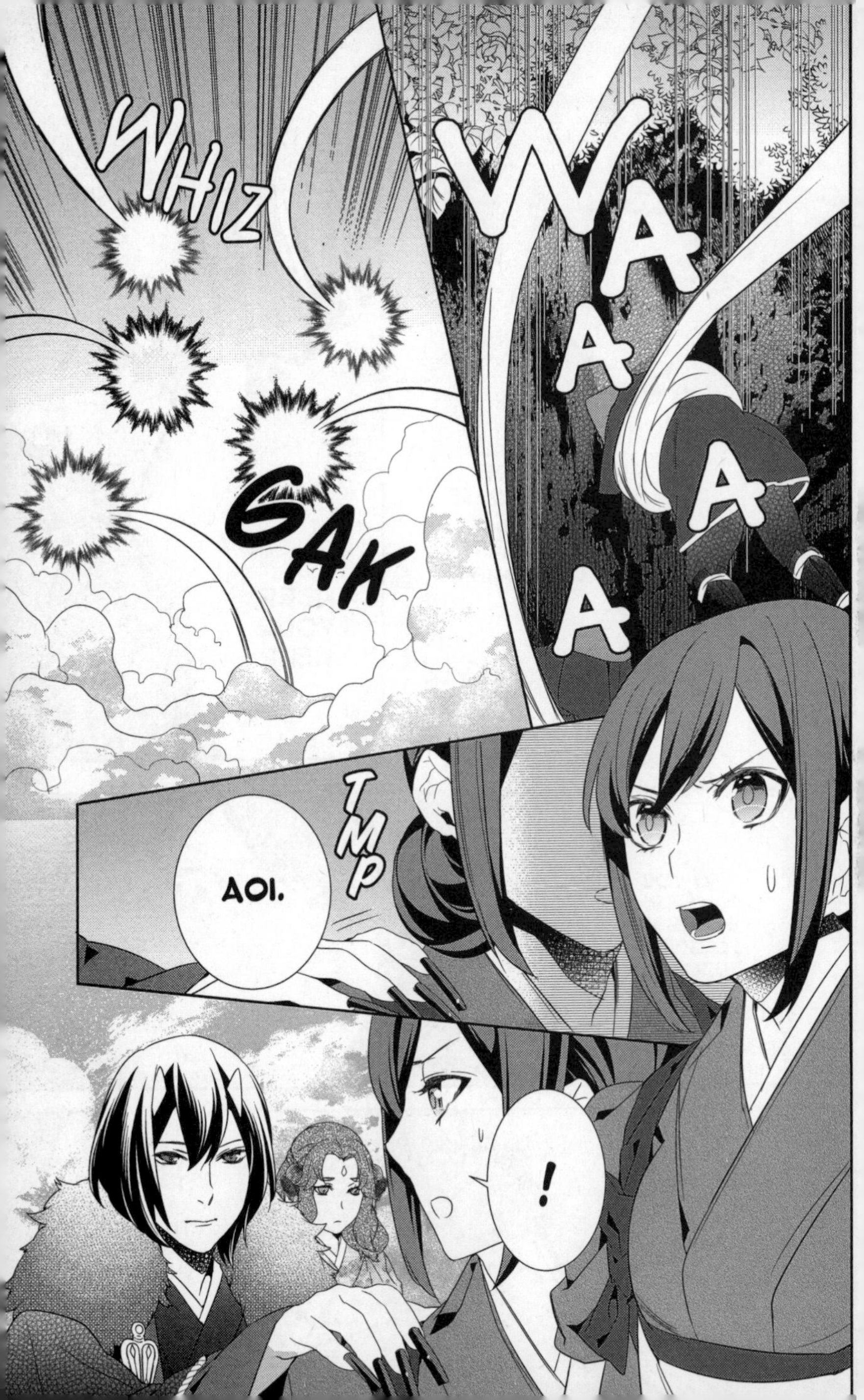
WAAAA
WHIZ
SAK
TMP
AOI.
!

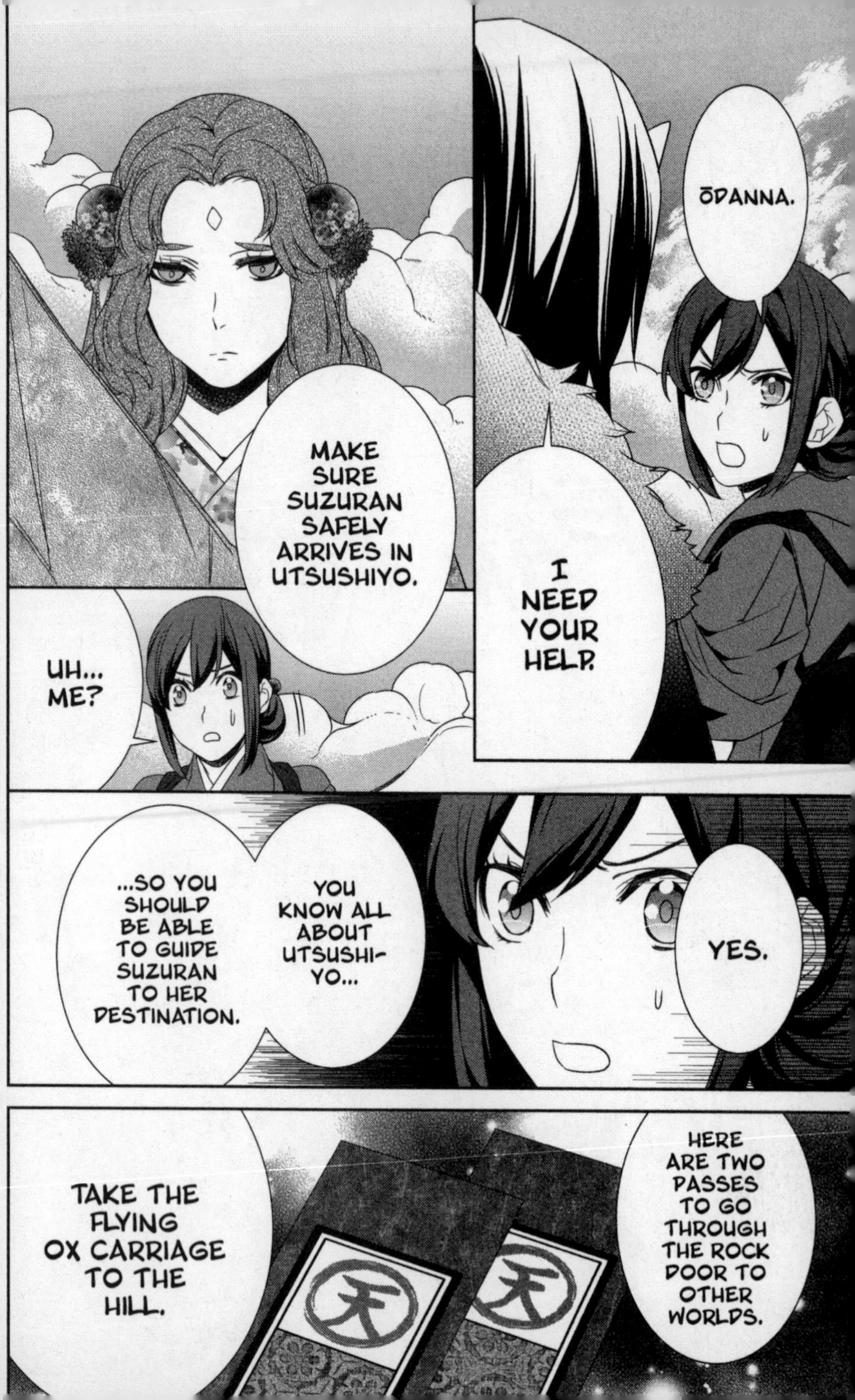
ŌDANNA.
I NEED YOUR HELP.
MAKE SURE SUZURAN SAFELY ARRIVES IN UTSUSHIYO.
UH... ME?
YES.
YOU KNOW ALL ABOUT UTSUSHI-YO...
...SO YOU SHOULD BE ABLE TO GUIDE SUZURAN TO HER DESTINATION.
HERE ARE TWO PASSES TO GO THROUGH THE ROCK DOOR TO OTHER WORLDS.
TAKE THE FLYING OX CARRIAGE TO THE HILL.
天
天

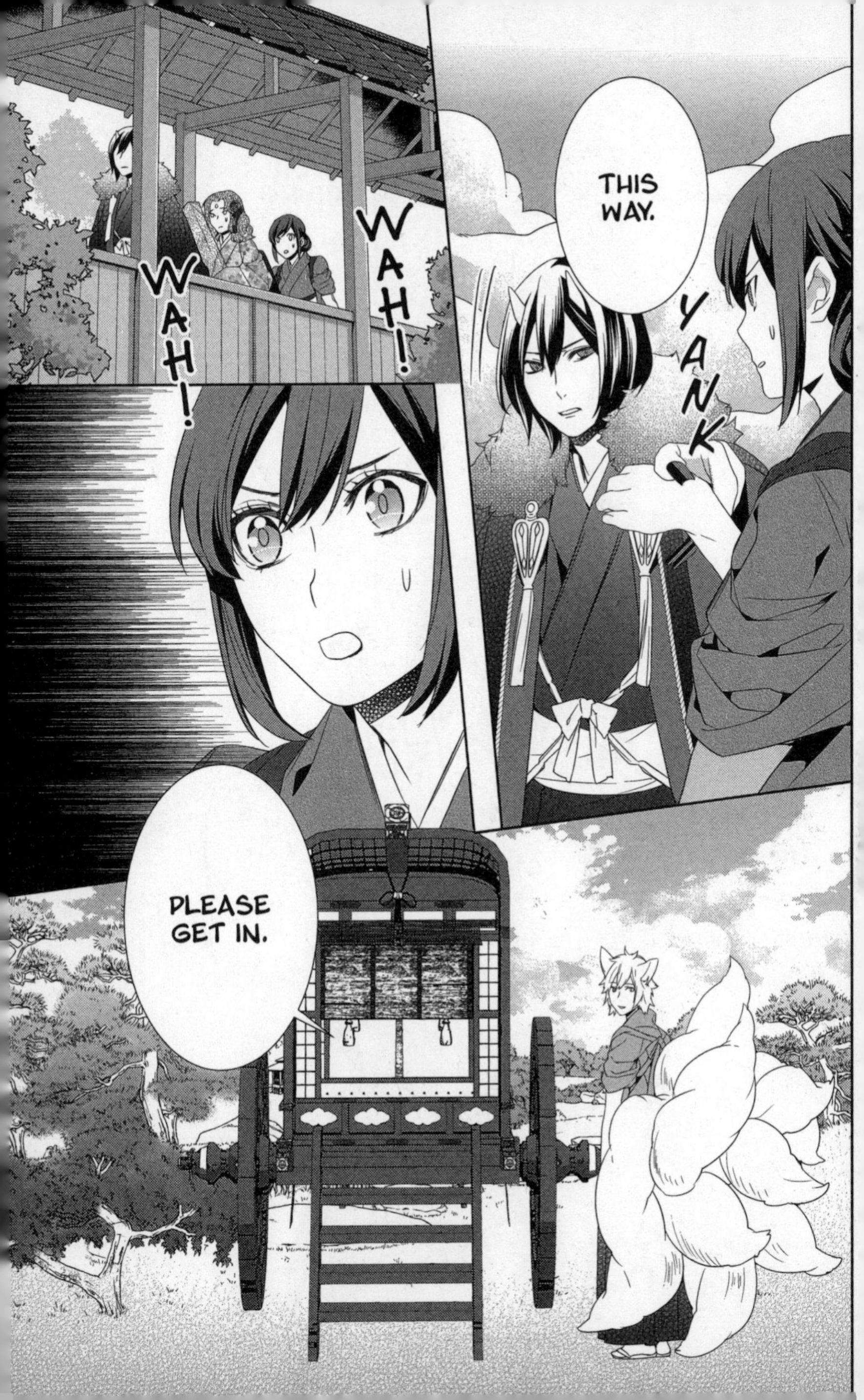

THIS WAY.
YANK
WAH!
WAH!
PLEASE GET IN.

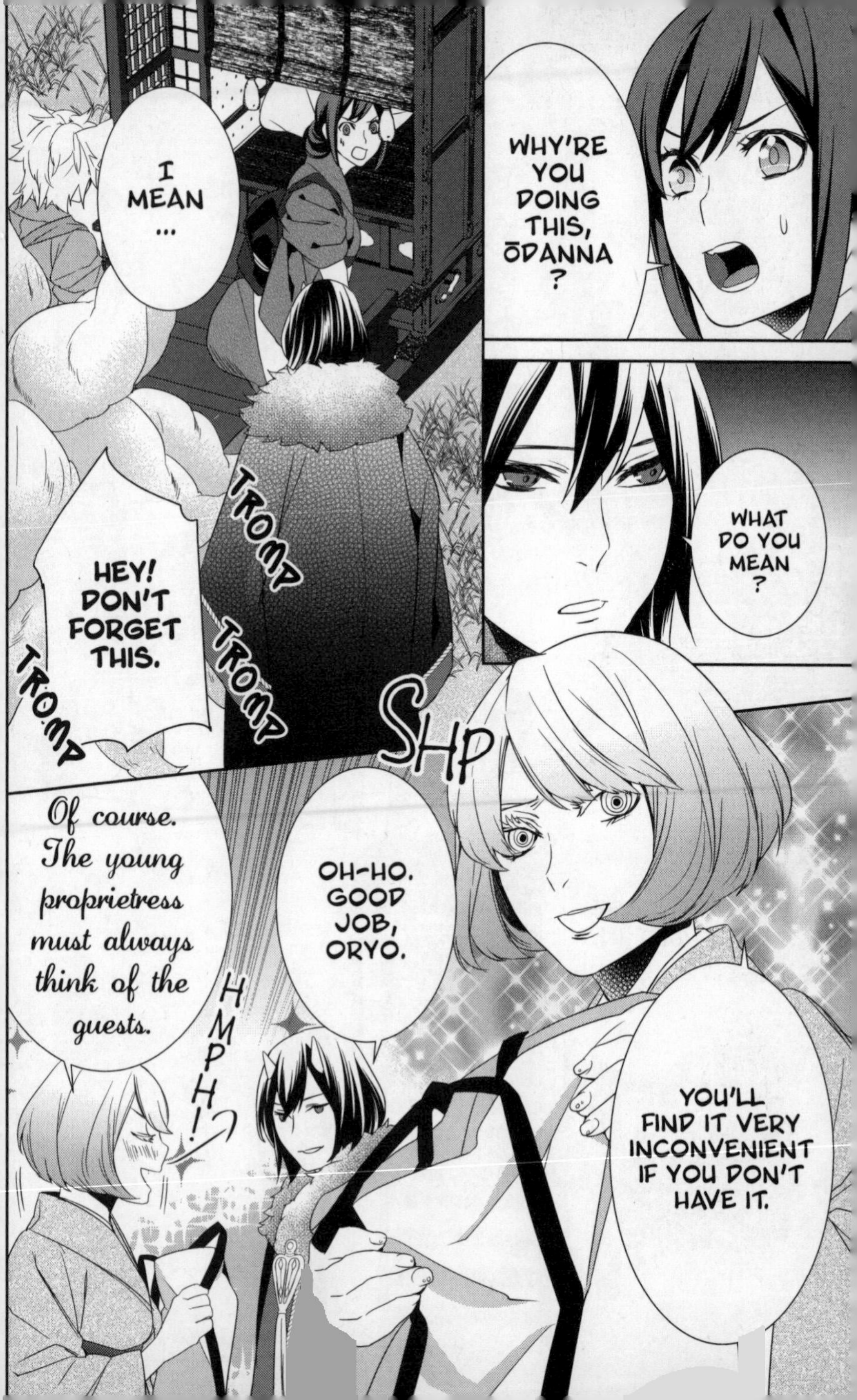
WHY'RE YOU DOING THIS, ŌDANNA?
WHAT DO YOU MEAN?
I MEAN...
TROMP
TROMP
HEY! DON'T FORGET THIS.
TROMP
SHP
YOU'LL FIND IT VERY INCONVENIENT IF YOU DON'T HAVE IT.
OH-HO. GOOD JOB, ORYO.
HMPH!
Of course. The young proprietress must always think of the guests.

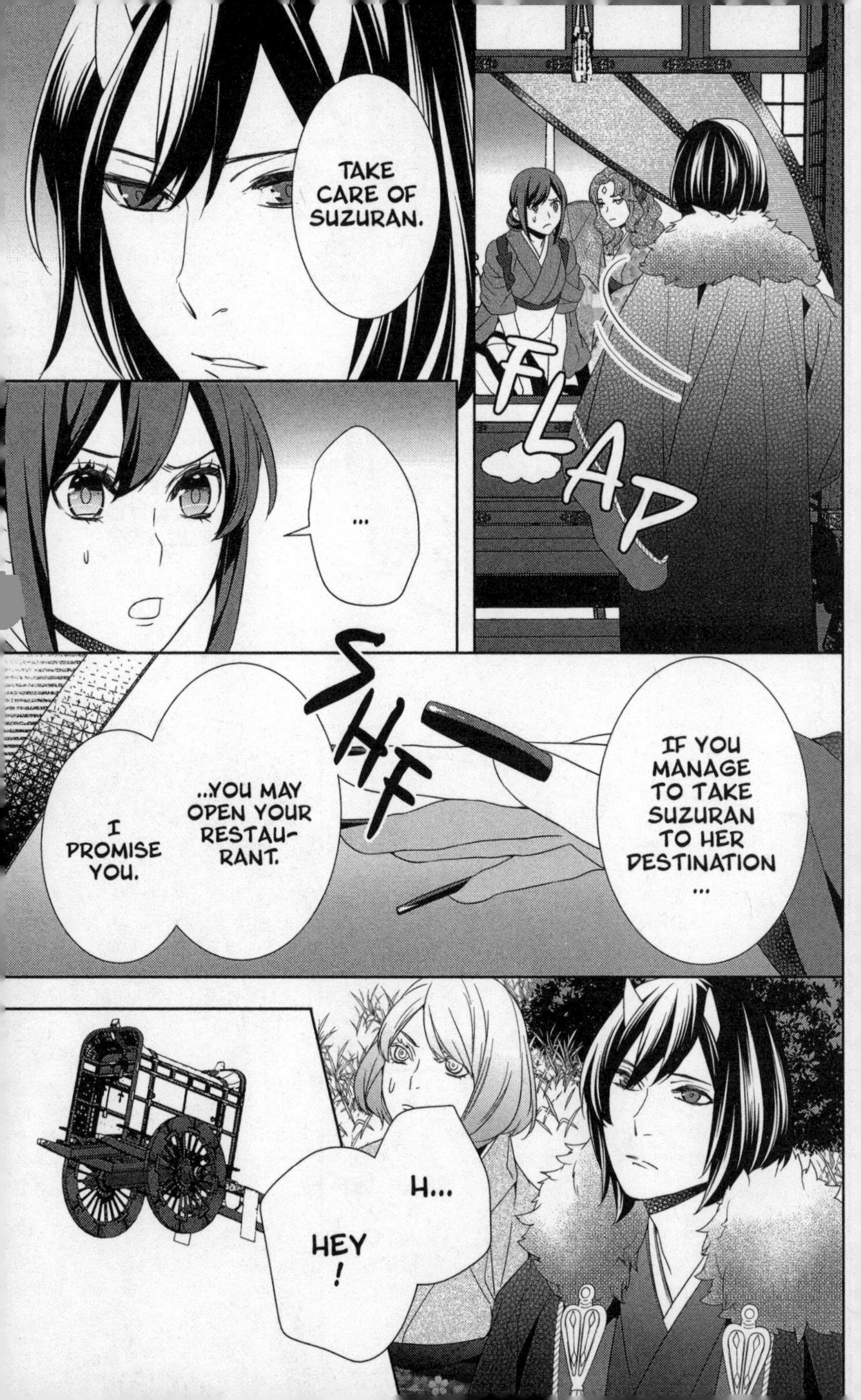
FLAP
TAKE CARE OF SUZURAN.
...
SHF
IF YOU MANAGE TO TAKE SUZURAN TO HER DESTINATION ...
...YOU MAY OPEN YOUR RESTAU-RANT.
I PROMISE YOU.
H... HEY!

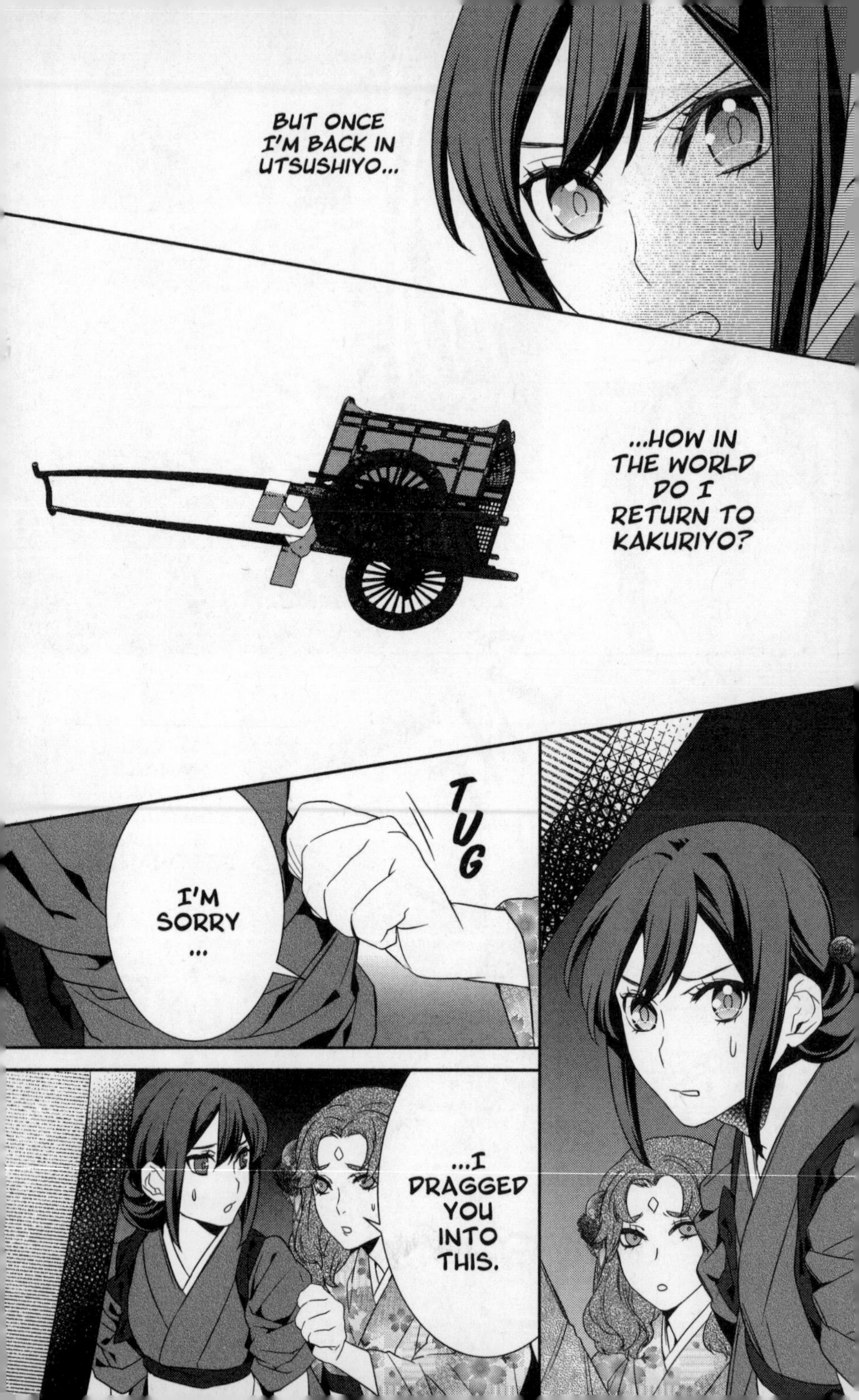
BUT ONCE I'M BACK IN UTSUSHIYO...
...HOW IN THE WORLD DO I RETURN TO KAKURIYO?
TUG
I'M SORRY ...
...I DRAGGED YOU INTO THIS.

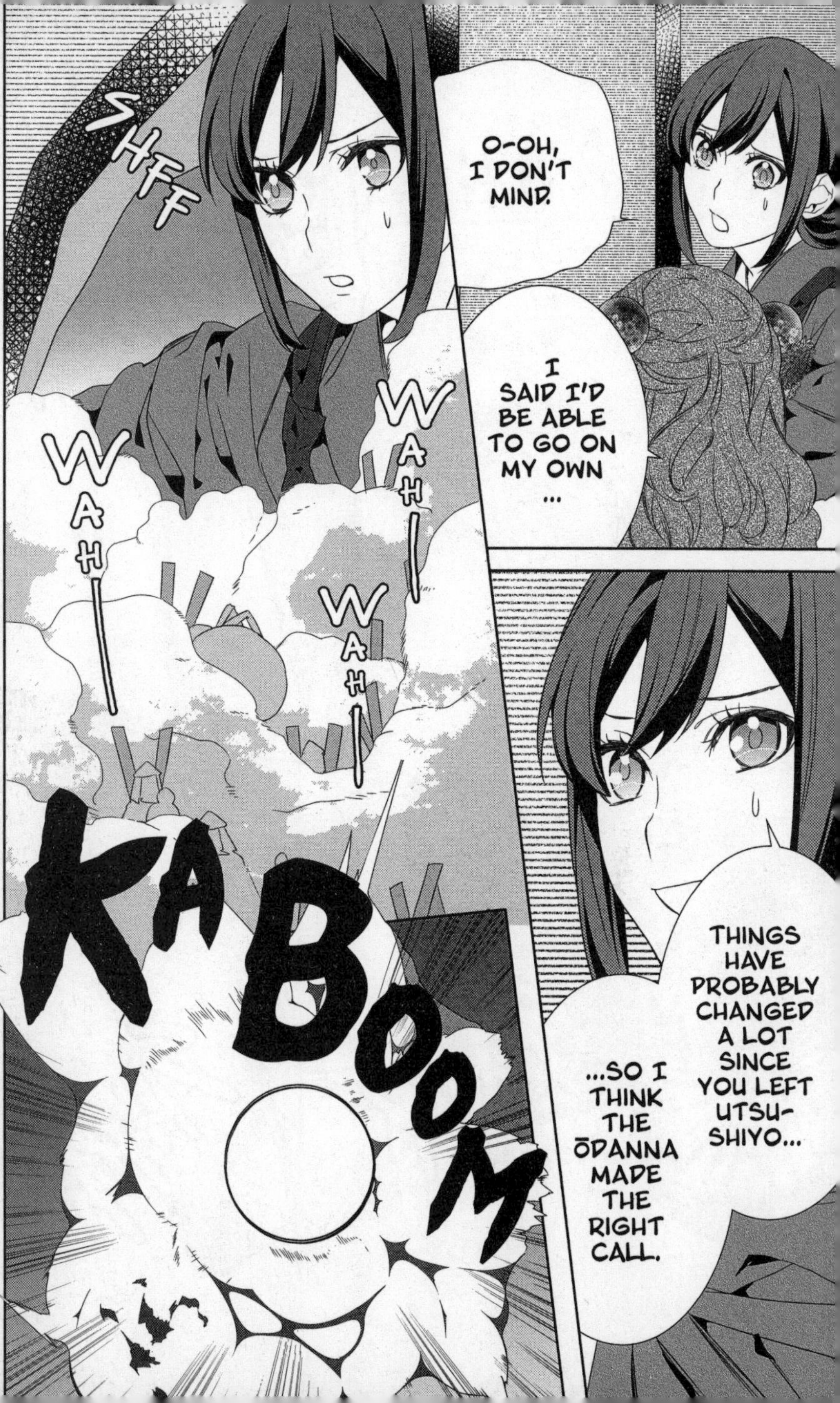
O-OH, I DON'T MIND.
I SAID I'D BE ABLE TO GO ON MY OWN ...
THINGS HAVE PROBABLY CHANGED A LOT SINCE YOU LEFT UTSU-SHIYO...
...SO I THINK THE ŌDANNA MADE THE RIGHT CALL.
SHFF
WAH
WAH
WAH
KABOOM

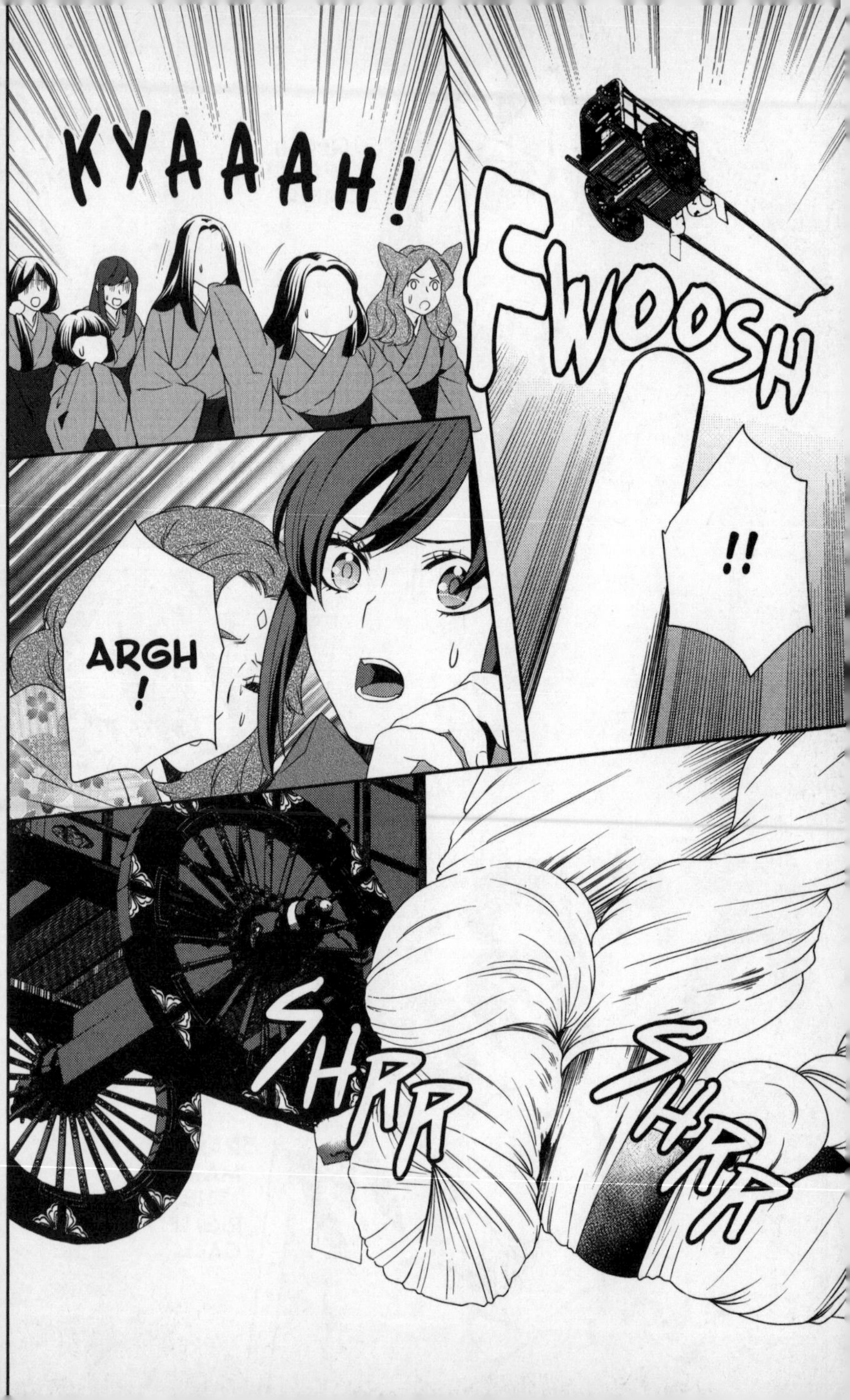
FWOOSH
!!
KYAAAH!
ARGH!
SHRR
SHRR

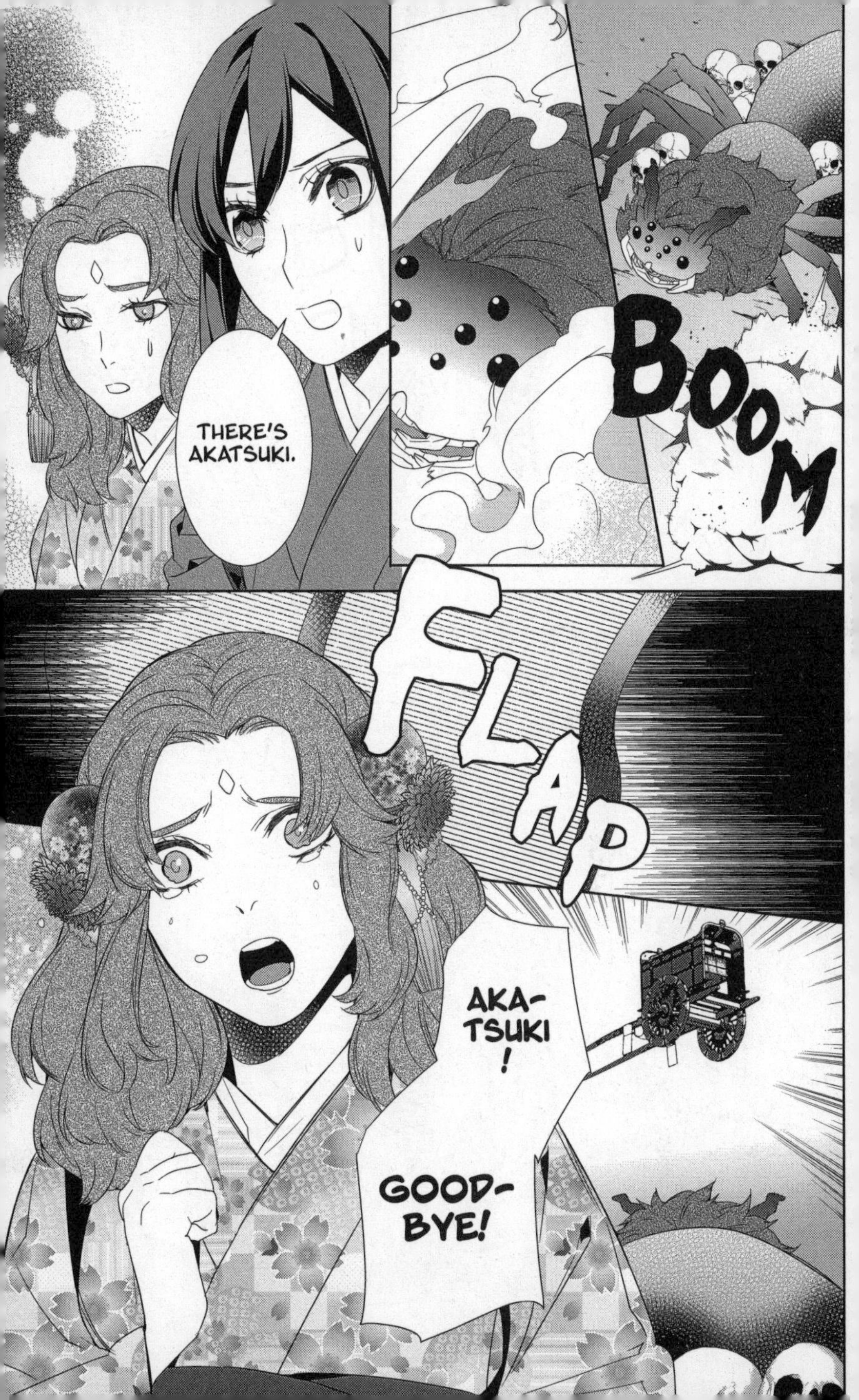
BOOM
THERE'S AKATSUKI.
FLAP
AKA-TSUKI!
GOOD-BYE!

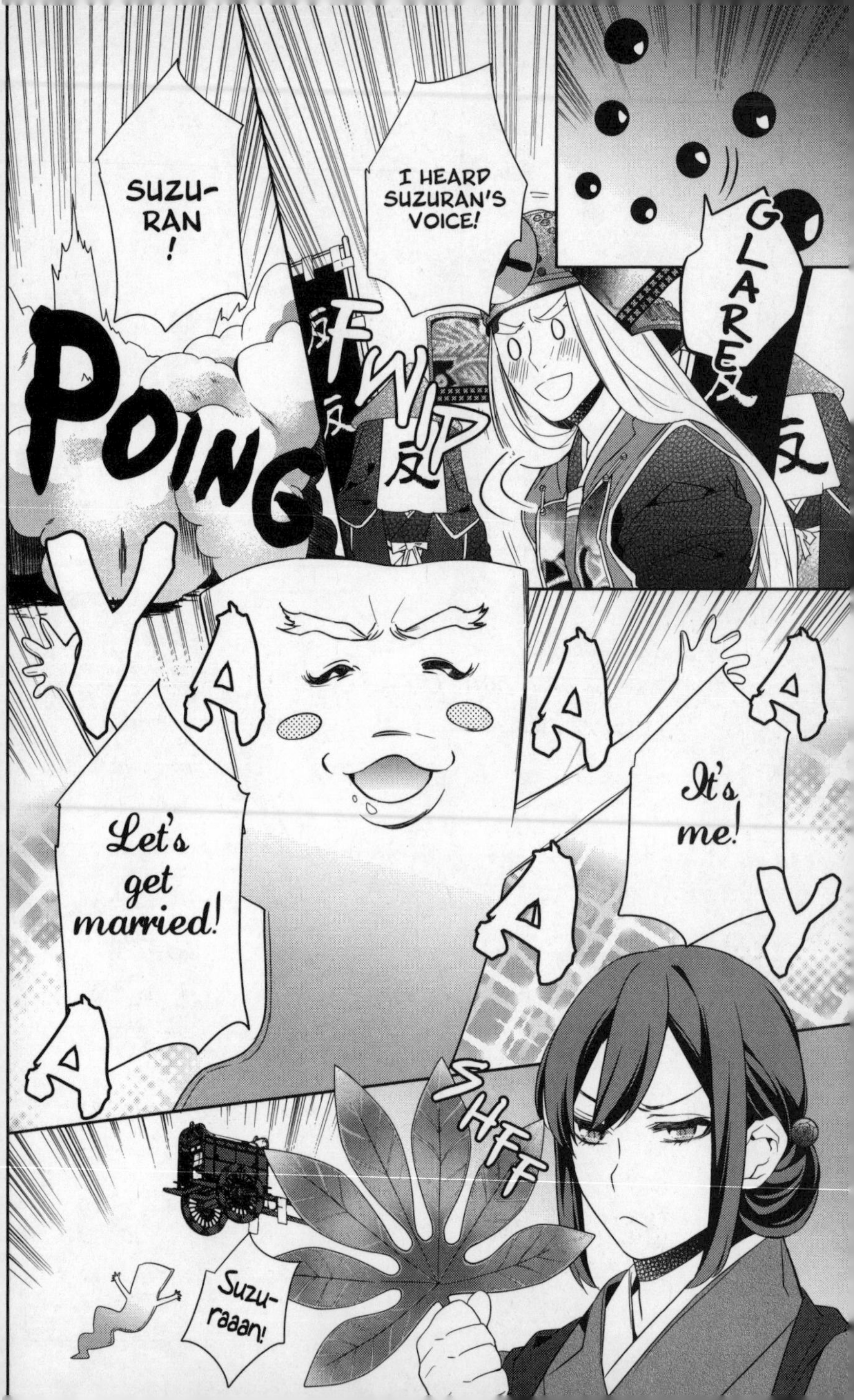
GLARE
I HEARD SUZURAN'S VOICE!
FWIP
SUZU-RAN!
POING
It's me!
Let's get married!
YAAAAAY
SHFF
Suzu-raaan!

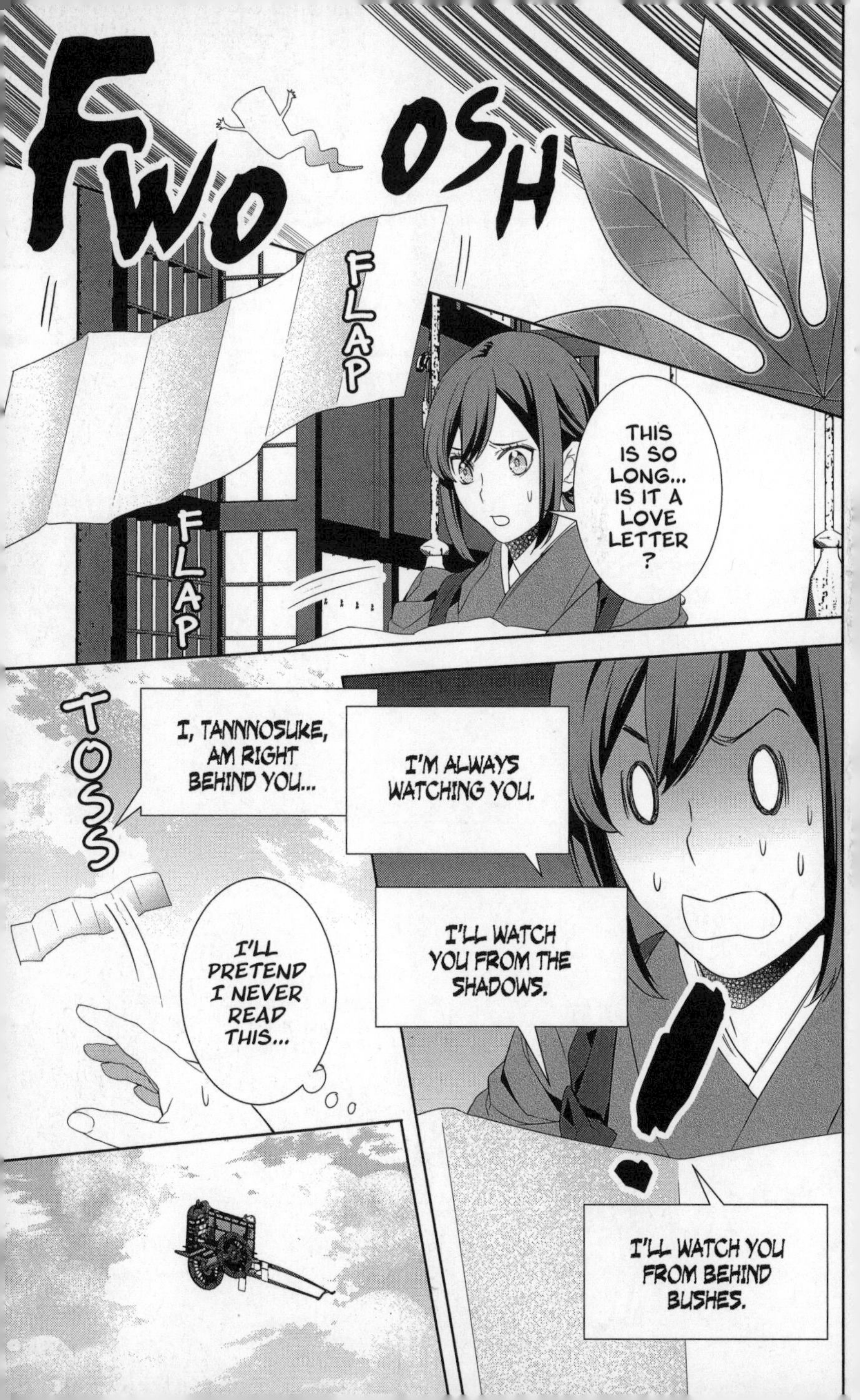
FWOOSH
THIS IS SO LONG... IS IT A LOVE LETTER?
FLAP
FLAP
I'M ALWAYS WATCHING YOU.
I'LL WATCH YOU FROM THE SHADOWS.
I'LL WATCH YOU FROM BEHIND BUSHES.
!
I, TANNOSUKE, AM RIGHT BEHIND YOU...
TOSS
I'LL PRETEND I NEVER READ THIS...

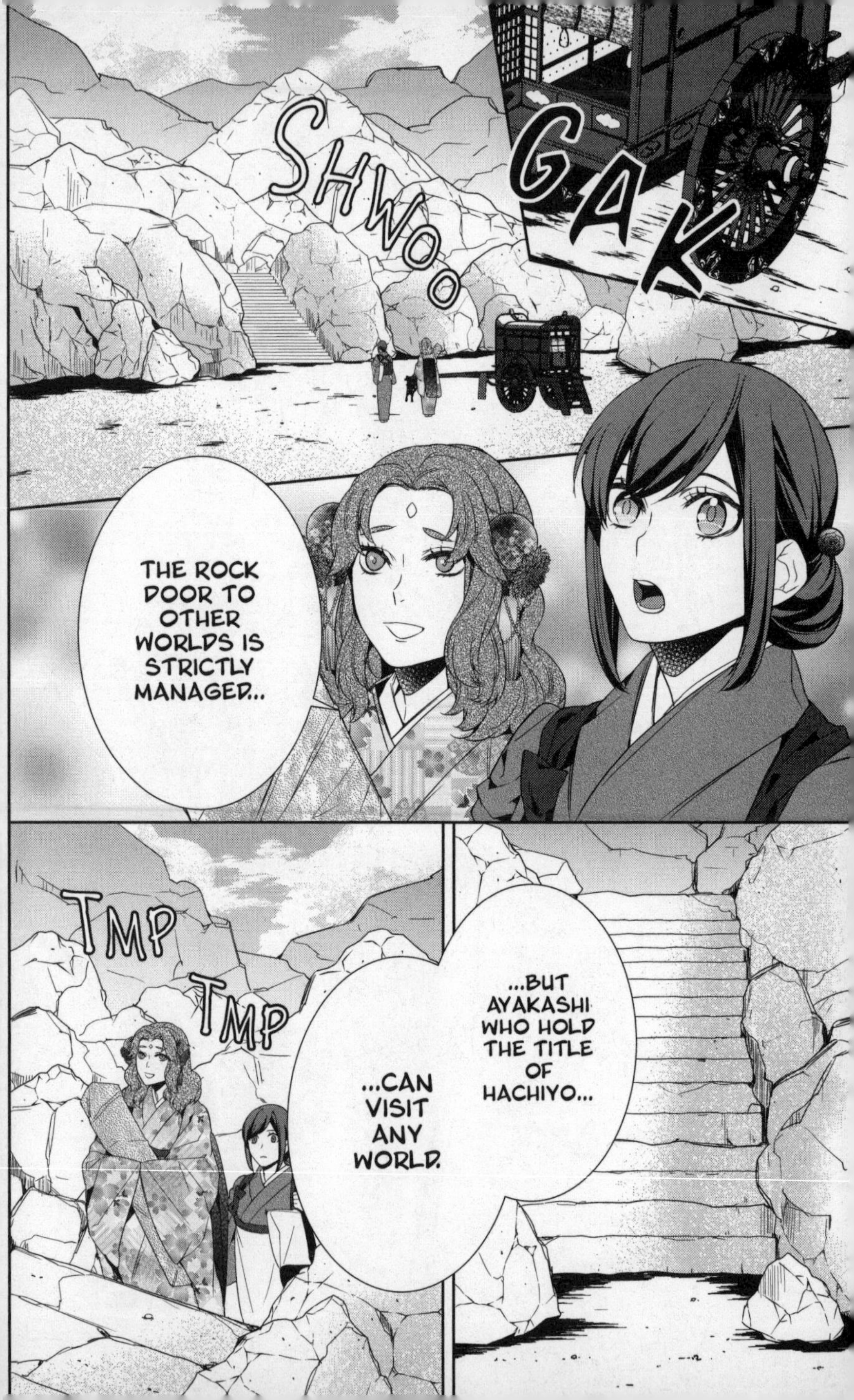
GAK
SHWOO
THE ROCK DOOR TO OTHER WORLDS IS STRICTLY MANAGED...
...BUT AYAKASHI WHO HOLD THE TITLE OF HACHIYO...
...CAN VISIT ANY WORLD.
TMP TMP

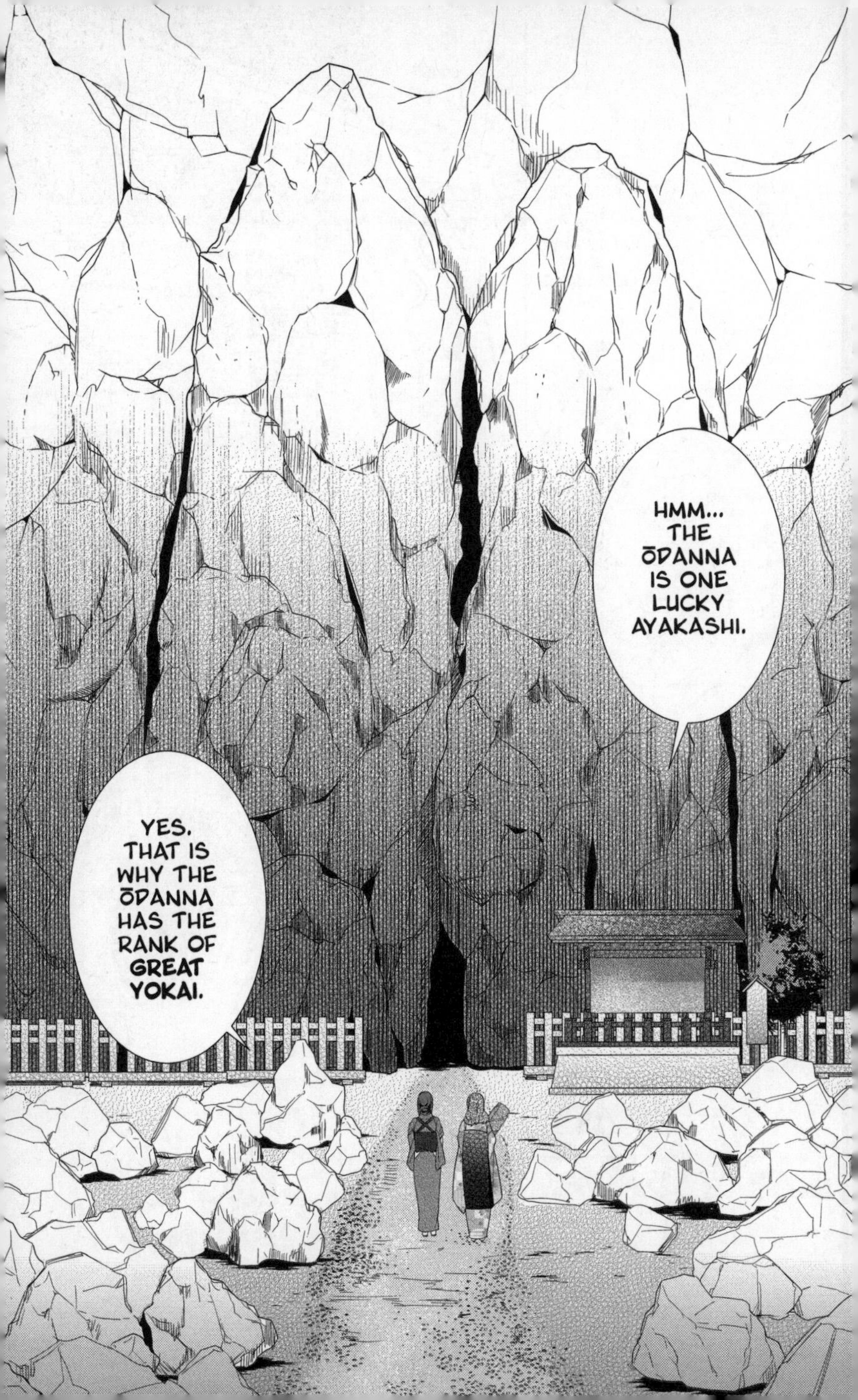
HMM... THE ŌDANNA IS ONE LUCKY AYAKASHI.
YES. THAT IS WHY THE ŌDANNA HAS THE RANK OF GREAT YOKAI.

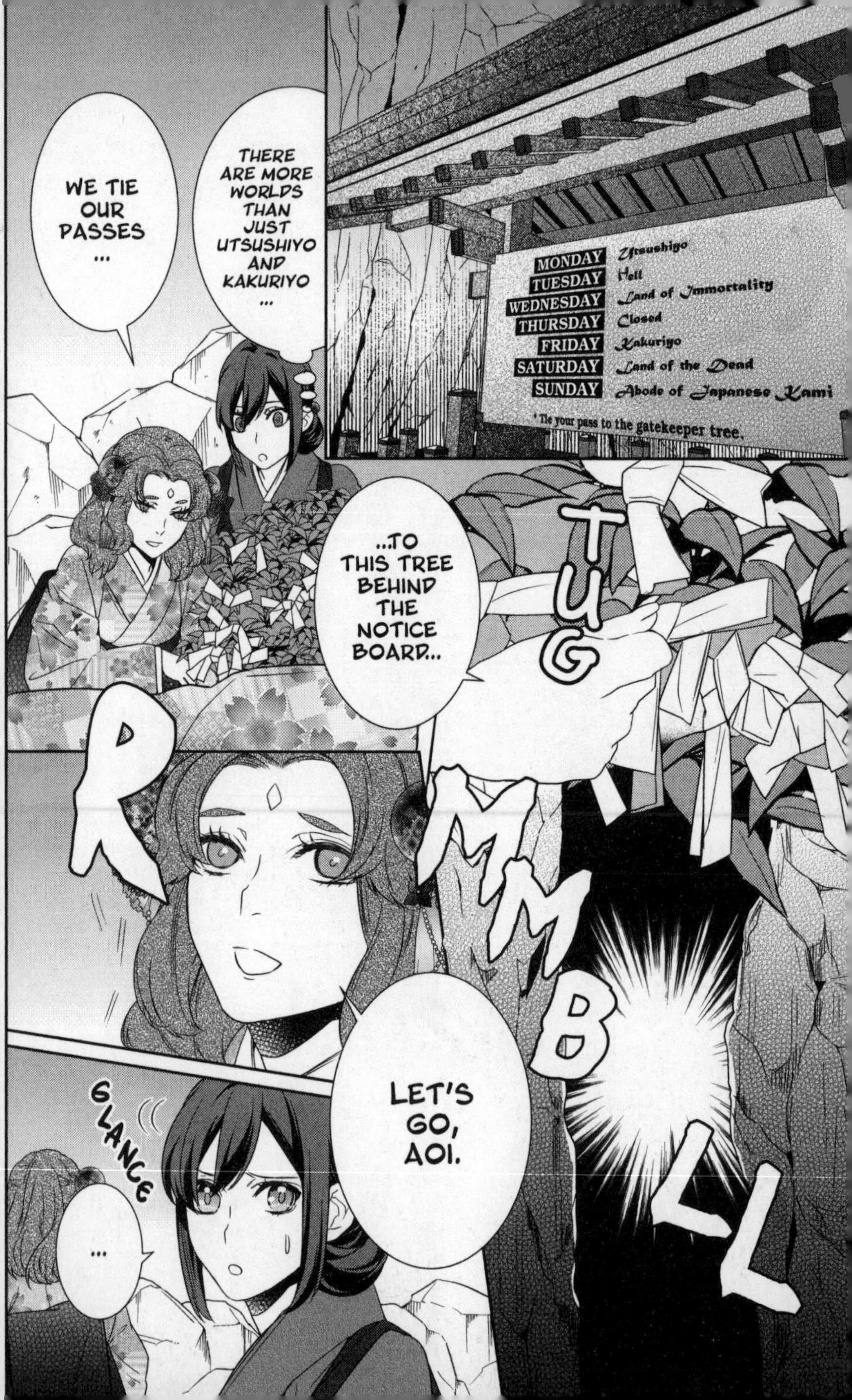
MONDAY Utsushiyo
TUESDAY Hell
WEDNESDAY Land of Immortality
THURSDAY Closed
FRIDAY Kakuriyo
SATURDAY Land of the Dead
SUNDAY Abode of Japanese Kami
* Tie your pass to the gatekeeper tree.
THERE ARE MORE WORLDS THAN JUST UTSUSHIYO AND KAKURIYO...
WE TIE OUR PASSES...
TUG
...TO THIS TREE BEHIND THE NOTICE BOARD...
RUMMBLL
LET'S GO, AOI.
GLANCE
...

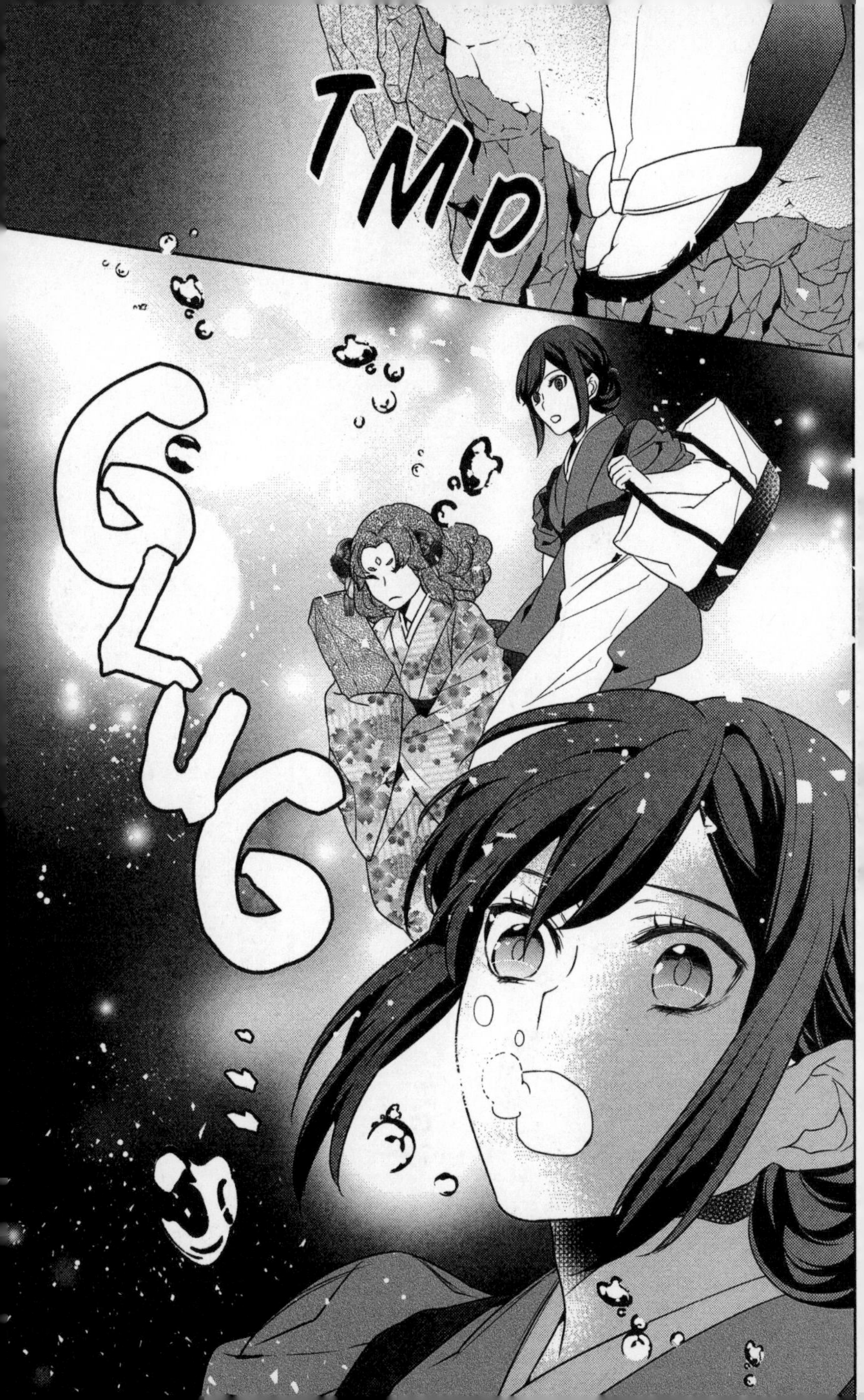
TMP
GLUG

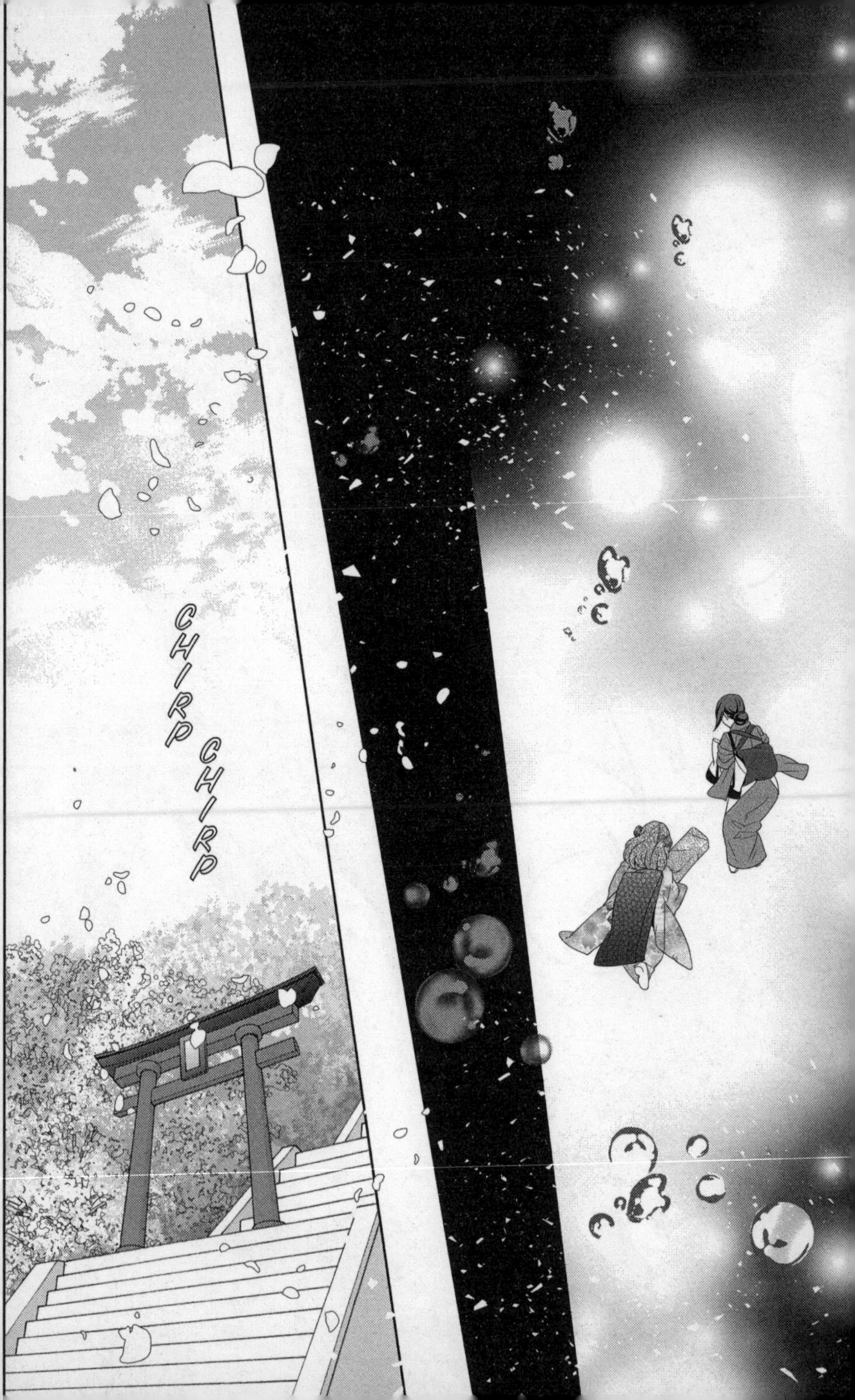
CHIRP CHIRP

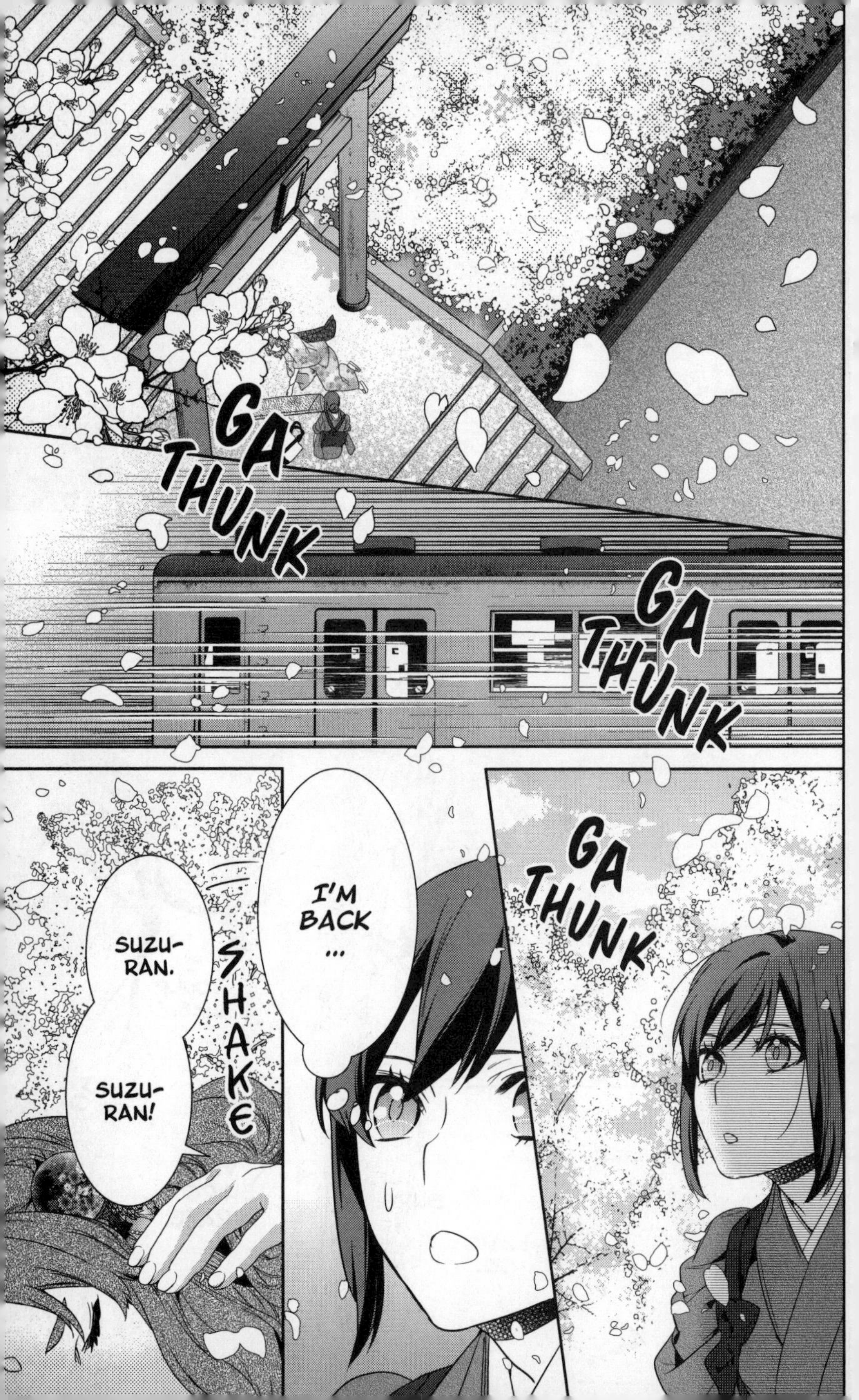
GA THUNK
GA THUNK
GA THUNK
I'M BACK ...
SUZU-RAN.
SHAKE
SUZU-RAN!

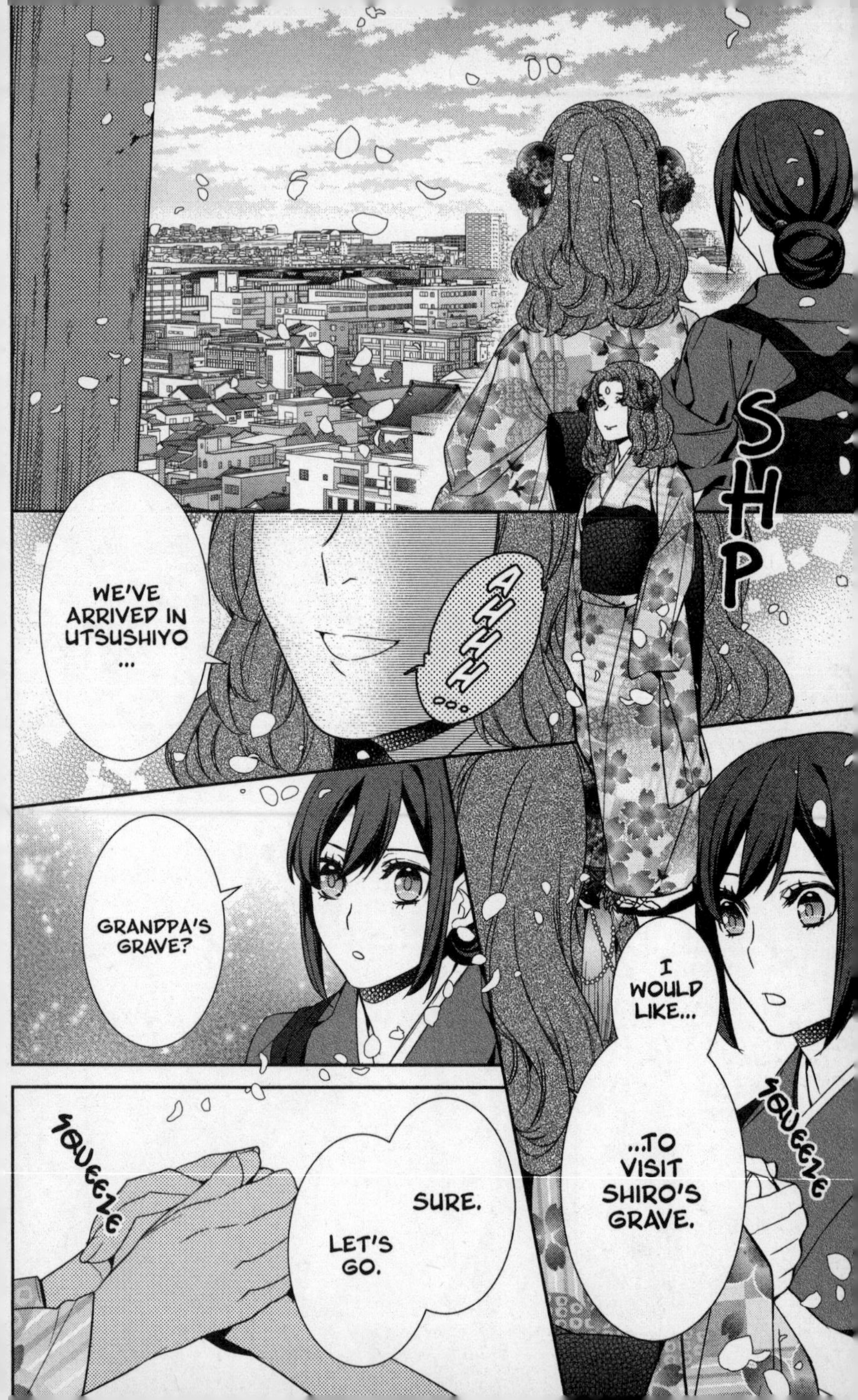
SHP
AHHH...
WE'VE ARRIVED IN UTSUSHIYO ...
I WOULD LIKE...
...TO VISIT SHIRO'S GRAVE.
SQUEEZE
GRANDPA'S GRAVE?
SQUEEZE
SURE. LET'S GO.

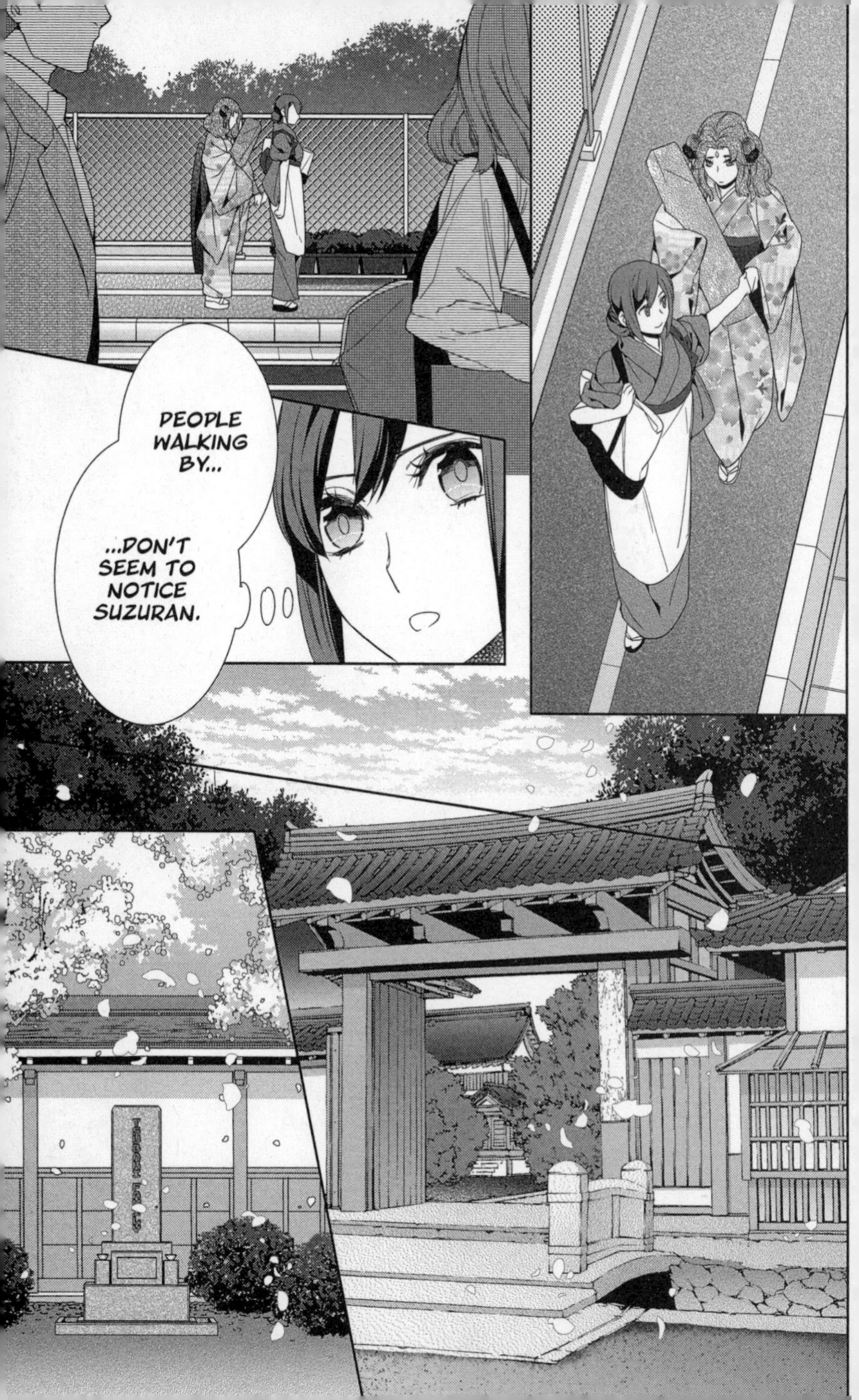
PEOPLE WALKING BY...
...DON'T SEEM TO NOTICE SUZURAN.

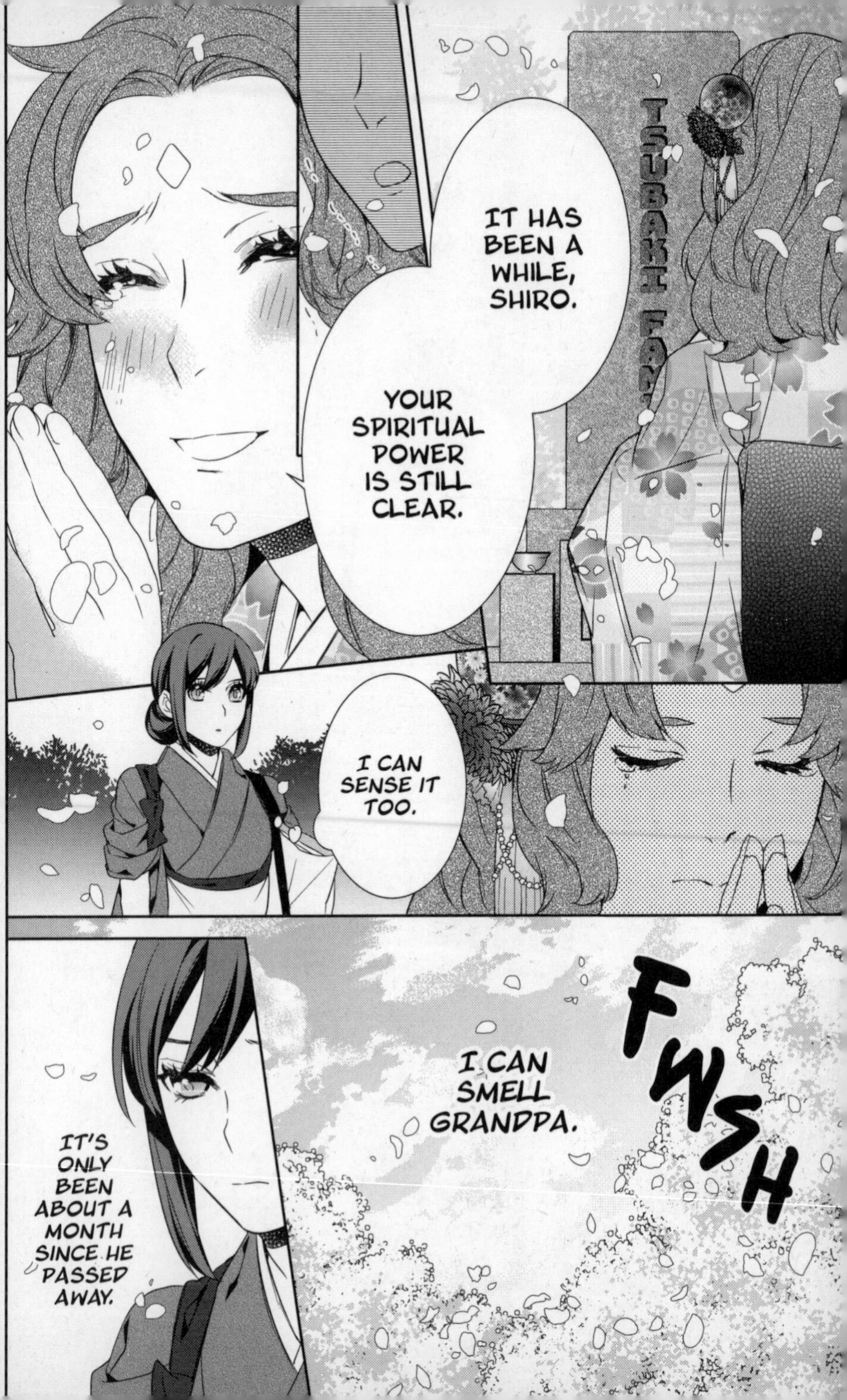
TSUBAKI
IT HAS BEEN A WHILE, SHIRO.
YOUR SPIRITUAL POWER IS STILL CLEAR.
I CAN SENSE IT TOO.
FWSH
I CAN SMELL GRANDPA.
IT'S ONLY BEEN ABOUT A MONTH SINCE HE PASSED AWAY.

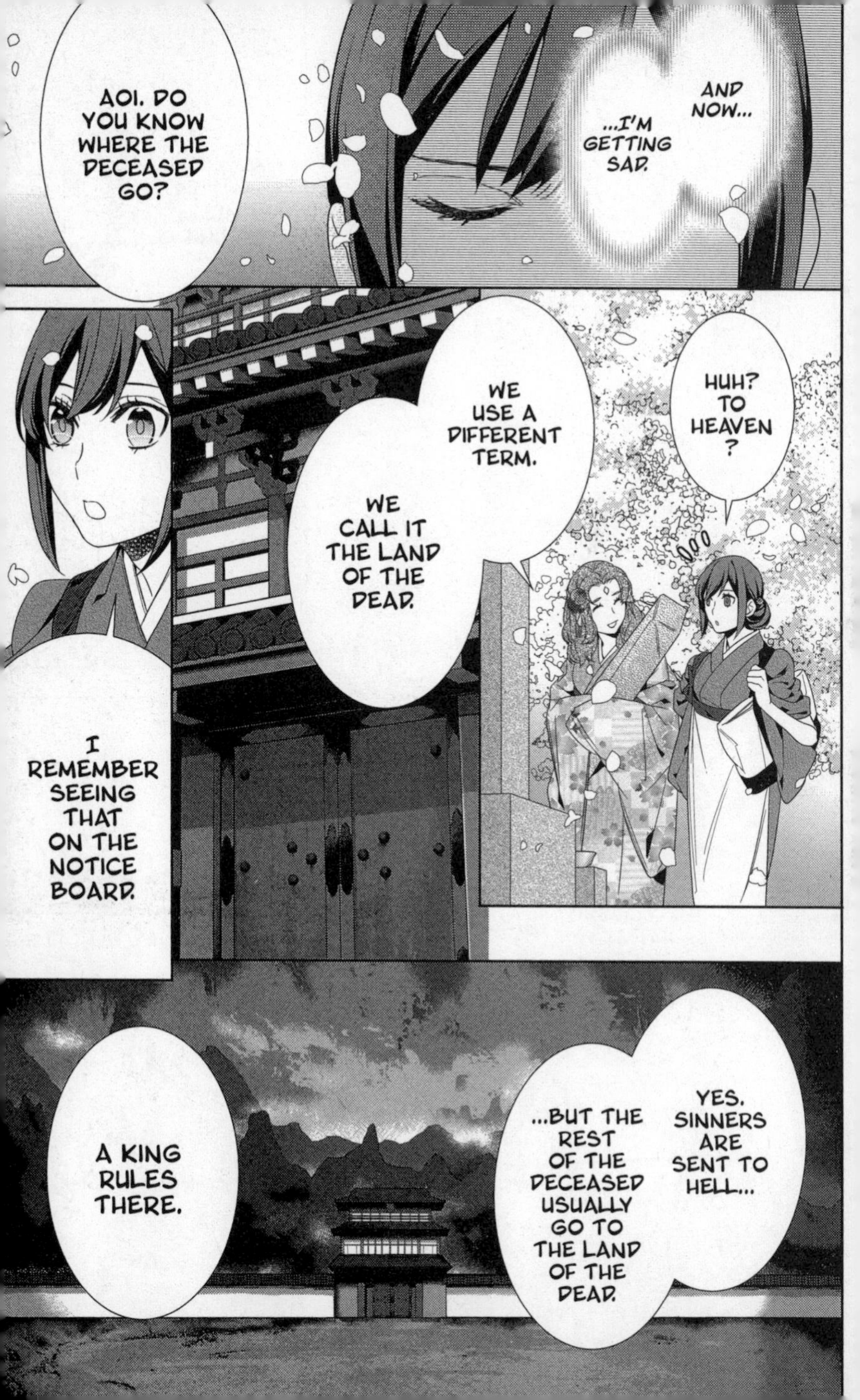
AND NOW...
...I'M GETTING SAD.
AOI. DO YOU KNOW WHERE THE DECEASED GO?
HUH? TO HEAVEN?
WE USE A DIFFERENT TERM.
WE CALL IT THE LAND OF THE DEAD.
I REMEMBER SEEING THAT ON THE NOTICE BOARD.
YES. SINNERS ARE SENT TO HELL...
...BUT THE REST OF THE DECEASED USUALLY GO TO THE LAND OF THE DEAD.
A KING RULES THERE.

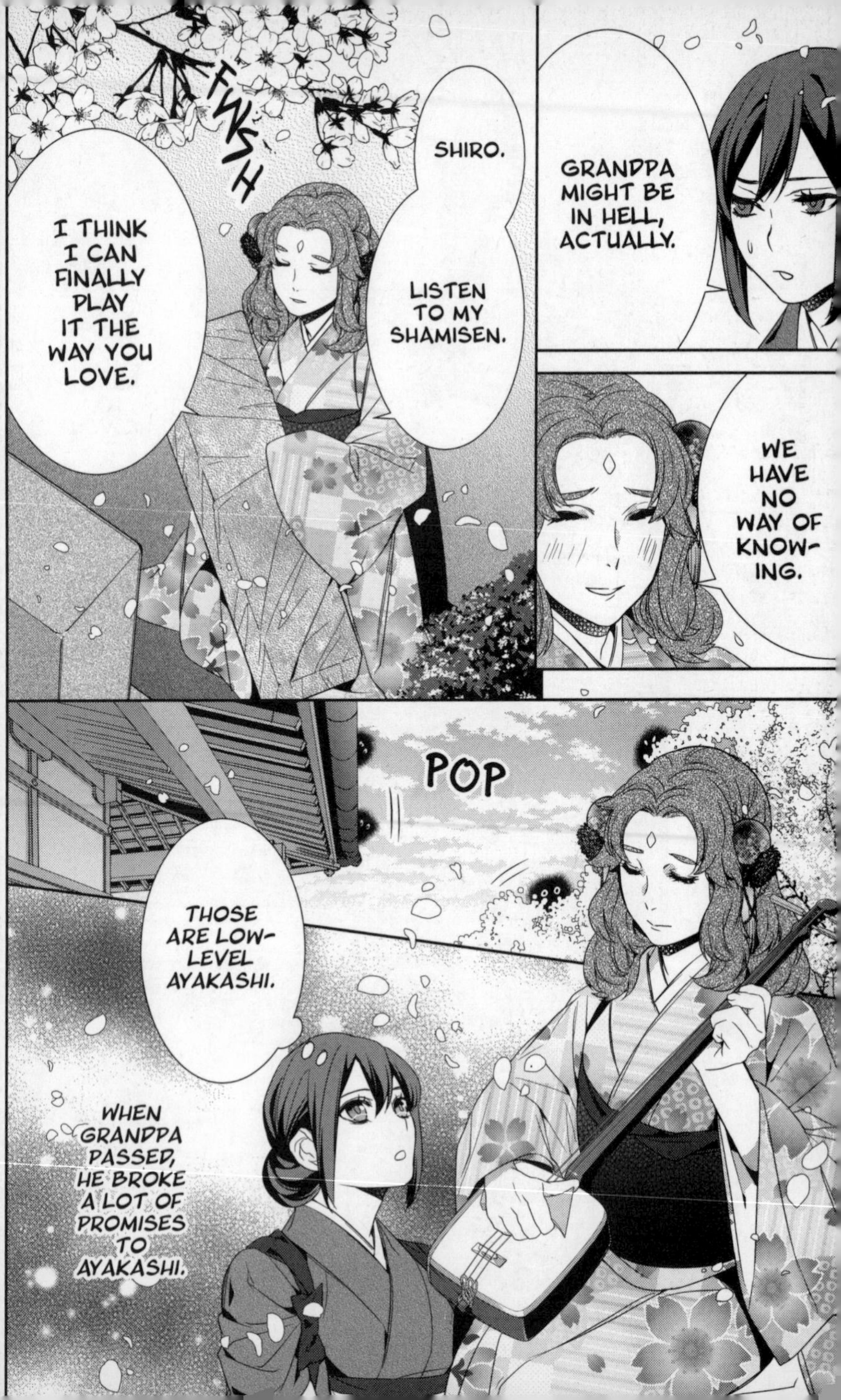
GRANDPA MIGHT BE IN HELL, ACTUALLY.
WE HAVE NO WAY OF KNOW-ING.
FWSH
SHIRO.
LISTEN TO MY SHAMISEN.
I THINK I CAN FINALLY PLAY IT THE WAY YOU LOVE.
POP
THOSE ARE LOW-LEVEL AYAKASHI.
WHEN GRANDPA PASSED, HE BROKE A LOT OF PROMISES TO AYAKASHI.

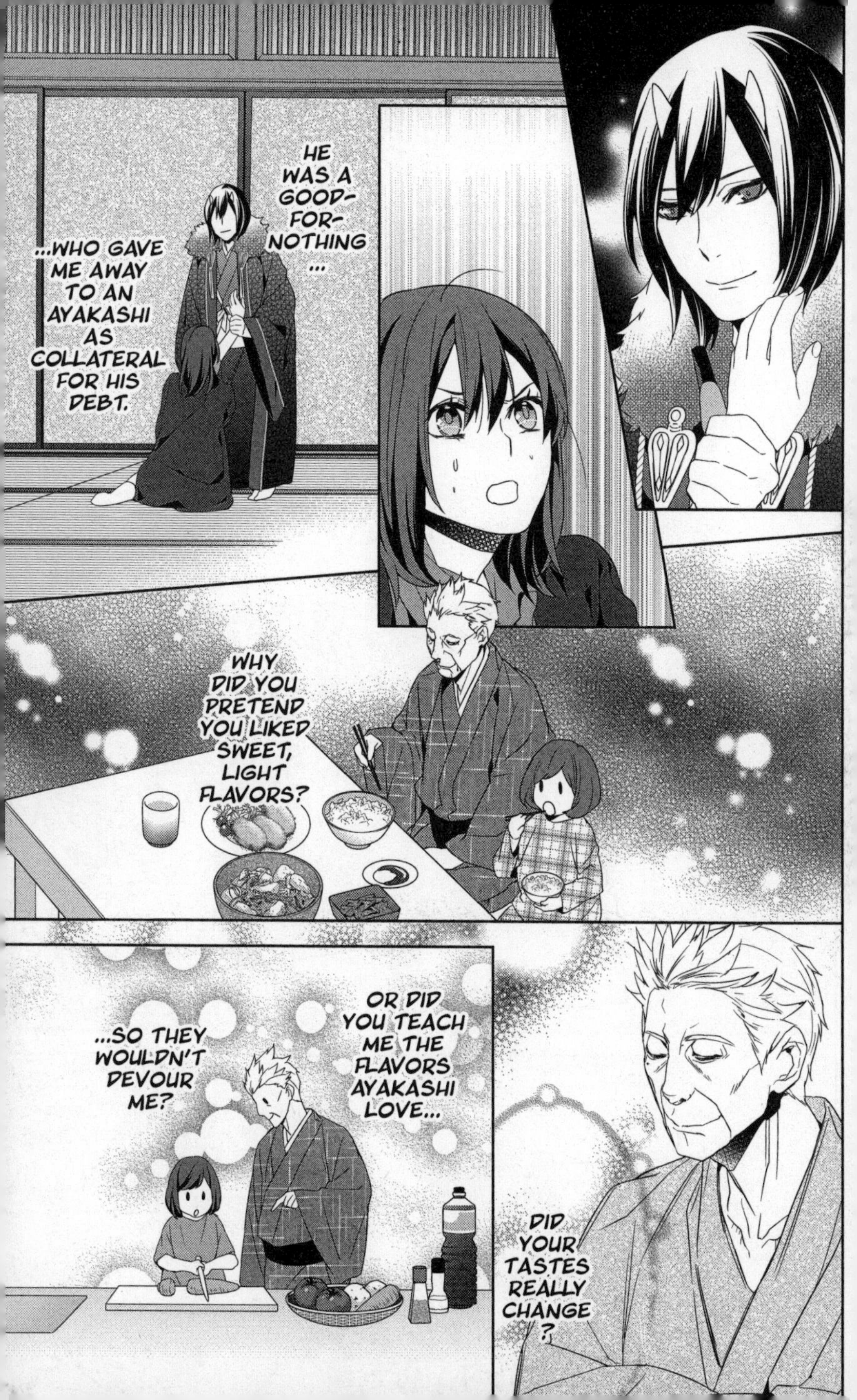
HE WAS A GOOD-FOR-NOTHING...
...WHO GAVE ME AWAY TO AN AYAKASHI AS COLLATERAL FOR HIS DEBT.
WHY DID YOU PRETEND YOU LIKED SWEET, LIGHT FLAVORS?
DID YOUR TASTES REALLY CHANGE?
OR DID YOU TEACH ME THE FLAVORS AYAKASHI LOVE...
...SO THEY WOULDN'T DEVOUR ME?

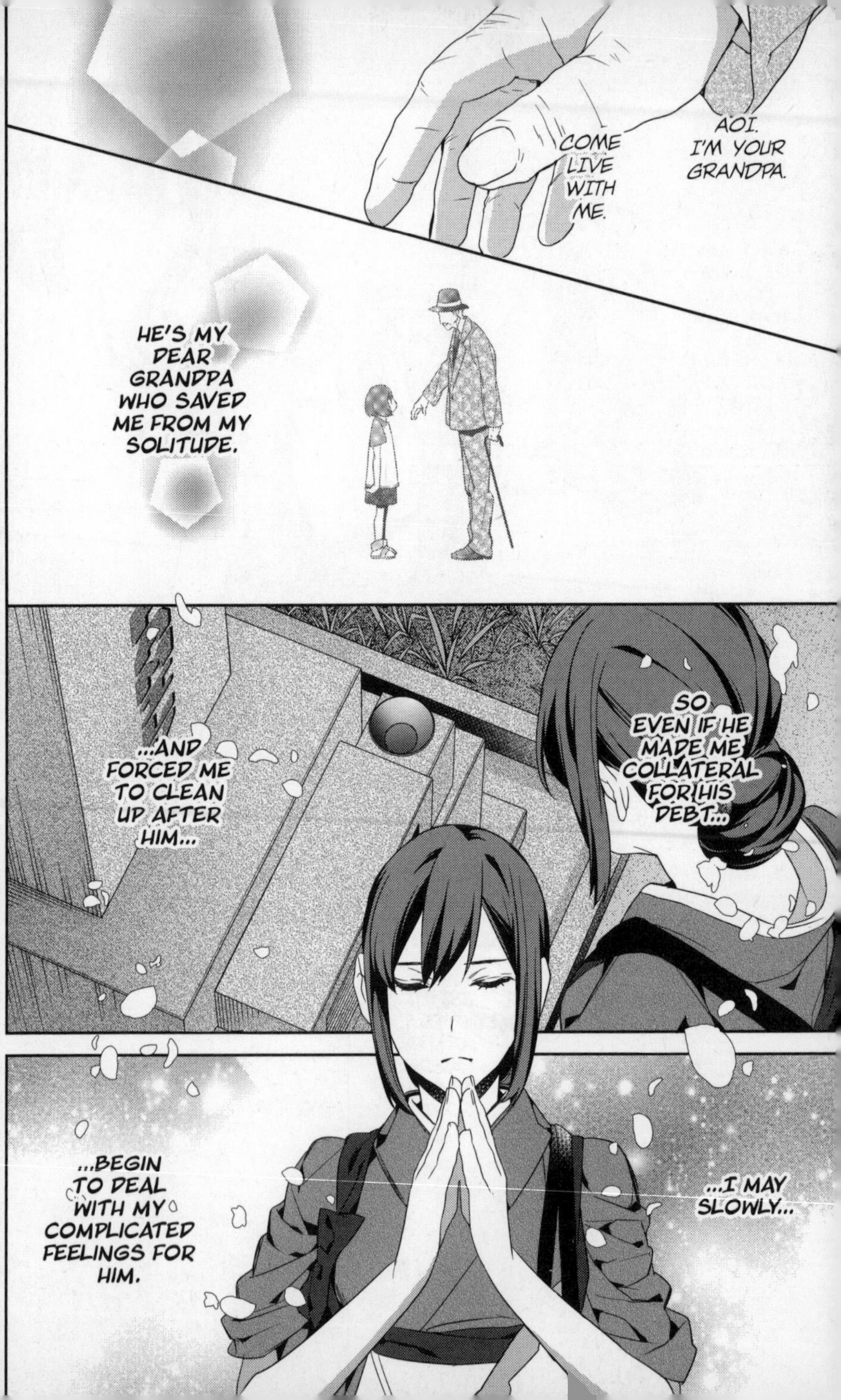
AOI. I'M YOUR GRANDPA.
COME LIVE WITH ME.
HE'S MY DEAR GRANDPA WHO SAVED ME FROM MY SOLITUDE.
SO EVEN IF HE MADE ME COLLATERAL FOR HIS DEBT...
...AND FORCED ME TO CLEAN UP AFTER HIM...
...I MAY SLOWLY...
...BEGIN TO DEAL WITH MY COMPLICATED FEELINGS FOR HIM.

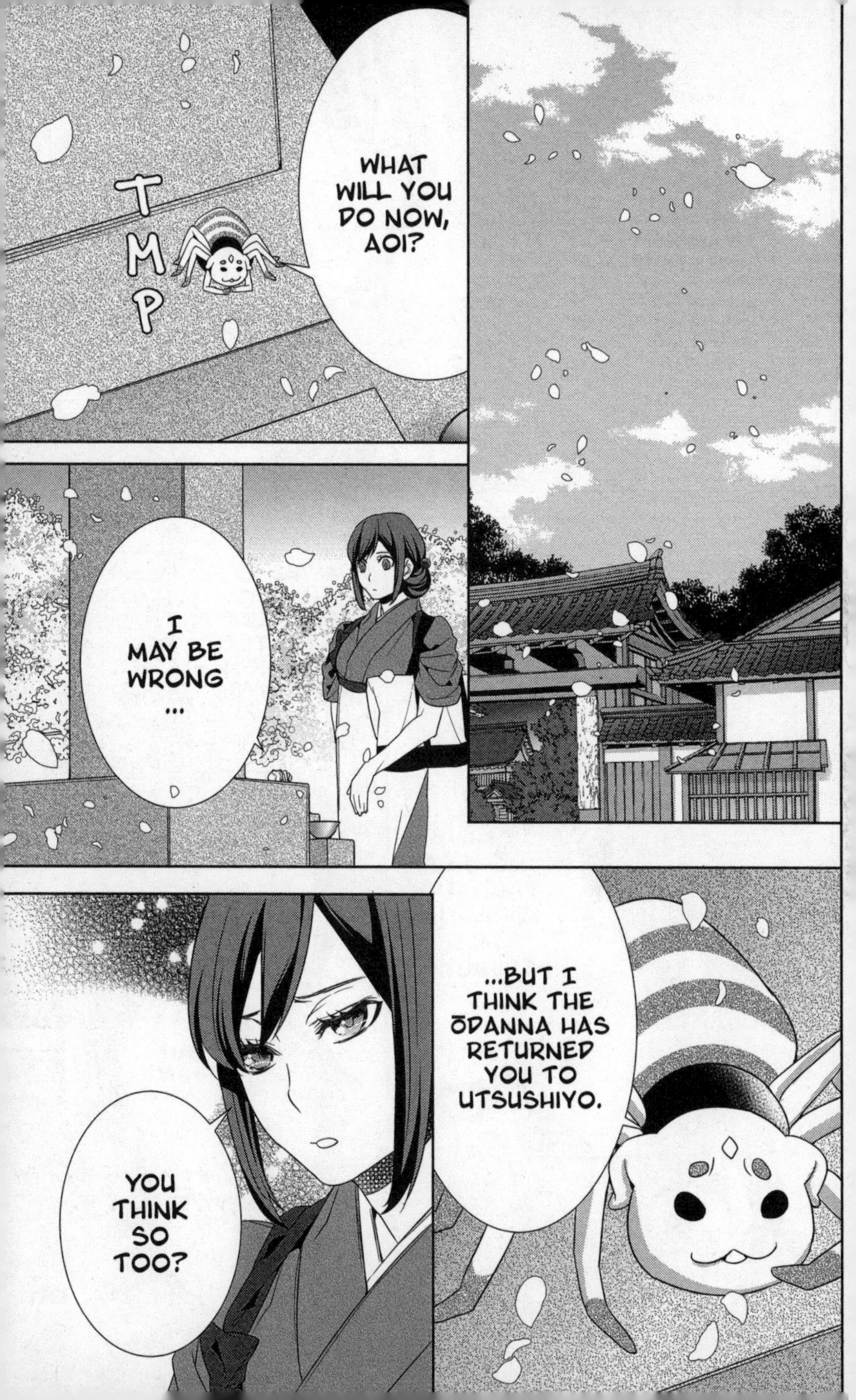
WHAT WILL YOU DO NOW, AOI?
TMP
I MAY BE WRONG ...
...BUT I THINK THE ŌDANNA HAS RETURNED YOU TO UTSUSHIYO.
YOU THINK SO TOO?

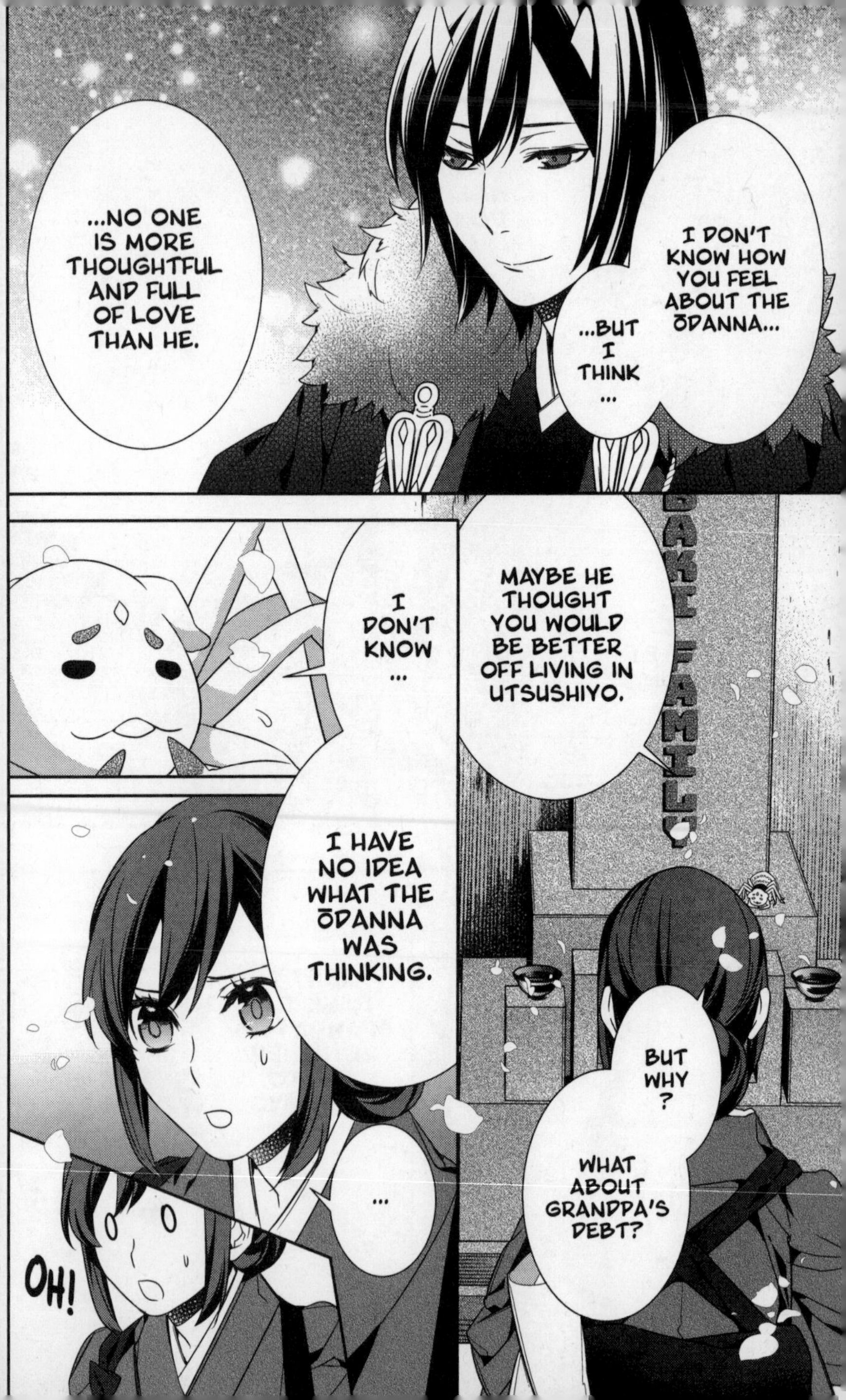

I DON'T KNOW HOW YOU FEEL ABOUT THE ŌDANNA...
...BUT I THINK ...
...NO ONE IS MORE THOUGHTFUL AND FULL OF LOVE THAN HE.
MAYBE HE THOUGHT YOU WOULD BE BETTER OFF LIVING IN UTSUSHIYO.
BUT WHY?
WHAT ABOUT GRANDPA'S DEBT?
I DON'T KNOW ...
I HAVE NO IDEA WHAT THE ŌDANNA WAS THINKING.
...
OH!

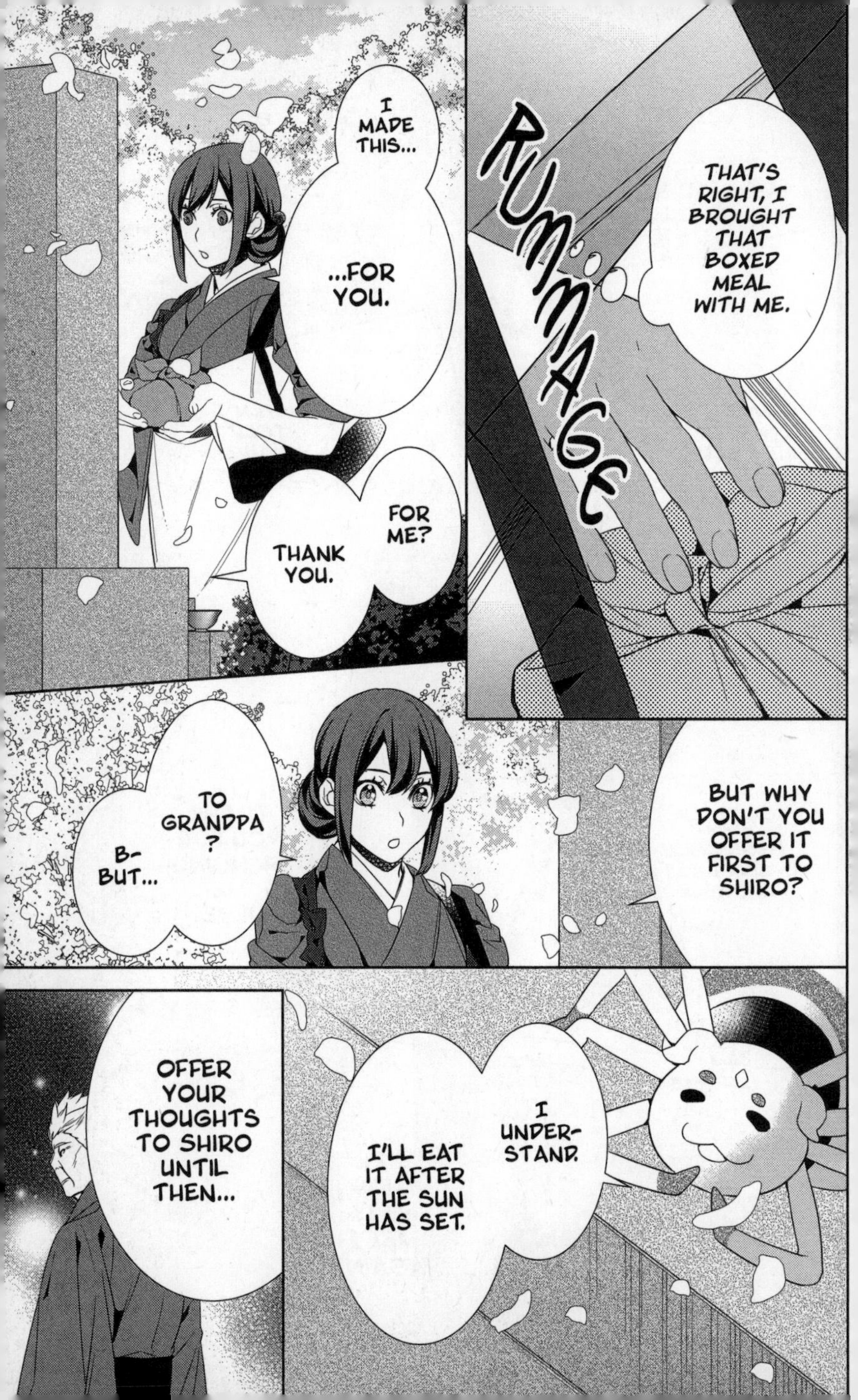
RUMMAGE
THAT'S RIGHT, I BROUGHT THAT BOXED MEAL WITH ME.
I MADE THIS... ...FOR YOU.
FOR ME?
THANK YOU.
BUT WHY DON'T YOU OFFER IT FIRST TO SHIRO?
TO GRANDPA?
B-BUT...
I UNDER-STAND.
I'LL EAT IT AFTER THE SUN HAS SET.
OFFER YOUR THOUGHTS TO SHIRO UNTIL THEN...

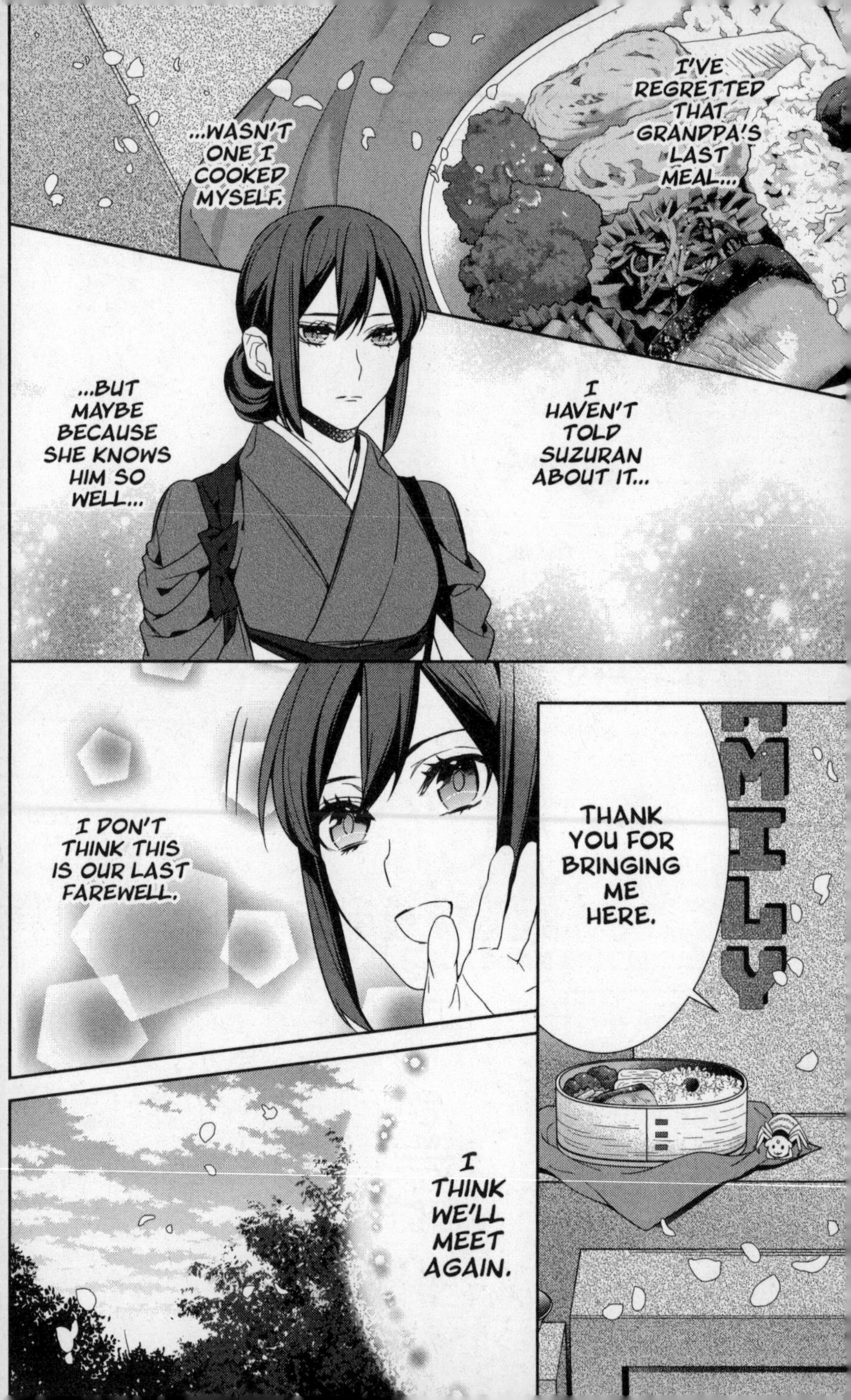

I'VE REGRETTED THAT GRANDPA'S LAST MEAL...
...WASN'T ONE I COOKED MYSELF.
I HAVEN'T TOLD SUZURAN ABOUT IT...
...BUT MAYBE BECAUSE SHE KNOWS HIM SO WELL...
THANK YOU FOR BRINGING ME HERE.
I DON'T THINK THIS IS OUR LAST FAREWELL.
I THINK WE'LL MEET AGAIN.

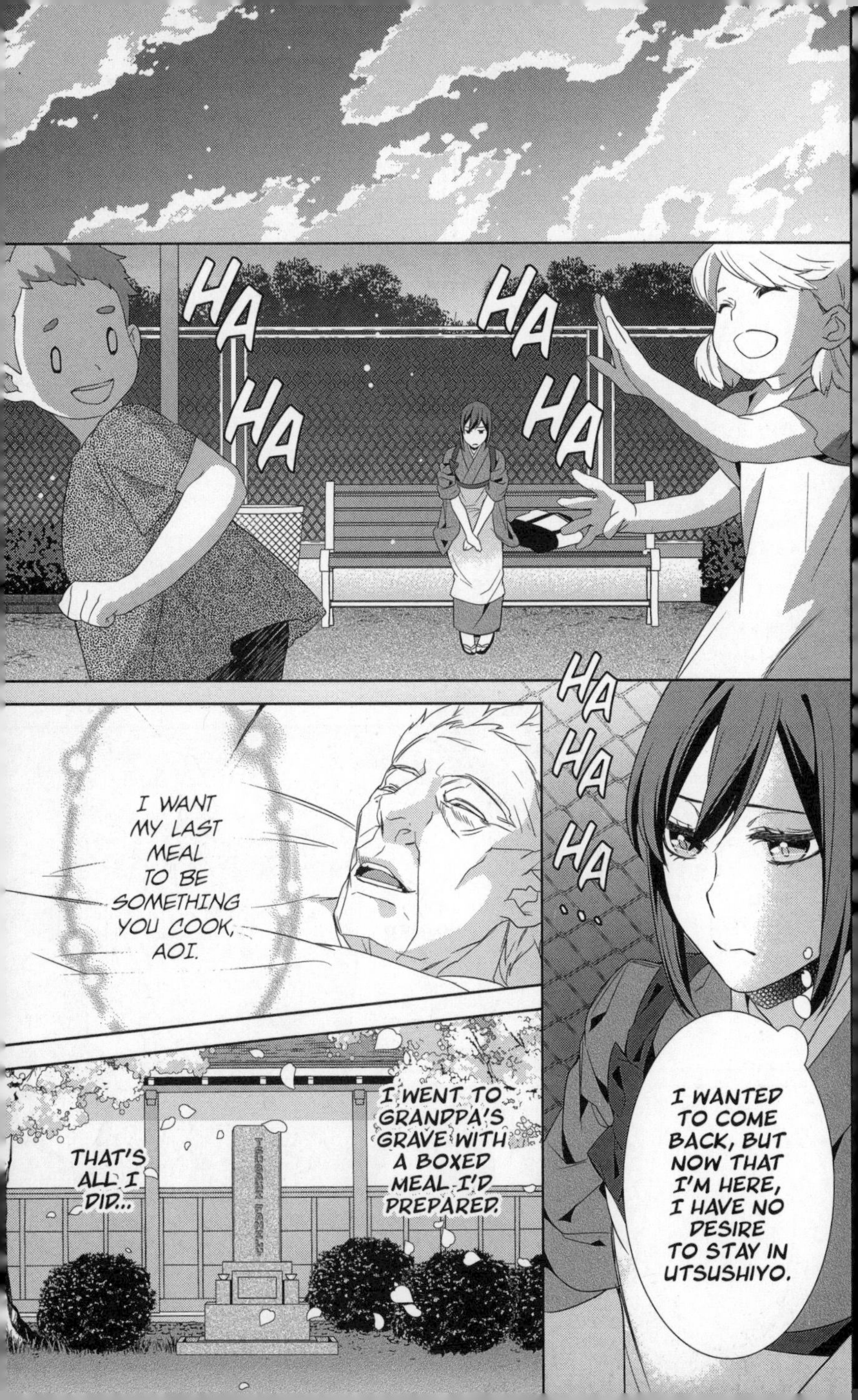
HA HA HA
HA HA
HA HA HA HA...
I WANTED TO COME BACK, BUT NOW THAT I'M HERE, I HAVE NO DESIRE TO STAY IN UTSUSHIYO.
I WANT MY LAST MEAL TO BE SOMETHING YOU COOK, AOI.
I WENT TO GRANDPA'S GRAVE WITH A BOXED MEAL I'D PREPARED.
THAT'S ALL I DID...

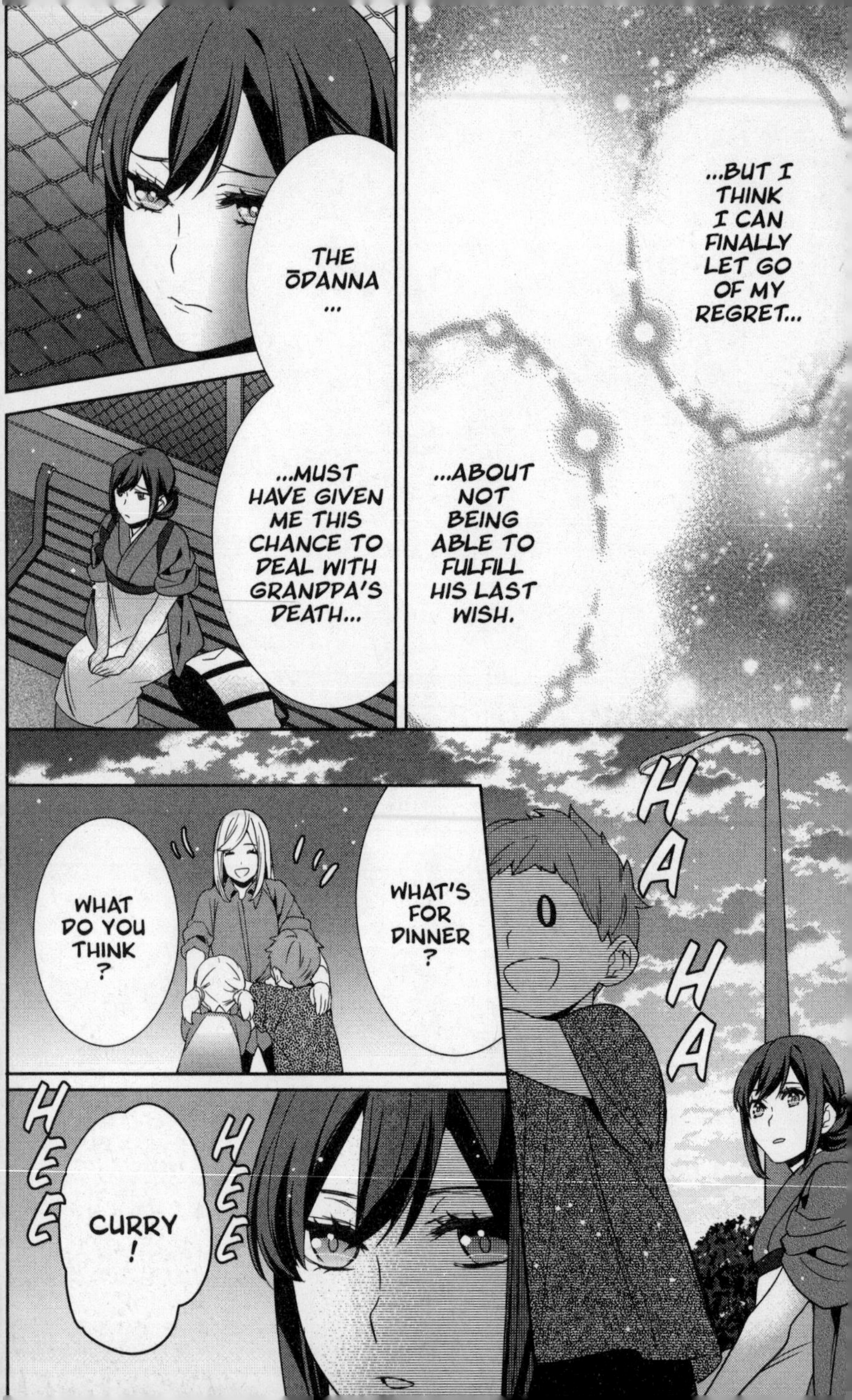

...BUT I THINK I CAN FINALLY LET GO OF MY REGRET...
...ABOUT NOT BEING ABLE TO FULFILL HIS LAST WISH.
THE ŌDANNA...
...MUST HAVE GIVEN ME THIS CHANCE TO DEAL WITH GRANDPA'S DEATH...
HA HA HA
WHAT'S FOR DINNER?
WHAT DO YOU THINK?
HEE HEE
CURRY!
HEE HEE

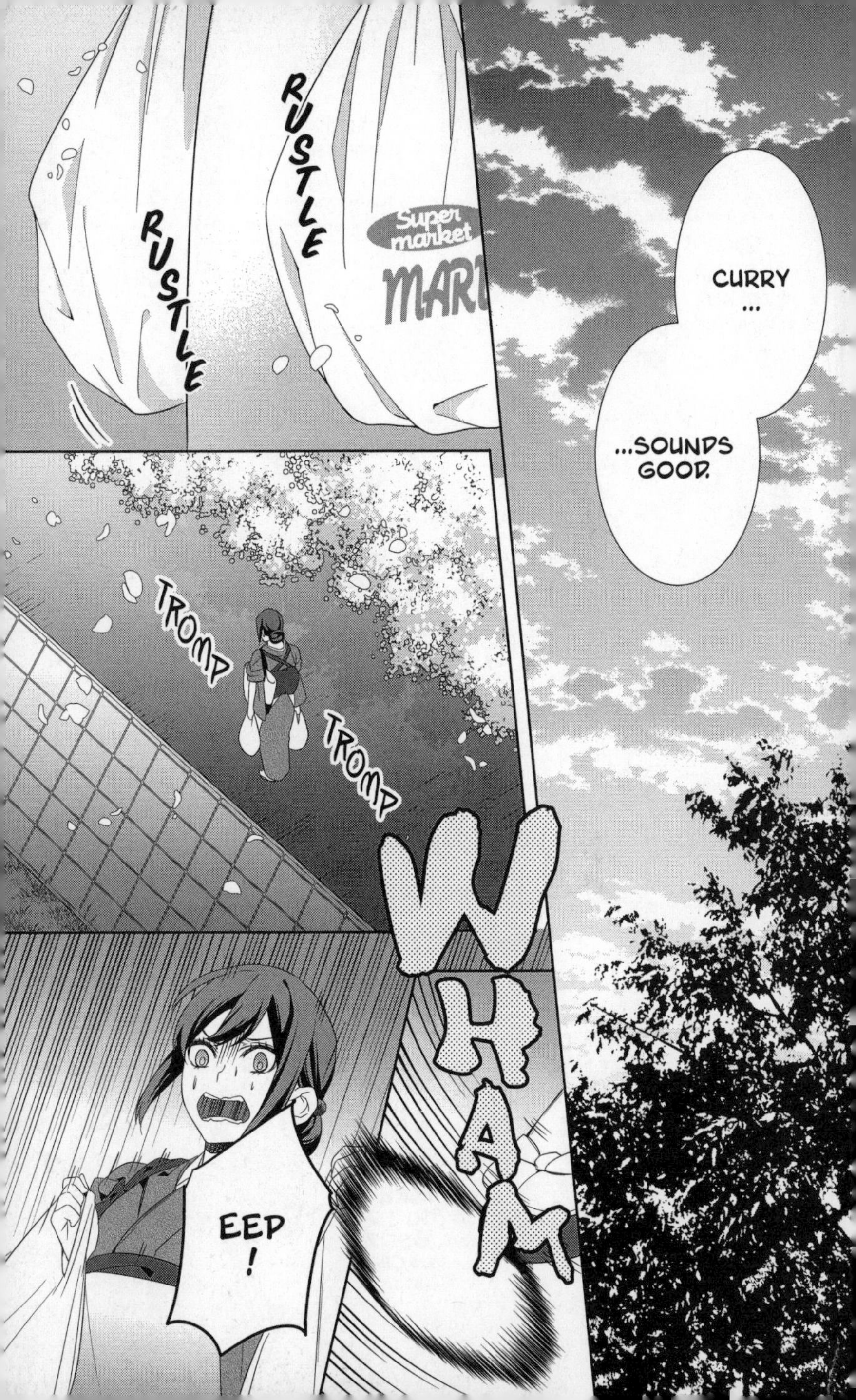
CURRY ...
...SOUNDS GOOD.
RUSTLE
Super market
MART
RUSTLE
TROMP
TROMP
WHAM
EEP!

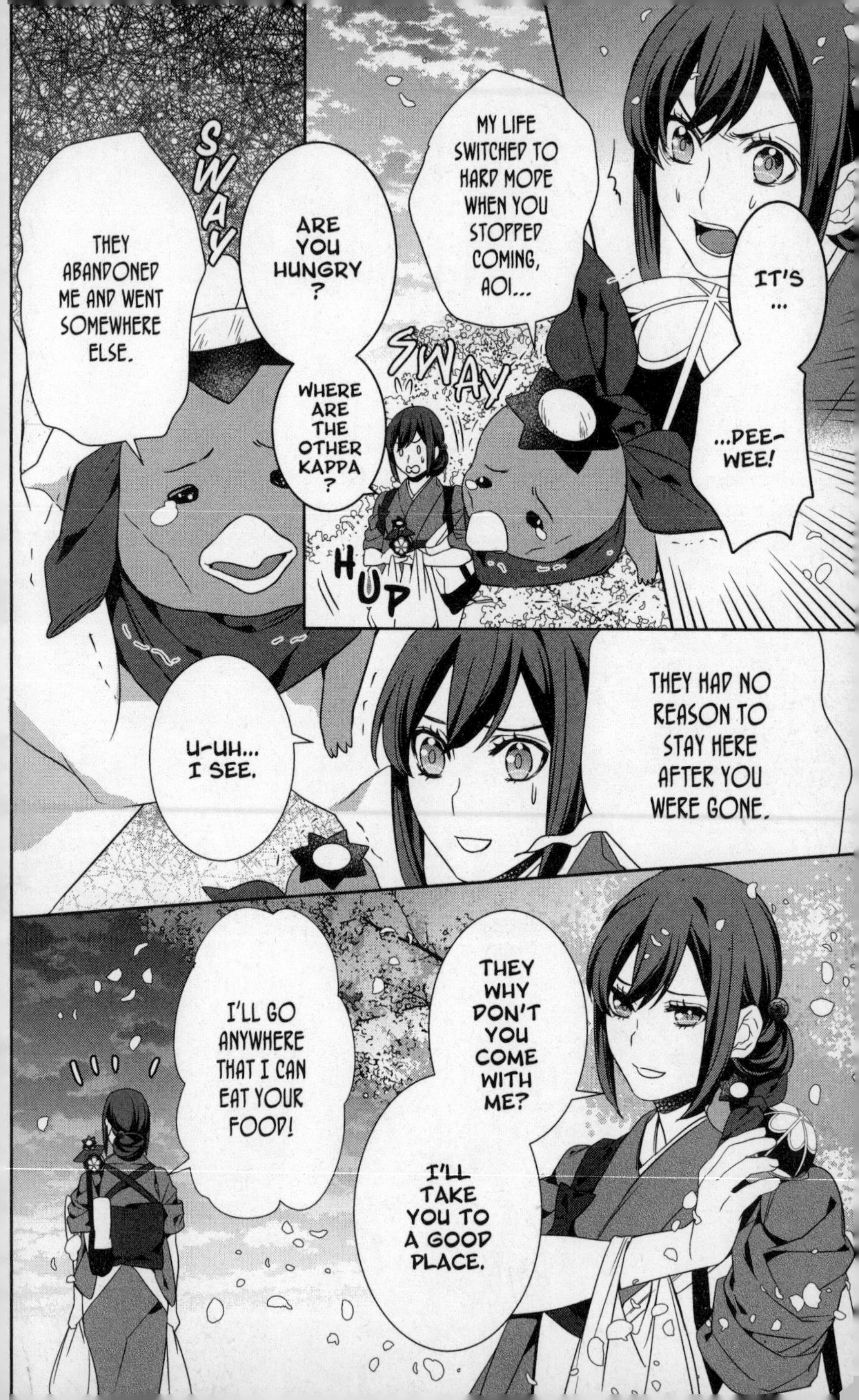
IT'S ...
...PEE-WEE!
MY LIFE SWITCHED TO HARD MODE WHEN YOU STOPPED COMING, AOI...
SWAY
ARE YOU HUNGRY?
WHERE ARE THE OTHER KAPPA?
HUP
SWAY
THEY ABANDONED ME AND WENT SOMEWHERE ELSE.
THEY HAD NO REASON TO STAY HERE AFTER YOU WERE GONE.
U-UH... I SEE.
THEY WHY DON'T YOU COME WITH ME?
I'LL TAKE YOU TO A GOOD PLACE.
I'LL GO ANYWHERE THAT I CAN EAT YOUR FOOD!

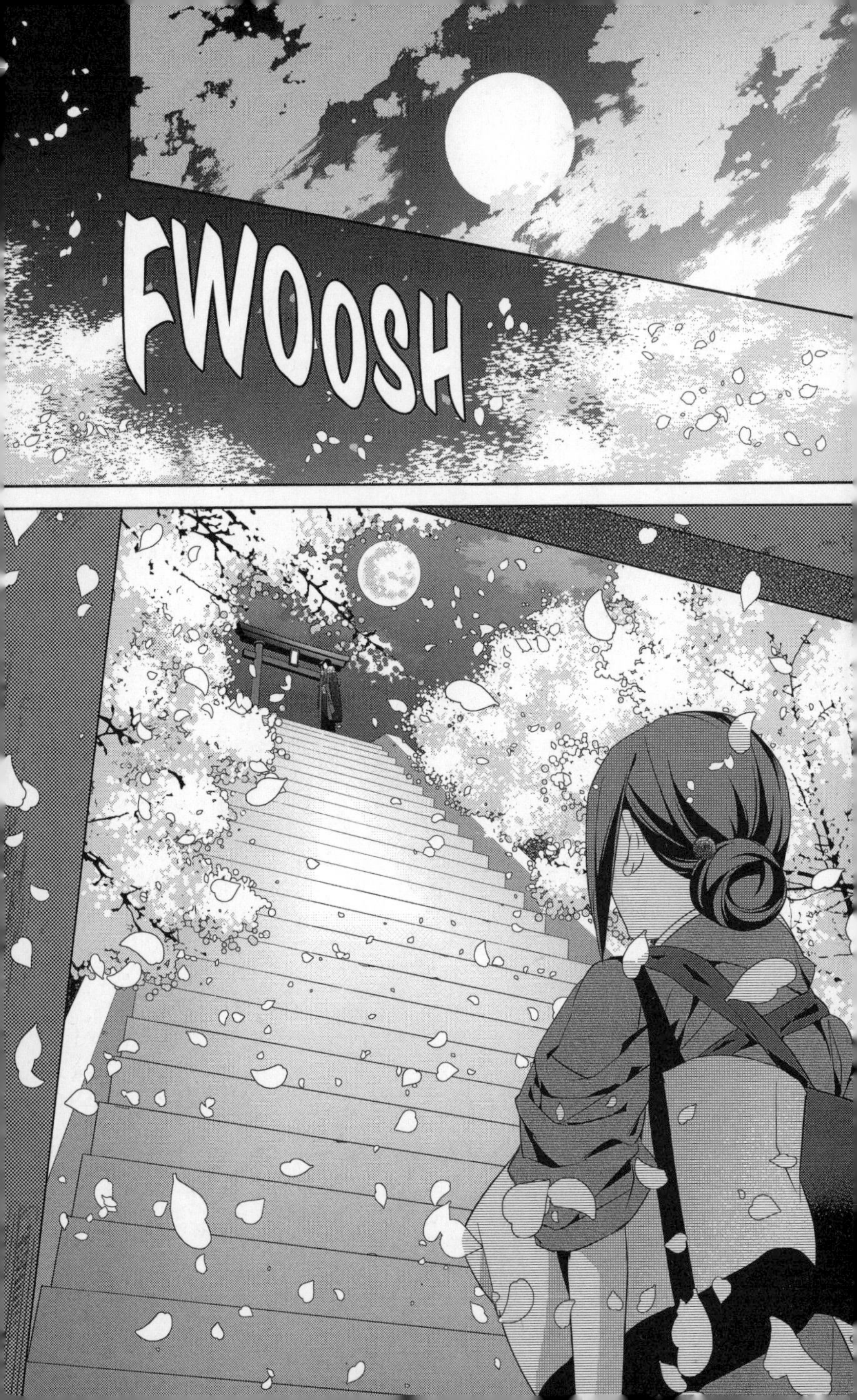
FWOOSH

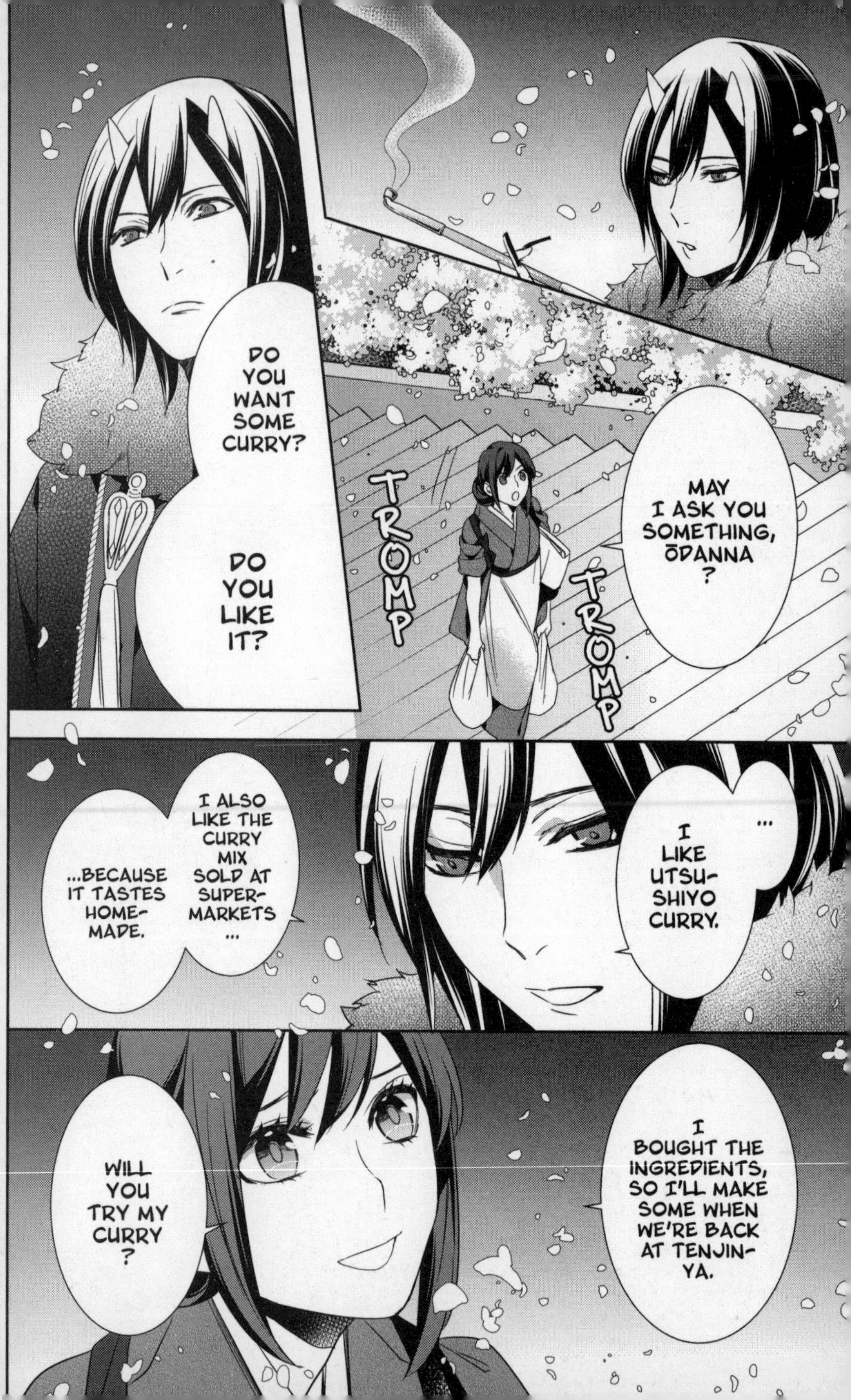
MAY I ASK YOU SOMETHING, ŌDANNA?
TROMP
TROMP
DO YOU WANT SOME CURRY?
DO YOU LIKE IT?
... I LIKE UTSUSHIYO CURRY.
I ALSO LIKE THE CURRY MIX SOLD AT SUPERMARKETS...
...BECAUSE IT TASTES HOMEMADE.
I BOUGHT THE INGREDIENTS, SO I'LL MAKE SOME WHEN WE'RE BACK AT TENJIN-YA.
WILL YOU TRY MY CURRY?

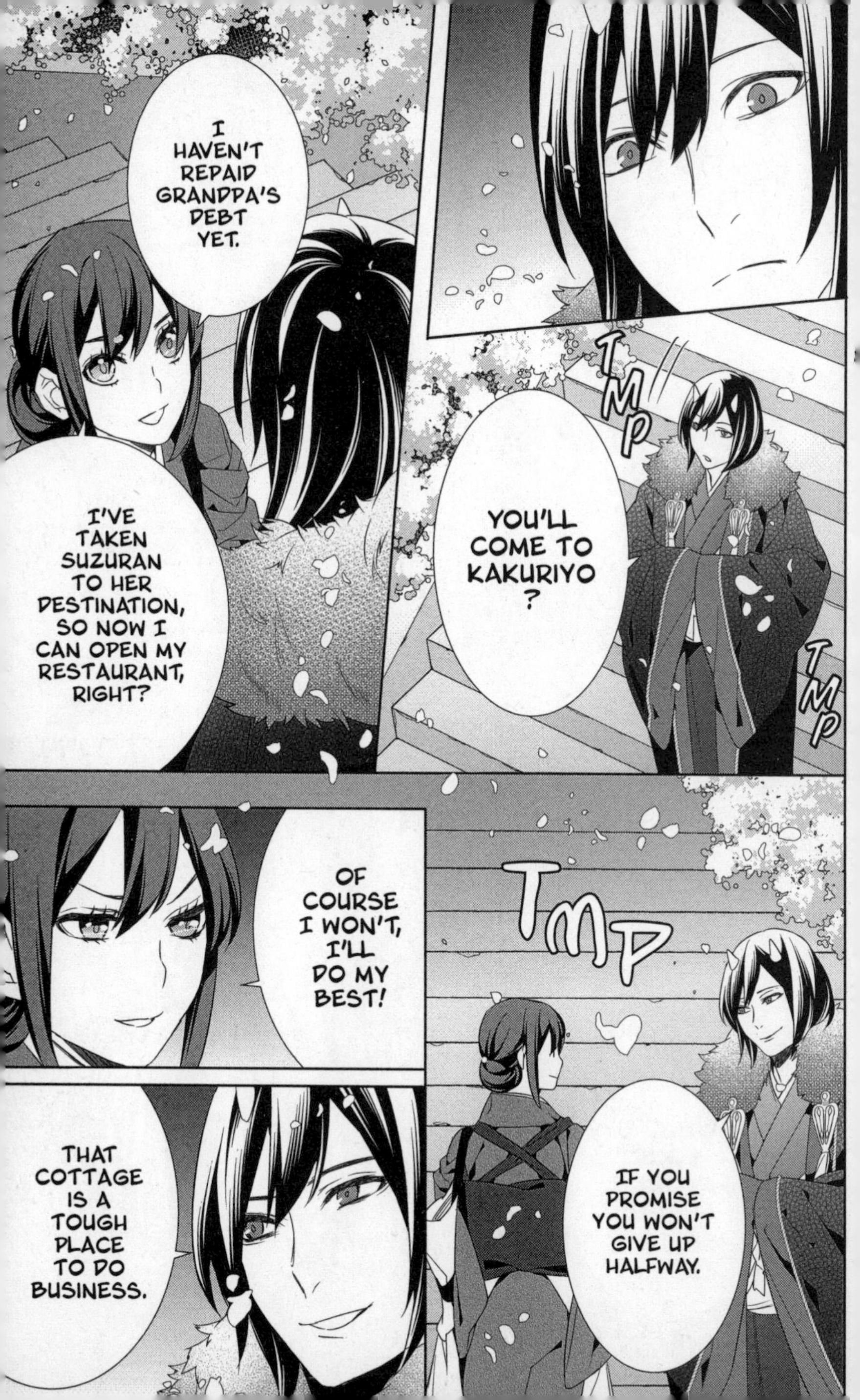
TMP
YOU'LL COME TO KAKURIYO ?
TMP
I HAVEN'T REPAID GRANDPA'S DEBT YET.
I'VE TAKEN SUZURAN TO HER DESTINATION, SO NOW I CAN OPEN MY RESTAURANT, RIGHT?
TMP
IF YOU PROMISE YOU WON'T GIVE UP HALFWAY.
OF COURSE I WON'T, I'LL DO MY BEST!
THAT COTTAGE IS A TOUGH PLACE TO DO BUSINESS.

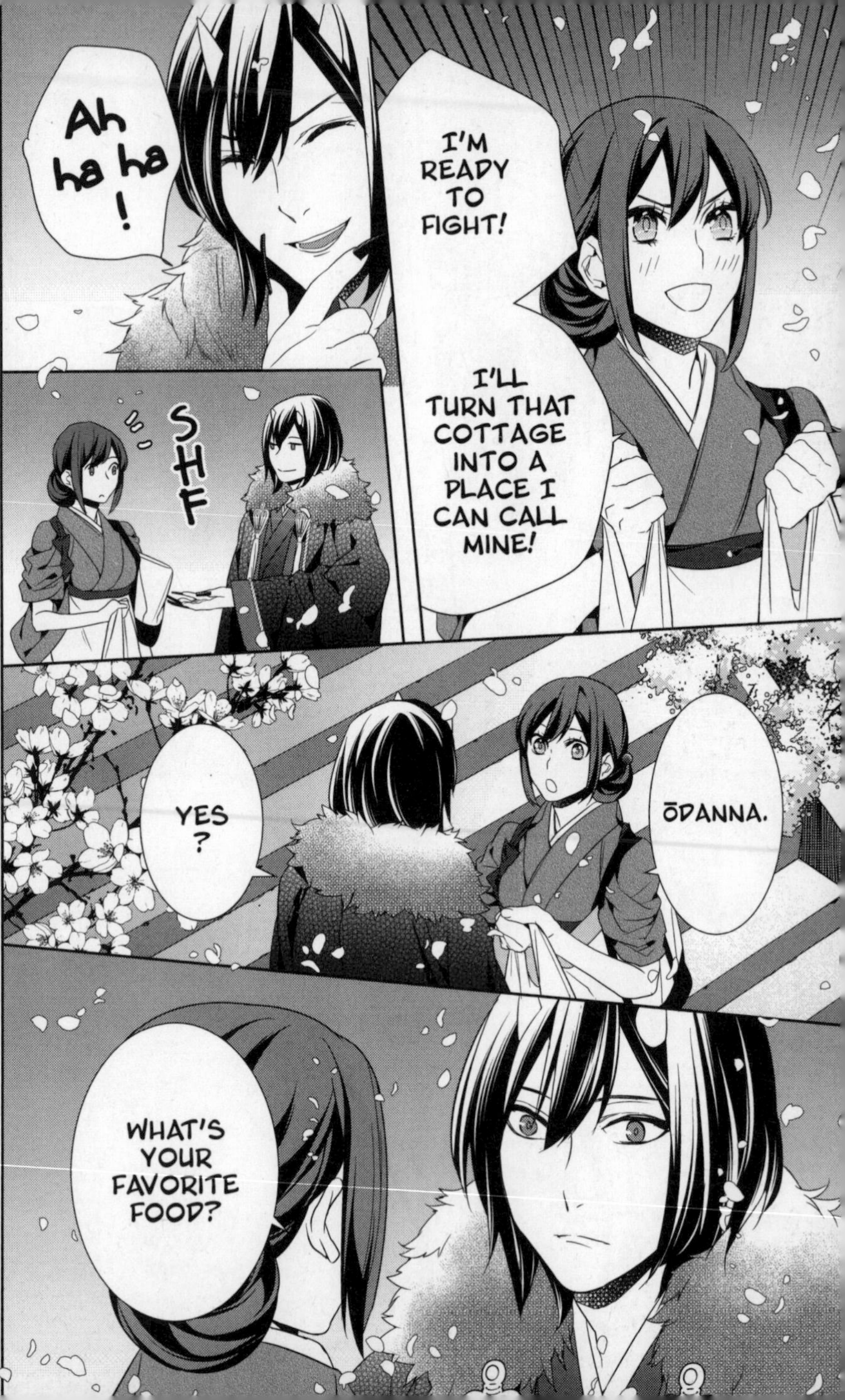
I'M READY TO FIGHT!
I'LL TURN THAT COTTAGE INTO A PLACE I CAN CALL MINE!
Ah ha ha!
SHF
ŌDANNA.
YES?
WHAT'S YOUR FAVORITE FOOD?

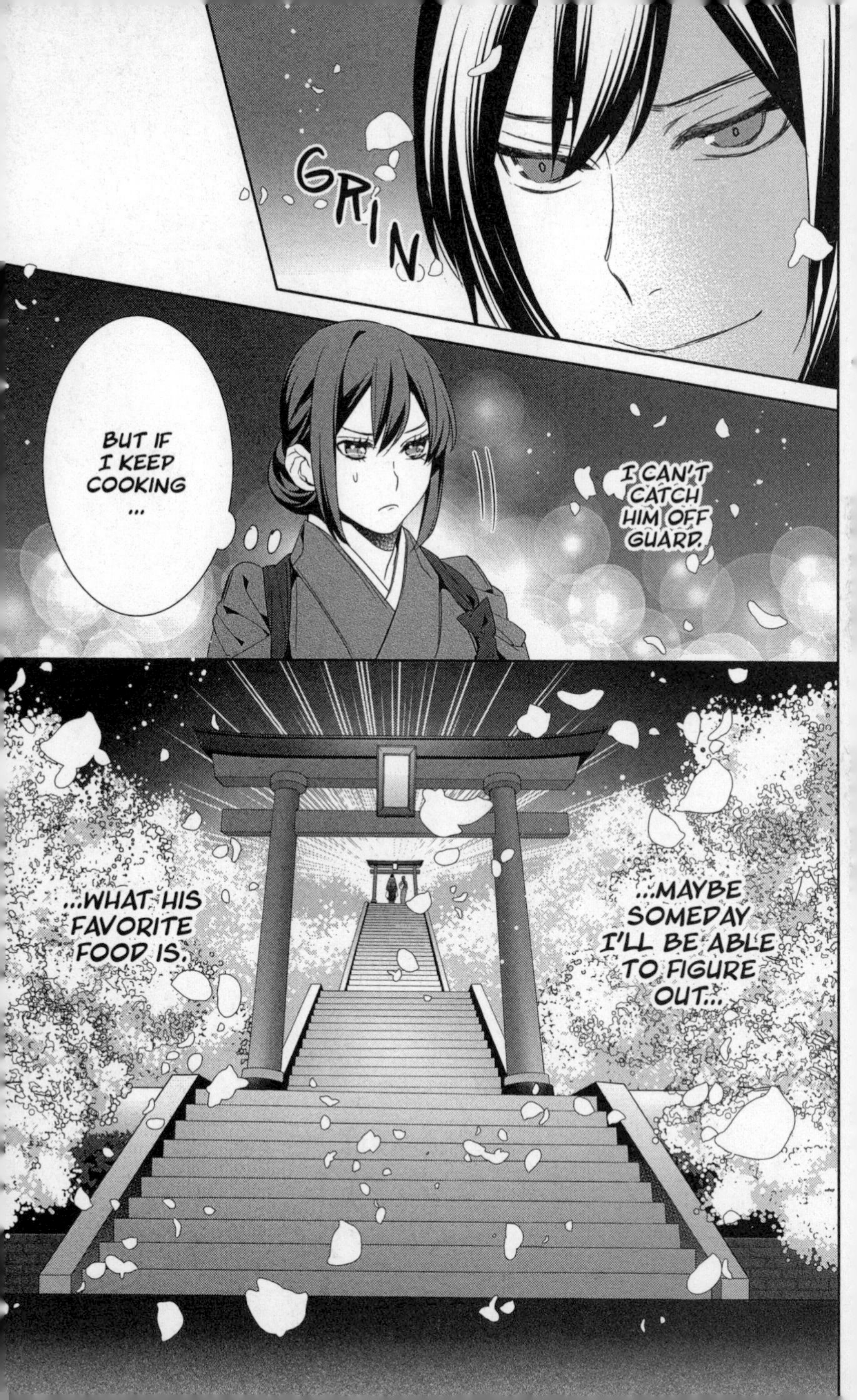
GRIN
I CAN'T CATCH HIM OFF GUARD.
BUT IF I KEEP COOKING ...
...MAYBE SOMEDAY I'LL BE ABLE TO FIGURE OUT...
...WHAT HIS FAVORITE FOOD IS.

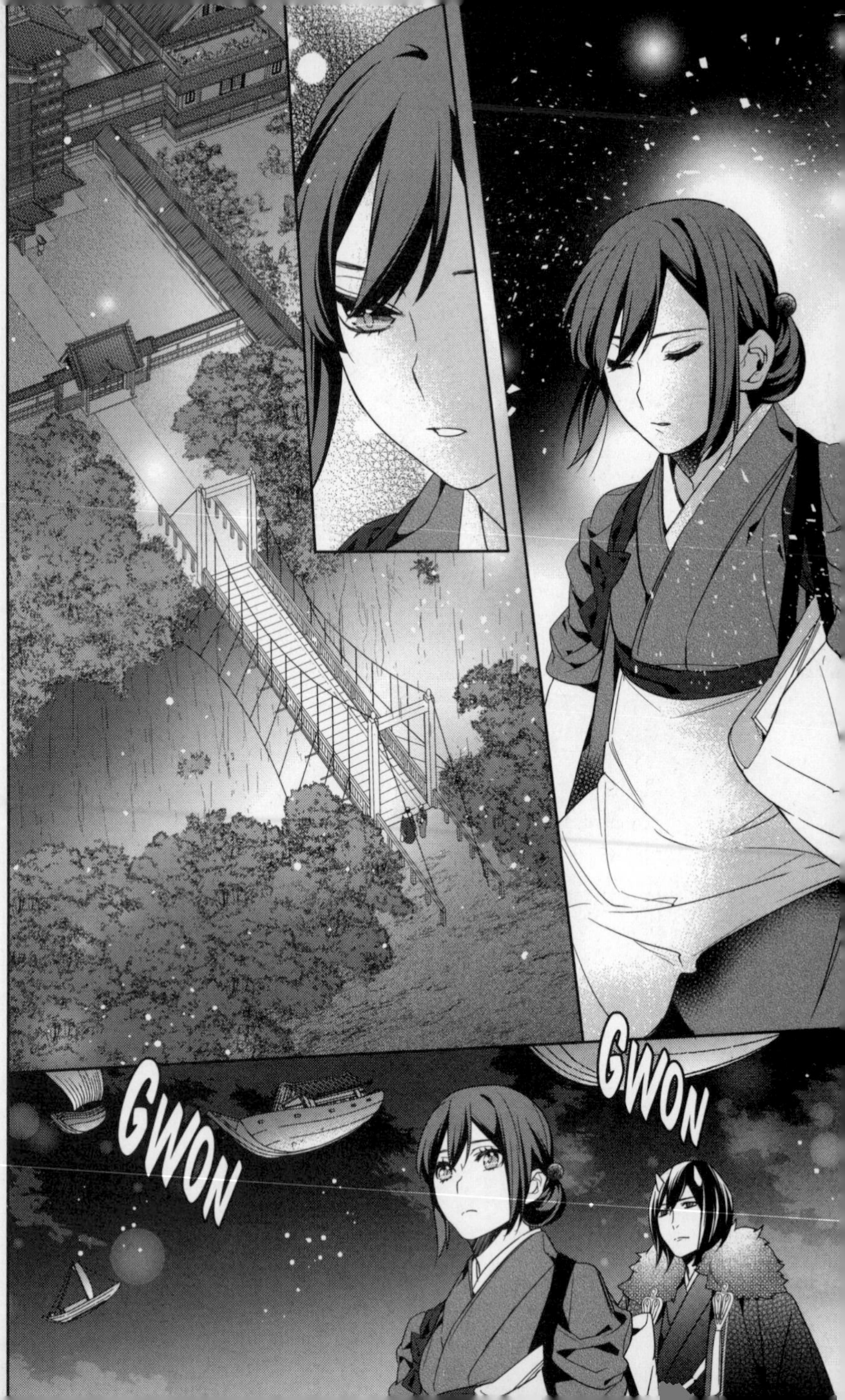
GWON
GWON

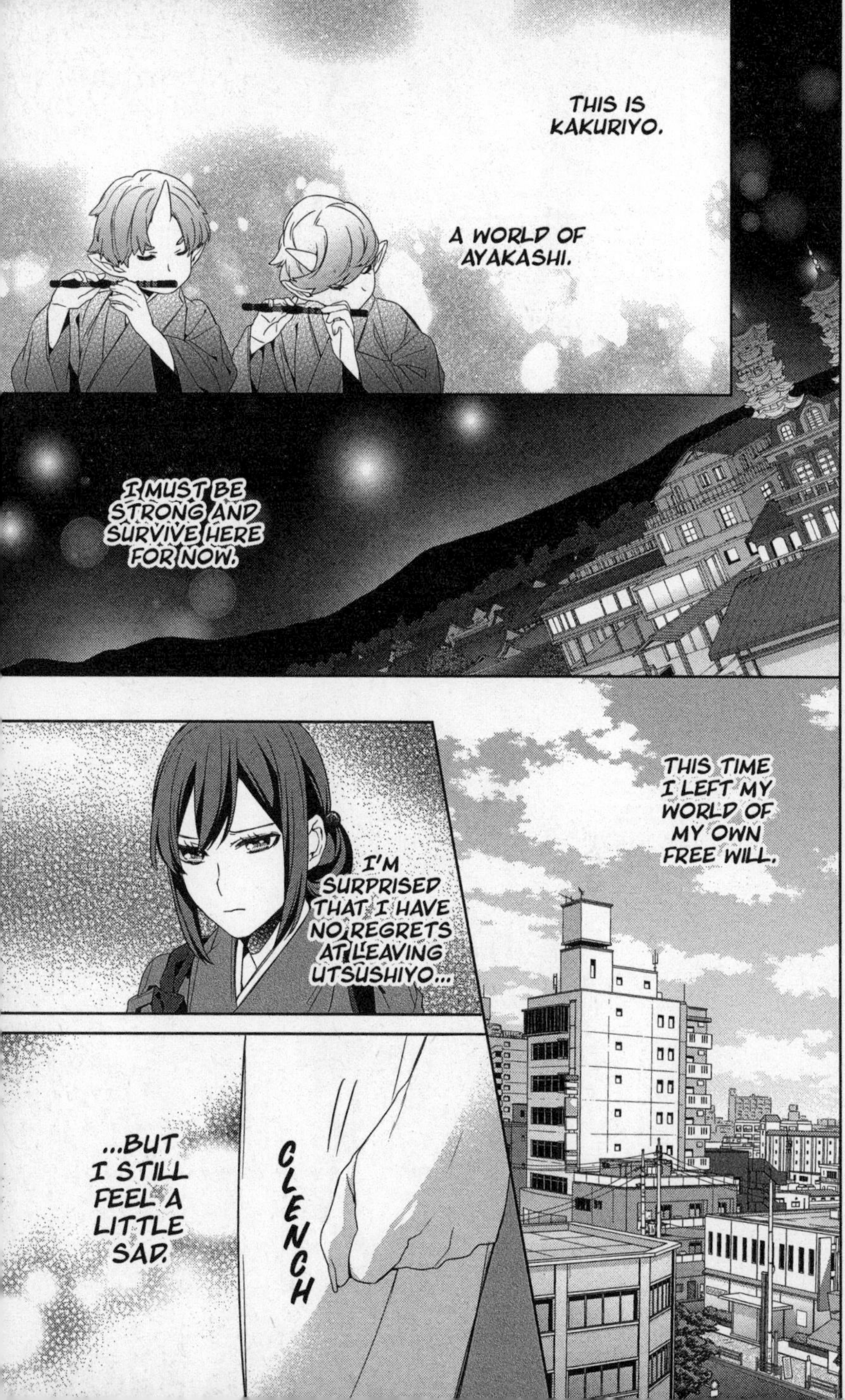
THIS IS KAKURIYO.
A WORLD OF AYAKASHI.
I MUST BE STRONG AND SURVIVE HERE FOR NOW.
THIS TIME I LEFT MY WORLD OF MY OWN FREE WILL.
I'M SURPRISED THAT I HAVE NO REGRETS AT LEAVING UTSUSHIYO...
...BUT I STILL FEEL A LITTLE SAD.
CLENCH

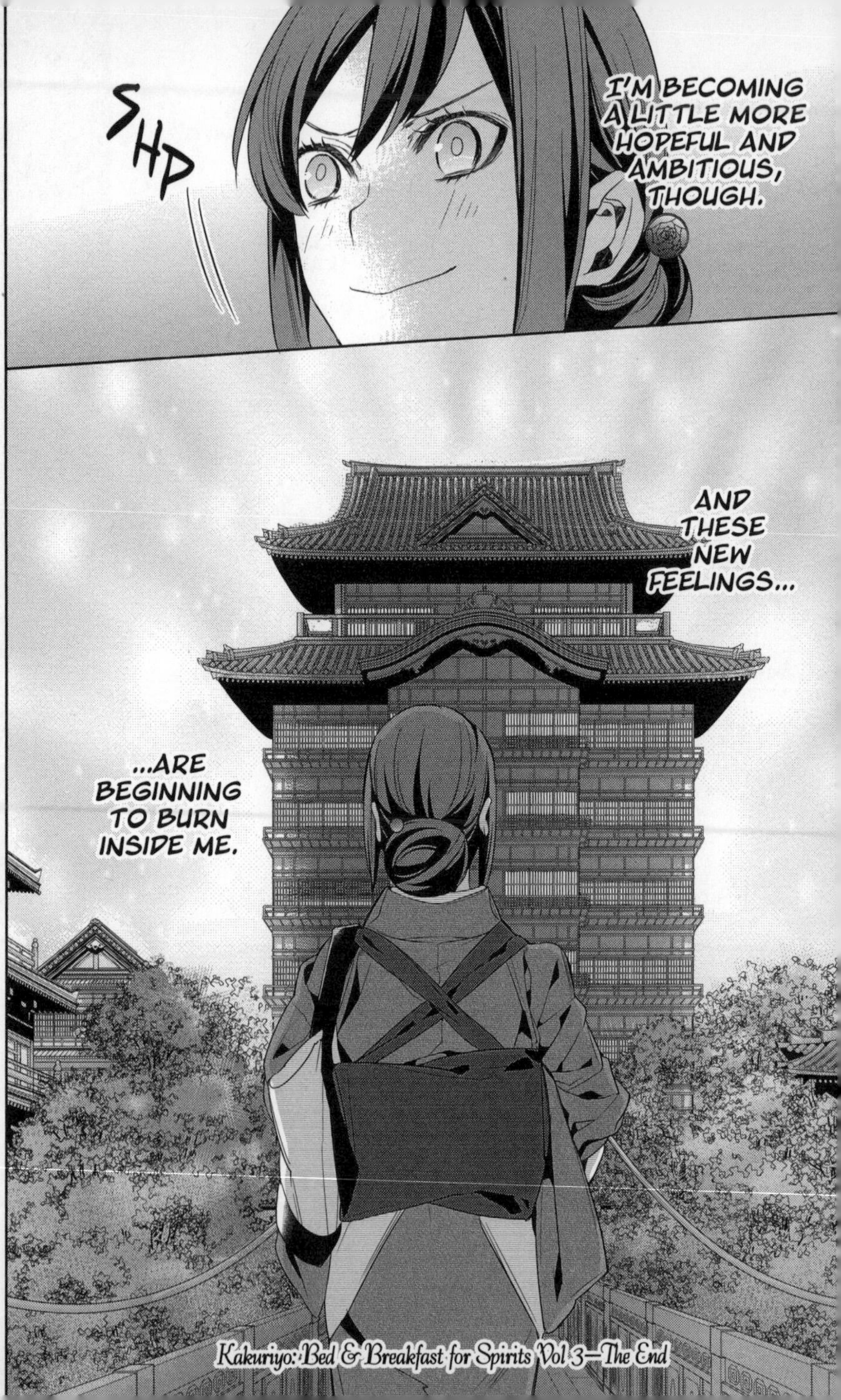
I'M BECOMING A LITTLE MORE HOPEFUL AND AMBITIOUS, THOUGH.
SHP
AND THESE NEW FEELINGS...
...ARE BEGINNING TO BURN INSIDE ME.
Kakuriyo: Bed & Breakfast for Spirits Vol 3—The End

Kakuriyo
Bed & Breakfast for Spirits

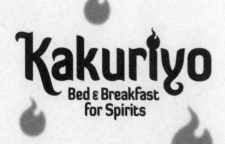

END NOTES

PAGE 44, PANEL 3
Shiizakana
Literally "strong snack" in Japanese. Shiizakana can be a strongly flavored side dish intended to be accompanied by sake, or a more substantial dish like hot pot.

PAGE 118, PANEL 2
Cough drops
A traditional form of cough drop is made from long rolls of soft candy that are sliced into bite-sized pieces.

PAGE 9, PANEL 2
Wall demons
Nurikabe in Japanese. Ayakashi that only appear at night. They create an invisible wall that prevents humans from going forward, as if the nurikabe are blocking the entire width of the road.

PAGE 23, PANEL 4
Mamedaifuku
Daifuku are soft rice cakes filled with sweet red bean paste. *Mamedaifuku* additionally have red peas or soybeans mixed into the outer soft rice cake.

PAGE 41, PANEL 6
Kaiseki course
Kaiseki cuisine is the haute cuisine of Japan. A kaiseki course meal focuses on seasonal ingredients over multiple courses, so menus vary depending on the time of year.

Kakuriyo
Bed & Breakfast
for Spirits

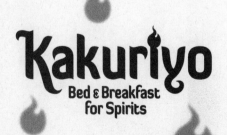

Kakuriyo
Bed & Breakfast
for Spirits

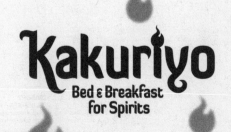

Kakuriyo
Bed & Breakfast for Spirits

3

SHOJO BEAT EDITION

Art by **Waco Ioka**
Original story by **Midori Yuma**
Character design by **Laruha**

English Translation & Adaptation **Tomo Kimura**
Touch-up Art & Lettering **Joanna Estep**
Design **Alice Lewis**
Editor **Pancha Diaz**

KAKURIYO NO YADOMESHI AYAKASHIOYADO NI YOMEIRI SHIMASU, Vol. 3
©Waco Ioka 2017
©Midori Yuma 2017
©Laruha 2017
First published in Japan in 2017 by KADOKAWA CORPORATION, Tokyo.
English translation rights arranged with KADOKAWA CORPORATION, Tokyo.

Printed in the U.S.A.

Published by VIZ Media, LLC.
P.O. Box 77010
San Francisco, CA 94107

10 9 8 7 6 5 4 3 2 1
First printing, May 2019

viz.com

shojobeat.com

Kamisama Kiss

Story and art by **Julietta Suzuki**

What's a newly fledged godling to do?

Now a hit anime series!

Nanami Momozono is alone and homeless after her dad skips town to evade his gambling debts and the debt collectors kick her out of her apartment. So when a man she's just saved from a dog offers her his home, she jumps at the opportunity. But it turns out that his place is a shrine, and Nanami has unwittingly taken over his job as a local deity!

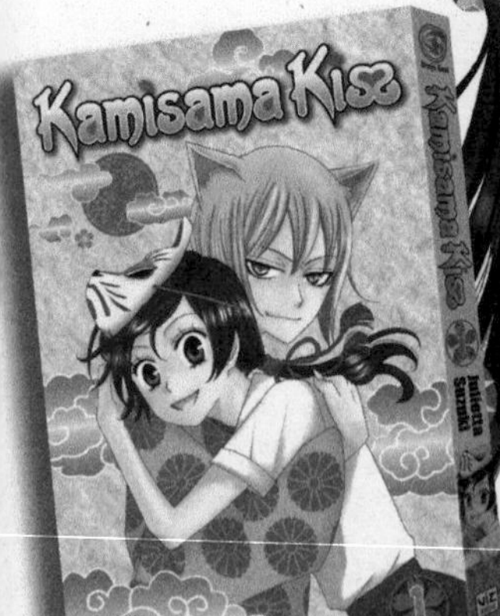

Kamisama Kiss
Kamisama Kiss
Julietta Suzuki
1
Story & Art by
Julietta Suzuki

Available now!

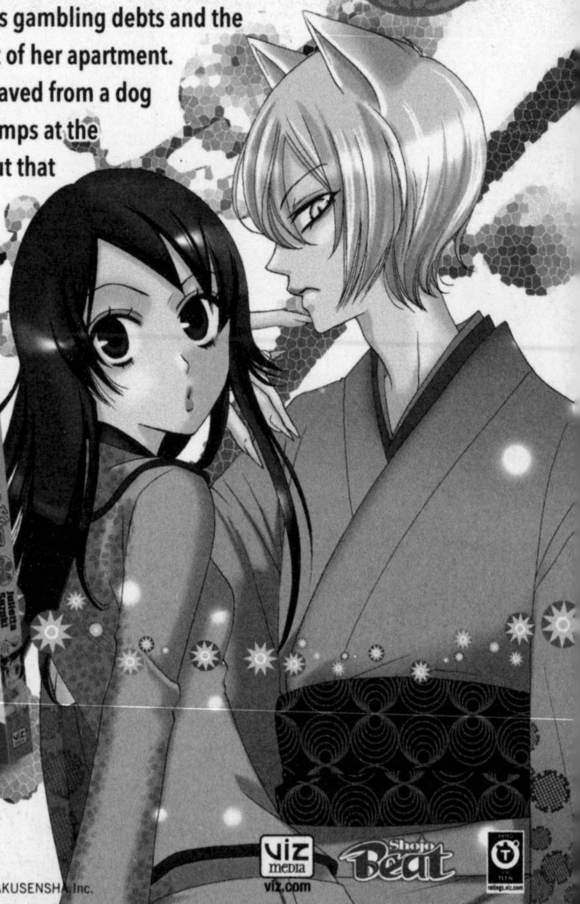

VIZ media viz.com Shojo Beat

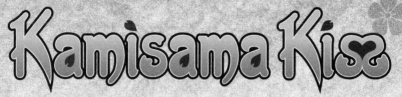

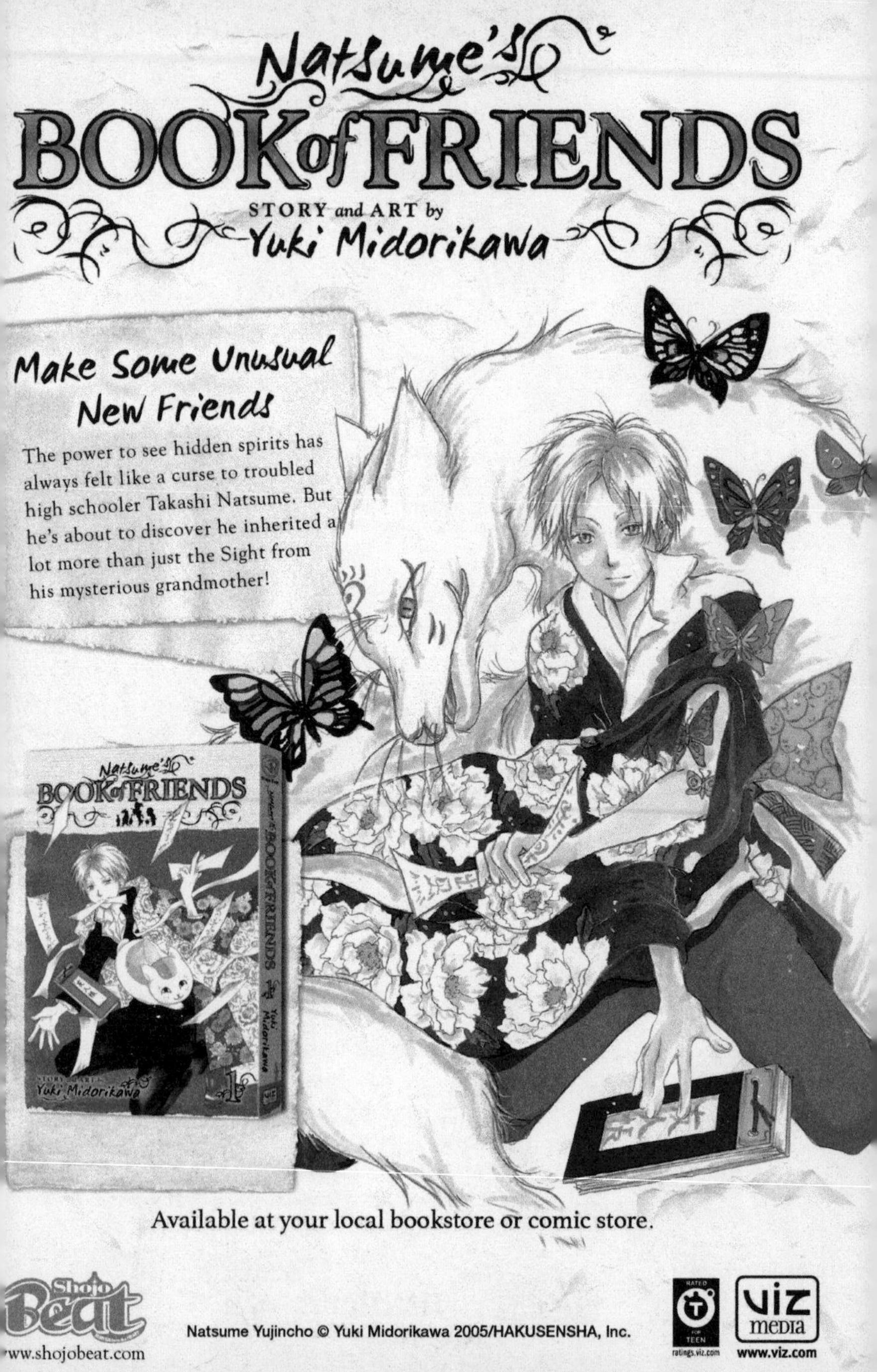
Natsume's BOOK of FRIENDS
STORY and ART by
Yuki Midorikawa
Make Some Unusual New Friends
The power to see hidden spirits has always felt like a curse to troubled high schooler Takashi Natsume. But he's about to discover he inherited a lot more than just the Sight from his mysterious grandmother!
Natsume's BOOK of FRIENDS
Yuki Midorikawa
Available at your local bookstore or comic store.
Shojo Beat
www.shojobeat.com
Natsume Yujincho © Yuki Midorikawa 2005/HAKUSENSHA, Inc.
RATED T FOR TEEN
ratings.viz.com
VIZ media
www.viz.com

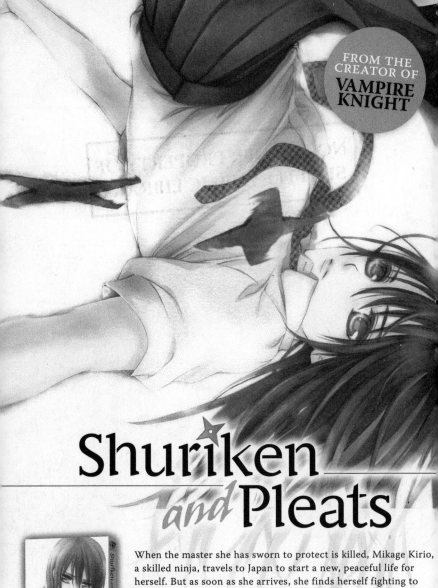

This is the last page.

Kakuriyo: Bed & Breakfast for Spirits has been printed in the original Japanese format to preserve the orientation of the artwork.

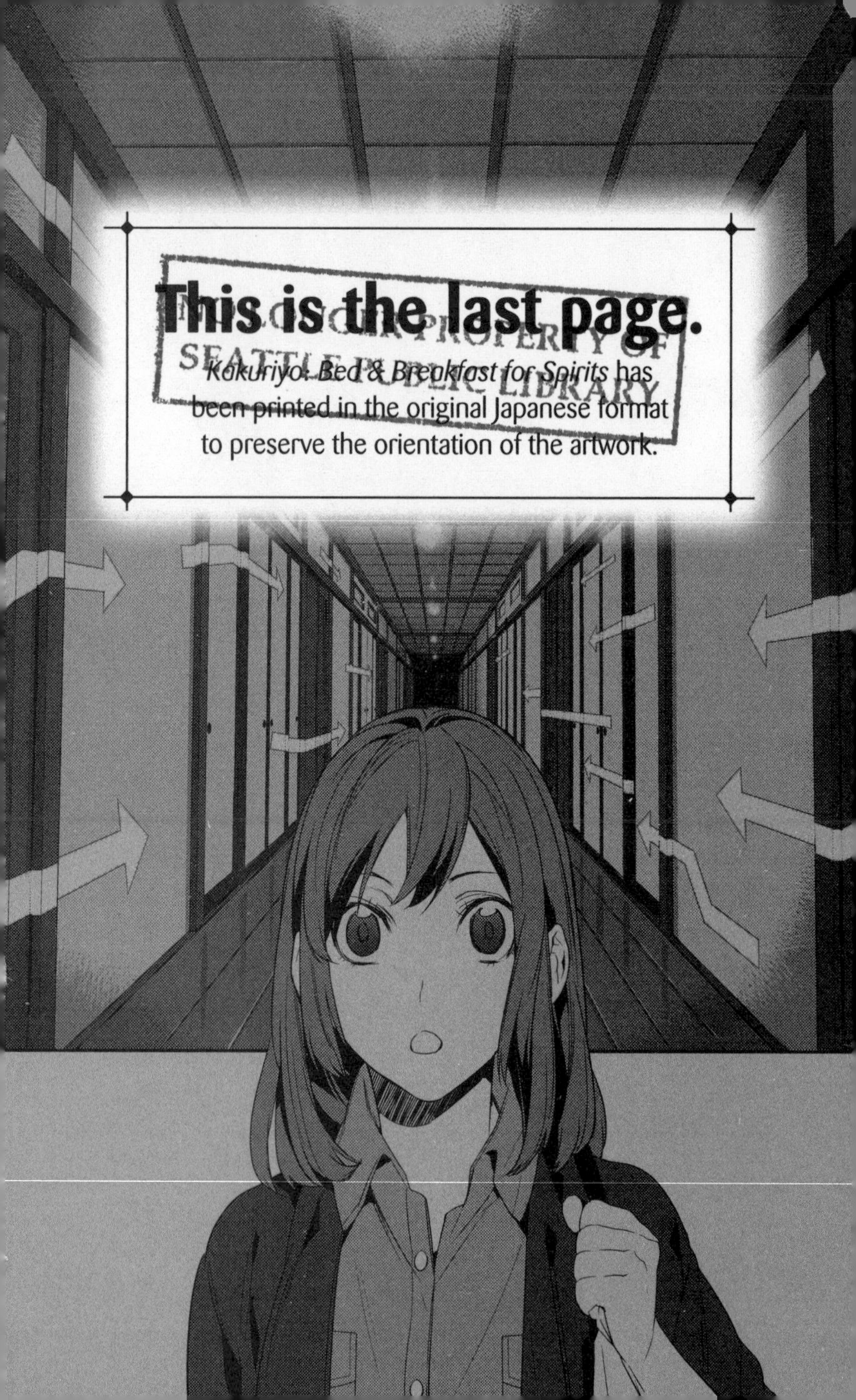